the CHILD CATCHERS

the CHILD CATCHERS

Rescue, Trafficking, *and the* New Gospel *of* Adoption

KATHRYN JOYCE

PUBLICAFFAIRS
New York

Published in the United States by PublicAffairs™,
a Member of the Perseus Books Group

Printed in the United States of America.

PublicAffairs books are available at special discounts for bulk purchases in the U.S. by corporations, institutions, and other organizations. For more information, please contact the Special Markets Department at the Perseus Books Group, 2300 Chestnut Street, Suite 200, Philadelphia, PA 19103, call (800) 810-4145, ext. 5000, or e-mail special.markets@perseusbooks.com.

Book Design by Cynthia Young

Library of Congress Cataloging-in-Publication Data
Joyce, Kathryn, 1979–
The child catchers : rescue, trafficking, and the new gospel of adoption / Kathryn Joyce.
    p. cm.
Includes bibliographical references and index.
ISBN 978-1-58648-942-7 (hardcover) — ISBN 978-1-58648-943-4 (e-book)
1. Adoption—Religious aspects—Christianity.   2. Abortion—Religious aspects—Christianity.   I. Title.
HV875.26.J6 2013
362.734—dc23
                                                2012044316

First Edition

10 9 8 7 6 5 4 3 2 1

For my family

"It is one hundred years since our children left."

—attributed to town records of Hamelin, 1384

CONTENTS

PREFACE

Before I met Sharon I didn't think about adoption as something that evangelical Christians particularly cared about, or at least not in families like Sharon's—large, homeschooling families in which the parents already have lots of biological children. Sharon isn't the sort of person you visualize when you think of an adoptive mother yearning for the child she's adopting to "come home," as they say in the adoption world. After all, Sharon wasn't infertile. In keeping with her religious beliefs and as part of an evangelical movement that promotes prolific fertility, she had already had seven children biologically, and now in her mid-fifties, she was no longer particularly young.

I first got to know Sharon, who asked me not to use her real name, in the spring of 2007 when I was reporting on a group of evangelicals who didn't believe in contraception but thought Christians should accept as many children as God gave them—hence Sharon's seven. We met at a celebration hosted in Virginia by a fundamentalist homeschooling publisher, a sort of training ground for some of the people who would go on to become Tea Party activists several years down the line. (True to form, many of the men at the event walked the grounds in tricorner hats and kneesocks while the women donned colonial gowns.)

Sharon, a homemaking wife to a gentle and soft-spoken pest exterminator, was an eagerly outgoing woman with shoulder-length brown hair, a frank, makeup-free face, and a playful enthusiasm for culture-war sparring. We struck up a strange friendship, exchanging scores of e-mails, letters, and calls over several years, much of it concerning the difference in our world views: Sharon is an avid evangelizer and adheres to the self-described "patriarchy movement," while I am a secular, feminist journalist who covers religion and reproductive rights. We argued a lot about abortion.

In time Sharon, who struck me as a lifelong spiritual dabbler, trying on a dozen denominations and New Age paths before returning to the conservative Baptist beliefs of her childhood, developed a new calling. As 2007 rolled into 2008, Sharon became increasingly "convicted" that God was calling her to adopt more children into her family—possibly a brother and sister from an orphanage outside Monrovia, Liberia, or maybe a blind girl from Guatemala, or one of several infants recently born in the United States. She found these children by looking online at the websites of various Christian adoption agencies and ministries, which seemed to grow in number by the week.

The family created a blog that referenced a verse of scripture that was increasingly important in evangelical circles, James 1:27: "Pure religion is this, to help the widows and orphans in their need." They began asking friends and family for donations to help defray the tens of thousands of dollars in adoption costs needed to "bring an orphan home."

But Sharon was slightly behind the curve in the places from which she was seeking to adopt. When she began looking into Guatemala, the country was on the cusp of shutting down its huge adoption program, which had been sending adoptable children to the United States at a rate of one in every one hundred Guatemalan children born. That booming system, fueled by a seemingly insatiable demand from prospective US parents, had led to a number of abuses, including coercion of Guatemalan families, child buying, and even kidnapping. Things didn't look much better in Liberia, which had become an adoption cause célèbre in the Christian anticontraception movement that Sharon followed and a particular trend in her own southern city. One of Sharon's friends, she claimed, had adopted fourteen children from Liberia, and members of several churches in nearby suburbs adopted almost all the members of a Liberian orphanage group. In 2009, however, just as had happened in Guatemala, Liberia's government suspended international adoption there as well. They were responding to numerous complaints about unethical adoption practices, including allegations of child trafficking after one unlicensed US Christian adoption ministry—the same ministry Sharon had hoped to use for her adoptions—was accused of trying to fly children out of the country without authorization.

Undaunted, Sharon began trying to adopt domestically, within the United States, spurred on by the experience of friends who had received a newborn baby within three days of applying thanks to a new "Safe Haven" program that allowed mothers to abandon children to public authorities without penalty and without the formalities (or safeguards) of officially relinquishing for adoption. "I will make you the first to know that my husband agreed today to pursue a newborn domestic adoption in Florida," she wrote me triumphantly one day. Not long after came another message, asking me whether I thought it would be wrong "to attempt to talk a woman out of an abortion and ask her to let me adopt the child instead?"

I hadn't thought about it much before, but when Sharon asked the question, I realized I did think it was wrong. Sharon countered with an argument borrowed from one of her new "adoption friends," someone she had met through an online community of women who had adopted or were seeking to. The friend assured her that "When you take one of these children, you are literally saving them from the ghetto life in America." Sharon began to support programs that encouraged women with unplanned pregnancies to carry the pregnancy to term and relinquish the child for adoption.

She also compiled a "birthmother letter" and a packet of information about her family, including photos of their children and house as well as descriptions of the lifestyle they could offer. She sent it out to Christian adoption agencies and updated the fundraising widget on her website. She quarreled with friends and neighbors when they lagged in writing reference letters for her home study—part of the adoption agency approval process—and began writing me using the acronyms of the adoption world: AA for African American or SN for special needs.

She alerted me in excitement every time a new possibility for adoption emerged, each of which might send her off to Florida or Texas or Utah at a moment's notice. She became invested in one potential child after another, leaping quickly from news that a child might be available to imagining the child in her family and then being crushed when the birthmother chose another couple, as often happens in domestic adoption.

Sharon's "best adoption friend," a woman who had adopted multiple times, wrote her in sympathy, telling her to hold out hope—more babies were being born every week—and if she wasn't chosen, that meant that this was not meant to be her baby. "God knows when each child is conceived where they will grow up and once you have YOUR baby you will understand what I am saying," she comforted.

When Sharon received another rejection, she cried and came down with headaches. She wrote me that she was exhausted with the entire process and didn't think she could continue. But she always came up looking for other options.

Part of me was baffled by Sharon's fervor, and part of me recoiled, though at first I couldn't understand why. I wondered why Sharon was throwing herself into such a punishing process when she had seven children at home. The tears she shed over kids who went to other adoptive parents would have seemed more understandable coming from an infertile couple who had been passed over and were mourning yet another lost possibility to parent. If her motivation was to save orphans in need, why did she seem more disappointed than relieved when children she had looked at were adopted elsewhere?

After my long discussions with Sharon I began to notice adoption more and more as I reported on conservative Christian social movements. As I looked more closely and spoke to more people involved in adoption—whether those seeking to adopt, like Sharon, or parents whose children were sent for adoption, or adoptees themselves—I came to realize that Sharon's convictions were part of a larger picture in evangelical America. Across the United States a much wider spectrum of evangelical churches than just Sharon's very conservative community had begun to view adoption as a perfect storm of a cause: a way for conservative churches to get involved in poverty and social justice issues that they had ceded years before to liberal denominations, an extension of pro-life politics and a decisive rebuttal to the taunt that Christians should adopt all those extra children they want women to have, and, more quietly, as a window for evangelizing, as Christians get to "bring the mission field home" and pass on the gospel to a new population of children, effectively saving them twice. What that meant on the ground was that churches were witnessing what they called a "viral" movement, with adoption becoming so popular in conservative, largely white, and often southern congregations that some churches saw their members collectively adopt upward of one hundred children in just a few years. This was matched by increasingly direct support from pastors and dozens of emerging Christian adoption ministries, conferences, and coalition groups.

Before 2010, if people connected evangelicals and adoption at all, it was probably to consider the rhetorical role that adoption plays in the antiabortion movement: that women who find themselves with an unplanned, unwanted pregnancy should carry to term and give the child up for adoption instead. Aside from Sharon, this was also my introduction—although from the other side. I learned about the women who had relinquished children for adoption through "crisis pregnancy centers" and maternity homes dedicated to ensuring that women "choose life" and then, ideally, choose adoption as well. I heard how many women not only grieved their child's adoption profoundly but sometimes experienced it as a loss worse than a loved one's death.

But the Christian adoption movement had a larger vision than just promoting adoption as an "abortion alternative." It envisioned a new, compassionate role for conservative Christians in addressing what has become known as the global "orphan crisis": the idea that there are hundreds of millions of orphaned children across the world who are in need of American help and waiting to be adopted. An evangelical movement seeking a new way to engage in social issues affirmed this message wholesale, sending tens of thousands of evangelicals overseas to adopt, not so they could start a family in the wake of infertility but instead in answer to a biblical mandate to care for orphans.

The orphans Christians seek to save, however, are a complicated category—most often not children lacking family but rather children whose parents are poor and live in countries where the social services infrastructure for child welfare is limited to orphanages that families may turn to in a season of need. The new Christian adoption movement has so fervently urged evangelical couples to look for orphans to save that it has inspired the creation of more "orphans" to fill that role: children fraudulently passed off as though they have no family, with their personal records laundered to create what reformers call a "manufactured" or "paper orphan." People with good intentions have become a market, the demand side of an industry that can be as profit-driven as any other, and they have significant cash to spend. The adoption system adapted itself to cater to their demand, but most would-be adopters, wrapped in the enthusiasm of their new calling, didn't recognize the problems: that children often came into the adoption system through false representations or implied offers of payment to their families, that some children were sent abroad without their parents' permission, that in an overwhelming number of cases children were relinquished because of poverty alone, when a fraction of the huge sums adopting parents were paying to agencies could have brought birth families out of poverty many times over. By the time many adoptive parents found out that their new children were not the orphans they were said to be, some also realized that gag clauses in their agency contracts blocked them from publicly warning others. What's more, a new crisis arose that threatens to derail international adoption completely: just as the Christian adoption movement began to gain steam, international adoption entered a period of pitched decline.

My initial questions about what was motivating Sharon led me on an investigation to discover where the larger movement had come from, what was driving it, and what its influence had led to. In the course of my reporting over four years I have conducted more than two hundred interviews, traveled in four countries, and read deeply into the history of adoption.

I looked at the saga of Idaho missionary Laura Silsby, who was arrested shortly after the 2010 earthquake in Haiti for trying to transport children out of the country as well as the very similar efforts of a kindly Alabama pastor who did not make headline news. I covered the evolution of the Christian adoption movement from the Southern Baptist Theological Seminary in Kentucky to Rick Warren's Saddleback Church in southern California. I spoke with dozens of US birthmothers who relinquished children in coercive adoptions and who feel that their experiences constitute an invisible chapter in women's history. In Ethiopia I surveyed a country in the midst of an "adoption boom," speaking with parties on all three sides of a fraudulent adoption and examining the rising profession of "adoption searchers"—private investigators hired by adoptive parents who suspect that their children's backstories may be untrue. In Liberia I examined the fallout from a postboom country, where adoptions flourished in the wake of conflict and where children were adopted to homes often tragically unprepared for their needs. In Rwanda I explored a church-state orphan-care collaboration that may defy the traditional "boom-bust" adoption industry model and that points to a cautiously optimistic way forward. And in South Korea I found an unlikely coalition of women who are challenging the root cause of why many mothers give their children up for adoption when they would keep them if they could.

ONE DAY SHARON got the news she was waiting for and adopted a healthy black baby girl from a mother living in Texas. But soon after the first adoption was finished, she was looking to adopt again. She remained interested in adopting the two children she had looked at from Liberia, periodically sending me updates on her "Liberian kids," while also keeping her eyes open for other opportunities in the United States. In the end Sharon adopted three children within about a year and a half: the baby girl from Texas, a Liberian boy who came to Sharon's home after his original adoptive family disrupted his adoption, and a baby boy with extreme special needs, having been born intersexed (with "ambiguous genitalia") and facing a plethora of health issues, including spina bifida, club feet, and spinal cord problems. Sharon and her husband depleted their retirement savings on the first two adoptions and completed the third with aid from a Christian ministry that helps fund evangelicals' adoptions.

In the middle of these adoptions they considered other children as well. They drove across the country to visit an autistic boy in foster care—in the end it did not work out—and took in a disabled child from Washington State who they later had to return due to bureaucratic complications. The boy from the disrupted Liberian adoption cried each time one of the children was sent back. From time to time Sharon would tell me she had "a couple other kids in the paperwork process." She began speaking about one day opening her own adoption agency or orphan ministry.

At some point the family sent the Liberian adoptee to a home for troubled boys in Missouri, citing his emotional unresponsiveness, his difficult behavior, and his failure to bond with the family. When I visited Sharon in 2011 she spent most of my visit on the phone with doctors, discussing state medical coverage for her youngest son's unremitting health problems; his breathing was so labored that he seemed unable to concentrate on anything else. She told me the family was eager to adopt an HIV-positive teenager from Ukraine next.

Sharon's adoption projects were my first introduction to the world of the Christian adoption movement, a movement that was evolving and becoming increasingly important in many Christian denominations even as I was reporting on it. But looking back now, Sharon's experiences already illuminated a number of the troubling outcomes of making adoption a faith-driven cause: the urge to push adoption on women with unplanned pregnancies, often amounting to coercion that treats single mothers as the source of a product; a rush to trending countries where adoption has become a boom industry, creating an incentive for child finders to recruit "orphans" from intact families; involvement with agencies, sometimes unlicensed, that place their mission above the laws of sovereign nations; and an enthusiasm to "rescue" as many children as possible that may outpace a family's ability to give them the best care, often leading to the tragic dissolution of yet another home for an already traumatized child.

Although not all evangelicals who follow the call to adopt take it as far as Sharon did—and many others go far further—all of them are entering an industry that even adoption professionals describe as an ethical "Wild West": a field in which humanitarian concerns are intertwined with and frequently overridden by business imperatives and where naive would-be parents enter agreements in blind trust, certain they're saving the life of an orphan.

Adoption is often described as a "win-win" solution—for a child in need of a home and for adoptive parents longing for a son or a daughter to raise. However, in the fuller equation adoption is too often a zero-sum game, in which the happiness of one family comes at the expense of another, particularly that of birthmothers and birth families, both in the United States and overseas, whose choice to relinquish for adoption is sometimes no choice at all. Despite the varied but largely altruistic motivations of evangelical adoption advocates, as a movement it is directing hundreds of millions of dollars into a system that already responds acutely to Western demand—demand that can't be filled, at least not ethically or under current law. What that can mean for tens of thousands of loving but impoverished parents in the developing world is that they become the supply side of a multi-billion-dollar global industry driven not just by infertility but now also by pulpit commands.

The Christian adoption movement's rapid rise and the complicated scandals it has been party to provide lessons that are not limited to the faith-based sphere. This book focuses on evangelical Christians as the dominant group in adoption today, promoting an agenda that shapes larger trends. However, many of the same complexities are present in all adoptions, domestic and international, religious and secular. Although the Christian movement has led to particular problems and may be more blinded by the certainty that what they are doing is right and even divinely ordained, the movement's failures reflect the broader problems in the adoption industry as well as the intricate moral balance of how Americans and Westerners should engage in child welfare missions on the global stage.

"If you want to look at what's wrong with international adoption, state adoption, and Christian adoption," one agency director told me, "it all has to do with how they treat birthmothers. The common denominator in all of these is that the birthmother is invisible." When you get that, one adoptive parent wrote, it changes everything. Or, as another told me, "It's like the Wizard of Oz. You open the door and either you have to accept it's a house of cards or you stay in denial. There's absolutely no middle ground."

When I titled this book *The Child Catchers,* I thought of the tension between two possible interpretations of that phrase: a savior catching a child falling in midair and bringing him to safety or the darker image of some-one's offspring being snatched away from her family and home. It's the same tension that underlies the dueling narratives about the institution of modern adoption, often viewed as an unqualified good or an unqualified evil, purely rescue or purely theft. The truth, as usual, probably lies some-where in between, a different answer from case to case. But the rise of the Christian adoption movement threatens to tip that balance, bringing mil-lions of new advocates on board to fight on behalf of an industry too often marked by ambiguous goals and dirty money, turning poor countries' children into objects of salvation, then into objects of trade. That's not al-ways the story, but in the movement's short history, the sense of mission has frequently obscured the harm the industry can do, excusing missteps as the cost of doing God's work. It doesn't have to be that way, but figur-ing out how to do better means understanding what has gone wrong.

CHAPTER 1

New Life

On January 12, 2010, just before 5:00 in the afternoon, a 7.0 Richter earthquake rocked Haiti, the poorest country in the Western hemisphere. The streets of Port-au-Prince rippled like a blanket being shaken out. Cheap concrete buildings pancaked in on themselves, with broken bodies and phantom screams trapped within the suddenly stacked floors. The air was white with dust and debris, and bloodied victims, both alive and dead, lay everywhere. The second story of the presidential palace slid and shattered upon its own front steps. Major figures in the dominant Catholic Church, opposition politics, and international development were killed. Soon the smell of the dead—as many as three hundred thousand of them—filled the streets. Another three hundred thousand were estimated injured, and a quarter of a million homes were destroyed, leaving more than a million Haitians newly homeless. In the weeks that followed, tens of thousands to hundreds of thousands of victims were interred, by necessity, in mass graves dug into the hillsides surrounding the capital. It was a catastrophe of historic proportions, unlike anything seen in modern times: the death toll of the 2004 South Asian tsunami rolled into one country with a population just above that of New York City. But when the US media arrived, many came to talk about adoption.

Newspapers around the United States honed in on American parents who before the earthquake had been in the long process of adopting children from Haiti—parents who had been stymied for months or years while negotiating Haiti's complicated and greased-palm bureaucracy and now said they were in a state of "joyful panic" as their adoptions were

1

expedited, with the help of a joint US State Department and Department of Homeland Security program designed to get children who had been "in the adoption pipeline" out of the devastated country quickly.

Headlines drove home the earthquake's silver lining: "Hope and Heartbreak in Haiti," "Happy Endings for Some of Haiti's Children," "Daughter's Arrival Fulfills Family's Dreams." Stories about the earthquake were set in suburban homes in Texas or Maryland, as reporters pored over details of earthquake orphans' adjustment to life in the United States: running water, no rats in the bathroom, microwavable bacon.

At some point a shift happened, and the silver lining to Haiti's tragedy became the main story. Members of the media became involved in actively helping to generate more silver linings—more orphans brought "home" to the United States. To read the stories was to see a massive reimagining of where these children came from. Children were written about as though they had no unique past, no personal history deeper than their evident need. They were born again in tragedy, with the story of their "new lives," as newspapers routinely phrased it, beginning at the point when US parents intervened, at the crack of the earth's crust.

Before the earthquake adoptions from Haiti to the United States were relatively few, averaging between two and three hundred per year, but suddenly adopting Haitian children took on energy, prestige, and a sense of spiritual calling. Journalists reverentially sat with would-be adoptive parents or their supporters; one reported from the pews of a Tennessee church as the congregation passed photos of "our girls"—children in a Haitian orphanage who they had sponsored and now sought to get out of the country. Evangelical bloggers wrote about their conviction that "my child is waiting for me." Advocates traded statistics they had heard: if just a small percentage of American Christians would adopt a child, there would be no more orphans in Haiti. When emergency adoptions brought children to the United States, they gave thanks: "God is Good."

Adoption agencies reported an onslaught of applications to adopt from Haiti. Bethany Christian Services, the largest US adoption agency, announced they had received more applications for Haitian adoptions in January 2010 than they had in all of 2009, and adoption agencies across the United States received nearly twenty thousand inquiries for Haiti. Pop culture celebrities caught the fever too, with Queen Latifah telling the *Today Show*, "I wanna just go down there and get some of those babies. If you got a hook up, please get me a couple of Haitian kids. It's time. I'm ready."

It was hard not to come away with the impression that Americans were becoming the central figures in Haiti's drama, that Haiti's catastrophe was a foil against which US charity and quest for purpose could shine. Soon after the earthquake, in a crush at the Haitian airport, CNN's Soledad O'Brien described a heroic scene: "Tall, broad-shouldered American servicemen are walking around with tiny Haitian kids," she said, "and they are feeding them cold, clean water." Elsewhere in the airport a group of wealthy tech firm employees arrived with a private plane and an ambiguous determination to help, and they returned with a group of Americans carrying twenty-two Haitian babies and small children. The group boarded with no passport check, and the techies ascended into the air, high on a new sense of "meaning," O'Brien gushed.

When the plane landed in Fort Lauderdale, CNN rushed a live feed truck to meet it. O'Brien narrated as children disembarked and their new adoptive parents stood by in a hangar, then rushed onto the tarmac, "screaming with arms outstretched." Some children were scared; one yelled "Mommy." It's "an incredible human moment," reported O'Brien.

MEANWHILE, Haitian adults were being told to wait. The streets outside the US Embassy compound in Port-au-Prince were clogged with hundreds of prospective US adoptive parents, orphanage directors and their wards, as well as "loose children," reported notes from a January 21 teleconference held by US Citizenship and Immigration Services (USCIS). "Only adoption cases are being handled," a teleconference participant noted, and Haitians visiting the embassy for other reasons, such as preexisting visa and immigration applications, were turned away.

In the waters outside Haiti a fleet of US Coast Guard vessels moved into place, not just as part of a rescue mission but also in accordance with "Operation Vigilant Sentry," an anti-immigration military and US Department of Homeland Security strategy developed in 2003, to ensure that Haitian citizens didn't try to flee the destroyed capital by boat. Overhead an Air Force transport plane broadcast a statement in Creole from Haitian Ambassador to the United States Raymond Joseph, warning would-be refugees to stay away. "If you think you will reach the U.S. and all the doors will be wide open to you, that's not at all the case," Joseph's recorded message repeated. "They will intercept you right on the water, and send you back home where you came from." From an Air Force base in Florida, Homeland Security Secretary Janet Napolitano added, "Please do not have us divert our necessary rescue and relief efforts that are going into Haiti by trying to leave at this point."

"The message 'Don't come here, don't come here,' was being blared to adults," said Karen Dubinsky, a professor of global development studies at Queen's University in Canada and author of *Babies without Borders: Adoption and Migration Across the Americas*, "at the same time that this counter narrative is building about how we'll take the children."

In the United States some of the scores of adoption agencies with ties to Haitian orphanages, evangelical Christians newly mobilized around adoption, and sympathetic politicians led the charge for expedited adoptions of the country's alleged pre-earthquake population of four hundred thousand or more orphans. This figure was widely reported, despite a clarification from UNICEF—the United Nations Children's Fund, one of the UN's humanitarian arms—that likely there had been only fifty thousand orphans, in the widely understood sense of the word. Others had lost only one parent or lived with extended family. Identifying which children fit which category was a matter of painstaking investigation nearly impossible in the aftermath of the disaster. Nevertheless, adoption advocates soon embellished the already bloated numbers, stating that as many as one million children in Haiti—a full ninth of the country's total population—were now orphaned.

Long-standing religious relief organizations joined with upstart Haiti orphan missions to call for a reenactment of the 1960s anti-Communist "Operation Pedro (or Peter) Pan" that had spirited more than fourteen thousand children out of Castro's Cuba and into mostly Catholic homes in the United States.* The revival Catholic groups proposed for Haiti, "Operation Pierre Pan," was enveloped in the language of emergency, with impassioned calls to "get the children out," as if they were boarding the last plane off the island. It was language that recalled another mission, the 1975 "Operation Babylift" evacuation of thirty-three hundred Vietnamese children to North America and Europe just before the Fall of Saigon. Evangelical activists suggested that any aid planes delivering supplies to Haiti should return to the United States "load[ed] up with orphans."

---

*Interestingly, the ideological battle at stake in this mission has carried over even to how it is named. Many US advocates refer to the mission as "Operation Pedro Pan" to depict it as a local Cuban initiative to send their children out of harm's way, while many Cubans refer to it as "Operation Peter Pan" to underscore what they see as its imperialistic roots in the United States.

But rather than saving children from Communism or an impending military attack, this time the urgency seemed to center on saving children from Haiti itself. "Haiti cannot feed its children," one US orphanage director, Harold Nungester of H.I.S. Home for Children, argued in the *Wall Street Journal*. "The best way to service them is to get them out."

Again and again Haitian children were characterized as prisoners in a backward nation, their ambiguous orphanhood overshadowed by their status as victims. Few asked where these children came from, if they had surviving family and friends in Haiti who were looking for them, or if they wanted to leave their country. As it would turn out, many were not actually orphans.

On some adoptive parent forums, noted the website Racialicious, which covers racial politics in the United States, commenters fretted about what would happen to children in a country where "survival of the fittest" had replaced the rule of order. The racial dynamics of the prevailing attitude toward the Haitian orphans were stark in their implication that Haiti, a nation birthed by a slave rebellion, had become a sort of animal kingdom from which children must be rescued, lest, Racialicious interpreted, "they won't even grow up to be human beings."

"Those children in five or ten years, what are they going to become?" Pastor Pierre Alexis, director of another Port-au-Prince orphanage, Maison des Enfants de Dieu, asked me. Haiti's children are the future and the country's resource, he continued, "But everyone knows when you have a resource and you don't use it in a proper way, it becomes a problem." The best option for them, he said, is to get them adopted. "There is no other plan for the children." As if in response, Haiti's prime minister, Jean-Max Bellerive, asked the *Wall Street Journal*, "How can we rebuild a nation if the only chance that parents have to give their children a future is to part with them?"

In the US the Adoptees of Color Roundtable, an organization of adult adoptees, released a statement in late January characterizing the adoption rush in Haiti as a colonialist and racist movement that disregarded Haitian family structures in favor of Western parents' sense of entitlement to developing nations' children. "For more than fifty years, 'orphaned children' have been shipped from areas of war, natural disasters, and poverty to supposedly better lives in Europe and North America," the Roundtable statement read. "We seek to challenge those who abuse the phrase 'Every child deserves a family' to rethink how this phrase is used to justify the removal of children from Haiti." It was a statement that got at the heart of the conflicts surrounding international child adoption—conflicts that rarely surface in popular American discourse, in which adoption is generally understood as a "win-win" scenario: saintly parents creating their family from the wreckage of another, giving love and a home to a child that has neither. Another critic derided what he termed "the Moment," the fairytale photo-ops dominating cable news when adoptees first land on US soil, "as if they've arrived at the Promised Land." This narrative of adoption as child rescue usually drowns out the more critical interpretation—that adoption is an industry driven largely by money and Western demand, justified by a misguided savior complex that blinds Americans to orphans' existing family ties and assumes that tickets to America for a handful of children are an appropriate fix for an entire culture living in poverty. But in Haiti in early 2010, in the midst of this murky old fight, the critics' side of the story became suddenly, startlingly clear as a sped-up version of the same vigilante child-rescue efforts that have taken place in dozens of other countries unfolded on the public stage. For a brief, unique moment people watching from around the world understood what the other side meant.

IN THE THICK of the debate over where Haiti's children should go, on January 29 came news that ten American Baptists from a fledgling Idaho orphan ministry, New Life Children's Refuge, were caught at the border of the Dominican Republic attempting to transport thirty-three children, ranging from infancy to twelve years old, out of Haiti without permission or documentation. The group was arrested on suspicion of trafficking and kidnapping, and they were eventually charged with kidnapping and criminal conspiracy, leading to a bonanza of headline stories about American Christians "kidnapping for Jesus."

Self-declared missionary Laura Silsby, a struggling, forty-year-old entrepreneur from Idaho with a troubled financial past, led the group. She had been CEO of a failed personal shopping business and at the time of her arrest was on the wrong end of at least fourteen claims for unpaid wages. Silsby had been brought up as the daughter of a missionary minister in the Wesleyan Holiness Church, which prohibits dancing, television, and alcohol and expects women to wear long dresses and not cut their hair. She was a sharp student who graduated high school at fifteen and then earned a business administration degree from Washington State University.

By late 2009, however, Silsby was a divorced mother of three, entangled in a custody battle with her ex-husband and facing the fallout of her failed business. With her financial and personal life in collapse, she took several trips to Haiti and the Dominican Republic and started making plans to build an orphanage in the DR for Haitian children. She founded the New Life Children's Refuge in November 2009, and then, just one month before the earthquake, Silsby and her children abruptly moved out of their house in Meridian, Idaho, to a rental home as the bank prepared to foreclose.

Silsby belonged to Meridian's 890-member Central Valley Baptist Church, a congregation in the Southern Baptist Convention, a denomination wherein many churches in recent decades have promoted short-term mission trips among their flocks. Christians from these churches have traveled overseas in unprecedented numbers, paying thousands of dollars on "voluntourism" vacations to developing nations.* There they constructed buildings or wells or spent time at orphanages, playing with children and bringing back a taste for Ethiopian coffee at their church's postservice fellowship hour. Voluntourism frequently amounts to a de-professionalization of missionary work, a shift from career missionaries who learn the language, culture, and laws of the country to amateurs combining sightseeing and charity. The same sort of volunteer-centered agenda that is often present in short-term missions seems to have been a central component of the Silsby affair.

Shortly after the earthquake Paul Thompson, an acquaintance of Silsby's and the pastor of a neighboring Southern Baptist church, Eastside Baptist in Twin Falls, Idaho, sent an urgent e-mail to friends asking for fellow missionaries to join him and Silsby on a two- or three-week trip to Haiti. A group of ten missionaries assembled, mostly from the two

---

*"Voluntourism" has been criticized in recent years for doing more harm than good. A 2010 report by the Human Sciences Research Council on AIDS orphan tourism in Southern Africa found that global trends of voluntourism often centered around orphanages, with wealthy Westerners paying to spend time on their vacations or mission trips playing with institutionalized children. Too often, wrote report coauthors Linda Richter and Amy Norman, the emotional needs of the tourists are the key focus of these trips, as visitors seek personal fulfillment by forging immediate emotional connections with orphanage children. But after the tourists leave, the children suffer yet another abandonment, leading to a pattern of intense connection and loss that is detrimental to their emotional well-being and development.

churches, and they collected emergency donations in plastic tubs to carry with them to the Dominican Republic.

Silsby approached the earthquake with an entrepreneur's optimism. She already had plans to build an orphanage in the Dominican Republic, so to her the earthquake seemed a sign to begin work early. "God has laid upon our hearts the need to go now vs. waiting until the permanent facility is built," declared a planning document for New Life Children's Refuge that was posted on the Eastside Baptist website. On her arrival in the Dominican Republic on January 22, Silsby leased a forty-five-room hotel from the Dominican Catholic diocese—presumably paid for with donation money—and launched New Life's first project, the "Haitian Orphan Rescue Mission." The itinerary for the mission outlined a straightforward plan: "Drive bus from Santo Domingo into Port au Prince, Haiti and gather 100 orphans from the streets and collapsed orphanages, then return to the DR." The planning document explained that ultimately the venture would "provide opportunities for adoption through partnership with New Life Adoption Foundation," another as-yet-undeveloped arm of the operation that would work with US adoption agencies and provide grants "for loving Christian parents who would otherwise not be able to afford to adopt."

Though Silsby later claimed that she had never intended to put the children up for adoption, her plans for the orphanage included a beachfront cafe and seaside "villas for adopting parents to stay [in] while fulfilling requirement for [a] 60–90 day visit as well as [for] Christian volunteers/vacationing families," amenities that underscored her understanding of local Dominican adoption residency requirements. The document also described the group's goal to "equip each child" with the opportunity "for adoption into a loving Christian family" and help them find "new life in Christ." It asked Christians to pray that God "continue to grant favor with the Dominican government in allowing us to bring as many orphans as we can into the DR."

The promise of "new life"—meaning not just a new family but also a new faith—was an undercurrent in the broader crisis. To those who understood evangelical manners of speaking, the term "new life"—the inspiration for naming countless churches and ministries—seemed to cast adoption as one way of making new Christians. The promise of new life was often accompanied by statements implicitly disparaging aid that didn't take Haitians' spiritual well-being into account—help that saved only a body but not a soul. As Dan Cruver, head of evangelical adoption advocacy group Together for Adoption, attested at a Christian adoption conference later that spring, after arguing that shipments of water bottles had only compounded Haiti's worries by creating a mountain of trash, "Relief, as important as it is, is not the answer. What is the answer is the church."

Overt evangelism was common in the many orphanages attempting to evacuate Haitian orphans. A Miami-based orphanage, His House, which coordinated adoptions for children airlifted from Haiti after the earthquake, described its mission as turning children into "Christ-like persons." The Texas ministry For His Glory Adoption Outreach, meanwhile, considered Haiti to be a country "dedicated to Satan in a contractual form," a reference to the apocryphal "pact with the devil" that Haiti's independence fighters are said to have made in exchange for freedom from French rule. For His Glory aimed to fulfill the Bible's Great Commission mandate, the charge that Christians evangelize the world, by placing orphans in Christian homes. Kim Harmon, president of For His Glory, personally adopted six of her eight children from the Port-au-Prince orphanage Maison des Enfants de Dieu, which her organization supports. "We want our children to be adopted by Christian families because we want them to be God's servants," Maison's director Pastor Pierre Alexis told me. "I know [God] likes it when we are feeding them, but He likes better—He loves—when the children are growing as His servants."

These evangelical motivations went largely unremarked in news media coverage of orphanages seeking to evacuate their wards. It was as if a consensus had been reached that Haiti—a seeming hellscape where children were fed mud cakes by their starving parents, or were sold into child slavery as *restaveks** in a country whose very name evoked voodoo, the underworld, and death—might need a level of evangelism that wouldn't be tolerated in a more developed country. In some cases journalists were explicitly embedded with evangelical orphanage workers. That spring, with the help of Christian film producers from Discover the Journey, an advocacy-oriented documentary group that creates videos about subjects like child soldiers, CNN's Soledad O'Brien made a TV documentary, *Rescued*, about an evangelical orphanage in Haiti called the Lighthouse. There, volunteers came, she wrote, "moved by a desire to leave behind their plastic lives, grasp meaning, and pursue God's grace." In a special preview for a group of evangelical adoption advocates, a Discover the

---

*Restaveks are children sent to live as unpaid domestics for relatives or other families.

Journey staffer asked the audience to help spread the word about the film, offering in exchange her winking assurance that O'Brien will "come out a believer."*

Despite the public fervor to adopt "earthquake orphans," the logistics of the adoptions themselves proved difficult. The quake had destroyed the Port-au-Prince building containing the vast majority of adoption paperwork for Haiti's children and killed the judge who oversaw adoptions. But on January 18, just days before Silsby and her mission were to arrive in the Dominican Republic, the US State Department and Department of Homeland Security responded to these complications by announcing its "humanitarian parole" policy, which would ultimately expedite the emigration of more than 1,150 "orphaned children" who had been matched with US parents on temporary authorization papers. Adoption advocates, however, pushed for even more measures to open and speed up the process. Although the devastation had rendered the Haitian government incapable of tracking either institutionalized or newly "unaccompanied" children's existing family connections, adoption advocates pressed to expand the humanitarian parole program to thousands of other children—to get children out of Haiti first and investigate whether those children had surviving families later, after they were safe in the United States, no matter that children of unclear origin taken to America are rarely returned. "The paperwork can wait," summarized a headline in the *Times* of London, "everybody wins with adoption."

Conversely, UNICEF, along with other aid groups like Save the Children and World Vision, called for an adoption moratorium until Haitian officials could determine which unaccompanied children were legitimate orphans, citing fears of child trafficking and misguided salvation missions. In response some adoption advocates charged that this goal made the perfect the enemy of the good; they accused UNICEF of leaving chil-

---

*O'Brien seems to have become a believer in at least one sense, repeating in an essay on CNN.com a motivational story that has been widely adapted as the driving parable in the Christian adoption movement: the "starfish story." This tale tells of a young boy rescuing a coastline of beached starfish by throwing them back in the water, one at a time, when a naysaying older man scoffs that he can never save them all. "It matters to the one," the boy replies in a sentiment that has become the anthem of the movement.

dren to suffer in the name of bureaucracy and "flexing their muscles" to harass Christian orphanages.

Such claims weren't new to UNICEF, long a *bête noire* of the adoption community and frequently accused of being so anti-adoption that it would rather see children die in institutions than be adopted to the United States. UNICEF's official stance is that international adoption is a good option for some children and preferable to orphanage care but that in-country options, such as reuniting children with their birth families or placing them with domestic adoptive parents, must be exhausted first. This hierarchy of options, known as "the principle of subsidiarity," also guides the Hague Adoption Convention, an international compact drawn to prevent adoption trafficking and corruption. Nonetheless, UNICEF still garnered special disdain among the Christian adoption advocates who flocked to the country after the quake.

Dixie Bickel, director of God's Littlest Angels orphanage in Fermate, outside Port-au-Prince, charged that "UNICEF appears to be the only organization that we're aware of that is currently working in Haiti that isn't working for the good of the children," while Randy Bohlender, founder of the Christian adoption ministry the Zoe Foundation, called UNICEF's subsidiarity principle "nation-pandering," a statement implying that Haiti shouldn't control what happened to its children.

Vision Forum Ministries, a far-right offshoot of a fundamentalist Texas homeschooling publisher that had assembled a Haitian rescue mission of its own, asserted that "Haiti's Children [are being] Held Hostage by UNICEF's Agenda." The group went on to make the wild claim that UNICEF would soon move from preventing adoptions to sterilizing Haitians.

The accusations built to such a pitch that Susan Bissell, UNICEF chief of child protection, spent much of her time addressing them in postearthquake interviews. "UNICEF is very much in favor of international adoption with the right system in place at the right time for the right children," Bissell repeated to me. "UNICEF isn't saying this stuff. There are international conventions that lay this out, and we're just compliant."

But adoption organizations and right-wing Christian ministries weren't the only source of attacks on UNICEF. Senator Mary Landrieu, a Louisiana Democrat who has made adoption her signature issue, threw down the gauntlet when she argued to expand the State Department's humanitarian parole program to other Haitian children. "Either UNICEF is going to change or have a very difficult time getting support from the U.S. Congress," she said. "Americans take this call very seriously."

WHEN THEIR BUS ARRIVED in Haiti on January 25, Laura Silsby and her team began knocking on doors around the devastated neighborhoods of Port-au-Prince, leaving flyers in one city slum, Citron, which was damaged by the earthquake, and one mountain village, Calebasse, which wasn't. Their flyer solicited "children who have lost their mother and father in the earthquake or have no one to love or care for them" and proclaimed that Silsby and her group "love God, and He has given us tremendous love for the children of Haiti." It also claimed that the group had permission from the Haitian government to take one hundred children to the Dominican Republic.

In Calebasse Silsby and her team enlisted a young English-speaking man in the village to assemble the town's five hundred residents on a soccer field so the missionaries could hand out their flyer, which showed the Dominican hotel and its swimming pool, and described the fields and school the children would have access to at the orphanage that they planned to build. One Calebasse mother, Maggie Moise, later told a *Guardian* reporter that a member of the group had assured her she would have access to her children. So she signed the paper that the missionaries presented, reasoning that Haiti would be a difficult place to live in for some time. Other parents in Calebasse later said that they hadn't realized they were relinquishing their children to a group who might put them up for international adoption, presenting *New York Times* reporters with school photos and awards for their children as testament that they never intended to let them go permanently.

In earthquake-ravaged Citron a Haitian pastor from Atlanta, Jean Sainvil of the Haiti Sharing Jesus Ministries, helped Silsby gather children, some of whom thought they were going on a holiday. Some parents seemed to believe it was an educational program or a temporary relief effort to keep the children safe in the Dominican Republic. One father told the *Wall Street Journal* that he had given his five-year-old son to Silsby because "the chance to educate a child is a chance for an entire family to prosper," an indication that he, like many in the developing world, did not understand the concept of Western adoption—that their children would not return. Another father, Regilus Chesnel, told the Associated Press that Pastor Sainvil had warned parents that epidemic disease was on its way and that the children could fall victim.

On January 28 twenty children got onto Silsby's bus in Calebasse along with another thirteen in Citron, their names written on pink tape stuck to their clothes. The group was stopped the next day at the Haitian-

Dominican border and questioned about the undocumented kids on the bus. The children were taken into custody by the relief group SOS Children's Villages International. One baby was hospitalized for dehydration, and others were hungry after a long drive and a night spent sleeping on the street. As it would turn out, the children were not orphans; according to SOS Children's Villages, all thirty-three had at least one living parent. One girl declared to the SOS workers, "I am not an orphan." Later all but one of the children were successfully reunited with their families, who had reacted to the situation varyingly. One mother had become catatonic when she was told she had accidentally sent her four children to be adopted. Conversely, those who had wanted their children cared for in the Dominican Republic didn't know how they could afford to feed them now that they were returned. Two years after the incident one of the Calebasse fathers remarked to the Associated Press that the parents had wanted to send their children off on the missionaries' bus to get them away from the general chaos after the earthquake and that if any children had stayed behind, it was only because there wasn't enough room.

The missionaries were escorted back to Port-au-Prince, where Silsby was questioned. Eventually all of the adults were jailed. Silsby immediately began a defense of ignorance, claiming their hearts had been in the right place and they hadn't thought documentation for children would be required in the context of the emergency. "These people would never do something like this in their own country," Chief of Haiti's National Judicial Police Frantz Thermilus said of Silsby's group. "We must make it clear they cannot do such things in ours."

Haiti's adoption system had been problematic even before the earthquake, however. A 2005 UNICEF report declared Haiti's adoption program "untransparent." Many children in Haiti, as in other developing nations, are placed in crèches, or orphanages, because of their families' poverty alone, meaning that orphanages can serve both as homes for truly parentless orphans and as de facto boarding schools for children whose parents can't afford to feed or care for them but who may continue to visit them and still consider them part of the family. In part because of the proliferation of crèches and also due to a lack of education or language and cultural barriers, some parents may inadvertently relinquish parental consent for their children without realizing the full implications—or, worse, may not relinquish it at all before their children are sent abroad. A group of three doctors and a social worker who went to Haiti shortly after the earthquake wrote in the *New England Journal of Medicine* that "Desperately poor families have often felt compelled to place children in residential care facilities, only to return later and find that they have been given away for adoption."

International adoption financially sustains many orphanages, as adoption agencies share with them a percentage of fees, which for Haiti often range from $10,000 to $25,000, paid by adoptive parents in the United States or Europe. Further, prospective adopters frequently pay monthly care stipends of several hundred dollars while a child is still in the orphanage. The money can become a powerful enticement to favor international adoptions over finding domestic adoptive parents for children or helping existing family reclaim them. Considering all of the middlemen involved—lawyers, civil servants, orphanage staff, facilitators, notaries, and more—some estimates value Haiti's adoption business at $20 million per year, making it one of the more profitable industries in a country where approximately 80 percent of the population lives on less than $2 a day.

Susie Krabacher is the director of Mercy and Sharing, a long-running Christian orphanage in Haiti that doesn't conduct adoptions. According to Krabacher, after the earthquake unethical adoption and child sponsorship programs became "the biggest money-making operation in Haiti," with real and fake orphanages "popping up everywhere." In the case of fake orphanages, savvy Haitians tried to capitalize on Westerners' interest by rounding up neighborhood kids to play the part of orphans when tourists came by in order to solicit donations. In the real orphanages staff made blunt suggestions that parents struggling to feed their children should give one up. Krabacher estimated that among Mercy and Sharing's own 181 employees, "We've got 90 percent who would have to look at the option of giving up a child if they didn't have a job."

Sometimes the death of a family member precipitates such relinquishments, as families spend their last $75 on a coffin to bury the dead—a nonnegotiable rite in Haitian culture. Sometimes it's the drain of sending one child to school at the expense of feeding the others so that the one child might eventually bring the family out of poverty. There's a word-of-mouth component as well, as people in positions to counsel parents, such as church pastors, have been known to call orphanages and tell them when a young woman is pregnant as well as to help convince the expectant mother to relinquish her child in exchange for a cut of the adoption fee. It's not uncommon, Krabacher said, for women working in orphanages to place their own children for adoption, meaning that some nannies are actually tending their own children until the day they are adopted away. "The people almost never really want to give up the child,"

Krabacher told me. "When they do it, it's because they think they're going to save the other three at home."

IN PICTURES TAKEN after her arrest, Laura Silsby appeared as a resolute woman with a youthful, freckled face and shoulder-length brown hair, wearing sleeveless blouses and denim shorts in the Caribbean sun. Picturing her in the calling she had imagined for herself was easy—a vision of an orphanage director making a fresh start in a simple life, moving between the developing world of orphanage children and the first world of adoptive parents she would cater to as they brunched by the beach at Silsby's seaside villas. It likely didn't hurt that this life would track with the increasingly visible representation in Christian movies and media of white evangelicals saving black children, from *The Blind Side*'s sassy Memphis adoptive mom to *Machine Gun Preacher*'s gun-toting savior of Ugandan child soldiers, both careening into danger to save children in need.

Throughout their imprisonment the American missionaries claimed they had acted in good faith, believing they had government permission to transport the children. In reality at least Silsby had received repeated warnings that her plan was unethical and illegal. Prior to taking the children Silsby had contacted Dixie Bickel, director of the God's Littlest Angels orphanage, who claimed she told Silsby that "UNICEF and [Haitian Social Services] are waiting to crucify somebody like you, taking children out of Haiti."

Before carrying out her plans, Silsby had also spoken to a US journalist, Anne-Christine d'Adesky of *Haiti Vox Bulletin,* explaining that they had a letter from a Dominican government minister authorizing their transport of one hundred children and "connections" that would help her cross the border. Although d'Adesky had warned Silsby that such a letter was inadequate authorization, Silsby was unfazed. "Throughout our conversation," d'Adesky later wrote, "she repeatedly referred to God having called her to rescue the Haitian children. God had spoken to her. If God wanted them to succeed, they would."

When Silsby had spoken to a Port-au-Prince school official about her plan, the official had told her that it was "unconscionable." Another orphanage director, Hal Nungester from H.I.S. Home for Children, told *CBS News* that Silsby had approached their orphanage, seeking one hundred orphans to take to the Dominican Republic. "They had no paperwork. They had no authorization from the U.S. government, from the Haitian government, or from anyone involved. They were just taking kids. That fits right in with what I would classify as child trafficking," Nungester said.

A Dominican official, Carlos Castillo of the DR's consulate in Port-au-Prince, had met with Silsby soon after she and her group arrived in Haiti. Castillo had warned her that she didn't have sufficient documentation to transport children from Haiti to the DR. "She told me she would try to reach the border in order to cross," Castillo told the *Wall Street Journal*. "I told her not to do that without the necessary documents because she could be accused of trafficking children." Regardless, Silsby offered Castillo's business card when she reached the Dominican border, claiming he had authorized her passage.

A police officer later alleged that he had stopped Silsby's bus of children several days before their arrest and had told them that their plan was illegal. Despite these many warnings as well as the fact that Silsby had shown a savvy understanding of the residency requirements for adoptive parents coming to the Dominican Republic, she would go on to claim ignorance of Haiti's adoption laws.

Silsby had also contacted a Kentucky couple, Richard and Malinda Pickett, who were in the midst of adopting three children from a Port-au-Prince orphanage, and offered to pick the children up for them. The Picketts, fearful she would jeopardize the proper legal proceedings of their adoptions, told Silsby to leave the children where they were. However, Silsby went to their orphanage anyway, claiming to be Malinda's friend. When she learned that the children were no longer in residence, she asked the staff if there were any others she could take instead.

Silsby made the same inquiry at other orphanages, which, to her distress, refused to give her any of their wards. Richard Pickett later told a Kentucky television station that he thought Silsby had intended to use a "mild form of extortion" on him and his wife in the case that she had succeeded in picking up their children. "She asked for kids at each of the orphanages, and at the end of the day when no one would give her any, she cried," he told the Associated Press. "Why would you cry after you see these kids are being taken care of?"

RUSSELL MOORE, dean of the school of theology at the Southern Baptist Theological Seminary in Louisville, Kentucky, and author of a book promoting adoption among Christians, worried that the Silsby scandal would "give a black eye to the orphan-care movement." Moore, a rising young star in the Southern Baptist Convention (SBC) who frequently guest hosts theologian Albert Mohler's radio show, dedicated his program on February 1, 2010 to the controversy. "I thought, 'Oh no, this is going to cause all kinds of derision to the orphan-care movement and to what the Holy Spirit is doing in churches all across America and all over the world in having a heart for orphans,'" Moore said.

Moore's guest, fellow adoption activist Jedd Medefind, president of the Christian Alliance for Orphans, described the incident as an embarrassment to the cause. At the time the Christian Alliance was promoting its annual conference as a way that "ordinary people can make a *lasting* difference for orphans—in Haiti or otherwise." Medefind had responded to the Silsby story with a *Christianity Today* op-ed entitled "Strong on Zeal, Thin in Knowledge," describing Silsby's actions as an aberration. "I think some folks who really oppose our approach to caring for children will kind of point to this very mistakenly as Exhibit A of reasons why a focus on adoption is not healthy and why you should leave caring for orphans just to governments and not allow ordinary people in the church to be involved," he told Moore.

Adoption professionals, like Tom DiFilipo of the adoption lobby group the Joint Council on International Children's Services, refused to acknowledge the connection at all, arguing that because the group was acting outside adoption law, they couldn't be planning adoptions. "What they were going to do with those kids I don't know," he told me, "but it sure as hell wasn't adoption. Their actions were wrong, clearly, and abhorrent in the way they went about this. It was equally abhorrent the way it was portrayed in the press that this was an adoption-related incident."

But in fact Silsby's failed mission looked less like the exception than the rule of the "orphan airlifts" taking place after the earthquake. When For His Glory Adoption Outreach attempted to evacuate 100 infants and young children out of Haiti just after the earthquake, ferrying them to the US embassy uninvited in the hopes that arriving with a busload of carsick children and CNN reporters would force the embassy's hand, a staffer justified it by saying, "The children do not want to go back to the orphanage. They want to go to America." They eventually ended up flying 110 orphans out of the country, including one for adoption by the agency's president, Kim Harmon. H.I.S. Home for Children, another evangelical organization, flew 67 to Miami and 50 to Orlando on military cargo planes.

Senator Amy Klobuchar, a Democrat from Minnesota who has made common cause with conservatives like Senator James Inhofe (R-OK) and former Senator Sam Brownback (R-KS) on adoption legislation, spoke at

Medefind's Christian Alliance for Orphans Summit later in 2010, boasting that her office had helped bring thirty-nine Haitian orphans to Minnesota despite the complications thrown in the works from "the Idaho people." Klobuchar later told me how, as part of the first senatorial group on the ground in Haiti, she had urged Haitian President René Préval to request that Minnesota's humanitarian parole cases be expedited and to revise the country's adoption and parental rights policies as part of reconstruction so as to clear the obstacles that were impeding more adoptions.

People began to speak in counterfactual terms of "repatriating" Haitian children to the United States or "reunifying" them with adoptive parents, despite the reality that none of the children were being returned to their home countries or families in any way except in the minds of prospective adoptive parents, who had already come to think of the children as their own. Others used the emotional language of a hostage situation. A Salt Lake City TV station reported that Stephen Studdert, a former Mormon mission president and Republican adviser to Presidents George H. W. Bush, Ronald Reagan, and Gerald Ford, had used his connections in Washington and "negotiated the release" of at least sixty-six orphans bound for Salt Lake City.

Although Haiti had taken the advice of UNICEF and Save the Children to close its doors to new adoptions temporarily, allowing only humanitarian parole cases to proceed, demand remained strong. When a rumor started in Indiana that three hundred Haitian child refugees would be brought to the state, Safe Families for Children, a Christian foster care alternative organization, aided by a local six thousand–member megachurch, recruited hundreds of volunteers to adopt them, even though no Haitian children were actually coming. Some adoption agencies continued to sign up applicants for Haitian adoptions or put people on "waiting lists." Others used the outpouring of interest to divert prospective adopters to other countries where they worked.

The US humanitarian parole program in Haiti allowed expedited adoptions for only two categories of children: those whose adoptions were all but completed before the earthquake and those who had recently been matched with prospective adoptive parents but who needed to be evacuated for their safety. But in practice, in the latter category the standard of proof was so low—such as children who had had any level of contact with a family in the United States—that other children ended up being transported under official US jurisdiction as well, including children from orphanages that were largely unaffected by the earthquake or those who had not been cleared for adoption at all. Two siblings whose adoption had previously been denied after their father objected—he had initially thought adoption was a chance for the children to go to school—were rushed out of Haiti on humanitarian parole after the earthquake, and their adoption was approved in a US court that didn't hear the Haitian family's arguments. "God got done in 10 days something human beings couldn't do in years," the adoptive father told the *New York Times*.

But perhaps the most famous case was that of twelve children sent to Pittsburgh on a military cargo plane commissioned by former Pennsylvania Governor Edward Rendell. On January 19, just one day after the US humanitarian parole program was announced, Rendell and Pennsylvania Representative Jason Altmire muscled through the evacuation of fifty-four children housed at a Christian orphanage, BRESMA, run by two young, photogenic Pittsburgh sisters, Jamie and Ali McMutrie. Rendell's position allowed him to land his plane at the chaotic Port-au-Prince airport in the same time period when a Doctors Without Borders flight was diverted three times to the Dominican Republic.

When Haitian officials only approved twenty-eight of the fifty-four BRESMA children to leave, the McMutrie sisters refused to budge. They insisted on taking all fifty-four. Governor Rendell and his wife, a circuit court judge, appealed to US diplomats in Haiti and contacts at the White House. Eventually they were allowed to take all of the children, including twelve whose families hadn't authorized their adoption. These twelve "orphans" would remain in legal limbo in a Pittsburgh Catholic institute for nearly a year while the International Red Cross found and contacted their families in Haiti. The mother of one of the children later told the *New York Times* that she hadn't known she wouldn't see her child again until she visited the orphanage several days after the evacuation to discover they were all gone. Even adoption advocates recognized that the mission had been poorly executed. "The exception made for these children was based on the political connections of Governor Rendell and the emotional response of the McMutrie sisters, when it should have been based on a plan that ensured permanent care for the children," argued a brief on postearthquake adoptions issued by the National Council for Adoption (NCFA), one of the two largest US adoption lobbying groups. (The NCFA had discouraged immediate adoption of new "orphans" after the earthquake in favor of children already in institutions and worried that vigilante rescue efforts would antagonize foreign governments into shutting down adoption permanently.)

An unnamed State Department official told the *New York Times* that "This wasn't supposed to happen this way," but the popularity of Rendell's rash mission outweighed such tepid bureaucratic rebukes. In the wake of Rendell's rescue operation Kathleen Strottman, executive director of the NGO the Congressional Coalition on Adoption, said that adoptive parents lobbied many government officials from other states, arguing, "Governor Rendell flew down there, why can't you?"

The rule bending wasn't limited to overzealous individuals, however. At the 2010 Adoption Policy Conference in New York Whitney Reitz, the USCIS staffer credited with crafting the "humanitarian parole" program, was reported by *Huffington Post* as saying, "The idea was to help the kids. And if we overlooked Hague"—the international adoption convention— "I don't think I'm going to apologize."

Reitz's colleague, USCIS spokesperson Chris Rhatigan, said the quote was taken from an off-the-record session meant to be attended only by adoptive parents. Otherwise Rhatigan defends the actions of USCIS staff as exemplary under the circumstances of a full-scale emergency, when US personnel were working under duress and long hours to get children out of the country: holding conference calls with adoption service providers, answering endless questions from panicked prospective adoptive parents, and even fielding adoptive parents' midnight calls as they passed through immigration in Miami with their new children. In their field office in Haiti, immigration officer Pius Bannis, who would be named the 2010 federal employee of the year for his work during the crisis, worked twenty-hour days for two weeks as he helped document hundreds of Haitian children for adoption, some of whom stayed at the embassy in a makeshift day care. "Very extraordinary measures were taken to save the lives of over 1,100 children," Rhatigan said. "In light of the emergency situation, I think they did everything they possibly could have."

In the end some 2,100 children were adopted out of Haiti after the earthquake, including more than 1,150 children to the United States and about 900 more to Europe and Canada. It's not a huge number, but it was double the country's normal standard and a sizable percentage of international adoptions to the United States in 2010. About 350 of the children sent to the United States represented adoption cases that were nearly final, whereas the remainder—the vast majority of the humanitarian parole cases—were in the second, more ambiguous category. "This acute augmentation in figures shows that inter-country adoptions were disturbingly 'over' prioritized during the emergency," a report from International Social Services concluded. The report also found that the expedited procedures "resulted in what one can only describe as chaos for all parties involved," with no Haitian oversight body, no investigation of children's surviving family, and with Haitian government officials who were as disconnected from adoption policy as the minister of agriculture being called upon to approve children's adoption paperwork.

After the Haiti earthquake, several congressional bills were proposed, and Christian bloggers lobbied hard for them. There was the HOPE Act— an acronym for Haitian Orphan Placement Effort—that was sponsored by Republican Representative Peter Hoekstra of Michigan. This bill sought to expand humanitarian parole adoptions to children who hadn't been in the process of being adopted. And there was the Help HAITI Act, introduced by Republican Representative Jeff Fortenberry of Nebraska, an antiabortion stalwart whose bill aimed to "help Haiti" by expediting permanent resident status and, thus, eventually citizenship for Haitian adoptees rushed into the country under humanitarian parole. Controversy almost struck down the bill in late November 2010, when an unnamed Democratic aide told *Congressional Quarterly* that Democrats were considering tying the bill to President Obama's DREAM Act, which would have created a path to legal residency for undocumented children whose parents had brought them into the country. Conservatives reacted with outrage, with *Rightwing News* sputtering, "Think of it . . . if Republicans vote against the DREAM Act . . . they would also be voting AGAINST the orphans." Once again the lines between which sorts of poor people from developing countries deserved Americans' help were clearly drawn.

"This [bill] is about Haitian orphans and their adoptive American families," said Fortenberry, seemingly unaware of how that definition conflicted with the bill title's larger promise to "Help Haiti." "To leverage that bill for a highly controversial immigration measure was just wrong." The bill passed, without any association with the DREAM Act, on December 1. Fortenberry called it a "Christmas present" for adoptive families.

GOVERNMENT OFFICIALS often bend to pressure from constituents when it comes to adoption, seizing the opportunity for an easy PR boost and not recognizing the rationale behind adoption restrictions. As Karen Moline, a board member of Parents for Ethical Adoption Reform (PEAR), an adoptive parents' advocacy group, said, "Congress's slant is that international adoption is good, let's get those kids out. They don't understand the business aspect of it, just the humanitarian side."

But at least for a short time the Silsby affair changed the script for how adoption ethics are discussed, bringing a critique of Western imperialism—

a topic usually reserved for academia—into the public sphere. For Moline, "Laura Silsby did a good thing. She put a face to the worst part of what international adoption can be, which is entitlement" to poorer countries' children.

Karen Dubinsky said that the long-standing debate over international adoption is often interpreted in binary terms, seen as either solely rescue or solely kidnapping. The Silsby affair brought these discussions into sharp relief. "Usually things are more subtle than that, but this was one of those moments where the battle lines became incredibly stark," said Dubinksy. "What they tried to do has been done a million times in human history, especially after disaster. . . . It's become seamless: disaster happens, and we in the West show up with bottled water, and we'll take your children."

It had happened five years earlier, in Indonesia's Banda Aceh province after the 2004 tsunami, when the Virginia-based missionary group WorldHelp announced its intention to adopt 300 Muslim tsunami orphans into a US Christian orphanage so the group could "plant Christian principles as early as possible." And it had happened again in 2007, when a French charity, Zoe's Ark, was accused of kidnapping 103 children from Chad, children they claimed were Sudanese war orphans when in fact many were local Chadian kids with families. (Group members were initially sentenced to eight years' hard labor but were later pardoned by Chadian President Idriss Déby. They faced trial in France in December 2012.)

However, by 2010 the disconnected missions of various Christian ministries had become a cause, and in Haiti the seams of the typically seamless narrative—disaster abroad followed by American adoptions—were unusually visible. With Haiti's government in a state of sudden and obvious devastation and its sovereignty disputed on all sides, the fate of the country's children became a line in the sand. "Silsby had the misfortune to arrive on the scene at this particular moment," Dubinsky said.

Silsby seemed to recognize this too, appearing indignant in her defense that she was being punished for something so many had done before. In an affidavit she would later file when her ex-husband sued for full custody of their children, Silsby downplayed the scandal, explaining, "We learned ours was only one of many groups bringing children out of Haiti without documentation or incident."

In their public statements, though, Silsby and the missionaries maintained that they had been called by God. Silsby's former live-in nanny, twenty-four-year-old Charisa Coulter, whom Silsby had made codirector of New Life Children's Refuge, echoed this: "We are 10 Christians who obeyed God's calling," she said. "We went to help the nation of Haiti and their children and for reasons unknown to us, it did not go the way we planned."

In the first days after the arrests the missionaries added a mystique of martyrdom when they said simply, "Philippians 1" when television reporters asked them about the allegations against them, a reference to the Apostle Paul's letter from prison and an implication that they had been jailed for their beliefs. They sang hymns as they were driven back to jail after being formally charged. And when a *Time* magazine journalist visited them in jail in mid-February, the missionaries told the reporter, "The Philistines won, the Philistines won."

The Central Valley and Eastside Baptist Churches in Idaho posted announcements that the team had been "falsely arrested" over a "misunderstanding," and some Christian groups decried the arrest as persecution for their faith. (Pastor Paul Thompson of Eastside Baptist, one of the jailed missionaries, would later let loose with a series of accusations that UNICEF had orchestrated the arrests as part of a campaign of spiritual warfare, claims that UNICEF tersely denied in full.)

But most Christian groups kept their distance, and some even rebuked the church culture that inspired Silsby. Fritz Gutwein, a US Baptist minister and adoptive parent with a background in Haiti, wrote a polemical essay for the *Associated Baptist Press* arguing that the prosecution of Silsby's team was good for the US evangelical church, which he saw as embracing a heretical and reckless attitude about adoption. If the missionaries were duped at all, Gutwein wrote, "They were duped by the peculiar strain of American evangelicalism that seems to think the United States is God's chosen country and that seeks conversions by any and all means, including adoption. . . . This has been taken to the extreme by theologians and pastors who encourage infertile couples to have the family of their dreams and expand the Kingdom *at the same time* by adopting a child from another culture and heritage and replacing that heritage and faith with their own." The Silsby saga turned even seedier when Jorge Puello, a US-born man living in the Dominican Republic who volunteered to represent Silsby's group, posing as an attorney and using an alias, turned out to be wanted for questioning concerning human trafficking and child prostitution in both the United States and El Salvador. (In 2011 Puello—charged under the name Jorge Torres—was sentenced to three years in US federal prison after pleading guilty to separate, earlier charges of alien smuggling.)

The mood in Haiti shifted more decisively against the missionaries. When a Minnesota adoptive mother came to the country to pick up her new adoptive son and five other children who had lived at the Children of the Promise orphanage—an undamaged orphanage ninety miles outside the capital that nonetheless evacuated children under humanitarian parole—a group of men surrounded her at the airport, demanding to see her paperwork. "They started screaming at us that they are Haitian children," a volunteer with the group told CNN, "and who do we think we are taking their kids from their country, and these missionaries can't be stealing kids." Central Valley Baptist Church posted an acknowledgement on their website that Silsby's group had made mistakes and asked the Haitian prime minister to forgive them. Charisa Coulter was released from jail in March, and Silsby, who was eventually convicted of the separate, lesser charge of arranging illegal travel, was released for time served in May.

Prime Minister Bellerive spoke to the circus aspect of the Silsby trial and how it had subsumed a majority of public attention around the larger crisis. "I believe it's a distraction for the Haitian people," he said, "because they are talking more now about 10 people than they are about one million people suffering in the streets." A Haitian man living on the grounds of the courthouse where Silsby was tried agreed, telling *ABC News* that "These people are American. The whole world just wants to know what will happen to the Americans."

EVEN AFTER the very public Silsby affair, the lessons that Christian adoption advocates might have been expected to learn didn't seem to take. Whereas Silsby became a villain or at least an embarrassment in the eyes of most observers—an opportunist who used the earthquake to reinvent herself, trampling on another country's laws and families in a quest to appear heroic—things aren't always as clear-cut. Silsby wasn't the renegade bad apple that adoption advocates sought to portray her as but rather the person who took prevailing practices to their logical end: the sense, as one critic put it, that "I'm on a mission. I have every right to be on this mission. The rules are stupid because I know better." Other orphan-rescue missions happening almost simultaneous to the scandal displayed a similar disregard for the law, but it was a disregard that could be harder to recognize coming from a more likable advocate—one like Tom Benz.

In February 2010, just weeks after Silsby's arrest, Benz, a kindly fifty-seven-year-old evangelical pastor, announced a new plan on the website of his ministry, Bridges of Faith. In coming weeks, he wrote, they would "airlift 50 to 150 orphans" to the ministry's 140-acre prayer and retreat center, BridgeStone, a sprawling campus of cabins and recreational amenities set among the cotton fields and Confederate graveyards between Montgomery and Birmingham. It would be the ministry's pilot program, Haiti OrphansNoMore, hosting Haitian children for three months in Alabama to help them learn English, "immerse them in the gospel," and "incubate adoptions" with the scores of local families Benz had signed up in the days after the earthquake. He appealed to donors to sponsor children at $200 each, the cost of processing their passports, which Benz, an excitable man easily stirred to poetry, called their "passport to the future." "Think of how many orphans will find forever homes!!" he wrote. "Will you help a child receive their passport to the U.S. and to a new life in Christ?" According to Benz's plan, after a ninety-day residency in Alabama, children picked for adoption would return to Haiti temporarily to live at a new transition home he would establish and then prepare to move to America.

Benz, a wide-smiling man with a buzz cut and a self-deprecating style, was confident the plan would work. Bridges of Faith had long run a missionary summer camp for orphans in Ukraine (as well as an unwed mothers' home in Kentucky). For two years he had been mulling over plans for a sort of "hosting program" for Ukrainian orphans with the goal of getting Alabama Christians to adopt them. It was part of the reason he and his wife, Larissa, a Ukrainian evangelical, had bought the BridgeStone camp, at a bargain price of $450,000, from the local Assemblies of God Church.

When Benz met Larissa he had been regional director for the International Bible Society, traveling widely and distributing Bibles in former Soviet bloc countries and other countries he can't name—missionary code for Muslim nations where evangelizing is forbidden. When he was assigned to visit an orphanage in Eastern Ukraine, he had planned to stop in quickly then hit the beaches of the Black Sea. Instead, he said, "within twenty-four hours those kids had crawled inside my heart and changed my life." Larissa became a translator for Benz, and in time they married and Benz adopted her twelve-year-old son. He came to believe that the Bible charged him to do something for other children, like in James 1:27, a popular verse of scripture that calls caring for widows and orphans "pure religion," or Matthew 25:40, when Jesus talks about helping "the least of these." "We don't want just to be Christians who sit in the church," Benz explained to me. "Our faith needs to have legs and hands— that we actually do something with our faith."

In 1995 Benz started his own ministry, Bridges of Faith, that would take hundreds of US Christians on short-term mission trips to Ukraine.

There they planted churches and worked with children who were aging out of Ukrainian orphanages. His goal is to change the statistics he repeats to all comers: that the majority of children who graduate from institutional care in Ukraine end up in trouble: the boys in organized crime, drug dealing, or prison, and the girls in prostitution, both at risk for substance abuse and suicide. In any group he assembles Benz always pauses for dramatic effect before he asks people to envision 60 percent of the girls in front of them growing up to be prostitutes. "But every child that is adopted," he tells them, "gets snatched out of those statistics."

Other adoption officials working in Ukraine say this is misleading, that the 60 percent figure only applies to a subset of orphanage children, those who opt out of government-sponsored education or job-training programs. But regardless of how many face the worst outcomes, all orphanage graduates contend with real, if more pedestrian challenges when they transition to independent lives, coming, as they do, out of institutions where they have never cooked for themselves, done laundry, or seen a functioning family.

After the earthquake Benz assumed that his familiarity with Ukraine's bleak narrative would translate neatly to the Haitian orphan crisis. When the quake hit Haiti—"Hay-dee," in Benz's Kentucky-bred drawl—he and Larissa felt God calling them to reassess their plans. They began to imagine the beds at BridgeStone filled with Haitian children instead of Ukrainians.

Providence aside, initiating the BridgeStone retreat with Haitian children made good PR sense. After Benz announced the need for extensive renovations to ready BridgeStone for Haitian orphans, he was overwhelmed with volunteer support and donations. Miles of new plumbing and electrical wire were laid for the center's twenty-two aging and weather-beaten cabins, and three new permanent staff buildings began construction, including one for Benz and his family to move into and another for his father—almost all with donated materials and labor. Volunteers made extensive capital improvements to the camp that benefited the ministry's ability to generate income from rent-paying church groups. Understanding the volunteers' motivations was easy: hard work on the grounds of BridgeStone seemed like a concrete way to do something for Haiti at a time when much of the country watched the nearby disaster with a sense of impotent despair. Benz's "army of volunteers" came from as far as the Carolinas and Iowa and as near as the local Auburn University football team.

While BridgeStone was being transformed, Benz continued to talk up his plan and sign up parents who wanted to adopt a Haitian child, an ad-hoc campaign that is far afield from how international adoptions are actually processed. "We've got more parents than we've got kids," Benz told me, predicting that "Most of the kids who come [to Alabama] will be returning." After a few weeks, though, Benz downgraded his estimates for the first group of Haitian kids coming from 150 to 50.

Benz was conscious of the tensions in Haiti over Western adoption efforts, but he gave them little thought. Because he had a friend who had connections at the State Department, Benz told me—and anyone else willing to listen—he was confident that he could wrangle the system by passing off his adoption scheme as a cultural exchange, "a foreign studies program, more or less." When I reminded him of the mission to "incubate adoptions," Benz laughed. "Well, that's absolutely part of our agenda, but you know, that's not the thing we're going to emphasize to the Haitian government! We'll emphasize the exchange part of it, the English studies."

It was hard to understand how Benz thought this plan—misleading the Haitian government about his intentions while he spoke openly about them to US journalists—would work. If the similarities between his plan and the Silsby scandal occurred to him, as both promised to Haitian officials a temporary trip for the children while simultaneously offering adoption opportunities to US parents, he didn't reveal it. He spoke of the Silsby affair as a mere "stumbling block" thrown in the road by people whose "hearts were in the right place, but their documents weren't."

In response to criticism that the crisis was being used to secure more adoptions for prospective US parents, thus serving their needs more than Haiti's or the children's, Benz repeated his standard disclaimer: "What I shared with people, in Haiti or Ukraine, is that I really don't care what nationality the adoptive family is. . . . My goal is not to get kids adopted in the US; my goal is to help orphans find great families in Christian homes." With a good-natured, conspiratorial chuckle, he delivered the punch line: "It just so happens that the place I work is the US, and the families I know are primarily in Alabama."

As time wore on and passports for the Haitian children were not forthcoming, BridgeStone's improvements continued with donated money and supplies: more housing for volunteers, overhauling existing buildings for staff, central heating and air in the cabins, four trailer homes donated by the local Air Force base that Benz gladly accepted along with a seventy-two-passenger bus that a church gave as a love offering.

Progress was slower back in Haiti. The estimated number of Haitian children coming to Alabama dropped again, this time from fifty to twenty-six. A Haitian pastor was helping to find and identify adoptable children to send, but communications were an ongoing problem and paperwork often got lost. The ETA for the children's arrival never seemed to change from three to four weeks out, but Benz remained optimistic, hinting at connections who could speed things along. "We made friends in Haiti—and in Haiti, a lot of things are based on friendships. Having a friend in the right place can make all the difference in the world," Benz told me with the confidence and excitement that had become so common among postquake rescue missionaries. He seemed to share the sense that the crisis could propel everyday people into action-hero roles and the shiver of giddy anticipation at the prospect of engaging a shady system, none of it quite real, as though making a deal or slipping a bribe would feel natural in the moment and unfold as though scripted. "I think if we make the right connections, we might walk in one day and walk out the next with their passports," he said. I could imagine the wink as he continued, "We might have to bless some people to make it happen!"

In May Benz announced that his primary partner in Haiti had "decided to bail out of the process" on the eve of submitting the group's paperwork to the State Department. In what seemed a familiar Plan B, Benz began calling other people they had met in Haiti, including For His Glory Adoption Outreach and their Port-au-Prince orphanage, Maison des Enfants de Dieu. By late May the number of children Benz told a local Alabama TV station he was expecting had dropped to ten. Then in September a fundraising missive pled for continued patience as the group sought to "bring children out of darkness and suffering into faith and life in Jesus Christ" despite all the hurdles that had been put in their path.

That was the last time Benz's newsletter mentioned Haiti. Soon thereafter "Haiti" dropped out of the title of the OrphansNoMore Project, and Benz began speaking about bringing children from other countries for adoption. In October his newsletter announced BridgeStone's pending open house to mark the launch of Benz's Ukrainian adoption program. At some point over the fall Benz's Haiti blog came down. Then in December 2010, almost a year after the earthquake, Benz welcomed his first group of Ukrainian orphans, whom he would come to call "the Christmas group," and announced his hopes that each one would find God's love and a forever home.

To a cynical eye the entire enterprise could appear as a massive bait and switch. Under the promise of forthcoming Haitian orphans, Benz had managed to elicit substantial donations and volunteer labor that transformed his BridgeStone property from a crumbling antique to a functioning, elaborate Christian retreat camp. But I can't imagine this is what Benz intended. I imagine him first bewildered that his Scooby-Doo plan to slip Haitian orphans across the border on benevolent but false premises didn't work out, then becoming depressed and then motivated to salvage the project with a return to the original plan: bringing Ukrainian kids to the Deep South.

This type of progression, leaping from one country to the next, has become a common spectacle in the international adoption world, where advocates lobby hard for the needs of children from a specific country, only to move swiftly to another nation when the hurdles of adopting from the first are too large. It's a cavalier approach that helps make the idea of "orphans" a hazy category for Americans—interchangeable across the world, defined most of all by their status as charity objects for prospective US parents. But to an advocate like Benz, that's just another way of saying there are always more children in need.

ALTHOUGH BENZ shifted the country he was working with, his approach remained largely the same. When the first group of children arrived for Christmas 2010—"ten gorgeous orphans," "ten beautiful orphans," Benz wrote to his supporters, seeming triumphant after so many disappointments in Haiti—he and his team took them on a whirlwind American adventure: to church, to eat lunch at the Montgomery mall food court, to buy sneakers, to an ice rink, to view a Christmas light display, and then to eat pizza. Prospective adoptive parents were invited to a meeting at the BridgeStone chapel with the Ukrainian adoption coordinator who had accompanied the group. At the end of their three-week visit Benz announced that all ten of the children were now in process to be adopted by Christian families who had visited them at BridgeStone. He told a local paper, "We want them to become Christians, yes, but we need them to find families."

A year later, in December 2011, BridgeStone welcomed its fourth group of Ukrainian children to Alabama. I came down to see it, entering BridgeStone through country roads flanked by salvage yards, trailer parks, and ranging fields of cotton, where short, brown stems anchored a delicate trail of fluff in the wan winter sun. As I arrived at the camp, half a dozen pale kids, who looked like they were between eight to twelve years old, ran over to my car, opening both front doors and shaking my hands enthusiastically, jabbering introductions in Ukrainian and Russian. In all likelihood the children knew their trip was a chance at adoption and were eager to make a strong first impression on any visitors who came. From my first minutes on the grounds of BridgeStone, it was clear to me that the thin line Benz had attempted to tread in Haiti was still the ministry's guiding principle: obscuring its ultimate adoption mission behind the façade of a cultural exchange.

In the visitor's office a volunteer named Chuck, a heavyset seventy-two-year-old from Virginia, gave me a form to fill out—name, age, and relationship with Jesus—and told me Rule Number One: "We don't use the 'a' word—adoption." "Since we are not an adoption agency, we do not exist in any way to arrange adoptions," the form read, warning that visitors must comply with the laws of the United States, Alabama, and Ukraine as well as common sense. "If someone even uses the 'a' word with a child, we must ask you to leave BridgeStone." It awkwardly continued with the notice that, despite this rule, the kids at BridgeStone were adoptable, and interested parents should talk to Benz or BridgeStone's project coordinator, Eric Carr, to find out how they could proceed. It was the same winking assurance that Benz had given not only to me but also to all of the local media he had spoken with about his plan to surreptitiously promote adoption of Haitian children while telling both the US and Haitian governments that it was only an English-language study exchange.

After Rule Number One, Chuck said, with the warm weariness of having repeated the same thing many times before, Bridges of Faith suggests visitors love on the orphans until it hurts, and then love them some more. It was a love-bombing approach, reflecting Benz's wish to give the children in a few weeks a gonzo dose of indulgent American childhood, a honeymoon adventure wherein a childlike Benz, acting as Santa Claus or maybe Willy Wonka, arranged elaborate outings and surprises for the kids. Former coach of the Auburn University football team Gene Chizik and former Mets pitcher Mark Fuller hosted one group of children at a nearby sports center to talk to them about God's plan for their lives; another group was invited into the bullpen of the Atlanta Braves; others rode in top model cars, racing at 120 mph; and in August a drop-in visit from the state police helicopter surprised one child with a birthday, Sasha, as he was playing in a field, lowering two troopers by rope to deliver the boy a birthday cake. In his newsletter updates Benz seemed overcome with wonderment. "We have no idea what eternal and indelible impact this gift had on young Sasha, a young man who daily feels the rejection and humiliation known only to orphans."

In the camp's main hall, in a dining area lined with three rows of sixty-foot foldout tables, covered in plastic tablecloths and Christmas knickknacks, I met Larissa Benz, a petite, attractive forty-seven-year-old in jeans and a burgundy leather jacket, her dark hair pulled into a neat ponytail. She introduced me to the staffers playing with the children— ten mostly preteen kids on loan from an orphanage in the Zaporizhya region of Ukraine who were learning to play kickball on the lawn outside the main hall. Watching from the benches were three Ukrainian women: Katya Chislova, BridgeStone's interpreter and orphan ministry leader; Julia, the orphanage representative sent to monitor the program; and Natasha, an independent adoption coordinator, there to talk to US parents who decide to adopt one of the children. Each group of ten children that Bridges of Faith brings over for a month-long stay costs more than $65,000 in fees, airfare, and expenses, including the round-trip travel fees for the Ukrainian adults accompanying them. As an independent agent among Ukraine's numerous adoption facilitators, Natasha, a platinum blonde in her twenties, came to Alabama unpaid (besides her airfare) but with the assumption that the trip will generate upon her return a number of adoptions and, thus, corresponding facilitators' fees— from $4,000 to $12,000 per child. The business implications were clear. A previous facilitator had been unable to come on this trip, Natasha told me, because he was too busy in Ukraine finalizing the adoptions that had resulted from a prior group. By September 2011, 85 percent of the first two groups of children BridgeStone had hosted were in the process of being adopted.

Climbing into a small white golf cart, Larissa gave me a tour of the property. It was a testament to the work that had been going on over the past two years, with its two sets of clustered cabins, numerous staff buildings and trailer homes, a rec room, chapel, and pool as well as a paintball field, horse barn, and manmade pond, all connected with two miles of rutted dirt roads. We arrived at CenterPoint, a unique construction of two modular trailer buildings the Air Force donated and connected by a central living area that one of BridgeStone's supporters designed. Center-Point is where the Ukrainian kids stay with their translator and a rotating group of American houseparents. When I visited, the houseparents were a willowy young woman in her twenties named Reagan and her husband Tee, a taciturn man in a baseball cap, who together had a two-year-old boy. They had come as a part of their church mission team after hearing about Benz's program through their homeschooling group. Perhaps unbeknownst to them, they had also been plucked as potential adoptive parents. Benz and the rest of the BridgeStone staff choose as houseparents young couples who already have children, in part so they will have parenting experience but also because they're people whom the BridgeStone group thinks would make good adoptive parents.

"We have a lot of people who come [thinking], 'Gosh, the mission field's come to Alabama!'" Benz explains. "'We can drive thirty minutes and reach out to kids'. . . . And then they come and fall in love with the kids and say, 'I'm going to take one home.'" "Fall in love" is a phrase in heavy rotation at BridgeStone, as staff discuss how they fall in love with each group of children. They want new volunteers to come and fall in love too.

It seemed to be working already. "The kids are very accepting," Reagan said with a soft smile. "They cling to you. From the moment we came in the youngest came up and put his arms around me. I thought it was going to be harder with the language barrier, but you figure it out."

But the fact of the children's easy affection gets back at BridgeStone's thin ethical line. As Larissa showed me the rest of the grounds, her phone rang. It was Tom—his ringtone on Larissa's phone sounds like the main riff of Muddy Waters's "Mannish Boy"—calling to meet up and take over my tour. He met us by the camp's manmade pond in an SUV with a cracked windshield—Benz at least was not getting rich off this program— beaming widely with a Bluetooth in his ear. He seemed guileless: quick to laugh at himself but smarter than the first impression he gives—of someone so open as to be naive, believing in his plan so completely that he can't imagine anyone seeing it differently. Within minutes of our meeting, Benz launched into the duality at the heart of his ministry: loudly touting its adoption promotion to US supporters but masquerading as a cultural exchange program when speaking to US or Ukrainian governments.

"Our program in Ukraine," he said, navigating deep rainwater trenches in the dirt roads, "if it were about adoption, it couldn't happen. . . . Everyone knows it's about adoption, but it can't be about adoption." He looked at me to see if I followed. Just as he had tried to do in Haiti, Benz has positioned Bridges of Faith as an educational opportunity for children to learn English and experience another country. Every time he brings a new group of children over, he said, the US embassy in Ukraine sends him an e-mail and hard-copy letter telling him that "You know this can't be about adoption."

The reason it can't be about adoption is because Ukraine has cause to enact limitations on its hosting exchanges. Although Ukraine has long sent children for international adoption in the United States, in recent years it has tried to replace this with domestic adoption by Ukrainian parents instead, as the nation's economy has grown and the country faces its own increasing infertility issues. In past years the pressure to find children for lucrative foreign adoptions has led to scandals, including a baby-selling scheme in which Ukrainian mothers' children were stolen after birth and offered for adoption as orphans. These days there are no healthy children under three years old available for international adoption from Ukraine, and very few under six.

But even the adoption of older children has run into problems. Although Benz doesn't officially call Bridges of Faith a hosting exchange, it is very similar to the hosting programs that have become ubiquitous in US Christian communities. In these programs, often organized through churches, families host Eastern European orphanage children for a few weeks or months, ostensibly as a foreign exchange program but in practice frequently as an informal adoption audition to see if they bond with the child. This host-to-adopt scenario is widespread despite the fact that the Ukrainian government retains all control over assigning children for adoption and forbids nongovernmental parties from circulating information or pictures about children available for adoption. Although the Ukrainian government has banned "preselection" of its children for adoption—in which foreign adopters request a specific child, likely one they had hosted, since no one outside the government is supposed to know children's adoption status—in reality government officials often look the other way when it comes to requests for older children, who are less in demand by Ukrainian parents.

But even though they're common, these programs can be harmful for both the adoptive parents and the children. Because the government, not hosting programs, controls adoptions, US families hosting children may be preparing to adopt children who aren't actually available.* But the greater danger is for the children, who are often all too aware that the trip may be an opportunity for adoption, having seen their friends undergo the process before. For those not chosen by host families, the repercussions can be severe, as the children feel rejected and face an increased risk for suicide.

In other words, there's a reason for all the rules that Benz breezily dismisses as bureaucracy. But because of these legal requirements, Benz said,

---

*In 1993 fifty-four Ukrainian children hosted by Christian families in the Chicago area were kept by their US hosts, who had been incorrectly told the children were all available for adoption. The incident led to international diplomatic tensions.

"When you go on our website you'll see very little about adoption. It's for that reason."

But on the ground it's all about adoption. Tom estimates that he spends four Sundays out of five speaking at churches to enlarge the circle of volunteers, prospective adoptive parents, and donors, including a local state senator who donated $25,000 to bring one group of children over. And behind the scenes in Ukraine it's about adoption too, as Benz and his Ukrainian staff work with orphanage directors to select children who are available for adoption to come to Alabama and meet potential parents.

"These kids are not told it's about adoption," Benz said with a boyish smirk, "because in Ukraine, it's not about adoption. But the kids all know. . . . They're all smarter than the government." Many orphanage kids have seen their friends go abroad, then get adopted shortly after their return. Adoptees sometimes call or Skype back to the orphanage to stay in touch with friends and tell them about their life in a new country. So when the orphan groups come to Alabama looking for families, Benz said, some kids will "suck up" to a family they like or petition the adoption co-ordinator, Natasha, to allow them to spend more time with a particular set of potential parents.

Acknowledging this seemed to spark some doubt in Benz as he re-flected on the August 2011 group that came, a group of preteen and teenage boys who had generated the fewest requests for adoption (possibly because girls are often favored in adoption). "The worst thing about these groups is sending them home," admitted Benz. Recalling their departure at the airport with sadness, he said, "I never got so many manly handshakes and manly hugs." But when the boys got through security, he continued, "they were bawling like babies," asking Larissa, "'What if I'm not adopted? What if I'm not adopted?'" Benz grew somber for a moment, thinking. "We're not supposed to talk about it, but some of them found out anyway."

BENZ ISN'T ONE of the bad guys in this book. On the contrary, he seems like a genuinely nice man with a sincere love of children. But Benz's type of eager, well-meaning naiveté is, in many respects, more dangerous for appearing so benign. Besides the fact that Benz's Haiti plans fell through before he could implement them and that he seems like such a nicer person, how much did his scheme differ from that of Laura Silsby? And how different is the strategy he eventually implemented in Ukraine, similarly misleading two governments as a result of his own confidence that getting children to America justifies bending the rules and the truth?

Benz's plans are an illustration of how temporary the lessons from Haiti can be, how common its ethical scandals are to other countries, and how supportive advocates nonetheless remain of adoption projects established as rescue operations. Tom Benz is undeniably a more sympathetic representative of the Christian adoption cause, giving voice to an urge to help children, an urge that many could share. However, his approach to adoption, whether from Haiti or Ukraine, was undertaken with the same beginners' zeal and faith that drove Laura Silsby: that his good intentions outweigh other countries' laws. It's a faith that is epidemic in the world of international adoption, particularly in the large and growing community that sees adoption not just as the means to build a family but also as a rescue mission assigned by God. Although in character Benz may be worlds away from Laura Silsby, in the larger picture that may be a distinction without a difference. In an international adoption field where scandals routinely originate from idealistic plans, good intentions simply aren't enough.

THAT NIGHT BENZ, Larissa, and I drove through dark country roads to one of the next closest towns, Millbrook, where BridgeStone's thirty-something project coordinator, Eric Carr, had helped plant a church at the local YMCA. Benz reflected on the exotic places his missionary work has taken him, from garbage dumps in Mexico City to jungles in the Philippines. "But nothing in my life strikes me as more sacred or more profound than bringing these kids," he said, expressing a hope that he can continue this work for the rest of his life.

Carr shares his sense of mission and has passed it on to his staff and a growing circle of volunteers. Many church members at Carr's small congregation at the Y are involved with BridgeStone. In addition to the three biological children Carr has with his wife, Wendy, they have three children adopted from foster care and a Ukrainian orphan on the way. They have taken their calling so seriously that they live in one of BridgeStone's donated trailers rent-free in lieu of salary for their work. Members of the congregation followed his lead: a number have become houseparents or volunteers at BridgeStone, and at least four families had already adopted through the year-old program or were in process. The state trooper who had flown in the surprise birthday cake for one group of children was himself a member of the congregation.

As Eric would tell me, adoption has become a guiding identity not just for his family but also for the church. "It's who we are, not what we do, which is a totally different thing. I could be a pastor, but we are about adoption." His statement offers a glimpse into what's driving Christians like the Benzes as well as Christians like Laura Silsby. Behind these seemingly disparate adoption activists is a growing movement that encourages Christians to see adoption as the ultimate emulation of Christ and an imperative for evangelicals who seek to do their part in the world.

When we left the Y that night, Eric, a lanky blond with a thoughtful drawl, piled a rag-tag collection of people into the battered family minivan: "ghetto-fabulous," he said wryly. Carr had run a coffee shop before Benz hired him, and he stressed that he knew his lifestyle—living in a trailer in the deep country and making his income between pastoring and odd construction jobs—is not what most would consider success. But his conviction that adoption was God's purpose for his life guided him. "I believe that's probably the clearest picture of the gospel: someone who literally doesn't know you or have to do anything for you, taking you in to love and care for you. That's the picture of Jesus." It hasn't always been easy, however. One of the children Eric and Wendy adopted from foster care, a fifteen-year-old girl who joined their family at ten, has struggled with emotional and psychological issues. According to Wendy, the daughter is now in a psychiatric facility, dealing with a diagnosis of depression with psychotic features, notably among which were threats to the family. "We found out a long time ago that we're not the answer," Wendy told me sadly. "Our love is not enough."

As he drove, Eric grew intent as he continued talking. Before he became a pastor, both he and Wendy had spent years in a spiritual wilderness, "pagans in the best sense," he said with a nostalgic sigh, living wild lives, separate from God. The minivan climbed over eighty miles per hour on the dark highway, and as he cornered a bend too fast, he grinned and deadpanned, "We're about to find out if we were right about the whole Jesus thing!"

He isn't sure about all the aspects of BridgeStone's ministry. He does realize that the $20,000 spent just on airfare for every group that comes to BridgeStone could probably make a larger impact in Ukraine—when he's gone there, Ukrainian officials have told him as much. However, he's also wary of critics who condemn a mission like this without doing anything themselves. But on the larger picture Eric has no doubts. "The Bible really talks about how we're adopted as sons because we're grafted in [to God's family] after we were separated because of our sin and our selfish nature," he said. "All we've ever done is sin and transgress the things He really wanted us to be, and He still loves us. The love of the father is unconditional."

When he talks to people about adoption, he tells them what he thinks is true: Christians aren't just called to adoption; they are commanded to it. Christians who don't get that, he began to reflect, and then stifled himself—he doesn't want to say "bad Christians." He thinks for a minute and starts again: "We seem to be known for everything but how we love."

CHAPTER 2

The Touchable Gospel

On a rainy morning in May 2012, as I crossed the university-sized campus of Saddleback Church in Lake Forest, California, the voice of Georgia Pastor Crawford Loritts boomed from the ground, turning the damp, empty walkways into an open-air chapel, his sermon piped through concrete speakers shaped like rocks and nestled at the base of palm trees. The Christian orphan-care and adoption movement, Loritts said, is not a passing fad like other social justice causes in the church's past. The movement cannot be allowed to become a seasonal attraction, rising and fading like a style of clothing, because adoption and orphan care is more than a cause. For many it has become the image of the gospel itself.

Loritts, a longtime staffer for Campus Crusade for Christ and the senior pastor of a megachurch outside Atlanta, was addressing the eighth annual summit of the Christian Alliance for Orphans, the hub and umbrella organization of the burgeoning orphan-care and adoption movement. The claims both Tom Benz and Laura Silsby made about being called by God to rescue orphans don't sound out of place in evangelical circles. There, it's hard to overstate the recent ubiquity of adoption and orphan talk, which is guided by several main convictions: that adoption mirrors Christian salvation; that it is an essential part of antiabortion politics; and that it constitutes a means of fulfilling the Great Commission—the biblical mandate, found most notably in Matthew 28:16–20, that Christians spread the gospel.

Like anyone else, church people are susceptible to trends and causes that pass in and out of fashion. These days, perhaps even more so than their secular counterparts. Just before I had turned onto the church compound, where Portola Parkway intersects Saddleback's "Purpose Drive," a campus road named for Pastor Rick Warren's best-selling book, *The Purpose Driven Life,* I spotted a weather-beaten sticker for "KONY 2012," the momentarily sensational campaign to marshal public support for capturing the brutal warlord Joseph Kony who, for roughly two decades, had forced Ugandan youth to become child soldiers in his Lord's Resistance Army. The sticker clung to a pole in the median, but the KONY campaign was all but forgotten two months after the instant viral success of its March 2012 video—a short, well-produced documentary that asked teens to spread the word about Uganda's child soldiers through stickers, Facebook updates, and rubber wristbands.

The impassioned KONY 2012 movement fizzled out almost as quickly as it had ignited, due in part to accusations that the movie (which turned out to be made by young evangelical activists from nearby San Diego, who had downplayed their faith to attract a wider audience) was misleading naive US youth about the facts on the ground in Uganda.* Other critics charged that the movie's call to action was ineffective and unethical, encouraging supporters to believe that buying branded merchandise and sharing the video with friends would actually help lead to Kony's capture. In truth Kony had long since decamped to plague other countries, and these days the surviving population in northern Uganda faces more pedestrian development challenges, issues that do not lend themselves as easily to viral Facebook videos.

But if the Christian adoption and orphan-care movement has become a fad, it's not one in danger of fading yet. Inside Saddleback's main worship center—just one of nearly twenty buildings on campus—an estimated two thousand people gathered for the Christian Alliance for Orphans Summit. Many were church pastors and adoption ministry leaders, and the 2012 summit had drawn more people than ever before, up from thirteen hundred in 2010 and thirty-eight at the Alliance's first meeting in 2004.

---

*As the criticism mounted, the activist who directed the documentary had a public breakdown and was hospitalized, further harming the film's credibility, if unfairly.

"This is the beginning of the end," Saddleback Pastor Rick Warren, a portly man in his late fifties who first gained fame for his Hawaiian shirt collection, told the crowd as he opened the summit. "It's the end of orphans in the world." The next day the audience cheered when Warren declared the route he envisioned for eradicating orphanhood: "When I say 'orphan care,'" he boomed, "it's adoption first, second, and last." After several years of high-profile scandals around international adoption, it was a strong affirmation of the continuing central role adoption plays in the movement.

Warren noted the concerted effort to promote adoption within Saddleback's own congregation. "Our initial goal was to have one thousand families—five hundred to adopt internationally and five hundred to adopt nationally. We've only been doing it a few years, and we're already over the five hundred mark," he said to applause. On stage Warren was framed by several hanging panels printed with Bible verses, including James 1:27, which states that helping widows and orphans is "pure religion." An unadorned wooden cross was hung at stage right in the customary, bloodless style of American megachurches, a lonely nod to simplicity among the church's elaborate array of amenities. Saddleback, one of the largest churches in America, has a weekly attendance of around twenty thousand people, and besides its high-tech worship hall, fitted with multiple cameras and an advanced video production booth set amid the ocean of seats, the campus includes four restaurants and cafes, two baptism pools, a movie theater, a three-wing children's complex as large as an elementary school, auxiliary adult classrooms, basketball and beach volleyball courts, and a skate park, not to mention the freestanding world headquarters for Saddleback's global-development arm. A full band setup for the worship team waited at stage left, and on the floor below it stood twelve easels displaying portraits of children of diverse racial backgrounds: orphans of the world, in need of Christian care.

Sitting in the large audience or standing to the side of the seats by the room's floor-to-ceiling wall of windows were scores of young, white parents who had taken part in this mission. They jogged black babies in Ergos and slings, the infants' hair braided competently or left natural. The men wore cause-related T-shirts and jeans. The women were variously in heels and $100 tans—classic Orange County style—or shredded jeans and camisoles hanging off tattooed shoulders. Youth volunteers scurried in packs, clad in oversized blue T-shirts that read, "ORPHAN," and from various vantage points in the aisles and risers of the worship hall video cameras streamed Warren's message out to many thousands more.

Together, Warren, his wife, Kay, and Saddleback Church are among the vanguard of what has become a national movement to end the "orphan crisis," one child at a time, while simultaneously exposing adoptees to Christianity. "If just one church in every four churches got one family to adopt, there would be no more orphans in America," Warren proposed. His Saddleback staff, some of whom have become national leaders in the movement, have an even larger equation in mind. As Elizabeth Styffe, director of Saddleback's Global Orphan Care Initiative, put it, "There are 163 million orphans [globally], but there are two billion people in the world who call themselves Christians. If you do the math, this is doable in our generation."

Although the Southern Baptist Convention has dominated the theological direction of the Christian adoption cause to date, and Saddleback is a Southern Baptist church, the movement represented at the summit cuts across evangelical distinctions. All groups and denominations, from Methodists to charismatic Christians to parachurch groups to homeschoolers, take up the mantle in their own way. Individual ministries and grant makers abound, with names like Redeeming Orphans, Orphan's Ransom, or The ABBA Fund, which, like many evangelical adoption organizations, references the Bible's Aramaic name for father. The ministries help born-again Christians pay the "ransom" of $20,000 to $35,000 or more in adoption fees by spreading the cost among the rest of their church or providing no-interest loans.

At the local level churches report a "contagious" spread of "adoption culture" that inspires fellow congregants to adopt, with even smaller congregations witnessing as many as one hundred adoptions in just a few years. Often parents adopt multiple children, and many adoptive families swell to eight or ten kids or more. The growth of adoption in churches is so rapid that it's led some Christian leaders to muse that church planters—Christians who help establish new, franchise-like branches of a church community—could build congregations this way.

The viral effect is intentional. Addressing an audience at the Southern Baptist Theological Seminary in 2010, The ABBA Fund's director of ministry development, Jason Kovacs, had counseled the crowd that the key to building a church-wide "adoption culture" is to "Get as many people in the church to adopt, and adopt as many kids as you can." He added that they should also "Pray that your pastor will adopt," noting the precedent a pastor can set.

One result has been the creation of "rainbow congregations" across the country, such as Louisville's Highview Baptist, where movement leader Russell Moore, author of the 2009 book *Adopted for Life: The Priority of Adoption for Christian Families & Churches* and a leading Southern Baptist theologian, is a preaching pastor. There, with the help of an active adoption ministry, members of the church have adopted some 140 children into the congregation. At a ceremony to celebrate them, Moore recalled, Highview's many adoptees toddled onto the stage with flags from their home countries. What brought Moore to tears was realizing that "most of the kids didn't recognize the flags [they were holding], but they all knew 'Jesus Loves Me.'"

Between expert-level pre-conference meetings and two days of main conference events, the May 2012 Alliance Summit stretched across half a week. The speaker list was a who's who of the Christian adoption movement. There was Russell Moore and Jason Kovacs; Dan Cruver, co-founder of the movement group Together for Adoption; Karyn Purvis, an attachment specialist from the TCU Institute of Child Development who's been called "the hurt child whisperer"; and Steven Curtis Chapman, the Christian contemporary music star and founder of the adoption ministry Show Hope, which gives grants of up to $7,000 for Christian families who want to adopt.

Nearly one hundred breakout sessions detailed many aspects of "orphan care," a broad spectrum of advocacy including adoption, child sponsorship, and promoting domestic adoption in developing countries. Attendees learned about starting adoption ministries in their home churches, using orphan care to reach the world's unsaved populations, and lobbying primers on important adoption legislation. At lunchtime a Christian singer-songwriter named Kristin Orphan—not herself an orphan, but an adoptive mother who founded the Finally Home Foundation—sang adoption-themed songs while young adoptees ran around in gauzy, traditional Ethiopian dress and adults browsed rows of exhibition booths, picking up adoption agency swag and Third World gifts: paper-bead necklaces, African coffee, and plush black baby dolls wearing white gossamer clothes. "It's like a day at the outlets," a pair of women in their thirties wearing tall heels told me as they lugged overstuffed conference bags, emblazoned with agency logos, back to their car.

The summit is the culmination of a year's worth of work for Jedd Medefind, the Alliance's thirty-seven-year-old president. A tall, thin man in jeans and a checkered shirt, Medefind has an angular face, a head-bobbing affability, and a slightly hesitant smile. He was chief of staff for Republican California Assemblyman Tim Leslie for six years before he served as special assistant to President George W. Bush and acting director of the White House Office of Faith-Based and Community Initiatives.

Medefind's program in Bush's White House was one of eleven federal agencies channeling government funds to private church and religious groups to address social issues ranging from prison reentry to drug abuse to the global AIDS epidemic. The faith-based initiatives program, started under President Bill Clinton and prioritized under Bush, has been controversial since its inception. During Bush's expansion of the program it was widely criticized for inefficiently privatizing social services, funneling money to ideological allies of the administration that were unprepared for serious social welfare work, and leaving employees and clients open to unwelcome evangelism and religious discrimination.

But on the whole this background in tapping churches for social service work is fitting experience for Medefind's current job—rallying Christians to address what has come to be known as the "orphan crisis," the idea that there are between 143 and 210 million orphaned children in the world and the implication that many, if not most, are in need of adoption.

A California native, Medefind asked the audience in Saddleback's worship center to take off their shoes and stretch before he began to speak. He then delivered a pointed message about making orphan care stand out in an era of information overload, making it a "touchable" gospel as tangible as a burning bush or, in the vernacular of this movement, as sharp as a baby's cry. Medefind called for a gospel that demonstrates how Christians still act on biblical commands: to help the least of these (Matthew 25:40), to be a father to the fatherless and set the lonely in families (Psalm 68:5–6), and to help widows and orphans (James 1:27). He asked everyone to hold hands as he brought a small baby on stage, clad in a pink pullover, with a purple ribbon tied around her head, which was tilted acutely to one side. A father of five, including one adoptee, Medefind held her expertly and confidently as he prayed, "Let us praise the God who made himself as present to the senses as this little baby; who is feel-able as these little fingers and toes; who smells like spit-up. As salty and warm as blood, as audible as a baby's cry at 2 a.m." He kissed the infant's head and walked offstage.

IT'S NOT THE FIRST TIME that adoption has been part of a grand project of salvation. From 1854 to 1929 between 100,000 and 250,000 children were sent west from New York and other East Coast cities to be "adopted"—though not necessarily adopted as we understand it today—

by Protestant farming families in what would become America's heartland. The project, known as the "Orphan Train" initiative of the Children's Aid Society (CAS), working with the New York Foundling Hospital, facilitated the placement of many homeless, abused, and abandoned children as well as children recruited from poor immigrant Catholic and Jewish families from the slums of New York City.

The children rode trains to farm towns as near as New Jersey and as far as the frontier territories of the Great Plains and, later, the West Coast. As they arrived at each destination they were displayed at church meetinghouses, where families looking variously for a new son or daughter or a cheap source of labor for the emerging agricultural industry looked them over and made their pick. "The main goal of the Emigration Plan was to remove children from slums, where opportunities were scant and 'immoral influences' plentiful, and to place them in 'good Christian homes,'" wrote Stephen O'Connor in the seminal history of the movement, *Orphan Trains: The Story of Charles Loring Brace and the Children He Saved and Failed.*

As many as 25 percent of the "orphans" had two living parents, and fewer than half were orphans with two dead parents. But this wasn't an accident. Among the immoral influences that CAS founder Charles Loring Brace saw waiting for children in New York City were the children's parents themselves. Brace, an abolitionist and a nineteenth-century progressive, also authored a book called *The Dangerous Classes of New York and Twenty Years' Work Among Them,* which described Brace's appraisal of his era's urban poor. His orphan train efforts were driven in part by a fear that the children of the poor were "growing up almost sure to be prostitutes and rogues!" as he wrote his sister in one letter. His orphan trains were sometimes filled after CAS representatives went into New York's tenement neighborhoods to recruit "orphans" from immigrant families. As for those families, O'Connor wrote that Brace "dismissed contemptuously those parents who stood in the way of what he thought were a child's best interests, including the removal of the child to a 'better' home."

This in itself was not without precedent. In the 1830s to 1850s devout Congregationalist missionaries from abolitionist churches in the Northeast—the same background Brace hailed from—began adopting children from the mission field in Jamaica, where slavery became illegal in 1838, said Gale Kenny, a religion scholar at Barnard College. Frustrated with the persistent influence of Baptist practices among the Jamaican adults they were evangelizing, the missionaries decided that "the only way they can have a real impact is if they focus on converting children, separating them from their parents and their culture to bring them up in their own homes," explains Kenny. The movement treated adoption as a civilizing project, assimilating Jamaican children who were born of freed slaves who had labored on sugar estates, into white, Christian culture. In one instance children were separated from their families to be raised at a missionary school built on a converted sugar plantation, where they farmed sugar cane in exchange for their tuition—perhaps a dubious improvement over the past.

Likewise, the orphan train movement's efforts to place children in families that would treat them as kin instead often resulted in placements that resembled employer-employee relationships or, worse, indentured servanthood. CAS had an extremely limited capacity to check up on placements, leading to many stories of abuse and runaways. The organization later performed a statistical analysis that found that only one-fifth of children placed from orphan trains had a family experience comparable to today's understanding of adoption.

But Brace's argument ran deeper than simply charity. In CAS fundraising appeals he stirred both his readers' sense of Christian philanthropy and their middle-class fears of a rising generation of poor, urban children taking over New York. These children, Brace wrote, "will soon form the great lower class of our city," influencing elections and bolstering the ranks of criminals. CAS promised that they were "draining the city of these children, by communicating with farmers, manufacturers, or families in the country" who could put these junior members of the dangerous classes "in the way of an honest living." It was an argument for adoption that sounds similar to some adoption rescue pitches today. In fact, Brace's *The Dangerous Classes* is a recommendation in the Christian Alliance for Orphans' online resource library.

After the orphan train program began in 1854, it grew increasingly popular until eventually, by the 1870s, it had spawned similar programs in other cities. O'Connor wrote that among genteel organizations, "the idea of rescuing 'friendless' children by finding homes for them became almost fashionable." One prominent women's magazine even regularly featured descriptions of poor and orphaned children, asking readers to take them in.

In the slums, however, there was a widespread suspicion that CAS was engaging in a Protestant plot to destroy the Catholic faith of Irish or Italian immigrants—akin to a form of ethnic cleansing. "Practically from its foundation, the Children's Aid Society was one of the Protestant relief organizations most hated by Catholics, largely because of its Emigration Plan, which was commonly seen as little more than institutionalized child snatching," wrote O'Connor. "A multipaneled cartoon in an Irish American newspaper portrayed one of the society's agents as a dour ghoul who only smiles when a westerner gives him $20 for a frightened Catholic newsboy." The final panel of the cartoon showed the newsboy transformed into a grown man, a Baptist minister nearly identical to the CAS agent who "rescued" him.

By contrast, Catholic relief programs that gained steam during this period emphasized helping poor children by aiding their impoverished parents to keep them. (Though at least one Catholic order running a hospital changed the names of abandoned Jewish children to present them as Catholic in their own form of conversion by fiat.)

In time, a preference for adopting young children and babies supplanted interest in older children whom the orphan trains had farmed out as a source of labor. By the late 1920s, as the movement was slowing down, most orphan train riders were infants, toddlers, and even newborns. After the orphan trains stopped running, another child-saving project began to gain more prominence: the effort to Christianize Native Americans by forcibly enrolling them in boarding schools, a mission that had been in place since the late 1800s, would become more aggressive from the 1950s through the '70s as the Child Welfare League of America's Indian Adoption Project. This project would relocate between 25 and 35 percent of all Native American children from reservations into the homes of white American adopters, orphanages, and foster homes. The blatant assimilationist aims of the Indian Adoption Project (similar to the forced mass adoption of indigenous children in Australia) resulted in the 1978 enactment of the Indian Child Welfare Act, which now severely restricts the adoption of Native American children outside their communities.

Eventually, as the drive to save children through adoption was directed overseas, the history of international adoption also became inextricably linked to Christian evangelism. In 1955 adoption first went beyond US borders in a significant way with the mission of Harry and Bertha Holt, evangelical farmers from eastern Oregon and an aggressively humble couple, he in overalls, she in long braids pinned to her crown. In 1954 they were moved while watching a film made by the evangelical relief group World Vision about Korea's "Amerasian" war orphans: the shunned and often abandoned biracial offspring of Korean mothers and US or British soldiers during and after the Korean War. Several months later Harry Holt found himself at the Grand Hotel in Tokyo, spending the night before boarding a connecting plane. He was halfway between his home in Creswell, Oregon, and his destination in a war-racked South Korea, where he was going to pick out eight orphans to raise.

After watching World Vision's movie, the Holts, deeply conservative Christians who were involved in child evangelism through the Good News Club, an organization that hosts after-school proselytizing meetings for elementary school children, wanted to help the Amerasian children in a more profound way than simply sending cash. They looked around their farmhouse and decided that, by squeezing their six biological children together, they had room for eight more.

In the hotel room Holt wondered and worried about where to begin his search for the children he and his wife would adopt. As his resolve wavered and he began to doubt his mission, he performed an exercise in bibliomancy common to many Christians in times of uncertainty or challenge. Kneeling in the dark beside the hotel bed, he opened his Bible at random and let his finger point the way to whatever message God had for him. It landed, incredibly, on Isaiah 43:5–7, which began, "Fear not for I am with thee." In a letter home to his wife, Holt emphasized the scripture's shocking relevance, italicizing key lines in the rest of the verse: "I will bring *thy seed from the east*, and gather thee from the west; I will say to the *north*, Give up; and to the *south*, Keep not back: bring my sons from far, and my daughters from the ends of the earth; Even every one that is called by my name: for I have created him for my glory, I have formed him; yea, I have made him." Just two years after the armistice ending Korea's civil war, which had lasted from 1950 to 1953, the reference to north and south seemed to resonate. In light of his larger undertaking Holt reflected on how the mandate to gather the "seed from the east" might mean more than just his eight children-to-be.

The verse would become perhaps the most important passage of Scripture to Holt and his wife for the rest of their lives; Bertha even went on to write three books that referenced it: *The Seed from the East, Created for God's Glory, Bring My Sons from Afar*. It would also forever change not only the lives of the approximately two hundred thousand Korean children adopted overseas and the families they joined in the United States and in Europe but also international adoption itself.

In rescuing these children, the Holts became America's first celebrity adoptive parents. Media gave their story heavy play not just for the spectacle of the grandfatherly Harry returning to the United States with eight babies and toddlers in tow but also for the legal mountains he and Bertha had moved to make it possible: lobbying for a special act of Congress permitting them to adopt four times as many children at once than was legally allowed. Their story was retold in television specials, a photo spread in *Life* magazine, and myriad newspaper articles. A senator's wife nominated Bertha Holt as Oregon's "mother of the year" (though she was disqualified because her biological children were too old, in 1966 Bertha did receive the national "American Mother of the Year" award from the American Mother's Committee). Journalists in Korea trailed Harry, a dark-haired man who often wore overalls or suspenders, and photographed him lying on the floor with a bevy of sweet-faced children crawling around him or as he led the toddlers in a line up a picturesque Korean hill. The couple was sure that the message Holt had received through Isaiah 43 wasn't limited to their eight adoptees but that "God was telling Harry" to do something more, "to assume the responsibility of getting the rest of those children into these homes that so obviously are open to adopting them."

The Holts appealed to Americans to save Korean orphans from the "cold and misery and darkness of Korea into the warmth and love of your homes." They also noted that they hoped "that every adopted child would become a born-again Christian." Interest continued to grow. By 1956 World Vision, which briefly partnered with Holt, published an ad in the *Los Angeles Times* offering "A Korean Orphan for You" to families who couldn't personally adopt but could join in the movement through sponsorship, becoming symbolic "Mother or Daddy to your own child in a Christian orphanage in Korea."

The Holts received requests for adoption by the hundreds and then the thousands. They began to organize regular chartered flights, with airplanes bearing as many as one hundred or more children at a time tucked into cardboard bassinets and occupying most seats in the cabin. The children became known as "mail-order babies," and some of the Holts' flights seemed designed to appeal to the public imagination, such as a widely covered "Thanksgiving Baby Lift." Many of the children underwent expedited procedures and benefited from the intensive involvement of supportive US politicians, who, then as now, were eager to be associated with missionaries bringing back planeloads of babies to the United States from a poorly understood Korean warfront. What would today be considered unusual practices reigned, such as quick proxy adoptions, where Holt adopted children on behalf of foreign parents, then transported the babies back to the United States to meet their families; "order-taking" that matched children to parents' desired age, race, and physical traits; and "prioritizing Christian fundamentalists as adoptive parents," as historian and Korean adoptee Tobias Hübinette wrote.

The Holts turned their basement into an adoption agency, asking of prospective adoptive parents few qualifications beyond a statement of faith. They also began to organize lobbying efforts, rallying thousands to write their representatives to pass special orphan legislation that would allow more adoptees to come. In Korea Harry's staff, including one of his adult daughters, traveled into the countryside, looking for "Amerasian" babies living with their mothers, and Harry began considering expanding his operations to Mexico as well. Meanwhile, at home Bertha rocked her eight new children two at a time for an hour each night, in a family expanded so large it resembled a small orphanage in itself.

Because the Holts' religion was such a huge part of their mission, unsurprisingly, the families they served were all Christians as well; until 1964 Holt placed its children exclusively with Christian families. Parents who had been denied adoption applications with other agencies "because of one thing or another," as Bertha Holt dismissively wrote in one of her several memoirs, *The Seed from the East*, completed adoptions with Holt. As such, social service agencies worried that the Holts' proxy adoptions were becoming a loophole for parents to bypass home-study requirements.

In 1958 a critical Child Welfare League of America worker, Arnold Lyslo (who ironically would head the League's Indian Adoption Project), wrote with dismay about meeting one Holt plane bearing 107 children that arrived in Portland, Oregon, two days after Christmas. Lyslo claimed to see cardboard boxes with holes in the ends that he thought had been used to hold infants on the ride and possibly be stacked. He was surprised by both the appearance of the adoptive parents—women so austere that he thought "these particular families [might be] of a strict religious sect"—and the explanation of one family that they had been approved for adoption on the basis of a letter of recommendation from their pastor and some brief financial statements. Many of the families, he wrote, seemed disappointed with the children they received, and he was concerned about how well they might parent.

> The expression on some of their faces were revealing that perhaps this was not the child that they had dreamed of, and they were still bewildered at the appearance of the child and his inability to make immediate response as they wished.
>
> I came away from this experience ill and almost as bewildered as some of the adoptive parents themselves—that this could happen to children and parents in the United States today! My worries for these children have never ceased, and one

can only hope and pray that they are doing as well as circumstances have allowed with such inadequate planning. I could only think how different this could have been with the participation of good social agencies who could work with these families to evaluate for their own good and the welfare of the child, their capacity to adopt a Korean child.

From the beginning there were problems, and not all of the adoptions turned out well. One child was returned to the Holts, another couple of children died, rumors spread in the media about physical abuse of adoptees, and one mother was charged with her adopted child's murder yet, within the year, was given two more babies by the Holts. A number of sick children died during the arduous trip from Korea to the United States or in transport from the flight to their homes. When a doctor reportedly insisted that the Holts' mission be investigated, Bertha answered with sharp conviction "that it was the Lord's work and that even the devil would not be able to stop it." She wrote extensively of what she felt were the anti-adoption attitudes of critics in government or social services, beginning what would become a long-standing narrative of adoption as a battle between saviors and obstructionists who think they know better.

Ultimately the Holts' ad hoc services for US Christian adoptive parents became the basis for the longest-standing international adoption agency in the world—and one of the largest: Holt International Children's Services. Today Holt has facilitated adoptions for more children than any other agency and is often considered the standard bearer for ethical adoption practices.

The Holts' influence and that of other, competing agencies that followed in their wake could be felt on the ground in Korea. The number of children's homes in the country had already leapt from 38 in 1945 to 215 in 1950. By 1957, after the war, there were 482 orphanages, most of them created by Westerners, which cared for nearly fifty thousand children. And as in other countries where a sponsorship model would become part of financing orphanages, the more children an institution held, the more donations they received from abroad.

It was the start of a system wherein, as Tobias Hübinette wrote, "foreign individuals and voluntary agencies considered themselves to be guardians of the country's children," as the conviction that they were called by God often justified their sense of ownership. The religious makeup of the adoption agencies working in South Korea as well as the adoptive parents lining up to adopt was so stark that even in 1988, thirty-three years after the Holts' adoptions, a US immigration officer working at the embassy in Seoul worried to journalist Matthew Rothschild, writing in the *Progressive*, that Christian parents might see adoption as "a quick means of spreading the gospel, a head start on proselytizing." In fact, the Holts' program became a force so formidable that it is often credited with starting not just Korean adoptions to the United States—though there had been scattered adoptions from Korea before the Holts' children—but also the institution of international adoption itself, endowing it from its inception with a strong evangelical mission to save children, both body and soul.

ALTHOUGH A NUMBER of Christians followed in the Holts' footsteps throughout the 1960s, '70s, and '80s, for many years a majority of evangelicals did not see adoption—or any other social justice cause—as their calling. The modern evangelical movement around adoption and orphan care, said Medefind, is in some way a return to forgotten convictions, as conservative Christians reclaim a social gospel message they abandoned decades ago. When former Fox News pundit Glenn Beck urged his viewers in 2010 to quit any church that mentions "social justice," which he claimed was code for Marxism, he was aping an old fight: the twentieth-century bifurcation of Christians into fundamentalists, who emphasized creed and doctrinal purity, and modernists, who focused on service, good works, and activism.

"In my interpretation," Medefind told me, "this is a false split. Historic Christianity has always emphasized certain convictions and certain actions, what you could call orthodoxy and orthopraxy. The one flows from the other." Recently, Medefind said, the evangelicals born of the twentieth century's fundamentalists have "re-embraced the Christian call to hold together Christian conviction with Christian service to people in need." According to this interpretation, the movement isn't a new social gospel but rather a return to a biblical tradition of orphan care that traces back to the days of the Roman Empire, when Christians were known for saving unwanted babies left to die outside city walls in what was a legal form of infanticide. "They were responding to the exact same need as people are today," Medefind said.

Russell Moore, however, is blunter. He told me that the anomaly isn't Christians caring for orphans now but rather the recent decades when Christians *didn't* care for orphans. Over the last fifty years the evangelical church "had become fat and materialistic and comfortable and self-focused," Moore stated. "I think there are several prongs of Christianity that are reawakening to their responsibility for social care and orphan care, with adoption care being part of that concern."

Medefind's Christian Alliance for Orphans was founded in 2004, beginning with little fanfare: its first meeting drew less than forty people. The movement gained momentum over the next few years, particularly with the entrance of Rick Warren, one of the most recognizable evangelical preachers in the United States, onto the global development scene in 2005. On the runaway success of his book, *The Purpose Driven Life*, which has been translated into more than fifty languages, as well as his pop-culture standing as a somewhat moderate evangelical figure, Warren had accumulated enough political clout to help shape trending concerns among US evangelicals. In 2002 he turned his attention to AIDS after his wife, Kay, read an article about AIDS orphans in Africa. Realizing that HIV/AIDS affected more diverse groups of people than they had thought, the Warrens began doing international aid work that eventually developed into Saddleback's trademark global ministry, the P.E.A.C.E. Plan. The plan aims to use local churches around the world to address the social needs of the poor in their own communities, bringing in teams of volunteer American missionaries to support churches in addressing five root problems: spiritual emptiness that breeds conflict, egocentric leadership, extreme poverty, global pandemics, and poor education. In 2010 Saddleback reached its 196th nation—more nations than are represented in the UN, Warren announced—making Saddleback "the first church in 2,000 years to literally go to every nation."

Saddleback's global focus then caught on in the larger evangelical community. In 2007 the Christian Alliance for Orphans, still in its infancy, held a small summit at the Focus on the Family headquarters in Colorado Springs, a city so filled with evangelical ministries that it is sometimes referred to as the Protestant Vatican. Warren attended and made an announcement that was hailed in national media as a sea change for conservative Christians: "We've got some people who only focus on moral purity and couldn't care less about the poor, the sick, the uneducated," said Warren. "And they haven't done zip for those people."

It was grandstanding, to be sure. Prior to learning about AIDS orphans, Kay Warren has admitted, she believed HIV/AIDS victims "deserved it" for living lives of sexual risk and sin, and Saddleback remains a strong and influential opponent of gay rights, famously partnering for a time with one of Uganda's most vehement homophobes, the condom-burning and gay porn–screening Pastor Martin Ssempa. Nonetheless, many Christians enthusiastically welcomed the opportunity to reposition themselves as fighting *for* something good instead of being known primarily for what they condemn. As Niels Hoogeveen, spokesperson for the adoption watchdog website Pound Pup Legacy, noted wryly, "Bashing gays is not really a purpose, but rescuing the orphans—that's a purpose."

Another influential undercurrent in the evangelicals' espousal of adoption as a central mission was the rhetoric of the decades-old culture war over abortion. After decades of hearing pro-choice accusations that pro-life activists only cared about children before they were born and being asked, "Who's going to care for all these unwanted children?" evangelicals began responding: we will. But what began as a half-hearted rejoinder, with Christians paying lip service to "the adoption option" on the anniversary of *Roe v. Wade,* the movement has transformed into a cause, with every adopted child seen as "a new son or daughter who escaped the abortionist's knife or the orphanage's grip to find at your knee the grace of a carpenter's Son," as Russell Moore wrote. (A chapter of Moore's book pits Joseph of Nazareth, who "adopted" Jesus, against Planned Parenthood, which he calls the "King Herod" of our day.)

After the 2007 Christian Alliance for Orphans meeting at Focus on the Family, the word went out across the country's churches and Christian networks. "Over the next six months," wrote Stephanie Simon in the *Los Angeles Times,* "Christian media will be saturated with stories and ads touting adoption and foster care as a scriptural imperative, an order direct from God. Tens of thousands of pastors will be urged to preach about the issue, set up support groups for couples considering taking in troubled kids, and even invite state child-welfare officials to talk to their congregations." The movement took off. By 2008 Focus on the Family, which has focused its advocacy most on adopting children already in the foster care system, predicted that the incidence of Christians adopting for religious reasons would become the norm within one decade; instead, it took only a few years.

Warren brought both presidential candidates in the 2008 election, Barack Obama and John McCain, to Saddleback for one of the church's trademark "Civil Forum" discussions. There, he got both politicians to commit to the idea of an emergency plan for the global "orphan crisis," similar to the President's Emergency Plan for AIDS Relief (PEPFAR), championed by President George W. Bush. That year Saddleback made orphan care one of its "signature issues," announcing its goal to adopt one thousand children among its congregation. In 2010 the church dedicated its Civil Forum explicitly to orphans and adoption. "Orphans and vulnerable children are not a cause," Warren said on the occasion, but rather "a biblical and social mandate we can't ignore."

Another watershed moment for the movement had also come in 2008, when Medefind became head of the White House office of faith-based initiatives. "It was kind of a perfect storm," said Tom DiFilipo, president and CEO of the Joint Council on International Children's Services (JCICS), an influential secular adoption lobby group that works extensively with the Christian Alliance. "We hit that moment when a movement really starts to ramp up, and get the attention of the public, and become more effective. People were in the right place at the right time."

Within a few years a number of movement books followed. Although there had been some earlier, fairly obscure books on the subject, like Michelle Gardner's 2003 memoir, *Adoption as a Ministry, Adoption as a Blessing,* the books riding the wave of the movement began to roll out one after the other, creating a growing library of books about "orphan theology." In addition to Russell Moore's *Adopted for Life,* there was Bishop W. C. Martin's *Small Town, Big Miracle: How Love Came to the Least of These* (2007), Tom Davis's *Fields of the Fatherless* (2008), Dan Cruver's *Reclaiming Adoption* (2010), Cheryl Ellicott's *This Means War: Equipping Christian Families for Fostercare or Adoption* (2010), Randy Bohlender's *The Spirit of Adoption* (2010), and Tony Merida and Rick Morton's *Orphanology* (2011). Scores of evangelical adoption or "orphan care" conferences were organized as well, passing orphan theology on to Christian activists.

Thousands of churches began to participate every November in "Orphan Sunday," an annual multimedia event that was originally created in Zambia but grew massive in the United States. On Orphan Sunday pastors dedicate their sermons to orphan and adoption issues and many screen a special concert organized by the Christian Alliance. Tens of thousands of Christian parents and youth groups participate in the Alliance's "Orphan's Table" activity, preparing a simple meal of mail-order boiled grains, letting children eat for a night the type of food that orphanage children typically receive. Other churches host orphan-empathy slumber parties in suburban parking lots to help teens understand what homelessness feels like.

In 2009 Moore helped codify the growing movement for at least a portion of its advocates when he drafted and helped pass a Southern Baptist resolution, "On Adoption and Orphan Care." This resolution called upon all sixteen million members of the denomination to become involved in adoption in one form or another, whether by adopting children themselves, donating money for other families' adoptions, or supporting the thousands of "adoption ministries" flourishing around the country.

The effect of all these developments on adoption agencies' business was evident within a few years. In 2010 the mammoth evangelical adoption agency Bethany Christian Services—the largest adoption agency in the United States, secular or religious, with total revenues in 2011 of almost $75 million—announced that its overall adoption placements had spiked 26 percent during the first half of the year, its international adoption numbers had increased 66 percent over the same period in 2009, and general adoption inquiries were up a whopping 95 percent. They attributed the leaps largely to the mobilization of churches around adoption and Bethany's own deepening partnerships with groups like the Alliance, Saddleback Church, and the Southern Baptist Convention (SBC). "We expect adoptions will continue to rise as new movements within the Christian community raise awareness and aid for the global orphan crisis," announced Bethany president and CEO Bill Blacquiere, who is also a Christian Alliance board member. In 2010 the agency joined the SBC to begin subsidizing pastors' adoption costs—the SBC through an endowment to provide $2,000 grants to adopting pastors and Bethany by granting $1,000 each to the first 25 that the SBC had approved, provided those pastors use Bethany for their adoption. In response, 140 Southern Baptist pastors and missionaries applied for the grants' initial round—double what organizers had anticipated.

Since its founding in 2004 the Christian Alliance has grown into a powerful coalition of more than one hundred "formerly competitive" conservative Christian organizations, including parachurch groups like Focus on the Family and Campus Crusade for Christ, adoption agencies like Bethany, adoption and orphan-care ministries like Hope for Orphans, as well as a nationwide network of churches like Saddleback. Even UNICEF, so often the target of adoption advocates, has felt compelled to reach out to the growing coalition, hosting a closed discussion in 2010 with six key US evangelical adoption leaders in an apparent effort to find common ground.

The movement has had influence outside the church as well. Adoption has become a moral asset on both sides of the political aisle: a way for liberals to neutralize abortion debates by proposing adoption as a "common ground" compromise as well as a way for conservatives to demonstrate their compassionate side, making their antiabortion activism seem more truly "pro-life," or "whole life," as one Bethany staffer coined it.

In 2008 megachurch Pastor Joel Hunter, a moderate evangelical frequently courted by Democrats, was featured in the *Wall Street Journal* when he called on federal programs to reduce abortions by promoting adoption. The same year the *Journal*'s trend-watching "Taste" section advised that Senator John McCain highlight his adopted Bangladeshi daughter as a way to boost his appeal with evangelicals. The girl who had once been the target of an ugly smear campaign during the 2000 Republican primary, when the Bush camp spread rumors that she was McCain's illegitimate black child, was now a political asset among the "values voters" flocking to adoption.

Two years later, at a 2010 conference at Liberty University in Lynchburg, Virginia, neo-Pentecostal leader Lou Engle, cofounder of the political prayer movement The Call, voiced a political goal as well, as investigative journalist Sarah Posner reported. "There is an explosion of adoption. If you talk to the millennials, they're all thinking: care for the poor, adoption. It's all in their DNA," Engle said.

"If the megachurches of America did this," he proposed, "[entering] the foster care system, we would be the answer, and we would get moral authority in this nation."

MOORE AND OTHER evangelical theologians are crafting an extensive orphan theology to undergird the movement, disseminating their ideas through Christian groups like the Family Research Council (FRC), Focus on the Family's political advocacy arm. Beyond the ubiquitous citation of James 1:27, which calls caring for widows and orphans "pure religion," is the notion of vertical and horizontal adoption: that Christians are adopted by God when they are born again (vertical adoption) and that they mirror this through their physical adoption of children on earth (horizontal adoption). Before adoption, all are equally orphans; afterward, all are Christian brothers. It's an idea taken from the biblical letters of the Apostle Paul, who wrote about Christians receiving "adoption as sons" and becoming heirs to God. As the first tenet of the SBC's 2009 adoption resolution put it: "In the gospel we have received the 'Spirit of adoption' whereby we are no longer spiritual orphans but are now beloved children of God and joint heirs with Christ." Or as the FRC put it, introducing a 2012 public lecture by Moore, "Adoption is a special topic for Christians. All who have united their lives to Jesus have something at stake in the adoption issue precisely because Jesus does." Adoption, advocates conclude, is the salvation message of the gospel itself, "the very heart of God."

However, Moore, a rising star in the SBC and perhaps the foremost leader crafting the ideas behind the movement, warned that the movement must maintain a balance between theology and practice. Without a theological grounding, he wrote, the adoption cause risks becoming "like one more cause wristband for compassionate conservative evangelicals to wear until the trend dies down." And without a practical, boots-on-the-ground expression of that theology, he warned, "the doctrine of adoption too easily becomes mere metaphor, just another way to say 'saved.'"

But in many ways, it has become a way to say saved, and Moore's book in effect popularized the evangelical metaphor—a long-standing tradition in some denominations, but new to others—that Christians are adoptees of God. As C. J. Mahaney, a prominent evangelical pastor, asserted in the preface to Moore's book: "I was adopted when I was eighteen years old. I wasn't an orphan, the way most people think of that term. . . . But I was in a condition far more serious: I was a stranger to the family of God."

That's also the message of Dan Cruver's contribution to the movement library, *Reclaiming Adoption: Missional Living Through the Rediscovery of Abba Father.* In it Cruver argues that vertical adoption is just shorthand for believers' union with Christ. It's a deceptively simple argument, but in reviewing *Reclaiming Adoption,* conservative Biola University theologian Fred Sanders suggested that the ideas Cruver and his peers are exploring "may have the momentum to reinvigorate evangelical systematic theology." This could push back against "an uncommonly mushy doctrine of God's universal fatherhood," which Sanders sees in liberal churches, with a more discriminating theology. The idea of fatherhood is a recurring theme in the movement's repeated references to Abba, or father, as in a special 2010 *Christianity Today* adoption issue, "Abba Changes Everything: Why Every Christian Is Called to Rescue Orphans," or in the hypnotic chorus of the 2010 Christian Alliance Summit theme song, in which a worship leader led the conference in repeating, "Abba, I belong to you, I belong to you, Abba, Father, God." The thrust of orphan theology is a reorientation or clarification of the idea—the "uncommonly mushy idea," as Sanders harrumphed—that all people are children of God, made in His image. Instead of this poetic standby, Sanders suggests that orphan theology enforces a higher standard, that only proper believers are actually God's children—adopted into the family when they are born again. If so, then adoption movement theologians are making the question of spiritual salvation inextricable from the worldly efforts of the evangelical adoption movement. Christian adopters are in this light the image of God, assuming His role to the children they adopt, with no distinction between taking a child in and saving her soul, the two a concurrent act. As Rick Warren explained, "What God does to us spiritually, He expects us to do to orphans physically: be born again and adopted."

It's an issue that's close to home for Moore. In 2002 he adopted two boys from what he describes as deplorable orphanage conditions in a mining town in Russia. The infant boys came from a country where some orphanages live up to the nightmare images that emerged from Eastern Europe after the fall of the Iron Curtain, when Romanian children were found dumped in emotionally sterile and physically squalid warehouses, neglected to the point of psychosis. Moore's experience meeting and later returning to pick up his sons in Russia seemed to shake him deeply. He wrote in *Adopted for Life* that adoption is on the one hand gospel, part of Christians' mission and inheritance from God, and on the other hand "war," a spiritual battle against unseen, evil forces (or "satanic powers," in the SBC resolution) that would obstruct the salvation of children like his, who are born into original sin and saved only by their adoption by God. ("Our birth father has fangs," Moore wrote. "And left to ourselves, we'll show ourselves to be as serpentine as he is.")

When Moore left his boys in the Russian orphanage to return home until the adoption paperwork was completed, he laid his hand on their heads in their cribs and quoted Scripture, John 14:18, when Jesus tells his disciples: "I will not leave you as orphans; I will come to you." He said the words came to him instinctively, that he hadn't intended to channel Christ. But to those reading about Moore's journey, his words weren't evidence of a savior complex; they were a roadmap.

WITH SO MUCH EMPHASIS on the parallels between saving children through adoption and saving souls through conversion, it's not surprising to find that the adoption cause has developed an acute missionary angle. In Moore's own church in Kentucky the emphasis is underscored by a matching set of full-wall world maps that depict the locations both of where the congregation sponsors missionaries and of where the adopted children in the congregation have come from, a gesture of equivalence that Moore believes, "signals to the congregation that adoption is a Great Commission activity." Dan Cruver is even blunter, writing in *Reclaiming Adoption* that "the *ultimate* purpose of human adoption by Christians, therefore, is not to give orphans parents, as important as that is. It is to place them in a Christian home that they might be positioned to receive the gospel."

Despite these overt calls to evangelize children, advocates like Moore, Cruver, and Medefind downplay the notion that invoking the Great Commission makes adoption a means of proselytizing. "If all we are doing in orphan care is taking children who are starving and abused and Christless and turning them into middle-class American evangelicals," Moore warned in one talk, "God help us." Instead, he elaborated to me, the Great Commission should be interpreted as Christians living in service to their neighbors and the world, spreading Christ's love by offering practical assistance.

Medefind makes the same argument. In the broad span of the evangelical community, he told me, the Great Commission mandate means different things. "Some groups emphasize the importance of sharing the gospel in every encounter, and others would take the line [attributed to] St. Francis: 'Preach the gospel always, use words when necessary,' meaning that to show love could be giving a cup to a thirsty child."

In any case, Moore told me, evangelicals are not "adopting in order to evangelize children" any more than they are "having babies in order to evangelize those children." Almost all parents, whether Christians or secular humanists, will try to pass their values on to their kids, he argues. But squaring this broader definition with the driving emphasis in so much of the movement's literature—that evangelizing, in the commonly understood sense, is part of the plan—is difficult. In fact, the SBC adoption resolution cites one justification for adoption in the denomination's historical concern "for the evangelism of children—including those who have no parents." And despite Moore's warning to advocates in a *Christianity Today* article that adoption is not "just a backdoor route to child evangelism," evangelism is there in abundance in Moore's own writings: when he says that adoption is "evangelistic to the core," as Christian adopters are "committing to years of gospel proclamation"; or that there is no dividing line between churches' adoption ministries and their evangelizing missionaries; or that adoption even opens up a new, "untilled" missionary field in witnessing to "unchurched" adoptive parents. "Through these ministries, you may find children being adopted on the earthly plane and parents being adopted in the heavenly plane," he wrote. In one anecdote in his book Moore clucked over a church that had established an annual mission trip to introduce orphanage children to potential US parents but wasn't, to his mind, being evangelistic enough. Their misunderstanding was tragic, Moore wrote, because "What better way is there to bring the good news of Christ than to see his unwanted little brothers and sisters placed in families where they'll be raised in the nurture and admonition of the Lord?"

The larger adoption movement is infused with the same philosophy. Moore's colleague Randy Stinson, dean of the Southern Baptist Theological Seminary's School of Church Ministries and president of the antifeminist Council on Biblical Manhood and Womanhood, discussed his and his wife's adoption of two Taiwanese girls as a means of "rescuing" the girls from "a situation of worshipping their ancestors." The ABBA Fund's mission statement calls adoption "'missions in reverse,' because it provides an opportunity to reach into our own cities and across the globe to bring children into homes where Jesus is present and the Gospel is proclaimed." Hopegivers International, a member of the Christian Alliance for Orphans, aims "to rescue one million orphaned, abandoned, and at-risk children who will be sharpened as Arrows for God, and launched back into society to proclaim the Good News of Jesus to the world." And the very membership agreement of the Alliance states its vision as "Every orphan experiencing God's unfailing love and knowing Jesus as Savior."

As might be expected, the subtleties of Moore's or Medefind's parsing of the Great Commission do not inhibit lay followers. Some simply proclaim adoption as a great way to make converts. Adoption is better than simply sending money, followers have suggested, because adopting gives an opportunity to save a soul that aid alone will not. As one Christian blogger wrote when arguing against simply sponsoring children in their home countries, "You cannot make a disciple out of a child you barely see."

Cheryl Ellicott, an evangelical foster care proponent, goes further yet in her book, *This Means War*. A foster mother to more than fifty, Ellicott wrote, "*Your main goal is not to raise well-adjusted children, but rather to bring the life-changing message of the Gospel to lost souls. If you work with a troubled, damaged child and he never becomes a successful or productive citizen, but he believes the Gospel and has a saving faith in Jesus Christ, you have succeeded. Adoption is a ministry to unsaved souls.*"

WALKING DOWN 55TH Street in New York City in 2011, I passed a young woman in her twenties wearing a T-shirt that read, simply, "143 million." To many New Yorkers the message might have been obscure, but in Nashville or Orange County or the suburbs of Minneapolis, it would have been old hat. Everyone in evangelical-dom knows about the orphan crisis and the significance of 143 million. In fact, for many this woman's T-shirt would be considered outdated. "143 million is old news," proclaimed Johnny Carr, national director of Church Partnerships for Bethany

Christian Services, in 2010, continuing, "163 million is the new number." Soon a new figure would upstage Carr's tally: 210 million orphans.

The numbers—whichever estimate is used—have become such an effective rallying cry for Christians involved in the adoption movement that the figure itself has become shorthand for a belief system: belief in the idea of the "orphan crisis" and a solution that prioritizes international adoption. As prospective adoptive parents routinely put it when announcing that they're adopting or that their child is "coming home," their adoption's larger significance is "143 million minus one."

But there's a problem with these numbers, just as there had been in the bloated estimates of Haitian orphans after the earthquake: they don't reflect reality. And that problem runs to the foundation of the Christian adoption movement. Initially, 143 million was a figure taken from a UN tally of "orphaned and vulnerable children" around the world, a category that doesn't represent the number of children living without parents but rather all children who have lost one parent or both and who are thus categorized as "vulnerable." Many of these children live with their surviving parent or with extended family in situations that, if they occurred to American kids, we would not refer to as orphanhood. The UN and US-AID have estimated the current number for 2012 to be 153 million total orphans and vulnerable children worldwide, which again means mostly "single orphans"—those who have lost only one parent and most likely still live with their immediate or extended family.

Only about 10 percent, or 17.8 million children in this figure, are "double orphans"—children who have lost both parents—but many of them likely live with their extended family. To complicate things further, many children counted in orphanages around the world are in fact still connected to their families, who may use the institutions as boarding schools during a dry season of poverty or a period of intense work, like an agricultural harvest. One Save the Children report found that 80 percent of children in orphanages worldwide have living family members. To complicate things even more, in the other direction, the numbers do not include many children who have living parents who do not care for them, like street children. But what is clear is that the numbers, at least when they're interpreted as an indication of children waiting to be adopted, are a complete fiction. What that means for the Christian adoption movement is that those flogging 143 (or 210) million on their chests, their blogs, or at conferences are laying claim on ideological grounds to tens or hundreds of millions of children who live with a parent or other family, ignoring the distinction between unparented "double orphans" and the much larger number of "vulnerable children," and implying that they all belong in American homes. "As soon as anyone quotes that figure," said Parents for Ethical Adoption Reform's Karen Moline, "you know they're the enemy of reality."

The idea of the crisis these numbers pose is so abstract that the actual figures have come to mean almost nothing. One adoptive father in the movement made the astonishing claim to the *Tuscaloosa News* that another 12 million children become orphans every single day. If this was true, then the 143 million figure would double in under two weeks and result in 4.4 billion orphans by the end of a single year—more than two-thirds of the world's entire population. To be fair, the father quoted was a lay follower of the movement and was repeating, probably incorrectly, a statistic he had heard somewhere along the line. But the fact that he passed it on without digesting its impossible meaning and that the newspaper printed it without question or comment gives an idea of the dimension in which discussions of the orphan crisis often take place.

In the popular imagination these hundreds of millions of orphans have become a mass of potential adoptees and a source of indignation when efforts to adopt a child are slow going or thwarted. How can it be so hard to adopt, prospective adoptive parents wonder, when there are hundreds of millions of children, waiting to be saved?

Susan Bissell, UNICEF's head of Child Protection, said that no good estimate exists of the actual number of "orphans" as Westerners think of them. "To my knowledge, there really is no accurate number of a child with no parents, no grandma, no aunty, all alone in the world," Bissell told me. "And you probably won't find one in the future." The task of identifying and estimating the number of orphans exists within a larger scenario, a crisis of documentation, in which 220 million children under the age of five across the developing world, not counting China, do not even have a birth certificate, making further attempts to track their histories and parentage a grueling and individualized process. But Americans, moved by the idea of the orphan crisis, and hoping to grow their own families, want fast and true numbers of children available for adoption. "I think the crisis that relates to adoption has this very murky definition that needs to be sorted out," Bissell continued. "If we had a definition that allowed us to 'datify' children who have no parents or extended family, you would have yourself a 'true orphan' in how that's understood. But the international community's definition of single and double orphans has evolved, and it's very confusing to all of us and to the public." "I think the crisis is something else," Bissell continued. "We have a child protection crisis, we have a violence crisis. It's a crisis of humanity."

Some members of the Christian orphan-care movement will acknowledge that the numbers are misleading. "There are not 145 million kids out there waiting for someone in America to adopt them," said Paul Myhill, president of the evangelical orphan ministry World Orphans, which he calls a "black sheep" in the field for its prioritization of in-country orphan care over international adoption. He calls the "143 million" rhetoric an example of "manipulative numbers." "The numbers *are* high," Myhill said, "but I think it's unfair to portray them to a world that doesn't understand the difference between a 'single orphan' and a 'double orphan' or an orphan in care and not in care. It's unfair to bat these statistics around without using all the qualifiers."

To complicate matters further, even this much smaller category of children who truly are in need of adoption often fall outside the parameters of what international adoptive parents are looking for. Most adoption demand in the United States continues to be for healthy infants or young children, whereas most of the children who are legitimately parentless or in need of an adoptive home are older, sicker, or more damaged from trauma than most families are willing to take. UNICEF estimates that 95 percent of the global orphan population is made up of children who are five years or older, but the overwhelming adoption demand is for children under five—long accounting for at least 85 percent of all adoptions.

Although a number of adoptive parents, particularly Christians, have declared a calling to adopt specifically older or special-needs kids—discussed in greater depth later in this book—the bulk of demand is still for young children, and aside from some groups' targeted advocacy for foster care adoptions, in general the larger movement does not distinguish between the types of children their followers are adopting. The misleading numbers continue to be used because they are effective in promoting both the cause and the business of Christian adoption, in which each child generates total adoption fees of around $20,000 to $35,000—and sometimes ranging as high as $50,000 or $60,000—to agencies and middlemen. In this light the 143 million rallying cry is tantamount to a free, industry-wide advertisement.

David Smolin, a constitutional law professor at Cumberland School of Law in Birmingham, Alabama, who studies adoption fraud, said the gap between adoption rhetoric and the realities of international adoption is a particular problem in the evangelical community. There, the rapidly growing demand for adoptable children is dwarfing the supply of young, healthy children and babies that most people want. "I'm told by people who work for agencies that evangelical Christian clients are often the most difficult to deal with," Smolin said, "because they really believe there are huge numbers of orphans who need to be adopted, and they just don't understand what the problem is: why is it taking so long? Why can't they get a child quickly? They just don't get it because of what they've been told."

Observers from the broader adoption community say the Christian movement, with its rhetoric of orphan rescue, has reinforced preexisting bad ideas about adoption. "It really permeates everything," said Shari Levine, executive director of the independent Oregon and Washington adoption agency Open Adoptions & Family Services. "A lot of the religiously affiliated agencies start from the adoptive parents' perspective and cast them as saviors and angels." The role of religious agencies pushing this perspective in the larger industry can be overwhelming, continued Levine, who said that religiously affiliated agencies, many advancing an explicitly evangelical mission, completely dominate some regional adoption events she attends. On the national scale some watchdogs estimate that roughly half of the entire US adoption industry is composed of evangelical agencies, although Smolin found the tally to be lower in his 2011 survey of around two hundred accredited adoption service providers. But even if numerically they don't constitute a majority, he said, the biggest and most powerful agencies, such as Bethany, are evangelical. And even agencies that don't explicitly identify as Christian use Christian imagery and reinforce the same mission-driven sensibility.

In 2012 Medefind told me he agreed that the movement had engaged in misleading statistics. In response, that July he released a white paper from the Christian Alliance for Orphans discussing how the numbers should be used in the future. In it Medefind warned that the statistics and even the term "orphan" were problematic, "reveal[ing] nothing about the distinct needs of individual children" or potentially misguiding churches, ministries, and everyday Christians seeking a good way to take action.

But other advocates have little use for clarification. Dr. Jane Aronson, a pediatrician whose work with adoptees has earned her the nickname "The Orphan Doctor," is also the founder and CEO of Worldwide Orphans Foundation, an active advocacy organization that frequently pairs with celebrities to spread awareness of the orphan crisis. She dismissed a question about the numbers in a letter to the Schuster Institute for Investigative Journalism, writing in response to an article by journalist E. J. Graff. "As for how many, I am, frankly, impatient with this question," Aronson wrote. "There are millions—probably hundreds of millions—of children living in this world without parental or familial care. Isn't that enough to know?"

For many followers of the movement that claim is more than enough. Online, Christian adoption and orphan-care advocates blog in numbers too great to follow about their family's "adoption journey," under titles like "Redeeming Orphans," "Adopting God's Dreams," "Addicted to Adoption," "We Have Room," "Throwing Starfish," or "Orphan's Ticket Home." Some indicate the range of countries evangelicals are adopting from: "Digging a Hole to China," "Blessings from Ethiopia," or, more recently, "Countdown to Congo." In this wide community enthusiasm for the movement is overwhelming. "Am I Showing Yet?" asked one prospective adoptive parent, describing her "adoption pregnancy." Another made an "ultrasound" image out of a map of China. Another blogged about a gap in the family portrait she had taken with her six children: an empty space that indicated there was another member of their family out there, waiting to be found. "I cannot get past that hole," she wrote. "But who? From where?" One ministry simply declared, "Adoption is the new pregnant."

Bloggers and readers raise money for their adoptions by selling custom T-shirts and soliciting donations "to help take one orphan out of the count by Orphan Sunday" or to "Bring an orphan home TODAY!!!" Many encourage each other as they go through the stressful international adoption process—often taking as long as two to three years to process paperwork and receive all approvals. Many write about orphans as a corporate entity: the plight of "the Orphan," as in, "the poor."

They defend each other and the cause. One Christian blogging couple was criticized for their story about destroying the Buddhist charm their adopted son was given as a memento from his orphanage caregivers. They responded by calling their critics an "orphan-hate group." Another used the occasion of Martin Luther King Jr. Day to complain about growing "intolerance" among global development organizations for the viewpoint that international adoption is a valid solution to the orphan crisis.

Offline, members of the adoption community, hoping to spread the movement at a grassroots level, gather at workshops for adoptive mothers, family adoption camps, and small-scale meet-ups put on by groups like Together for Adoption. Some even sign up for lifestyle options like the annual Ukrainian orphan missions cruise arranged by HopeHouse International, a Franklin, Tennessee, ministry that takes up to fifty US Christians on a river cruise of ten orphanages along the Dnipro River.

The momentum feeds on itself. In a Tuscaloosa, Alabama, church, fourteen families adopted simultaneously and formed a church adoption support group. One parent explained to the *Tuscaloosa News*, "It wasn't like a bunch of us got together and said 'Let's all adopt.'" Instead, she suggested, "I strongly believe it's the Holy Spirit working." It was a demonstration of the "contagious" adoption culture that movement leaders want to foster, as more and more Christians begin to feel "burdened" to bring home an orphan after reading or hearing about others' adoptions. Even Justin Bieber, the teen pop icon who has traded on his mostly wholesome Christian image, announced in 2010 that he hoped to travel to Romania to "show love to orphans."

A common savior narrative emerged on the blogs. Some parents seemed almost to fetishize the disparity between themselves and the children they sought to adopt. As one blogger wrote, "No one can get any poorer than our Bethie is. . . . We, by contrast, have all the power in the world." That focus seemed to slide from acknowledging poor children's struggles to denigrating kids the adoption movement kept referring to as "the least of these," as when another adoptive mother to six described herself as "a dumpster diving orphan lunatic" who was still "afflicted with my Orphan Obsession" after adopting four kids and birthing two. "I am already part of a tribe of women that by much of the world's standards have a disorder," she wrote. "We wake up at night with visions of orphans going through our heads" and are fixated, she continued, on "match-making" their friends with orphans they had seen pictures of online. "Like the woman diving headfirst for the day old bread and barely ripe red bell peppers we dream and obsess over capturing and saving human treasures from being thrust into a decaying dump where they will be lost forever."

SOMETIMES THE MOVEMENT'S focus on American Christians saving developing nations' orphans leads followers to extremes. In 2011 Katie Davis, a twenty-three-year old evangelical homecoming queen from the rich Nashville suburb of Brentwood, published an "as-told-to" memoir, *Kisses from Katie: A Story of Relentless Love and Redemption*, that detailed her move to Uganda after high school and her "adoption" of fourteen girls in the community where she volunteered—more than a dozen children for whom she has become legal guardian. Some of the girls aren't much younger than she is, making her motherhood of some of the children a theoretical question. On the cover is a picture of Davis, a pretty, young brunette, in a gray T-shirt, walking through a rural Ugandan village while thronged by smiling black girls with shaved heads, as deep-red dirt roads stretch behind them.

The book, praised by movement leaders like Jedd Medefind and Dan Cruver, is filled with the ostentatious modesty Christian pop literature often stumbles into, a cover-to-cover humblebrag. "I have absolutely no desire to write a book about myself," Davis nonetheless wrote. "This is a book about a Christ who is alive today and not only knows but cares about every hair on my head."

That tone changes, however, when she describes meeting the orphanage children in Uganda. Like the blogger above who compared adoptees to stale bread, Davis was acutely aware of her wards' destitution even as she strained to insist that she saw them through Christ's eyes:

> I think many people would have looked at them and seen only their filthy clothes, the ringworm on their heads, or the mucus that ended up in a crust around their nostrils. . . . I didn't see these things. The truth is, I saw myself in those little faces. I looked at them and felt this love that was unimaginable and knew that this is the way God sees me . . . small and dirty at His feet, and He who sits so high chooses to commune with me, to love me anyway. He blinds Himself to my sin and my filth. . . . I just sat right down on that cold, hard floor and snuggled my nose into their dirty necks and kissed their fungus-covered heads and didn't even see it. I was *in love*.

She rhapsodized about the children's large brown eyes, their chocolate-colored and ebony skin. She reveled in the fact of her "beautifully filthy" daughters, and she saw Jesus in the faces of her Ugandan neighbors, whom she believed were so desperately poor that they had become spiritually rich—rich enough to be satisfied with their lot. It's a romanticization of developing nations' poverty that, although it may be forgivable in the young, is endemic to the larger movement as well: praising the holy poor and implicitly praising oneself for entering their world. On more than one occasion Davis describes how recipients of her charity fell to their knees and reached out to hold a piece of her clothing. And as a crowning gesture of humility, after attesting that God doesn't see skin color, Davis declares, "in heaven I am going to be black; I have already asked God for it."

One of the most obvious undercurrents to the Christian adoption movement is the massive rise in transracial adoptions in white, evangelical communities, most conspicuously to churches in the South. Becca

McBride, a political science scholar and evangelical from the Nashville area who is studying the movement from the inside, said the viral effect of adoption demonstrated in her own church (home church to Steven Curtis Chapman) and in a number of other central Tennessee congregations has led to "a sort of wild side effect": the integration of churches solely through white members' adopted children of color. McBride told me that in one neighboring church in Brentwood, the same suburb Katie Davis hails from and the proposed location of the Christian Alliance's 2013 summit, the "bottom-up" growth of an orphan-care ministry in the church started after a few people adopted. Within five years fifteen or twenty more families had adopted, almost all from African countries, bringing a sudden racial diversification to the church. "The diversity that exists in many churches is imported diversity," McBride noted. "It's not because there are a lot of black families in our town, but because people have adopted black children."

But the distinction McBride recognizes—that adopting children of color into an otherwise white congregation is different from a locally integrated church, where adults are meeting each other on equal footing— seems lost on many international adoption advocates. In one session at the Christian Alliance for Orphans Summit at Saddleback, The ABBA Fund's Jason Kovacs told the audience enthusiastically, "God is the first transracial adoptive dad, did you know that?" repeating a common refrain in the movement that, in adoption, as in the gospel, there is "no Greek, no Jew" but only people who have joined God's family. "The world's largest transracial adoptive community is going to assemble in heaven," Kovacs added, beaming.

Rick Warren echoed him, criticizing people who don't adopt because of "pride of race." "God could not care less about human bloodlines," Warren said. "You'd better thank God that He isn't interested in bloodlines, because you couldn't get saved, because you're not a Jew, and they're the chosen people and we're not. . . . We have been grafted in— adopted into the family."

I had heard this message before. On a Friday night in late February 2010, Russell Moore preached an electric message in the campus chapel at the Southern Baptist Theological Seminary in Louisville, Kentucky. It was the opening night of the "Adopting for Life" conference, a weekend meeting convened around the message of Moore's book. There, on a quiet campus with its own Christian bookstore and formalwear shop, a charismatic Moore wore jeans and a sports jacket, joking in a cool Mississippi drawl about Johnny Cash and Viagra and teasing the earnest Christian singer-songwriter serving as conference worship leader over his taste in music. An audience of around six hundred young Christians, overwhelmingly white and middle class, laughed comfortably—a different generation from the buttoned-down Baptists of yesteryear. Moore had a modern message to match: denouncing evangelicals' historical antipathy to civil rights and the evangelical churches of his parents' era that had turned a blind eye to racism while focusing on "the fundamentals" of the faith.

"There was a time when a group of people could stand around a room like this, maybe even this room," Moore preached, "and say, 'We're not going to worry about civil rights because we are going to simply preach Christ and Him crucified. We're going to focus on the gospel.' . . . When in reality, if you are not standing up and saying to people convinced they are superior to other people by virtue of the color of their skin, then you are sinners in need of a common salvation through a common savior. You are not preaching the gospel." The same spiritual call that should have compelled Southern Baptists to support civil rights, Moore said, commands the contemporary church to get involved in the orphan crisis. Around the chapel audience members clad in fleece jackets and denim, efficiently tending to babies in the back pews, offered sober Amens.

It's a message that cuts close to home in the SBC, a denomination founded in 1845 in defense of slavery, when the Southern Baptists split from the abolitionist Baptists of the north. After the Civil War and for much of the twentieth century the SBC was a home for white supremacist thought, but for the last two decades the SBC, now the largest Protestant denomination in the United States and the second-largest Christian denomination after Catholicism, has been trying to rehabilitate its image. In 1995 it issued an apology for its historic support of slavery and segregation, and a number of resolutions since then have called for individual churches to increase black membership and leadership. In 2012 they even approved a voluntary name change for churches that want to distance themselves from the SBC's legacy of racism—from Southern Baptists to Great Commission Baptists. At the same annual convention New Orleans Pastor Reverend Fred Luter Jr. made history when he became the denomination's first black president.

On that Friday night in February 2010 Moore seemed to have the same goal in mind. "One of the reasons that the civil rights movement is a shame on evangelical churches," he preached in Louisville, "is because the civil rights movement had to stand and speak to people who claimed to believe in inerrant bibles and say, 'You are hypocrites. You do not believe what you say you believe, because if you believe that all of humanity comes from one blood, as you so vehemently say you believe, then how in the world could you claim to own another being?'"

In the reserved but emotional atmosphere of the seminary chapel, Moore's message seemed clear: evangelicals have a second chance to get it right—and in a specific way: by throwing themselves into an adoption movement that preaches a message of "one blood" under a God who doesn't see race, just Christians adopted into a "common culture." Moore wasn't the only one to see the opportunity. As Rick Morton, Moore's one-time SBC seminary colleague, wrote in *Orphanology: Awakening to Gospel-Centered Adoption and Orphan Care*, the orphan crisis "affords the church a tangible opportunity to live out a God-based ethic of racial relationships and to engage in racial reconciliation to its utmost."

But practically speaking that means the SBC is addressing its racism most prominently not by talking to black adults, who may have endured the effects of the church's institutional bias, or by making its congregations more appealing to people of color but instead by adopting children from other races and cultures—frequently, these days, from Africa. For Moore, who wrote dismissively about multicultural critiques of adoption, this is not a problem. "That's adoption," he wrote, describing his own approach of raising his adopted Russian sons to recognize that their heritage is no longer Russian but now Mississippian, trading Dostoevsky for Faulkner, borscht for red beans and rice. "We're part of a brand-new family, a new tribe, with a new story, a new identity."

The same idealism has undergirded interracial adoption since the 1970s, when white liberals were eager to have their families reflect their integrationist principles. "In the late 1960s," a UNICEF report on international adoption noted, "adoption became tinged with the ideology of 'solidarity with the Third World' then current in industrialized countries, implying practical manifestations of sharing responsibility for the burden facing the newly decolonized nations." By the '70s adoption had begun to resemble "mass exportations" of children, and agencies had arisen to broker the transactions. In response, leaders from foreign nations described the export of their children as a tragedy. And in 1972 the Association of Black Social Workers famously declared that emerging trends of interracial adoption of black children by white parents seemed more like theft than solidarity, and that white families, blind to the variety of oppressions nonwhite people face, could not adequately prepare black children to live in a racist world.

The statement was a foundational declaration in the competing narratives around adoption: as either rescue or kidnapping. "There was this fledgling attempt to make interracial adoption a good thing in the public view," recalls historian Karen Dubinsky, author of *Babies Without Borders*, "with white liberals saying that integrating our families is making our families look like how we want the world to look. When all of a sudden these cranky black social workers say, 'Stop stealing our children.' That's the way the history has tended to be remembered: that 'kidnapping' came along and spoiled all the fun."

Today's Christian adoption movement is meeting the same critique that secular, liberal interracial adoption met years ago: that rescuing children through adoption can leave them unrooted and estranged, caught between dueling identities and never quite at home. Lisa Marie Rollins, a performance artist, academic, and a transracial adoptee with Filipino and African American birth parents, was raised by conservative white evangelicals in Tacoma, Washington and experienced the disconnect that the black social workers had warned against. "My parents didn't have a language for racism," she said, recalling how her own adoption paperwork had obscured her black heritage, passing her off as part Mexican instead, leading her well-meaning parents to assure her that "You're not really black" when Rollins encountered prejudice. It's an attitude that Rollins calls a "veil of whiteness," which often lasts only until children grow into adolescence and begin to encounter for themselves America's systemic hostility toward people of color. In this context Russell Moore's quip about swapping his children's borscht for fried catfish seems not so much amusing as an erasure of heritage, not to mention a more seamless assimilation—of white adoptees blending into another white culture—than that which is available to adoptees of color. In any case, most adoptees these days aren't trading in their borscht but rather their fufu, injera, and rice—as well as the cultures behind these staples, each already long marginalized in a world dominated by the West.

Forty years later the same debate continues, as the evangelical adoption movement follows in the footsteps of its secular forerunners in attempting to deal with the conflicts inherent to cross-cultural adoption. Despite the overt racism present in some threads of US conservatism, most mainstream evangelical churches are eager to embrace diversity. In these churches there is often a concerted "color-blind" rhetoric that could put liberal college campuses of the 1990s to the test. However, the postracial ideal of colorblindness that originated with white liberals has largely been discredited—research has found that those claiming to "not see race" are more likely to engage in casual racism—in favor of recognizing structural racism and focusing strongly on how people's race affects their experiences and privilege. (To that point, evangelicals claiming "color-blindness" are equally vulnerable to overlooking obvious offenses, as in the case of one white adoption agency director, Merrily Ripley of Adoption Advocates International, a Christian mother of eighteen who runs a side business selling "golliwogs," black-skinned fabric dolls with exaggerated racial features in the minstrel tradition.)

But when adoptees or others raise questions about the new mass adoption of black children into white churches that, just a generation ago, defended segregation, many Christian advocates dismiss them as racists in their own right. In Russell Moore's words, such critics are "[George] Wallace's progressive heirs . . . standing in the orphanage door."

Other advocates simply dismiss questions of cultural sensitivity out of hand, like Tony Merida, coauthor with Rick Morton of *Orphanology*, who warns adoptive parents to expect opposition to their mission and implores them to not let themselves be swayed. "As our level of obedience to God increases," Morton explains, "so will the attack of the enemy."

The vision of adoption as a stepping stone to racial reconciliation goes beyond the SBC. In other churches, as in Moore's vision, adoption fills a multipurpose agenda: addressing race, abortion, evangelizing, and the need for Christians to do good works. In late April 2010, at Liberty University—a school founded by segregation defender Jerry Falwell—neo-Pentecostal "prayer warrior" Lou Engle, the preacher who described adoption as the ticket to gaining moral authority, led a group of charismatic Christians in a call for racial diversity at the Freedom Federation Summit. Engle brought on stage Bishop W. C. Martin, a white-haired African American pastor from a Texas hamlet called Possum Trot. Starting in the late nineties, Martin's church of two hundred members had followed the pastor and his wife in adopting seventy-two children out of foster care after Martin began preaching regular sermons that "God commands us to take care of the orphans," a story told in Martin's 2007 book, *Small Town, Big Miracle,* published by Focus on the Family press.

On stage in Lynchburg, Engle, a thin, mustached man whose weathered face crinkles easily to tearful exhortation, beseeched Martin "to pray right now all across this way for the most outrageous adoption movement to be released through the church." Martin took a microphone and belted out a prayer to the low throb of a bass guitar. A white crowd swayed, hands held aloft, as Engle directed them to break down into small groups to pray. "We're not starting with ending abortion. We're starting with praying to God for crisis pregnancy centers, pregnant mother's homes, and an adoption movement that will sweep the nation that the church leads to greater history. . . . Go ahead, pray to God. You're moving heaven tonight."

CHAPTER 3

Suffering Is Part of the Plan

With adoption becoming a cause on so many levels—tapped to solve the complicated questions of global poverty and child care, make restitution for racism, and give evangelicals a more positive way to express their antiabortion values—it was easy to miss an elemental problem: how the very language of the Christian adoption movement reinforces a claim of predestination, thereby aligning prospective adopters' desires with the will of God. The way Christians spoke about adoption began to justify the tragedy at its root. One ubiquitous figure of speech in adoption-land, that parents have "found" their children—meaning they were struck by a sense that a particular child they saw a picture of was "meant to be" their son or daughter—assumed a literal interpretation, as though the children had been misplaced in another family. Matthew Hutson, author of the 2012 book *The 7 Laws of Magical Thinking: How Irrational Beliefs Keep Us Happy, Healthy, and Sane,* diagnosed a form of "magical thinking" common to adoptive parents who felt so strong a connection to their adopted children that it feels "as if the universe conspired to make it happen." Hutson labeled this expression of magical thinking benevolent—the seemingly harmless idea that, as one recent adoption memoir put it, *Baby, We Were Meant for Each Other.* But in the Christian adoption movement that sort of comforting declaration, that adoptive families come to love their adopted children so deeply as to make the relationship seem fated, was becoming a source of theological assurance for adults who might otherwise question how adoption creates families in the wake of tremendous loss.

As the Heart for the Fatherless Ministry put it, adoption is "a costly, complex, emotional journey in which a child whom God has meant for a particular family from before the foundation of the world comes home." God, the author continued, "intended adopted children to be in the family that adopts them the same as children who come biologically." Many in the Christian adoption movement accept this argument so unquestioningly that they wrote about the children they were hoping to adopt as though the adoption was divinely scripted.

The claim to predestination is an unwitting description of one of the most significant problems with both domestic and international adoption: the enthusiasm of would-be parents for adoptable children has become a demand in search of a supply, a demand met by an industry that sometimes separates willing biological parents from their offspring, artificially creating "orphans" for adoptive parents to take in. That magical thinking has become so routine that an infant daughter requested by American parents can be labeled an "orphan" even as she kicks in her mother's womb. Most often these days this supply is found in the world's developing nations, but the story of the modern Christian adoption movement starts much closer to home.

IN JANUARY 2000 Reanne Mosley entered the New Beginnings Home for unwed mothers in Puyallup, Washington, ten miles southeast of Tacoma. At the time Mosley was nineteen and seven months pregnant, and her parents sought to distance her from the boyfriend who had impregnated her.

In a photograph from a scrapbook she began compiling while she was there, Reanne sits in an armchair reading a book on her first day at the home. She smiles widely at the camera, a pretty girl with thick, curly brown hair and a scrubbed complexion. Two months later, hugely pregnant, she posed with her mother the day before she gave birth. "I look sad," she said, studying the scrapbook, each page ornately decorated with gingham wrapping paper background and cutouts of Christmas trees and presents to mark holidays and special occasions. There is neat cursive text written in a square border around pictures of the son she gave birth to, repeating what the home told her he would be if she gave him up for adoption: the gift of life, "A Gift from God."

When I finally met Reanne in person in May 2012, after several years of phone calls and correspondence, the son she had had while at New Beginnings—and who had been adopted the next day—had recently turned twelve. Though Reanne, now a thirty-two-year-old hair stylist living in southern California, has since gotten married to a gentle and good-looking man named Josh and had two more children—aged seven and three, with a third on the way—she still counts her life by years out from that loss.

We met at a restaurant in an upscale outdoor mall in Irvine, California, so Reanne could talk out of earshot of her children, whom she feels are still too young to be told they have another brother. She had driven an hour from her home in Temecula, a handsome two-story stucco in a city of endless subdivisions ringed by the Santa Ana Mountains and halfway between Los Angeles and San Diego. The family had moved there two years before to be closer to the industry Josh worked in; he composes musical scores for the entertainment industry. Six weeks into her fourth pregnancy, Reanne looked like a Southern California bombshell, wearing a pink faux-lace-up shirt that matched her nails, sparkly hoop earrings, and her long brown hair in a blowout that fell into soft curls at her chest. As we walked to the restaurant a passing group of guys nodded, looking her up and down, and Reanne rolled her eyes. Picturing her twelve years younger was easy, but a lot has changed since then.

ON THE WEBSITE for the thirty-year-old New Beginnings Home and its sister organization, Youth With A Mission's Adoption Ministry, photographs of residents, a smiling sorority of young pregnant women wearing matching denim overalls and forming human pyramids, make the home look casual and even irreverent. One expectant mother is pictured in a T-shirt that reads, "I'm not fat, I'm knocked up."

A fundraising video for the home's benefactors offered a seamier narrative about the women being reformed within New Beginnings's walls, painting them as promiscuous or drug addled or caught up in "the college/youth lifestyle," as one former resident put it. But these hadn't been Reanne's problems. "There was nothing wrong with me," she told me when we first spoke in 2009. "I could have taken care of my child easily. I wasn't on drugs or an alcoholic. I was just young."

Though it's larger now, New Beginnings was then a compound of just two buildings: a southern-style farmhouse, where the houseparents' family slept, connected by a breezeway to a renovated barn, where resident pregnant women lived. On a cupola above the resident's home a weathervane in the shape of a stork carrying a bundled baby turned in the wind.

When Reanne's parents summarily dropped her off at New Beginnings, she felt unfairly abandoned and unsupported by her family. So it was no surprise that she was drawn to the image of family life presented by New Beginnings's founders and houseparents, Miles and Debi Musick. Reanne had become a born-again Christian only the month before arriving at the home, and the Musicks were conservative Christians who lived with their six children in the main house. In an early video Miles Musick was a beaming, mustached patriarch and Debi a maternal and soft-spoken brunette. They were missionaries with Youth With A Mission (YWAM), an international evangelical ministry with a thousand locations in 180 countries and ties to fundamentalist Christian politics. (YWAM's Washington, DC branch formerly owned the "C Street House" at the center of the 2009 Republican congressional sex scandals.) The Musicks had opened their first maternity home in Tacoma, and in the late 1990s they expanded to Puyallup Valley with support from YWAM and New Beginnings's individual donors, who have contributed close to two million dollars to the ministry since 2004. The Musicks brought a personal story to the ministry as well: three of their six children were adopted. Feeling estranged from her own family, the welcoming atmosphere the Musicks created and then their teachings on unwed motherhood swayed Reanne.

The Musicks told her that, on the one hand, if she decided to raise her child herself, she wouldn't fulfill her potential and go to college. On the other, they encouraged her to see her child as a divine gift she could bestow on infertile couples and to consider biblical stories of adoption. After all, they told her, Moses and even Jesus were adoptees of sorts. Many of the families associated with New Beginnings had adopted already. "They're telling you that God wants you to do it: look at Moses in the Bible. . . . They always refer to your child as a gift," Reanne recalled. "You go in there feeling worthless—how could you get pregnant outside of marriage? Then you hear that these other people have been waiting so long [for a child]. . . . They made me think I didn't deserve a child."

At the same time Reanne was increasingly isolated from people in her outside life. Testimonials on the New Beginnings's website feature young women gushing that Miles Musick was like "the father I never had," and Reanne said the Musicks generally see themselves as substitute parents for girls who grew up without enough discipline. House rules aimed to change this. Resident women had to make their phone calls in front of staff and adhere to a policy that requires any boyfriends of residents to submit to three interviews with houseparents before they can visit. Ostensibly this rule was in place to ensure that the men prove their dedication, but in practice, Reanne believes, it was also to make sure they don't interfere with adoption plans. Although Reanne's boyfriend called the

Musicks, he was never approved to visit; whenever he called to speak to Reanne, she said, they told him she was out.

There was a constant background hum of pressure in the home about who should raise the babies the residents were carrying, though Reanne was the only one actively considering adoption. The Musicks had her conduct an exercise that's common among maternity homes and crisis pregnancy centers: setting down on paper the things she was in a position to offer a child versus what the adoptive family could give. The advantages of adopters' two-parent home were stressed, whereas the situations of residents like Reanne were described in disastrous terms: they were "needy women" undergoing "crisis pregnancies." The Musicks gave Reanne a Christian book about teen pregnancy and adoption, *Bittersweet*. She also regularly heard testimony from the roommate she had been paired with, a birthmother who had relinquished her child for adoption the year before and constantly spoke of it to Reanne as a positive choice. (Continued support to women who relinquished for adoption was one of the perks of the home.)

Reanne said that she was first shown paperwork concerning her preliminary relinquishment of her future child on one of her first days in the home and that the Musicks took her to the office of a local attorney, Dennis Casey, to discuss the legal ramifications of adoption. Soon afterward the Musicks gave her a series of family profiles to look through: scrapbooks created by would-be adoptive parents to entice women to choose them. One stuck out to Reanne: that of Jeff and Chris Butler, a nearby evangelical couple with a teenage daughter. Jeff was a church leader described as "very involved in evangelism" and would later become a pastor; Chris was a stay-at-home mom. Their faith was reflected in the scrapbook, as the Butlers wrote of their sense that God wanted them to fulfill their desire for a large family through adoption. Both parents wrote letters addressed to a generic birthmother, praising the women reading their words for their courageous choice in carrying the pregnancy to term and their selflessness in preparing for adoption. The rest of the book was full of pictures of the house; the Butlers' daughter engaged in sports, music, and church activities; and the family on vacation in Lake Tahoe and Disneyland. If a birthmother chose them, the letters promised, they would always speak reverently of her to the child and "will be sure to tell of the great love you had, and the gift that you so graciously gave."

"Everything is so negative and subtle, and it starts to work on you," said Reanne. "I felt like I was walking around with a baby that wasn't mine. I was a birthmother before the child was born."

A MONTH BEFORE her due date, on February 16, Reanne signed pre-liminary relinquishment papers, allowing the Butlers to adopt her son. When Reanne met with Dennis Casey, who was representing the Butlers, she believed he was representing her as well. She also thought she was agreeing to an open adoption—a formal adoption contract that specifies a certain degree of continuing contact between the adoptive family and the birthmother, from them sending occasional pictures and updates about the child to ongoing visits with the family.

Debi Musick encouraged Reanne to plan activities with the Butlers so as to foster a relationship that Reanne believed was meant to continue as the child grew up: going to get an ultrasound together or having them take her to her prenatal checkups. In her last week of pregnancy Reanne gave voice to the doubts that she had been having while Chris Butler was driving her back from the doctor's office and said she "couldn't do this." Chris cried and left, and later called Debi Musick.

That's when the pressure turned ugly. The Musicks sat her down, Re-anne said, and asked her what her plan to parent was. They pointed to their own adopted daughter, then a toddler, and told Reanne that they didn't know what they would have done if someone had done to them what Reanne was considering doing to the Butlers: not following through on an adoption plan.

In a letter she wrote later she listed the arguments the Musicks made: "That placing your child for adoption was biblical, so God would bless me abundantly for my decision. That I had too much potential to be a single mother and God had big plans for me. That they had to hold me to what I said when I first moved in," and, finally, "That it shows you care more for your child when you place them for adoption." They told her that she had already signed the papers and that she was just being emo-tional. Reanne didn't know that consent documents for adoption are not legally binding in Washington state until after birth. "Everything was screaming at me to keep my child," Reanne said. "Absolutely I was emo-tional." She wishes now that she had asked what the difference was be-tween her emotions and those of the prospective adopters; after all, everyone was similarly attaching themselves to the baby growing inside her. But then, that week, Reanne's boyfriend broke his back in a car acci-dent, and the Musicks seized upon the news to convince her she really had no choice but to relinquish.

Through the stress of the conflict, Reanne became ill. She was diag-nosed with toxemia, and her legs swelled dramatically. Doctors had to break her water to induce labor and forcefully pulled out the baby, a boy I'll call Jason, born at nine and a quarter pounds. The New Beginnings staff was supposed to call Reanne's contacts when she went into labor, but she said they didn't call her boyfriend; he later told her that he had been calling all day and the staff wouldn't tell him where she was. Instead, Chris Butler was in the room with Reanne during labor, and after birth, when Debi Musick, Dennis Casey, and the rest of the Butler family came in, the nurse handed the baby directly to the Butlers before Reanne had a chance to hold him. The labor was traumatic and Reanne tore badly. After the birth she was put on heavy pain medication and sleeping pills. Her blood pressure had risen severely, and she developed postpartum preeclampsia, a form of hypertension. Her hospital records from the labor and the following day make repeated mention of maternal exhaustion.

She never did get a chance to hold Jason by herself, without the Butlers or Musicks present. He had been born after 5 p.m. in the evening, and the next morning, while Reanne was still under heavy pain medication, she was asked to sign consent papers granting the Butlers temporary custody until the adoption documents were filed in court. Then they took him home.

Reanne claims Dennis Casey had lied to her, telling her she had only twenty-four hours to change her mind and revoke her consent when, by state law in Washington, she should have had at least forty-eight, possibly longer, depending on when the papers were filed. She was still recovering in the hospital later that day when her boyfriend finally got through to say he didn't want to proceed with the adoption. Though Reanne agreed, she believed their window to object had expired, and she told him there was nothing they could do. Neither Casey, the Butlers, nor the Musicks responded to my repeated e-mails to explain their side of this story.

Casey would later defend himself, successfully, to the Washington Bar, asserting that he never represented Reanne and had made this clear to her and had not misrepresented her right to revoke consent. Reanne responds to this claim with a picture from her scrapbook, taken shortly after the birth. In it Casey, a dark-haired man in a striped sweater, leans over Reanne's hospital bed while the Butlers' daughter holds Jason in the foreground, smiling. "If he wasn't my lawyer, what's he doing in my room right after labor?" she demands. "They knew what they were doing, and they knew how to play it just right where I thought that I had no choice."

THE NEXT SIX MONTHS were a blur of emotional and physical pain, said Reanne. She was so depressed the first month that she barely ate, losing almost all of her baby weight in four weeks. She grappled with un-characteristic thoughts of suicide, and the Musicks' doctor prescribed her antidepressants. She returned to New Beginnings to recuperate and get her life together but soon began to rebel against the house rules: she was hanging around with outside friends, having phone calls that weren't monitored, and regularly skipping church. One day she left without per-mission to meet a friend to play tennis, and she didn't return, leaving most of her belongings in the home. Through the rest of the year she lived with friends and, later, on her own. She dabbled with drugs—something she had never done before. "I had [Jason] and then I lost it for a while," she said. "I didn't want to live anymore, and that's really out of character for me."

In Puyallup the Musicks filed a missing persons report, and then went through Reanne's things. They found her journal and, within it, an entry in which Reanne had been drafting a letter to her son. The pages, written in a looping, feminine script with a number of words scratched out and written over, echo the lessons Reanne had learned at New Beginnings. She wrote to her son that she was "happy to be involved in God's special plan for you." "It's not every day someone gets to give a life to someone," she had written, then crossed out. She tried again: "As much as I wanted to be selfish and keep you for myself, I knew that you would be better off with TWO loving parents, a sister, to protect you." The Musicks gave the jour-nal entry to the Butlers, presenting the scratched-out draft as a "dear son" letter they could share with Jason when he was older. To Reanne, the state of the pages, full of mistakes and rewrites—obviously not a final draft—is proof in itself that the letter was never intended for her son. She would never introduce herself in such a sloppy manner, she said indignantly.

It took six months for Mosley to pull herself out of depression and to meet the man, Josh, whom she would later marry. Josh's mother was ap-palled to hear what Reanne had gone through and set about to help her reclaim Jason. But Reanne, in so new a relationship and still angry at her own family for sending her away, still felt dependent on the maternity home for security and a place to stay. So she returned in early 2001, and the Musicks found her a place to stay with friends: another large adoptive family whose husband sits on New Beginnings's board.

There, Reanne had extensive contact with the Butlers and Jason for several months, meeting occasionally at the house she was staying in or at New Beginnings, playing with the baby and taking photos for her scrapbook. But around the summer of 2001 Reanne called the Butlers and left a message, asking to talk. They never returned the call, so Reanne thinks they understood why she was calling. To others in New Beginnings's circle, she had already begun to say that she thought she had been pressured to relinquish Jason. Although Reanne didn't know it then, she said the clock was running out on her window to contest the adoption legally, as some birthparents in Washington have up to two years to fight an adoption if they claim their consent was obtained by fraud, duress, or coercion.*

Soon after she called the Butlers the Musicks arrived at the home where Reanne was staying and, together with the couple who owned it, again sat her down. She said they warned that if she didn't stop what she was doing, she would have to pack up and leave the house immediately. They told her that if she hoped to see her son again, she should write a letter of apology to the Butlers at once. The family she was staying with would have to approve the letter before she sent it. "I didn't know I had recourse, that I could have gotten him back," she said. So she wrote the letter. Reading it more than a decade later, it's a painful document: a page of self-recrimination, as Reanne repeats what the Musicks were telling her: that she had been influenced by Josh's mother but she had again found God's peace regarding her decision and that she hoped she hadn't caused irreversible damage to their relationship.

"I cannot even imagine the heartache that you have gone through. I can say that God has again shown me the truth in all of this," Reanne wrote. "I am terribly sorry for all that has been done to you." The Butlers wrote her back, thanking her for the apology and offering to provide photos as time went on, but Reanne said only a few more came, and she would never be invited to visit Jason again.

In the days and weeks after, the New Beginnings staff mobilized to send Reanne on a six-month mission trip with their parent organization, Youth With A Mission's Discipleship Training School in Hawaii. There, they hoped, Reanne could transform her grief into a pro-adoption testimony on the tough but right choices that New Beginnings helps unwed mothers make, and then become an ambassador for the home. "They

---

*Under most circumstances birth parents in the state have only a year to contest an adoption they claim was coerced, but Native Americans have two years. Because Reanne's child had a small portion of Native American heritage from his father, she believes she might have been able to contest it on those grounds, although it's not clear whether or not the percentage of Native American ethnicity the child has would have been enough to qualify.

wanted me to be the girl out front, convincing all their other girls to choose adoption," she said.

A letter from a Discipleship Training School staffer in Tacoma lobbied to have the program take Reanne on short notice based on recent events "that led us to believe that we were [to] do everything possible to get her in a DTS immediately." An accompanying recommendation from Debi Musick, written in calligraphy, recommended Reanne on the basis that "she has been diligent to follow God's plan for her life" but that now "she needs to be separated for a while to seek God—and fulfill the call of God in her life."

After New Beginnings pulled strings for her to get into the program, they helped her write a fundraising letter to pay for it; the Butlers contributed $200. But although Reanne got to Hawaii, she didn't transform into a spokesperson for New Beginnings. Instead, she said, the solitude in Hawaii allowed her to realize that the sacrifices she had made at New Beginnings had nothing to do with her understanding of God. She left the program early and came home. Explaining her decision to the Musicks was the last time she ever spoke to them. The Butlers, once they knew Reanne wasn't coming around, cut off contact, closing the adoption.

REANNE BEGAN a years-long fight for her son that has involved court battles as well as restraining orders against both her and one of her in-laws, who have accompanied her during attempts to confront the Butlers at their home and church. The Butlers have told law enforcement officials that they've moved to evade Reanne's efforts to get news about Jason.

In conventional wisdom a story like this is usually framed as adoptive parents' worst nightmare—an angry birthmother appearing on their doorstep, demanding her child back. The scenario has been well worn on TV and film, where birthmothers are often depicted as unhinged, addicted, or gold diggers, fighting for a child they don't really deserve. But there's another side to the story.

Several months after Reanne dropped out of YWAM's discipleship training program, in April 2002, she wrote the Butlers a lengthy letter, describing the coercion she felt while at New Beginnings:

> I feel as through the decision to place my baby was forced upon me. I was made to feel that I could not take care of him in the way that he needed to be taken care of. I was in complete distress at the time and everyone around me was making me feel as though I was doing the

right thing and that God would bless me for what I have done. . . . I was made to feel sorry for you because I had already told you that I was going to place him with you and in doing this I would hurt you both. . . . Scripture was used to make me feel as though I was doing something that God wanted.

When she sent the letter, it was a month after the time when she could have conceivably brought a court case to contest the adoption on the grounds of coerced consent (were she to argue for a longer window of time based on the child's Native American heritage). By the time Reanne belatedly got legal advice, she realized how little recourse she had left. Despite her understanding that she had agreed to an open adoption—a significant matter in Washington, one of the very few states where open adoption agreements are legally enforceable—no legal agreement mandating ongoing contact with her son or updates from the Butlers had ever been written into the adoption papers. At nineteen and estranged from her parents, Reanne hadn't realized that the attorney New Beginning suggested was not there to protect her interests and said she hadn't fully understood what she was signing.

In 2009 Reanne filed a complaint against Dennis Casey with the Washington State Bar Association, charging that he had violated professional ethics by appearing to represent her as well as the Butlers, a charge she backed up by noting that the Musicks had taken her to his office before she had ever met the Butlers. A letter from Reanne's mother, with whom Reanne reconciled in the years after Jason's birth, testifies that she had thought the same. "If we had known Mr. Casey was not acting on her behalf as legal representation," she wrote the Bar, "we most certainly would have hired an attorney to represent Reanne. . . . We feel very much 'ripped' off and cheated that Reanne was lied to and betrayed."

In documents Casey supplied in his defense, he claims that he had told the nineteen-year-old Reanne that he did not represent her but rather the adopting parents and that she had a full forty-eight hours after her child's birth to change her mind—both claims that Reanne disputes. Casey filed as supporting evidence the pages the Musicks took from Reanne's journal, the "dear son" draft letter offered as proof that Reanne hadn't been misled. "Reanne's reaction to the adoption is very sad," Casey wrote to the Bar. "She had a good relationship with the Butlers until she began accusing them of defrauding her. . . . [Jason] will be ten years old in March. It is time to put the case to rest." Reanne said the Bar later told her that they were unable to find proof that Casey had represented them both. To me the Bar's disciplinary council could only confirm that no disciplinary record existed for Casey, indicating that Reanne's complaint was dismissed.

Reanne and her mother-in-law, Cynthia Mosley, made several attempts to confront the Butlers to get the updates and pictures that Reanne had been promised, including showing up twice at the Butlers' house in 2004, with Cynthia Mosley at one point waving a large white "prayer flag" and shouting that Reanne's baby had been stolen. Reanne said she knew she would never get Jason back at that point, but she wanted updates and assurance that Jason would not grow up thinking that she had abandoned him. "I just kept writing to them for my own sake, and to have documentation to show my son that no matter what, look how hard I tried. I want to be able to show him, for how many years I did come at these people. They'll have no room to say she didn't want you."

The Butlers filed a police report. Jeff Butler stated he "was very concerned for the safety of my family and the threat that Reanne will never stop fighting for our son." They requested a permanent thousand-foot restraining order for their home and church; a less restrictive, temporary order was granted. Not until Reanne went to court in response to the restraining order did she learn that she did not have an open adoption. "The first thing out of Dennis Casey's mouth was 'We don't have a formal adoption agreement,'" she said. "He was so quick to say it. I asked the judge, if we don't, then why do I have pictures with my son, why did I see him for the first year of his life? Why do I have their phone number, that I talked to them all the time? The judge looked over at them disgusted, but he said 'I don't have the power to do anything for you.' He just kept saying that over and over."

On another visit to the court, during which Reanne tried to gain access to Jason's adoption records—in most states laws mandate closed adoption records, a matter of long-standing protest by adoptees and birthmothers—a judge advised her to get a lawyer to take her case to Superior Court. But when Reanne contacted the three lawyers the judge suggested, she was told that it would cost as much as $100,000 in all—far more than she could afford.

Reanne wrote the Butlers' pastor to request that he help mediate some agreement with the family, then visited the social worker who had signed off on her adoption. The social worker called the Butlers and returned to Reanne with a message: they didn't want an open adoption or to send any photos, but "They said to tell you, 'Thank you for the gift.'"

IN 2010, in a suburban town near Tacoma, Reanne and Cynthia Mosley slowed down their car, then drove past the Butlers' house. Outside they saw Jason, a ten-year-old boy with olive-colored skin, riding a bike in the driveway. A number of his eight siblings—the Butlers went on to have another biological child and adopt six more—played nearby. It was the first time Reanne had seen him since he was one.

Inside the car Reanne and Cynthia conferred about whether they were going ahead with their plan. Reanne knew that Jason was aware that he was adopted—the Butlers are very public about their adopted children and their adoption advocacy—but she didn't know if he had ever been told about her, as the Butlers had promised. They waited five minutes and drove back, stopping next to the driveway as Jason slowly rode up to them. Reanne opened the door and said, "[Jason], I'm your mother." The boy looked at her and almost fell off his bike, then turned and pedaled toward the house.

Up the driveway Jeff Butler looked at the car and promptly called the children to come inside. "My name is Reanne Mosley," Reanne yelled, as the children filed into the house, "and I always wanted you." Within moments another car pulled up behind the two women, and then a police car—seemingly a demonstration of an emergency plan of action prepared, Reanne laughs grimly, in case "the psycho" showed up. "I'm sorry if they think I'm crazy," said Reanne, "but if you felt like your child was stolen, you'd show up too."

Reanne said Jeff Butler asked the police officer to sit inside with the children while the adults talked, for nearly two and a half hours, in the driveway. At one point Jason came back out of the house and sat on a basketball in the driveway, watching, until Butler told him to go back in. They asked Reanne to write an e-mail that Jeff's wife, Chris, could read when she returned home, to consider whether she would agree to meet. A couple days later they did meet, in the empty pews of the Butlers' church, where Reanne said Jeff apologized for the restraining order and Chris hugged Reanne, tearfully saying she had thought it would be easier for Reanne to move on if she didn't have to see pictures of her son growing up.

Reanne said Chris told her, "You never told us you didn't want to do it," to which Reanne replied with a question: why, then, had Chris cried during the ride to the prenatal checkup, after Reanne had voiced her misgivings, then called Debi Musick, triggering the avalanche of pressure that came afterward?

They gave her pictures of Jason and said they were eager to meet Re-anne's other children. But after the meeting the Butlers again stopped responding to Reanne's e-mails. The last time she was in Washington she asked them to meet, but they told her they weren't comfortable with it and that they weren't going to introduce her to Jason unless he asked them to. "It's hard to say if I'd played the game and stayed silent, and said, 'This is what God wants for [Jason's] life,' whether I'd have kept on receiving pictures and being a part of his life," Reanne said, reflecting on the reality that many adoptive parents close open adoptions, later claiming that the process has become confusing or painful for the child. "They still could have found any reason to cut me off because it became uncomfortable to them."

"They knew they were part of coercing me," Reanne believes. "Sure, they didn't hold a gun to my head and force me, but that's not the only way it's done. It's a lot more tricky, and it's done in a way that's hard to prove, by getting you to believe that what you're doing is right."

In an old video on the New Beginnings website, Chris Butler, her oldest daughter and baby Jason sit on a couch, with the side of someone else's arm just sticking into the frame. The video was originally made of the three of them plus Reanne, but almost all of Reanne has been cropped out of the picture. In what remains, Chris said that New Beginnings is "a wonderful ministry that God uses to bless lots of lives and make new beginnings of lots of lives."

In what Reanne remembers about making the video, she testified that adoption was wonderful, while constantly looking down at her son, sitting in his new mother's lap. "I looked like a wreck and I kept looking at him, saying, 'This is the best thing ever.'"

THE FACT THAT as recently as 2000 women could be pressured so severely to give up a child to atone for an unmarried pregnancy is hard to believe. If it sounds like something from another era, in a way that's because it is. In the decades between 1945 and 1972, when abortion was illegal and single motherhood taboo, women who became pregnant out of wedlock faced a small range of options: a shotgun wedding, raising the child alone in the face of overwhelming social condemnation, risking death or maiming through illegal abortion, or "going away" to homes for unwed mothers for the duration of their pregnancy, where they were pressured to relinquish their babies for adoption and return home as though nothing had happened. Overwhelmingly, women chose—or were forced to choose—the latter.

Some estimates hold that, during the era, a fifth of all children born to never-married white mothers were relinquished for adoption. In the general population 9 percent of unmarried women who became pregnant gave their children up. For women who were sent to maternity homes, that rate increased exponentially, with nearly 80 percent of residents relinquishing. In real numbers, during that era anywhere from the 1.5 million mothers officially documented to higher estimates of between 6 and 10 million relinquished their infants. Today most adoption agencies speak of that time as "the bad old days." Adoption reform advocates have a more biting name, calling it "the Baby Scoop Era" for what they see as the massive theft of millions of children.

Ann Fessler, a documentary historian and author of *The Girls Who Went Away: The Hidden History of Women Who Surrendered Children for Adoption in the Decades Before Roe v. Wade,* has meticulously chronicled the lives of women of the Baby Scoop Era. Fessler is herself an adoptee who came to the subject after first meeting a birthmother from the era at the age of forty and hearing about the lifetime of worry and grief the mother had endured since relinquishment—not knowing what had happened to her daughter or whether she would ever find out. Fessler considers the period a missing chapter of feminist history. "Despite the fact that I was invested in women's issues and considered myself part of the women's movement," she said, "this had never been brought up: women who wanted to be mothers, but didn't have that choice."

The coercion of that era was often brutal and unapologetic. Women whose families sent them either to unwed mothers' homes—dormitories reminiscent of Ireland's Magdalene Laundry asylums for "fallen women," run from the late eighteenth century through 1996—or affiliated "wage homes," where women earned their keep as unpaid domestics in individual families. Severe isolation and shaming were normal, as was withholding information from the women about their pregnancies and impending labor. Maternity home women were forbidden contact with friends or family or with the boyfriends who fathered their children; treated as servants for home benefactors; dropped off at hospitals to labor alone, apart from married mothers, sometimes without pain medication; and coerced to sign relinquishment papers while they were still drugged or recovering from labor. Many were pressured to deny that they knew the fathers of their children, deliberately misled about their right to keep their child or about services that could help them, and frequently refused a chance to see or hold their babies after birth. Some had their babies taken while they were sedated or were told that the babies had been stillborn but were never shown their bodies. "They wanted to keep us scared to death," said Karen Wilson-Buterbaugh, a former ward of the Florence Crittenton maternity home in Silver Spring, Maryland, and founder of the Baby Scoop Era Research Initiative, which compiles information about the period. "They didn't want us to be repeats. It was so traumatizing that many mothers don't remember the births."

When Wilson-Buterbaugh became pregnant in 1966 at the age of seventeen, her family sent her to a "wage home," where she worked as a servant for a wealthy family associated with Florence Crittenton in exchange for her room and board. By day she was brought to the maternity home to complete high school requirements. At night she lived in the made-up attic of her guardians' brownstone and sometimes served cocktails at their dinner parties, where she would overhear guests discuss her situation. After time spent in two wage homes, she grew depressed and requested to be transferred to the maternity home full time. There, she was instructed to identify herself only by her first name and last initial, both to maintain the secret of the pregnancy and to bolster a sense, explains Fessler, that "the person who went away to deliver the baby was someone else. And you could return home and be the person you always were"—to come back, as another Baby Scoop Era mother, Sandy Young, put it, a "born again virgin."

In 1967 Young had just graduated from high school in Illinois. Around her eighteenth birthday she became pregnant by the boyfriend she had been seeing all year. After keeping the pregnancy secret as long as she could, Young told her parents at Christmas. She adored her boyfriend and hoped their relationship would work out. Although she was legally an adult, state law in Illinois—which Young describes as having been a "chattel state" in which women were considered legal dependents of husbands or parents—determined that Young's pregnancy "incapacitated" her and that, therefore, her parents could make decisions for her. "We could be expelled from school, from college; there were morality clauses for teachers, you couldn't teach as a single mother; we couldn't get credit in our name, couldn't get a job or an apartment. Even if we had somehow managed to save our child from adoption," said Young, "unless our parents were behind us, we were toast, we'd lose the children anyway."

Her father disapproved of her boyfriend's family, so he decided to separate the couple. There was a large maternity home nearby, but Young's parents feared neighbors would recognize her; instead, he sent her to the Salvation Army's Booth Memorial maternity home in Saint Louis, 250 miles away.

Because she had already finished high school, Young was put to work at Booth Memorial, sweeping stairwells and dusting. Alongside one hundred other "wayward" girls, Young wasn't allowed to use her own name or wear her own clothes, and Booth Memorial staff closely monitored her contact with outsiders. When her delivery date arrived Young experienced childbirth alone in her hospital room, without pain medication but with a "Twilight Sleep" Scopolamine drug cocktail and a dangerously high amount of the labor-inducing drug pitocin, which left her bleeding heavily and on strict bed rest for eight days.

As Young sees it, "This was part of our punishment." During her recovery Young's boyfriend tried to see her at the hospital, but the maternity home had him arrested at the door. Young's parents were called, and she was sedated. At some point a nurse came and took her son. She doesn't believe she ever signed a surrender document. "When we left the homes, we left with not a piece of paper to show for anything," said Young. "Like that portion of our lives never happened. All we had to remind us of it was our stretch marks."

The experience left Young and millions of other mothers from the era suffering from something akin to posttraumatic stress disorder, so distraught from the experience of losing their first child that when they later had children within the safety of marriage, they feared that those children would be taken as well.

PART OF THE PUSH for women to relinquish babies for adoption back then came from rising concern about infertility in the postwar years—some adoption researchers suggest increased infertility could have resulted from sexually transmitted diseases among returning GIs—as the Baby Boom and popular media put a spotlight on couples unable to conceive. The rising desire—demand—for children inspired a cultural shift in attitudes toward adoption. Although it was still regarded a vaguely shameful secret, there began to be an emphasis on the adoption "supply chain," focusing less on finding homes for needy infants than finding babies for childless couples.

Facilitating this change was an ironic historical twist. Before the 1940s unwed mothers' homes had for decades been run by Christian charities, which had taught the women skills to support themselves and parent, and firmly believed that mother and child must be kept and supported together.

In the 1940s control of the homes shifted to social workers—just then emerging as a recognized class of professionals—who viewed illicit sex as a pathological disorder and unwed mothers as feeble minded or mentally ill. (More specifically, they viewed unwed white mothers as pathological. Unwed mothers of color were viewed as naturally and irredeemably promiscuous and, therefore, had the mixed blessing of being less likely to be pressured to relinquish their babies for adoption, as there was lesser demand for black babies, but more likely to be coerced into other forms of reproductive control.) Although the Christian-run homes had viewed single mothers as sinners in need of religious charity, now "professionalization" redefined what had simply been morally shameful into a social disease.

"We were deviant, unnatural, had to be cured," said Wilson-Buterbaugh. Her Baby Scoop Era Research Initiative has documented numerous sociological reports from the period that reveal the paternalistic and punitive orientation of the homes. Social workers noneuphemistically called resident birthmothers "inmates" and asserted that their role as social workers was to serve as disciplinarian parents to girls who had gotten pregnant on purpose. In a caseworker paper presented at the 1960 National Conference on Social Welfare, Dr. Marcel Heiman made exactly that argument, alleging that caseworkers must compensate for defective parental discipline in families in which a girl becomes pregnant out of wedlock by taking on the parents' role. "The caseworker must then be decisive, firm and unswerving in her pursuit of a healthy solution for the girl's problem. The 'I'm going to help you by standing by while you work it through' approach will not do. What is expected from the worker is precisely what the child expected but did not get from her parents—a decisive No! . . . An ambivalent mother, interfering with her daughter's ability to arrive at the decision to surrender her child, must be dealt with as though she (the girl's mother) were a child herself."

In light of the growing number of married couples seeking white babies to adopt as their own at the time, sociologist Clark E. Vincent, author of the 1961 book *Unmarried Mothers,* offered a chilling warning that maternity homes could become the hub of a market driven by supply and demand. "If the demand for adoptable babies continues to exceed the supply . . . then it is quite possible that, in the near future, unwed mothers will be 'punished' by having their children taken from them right after birth," he wrote. "A policy like this would not be executed—nor labeled explicitly—as 'punishment.' Rather, it would be implemented through such pressures and labels as: 'scientific findings,' 'the best interests of the child,' 'rehabilitation of the unwed mother,' and 'the stability of family and society.'"

"As far as people were concerned," said Fessler, "they were bad girls, sluts, not deserving of being mothers." The women were told that they would forget about their children. But in taking oral histories from more than one hundred mothers from that era, Fessler found that not only did mothers not forget; most suffered lifelong guilt and depression.

"It's a death: the baby is here, then the baby is gone," said Joe Soll, an adult adoptee and a New York City psychotherapist who runs a weekly support group for people affected by what's sometimes called adoption loss. "Many of these women suffer from PTSD. It's almost like unresolved grief. You can't go to a funeral, can't cry, can't grieve, must forget about it. You're told to make believe something that happened did not happen."

In fact, as research has shown, for some relinquishing a child for adoption is worse than death. A 1999 review in the *Journal of Obstetric, Gynecological and Neonatal Nursing* found that "Relinquishing mothers have more grief symptoms than women who have lost a child to death, including more denial; despair, atypical responses; and disturbances in sleep, appetite, and vigor."

Mirah Riben, vice president of communications for Origins-USA, a birthparents' organization, relinquished her child in 1967 when her Brooklyn Jewish family couldn't imagine another option for raising a child out of wedlock. Years later, after reuniting with her daughter and forming a relationship, the daughter died, and Riben was surprised to find the death easier to grieve than the initial separation through adoption. "It has been called a 'limbo loss,' a grief like mothers' whose children are missing in action," Riben said. "With death, there's closure—something that isn't there in adoption loss. It doesn't keep the wound open."

Sandy Young was told that her son would be in touch when he was eighteen, and she sent letters every year to the adoption agency for a file that the agency was supposed to be keeping in case mother and child both wanted to connect later in life. (Young was still living in Illinois when her son turned eighteen in the mid-eighties, and she said that thanks to the state's "chattel law," she had to have her then-husband—no relation to her son—give his permission for Young's son to contact her.) When her son did contact the agency at twenty-three, three days after his first child was born, she learned that none of her letters had been saved in their file.

The experience of reunification was intense and overwhelming, as it is for many mothers and their relinquished children, and ties of blood mattered more than either had been told. There would be periods of nonstop communication, as they realized they had the same physical tics and that he and one of Young's other sons, raised within her marriage, had been at the same military base at the same time, each hearing there was another guy on base who looked just like him. Then, painfully, there would be a "pullback," in which Young's son would stand her up after they had made plans to meet. "The intensity of the feelings was just too much for him," Young said.

After one such pullback, when Young was again left without contact, she searched online late into the night to see if she could find pictures of her son and his then-preteen daughter. She came across a photo of a girls' T-ball team, looking stern as they posed at a state championship game. "I'm looking at this picture, knowing one of these girls is my granddaughter, my firstborn son's firstborn child, and I'm scanning this picture desperately, for hours. I know she looks like me and I'm trying to pick out which one of these children is mine," recalled Young. "All of a sudden, all of the things I had buried for years erupted, and this animal wailing came over me like a tidal wave, and I couldn't stop. I was sitting alone in the closet in the middle of the night like a wounded animal. I was so embarrassed when I realized what I was doing, because it's so not me."

In the wake of that breakdown and desperate for support, she Googled the word "birthmother"—"the only word I knew," she said, "because the agency told me that's what I was." This was the genesis of her activism, enabled by the Internet, which Young calls "the absolute salvation of birthmothers, because we could go on and share our shame." In time, though, she lost the shame. The first letter she wrote to the editor of a local newspaper, identifying herself as a birthmother, she said, "was like putting on my scarlet letter myself."

Women of the Baby Scoop Era as well as later maternity home inmates who experienced similar coercion have become a small but dedicated army of reformers. Suz Bednarz is a Connecticut communications director who was sent to a maternity home contracted by a "grey-market" adoption agency, Easter House. There, she was threatened that her parents would be charged thousands of dollars if she tried to keep her baby. Later Bednarz helped shut the agency down and reunite more than sixty Easter House birthmothers with their children.

In other Western countries that had their own Baby Scoop Eras, notably Australia, Canada, and the United Kingdom, birthmothers and their advocates have had increasing success in getting official acknowledgement of their experiences, as multiple governments, hospitals, and churches have issued formal apologies for their role in "forced adoptions." In Canada several churches have begun an archival dig to determine their part in the coercion. In Australia ongoing advocacy by Baby Scoop Era mothers has resulted in public apologies from all but one of the eight state and territory governments, two Christian denominations, and one major hospital. In 2012 Australia's federal government pledged to form a committee to draft an apology on behalf of the nation as well, modeled on the formal 2008 apology Australia issued to recognize the forcible adoption of as many as one hundred thousand children removed from aboriginal and indigenous communities between 1869 and the 1970s, known as the "Stolen Generations." The Australian movement has helped create a social consensus in that country that adoption can be beneficial but can just as easily be coercive or abusive to natural families and that all attempts at family preservation must be exhausted before adoption is allowed.

The Australian example is a shockingly different understanding from that in the United States, where the default view of adoption is as a "win-win" scenario. From this perspective the experiences of birthparents are often treated with condescension or dismissal. This is perhaps best epitomized by actor and LGBT adoption advocate Rosie O'Donnell, who has written that she told her adopted son that God mistakenly put him in another woman's womb and that she had taught him to call birthmothers "tummy ladies." Or as actor and adoptive mother Edie Falco told Anderson Cooper in 2012, "The second you are handed a newborn it is yours. It doesn't matter what body it came out of."

In 2012 Falco's comment was absolutely unremarkable, a statement of conventional wisdom so universally accepted as to be bland. That this is so is a testament to how successful the adoption industry has been in shaping our attitudes and conversations on the subject. Adoptive parents—almost always a more privileged cohort than birthparents—have access to an adoption system that legitimizes their parenthood over that of the poorer women who birthed their children. The system masks that discomfiting fact by obscuring or denying the significant role of money in the adoption services sector, where domestic infant adoptions generally range from $15,000 up to $40,000; babies' adoption fees are sometimes bluntly scaled to reflect their race and health conditions; and large agencies may take in as much as $10 million annually. The perception of adoption as the ultimate form of charity diminishes all of these costs and profits. "You can thank the adoption industry for the idea that adoption is

noble," said Wilson-Buterbaugh. "They took on the media," she continues, noting successful public campaigns to alter the representation and
language of adoption, "and society bought it hook, line and sinker."

Indeed, it's no accident that discussions of adoption today often em-
body or emphasize an understanding of it as an uncomplicated good. In
the 1980s adoption agencies helped popularize what came to be known as
"positive adoption language," a new set of euphemistic terminology intended to remove any stigma from the ideas of being adopted or relinquishing a child for adoption. Instead of saying "relinquished" or "gave
up," advises a handout from the North American Council on Adoptable
Children, an adoptive parents' lobby group, use the phrase "made an
adoption plan." Instead of saying a mother "keeps" her child, say she
"parents" him or her; "not keeping" implies abandonment, and NACAC
wanted to emphasize the positive interpretation that "birth parents always
'keep' feelings for their children." And instead of saying "real" or "natural
parents," say "birthmother"* or "biological father," as adoptive families
are just as real. Some families celebrate "gotcha days"—the days on which
they adopted their child—in addition to or in place of birthdays. The significance of the language and the meanings it conveys has become so important that many adoptive parents express (or affect) outrage when
outsiders use the wrong terminology to ask about their children's biological ties.

The same hierarchy of values is implicit in the way many adoptive
parents construct their experiences—for example when they blog on websites with names like "Her Womb, Our Hearts." Although these names
and phrases bring the pain of infertility into sharp relief, they also reduce
birthmothers to a functioning body part, obscuring with sentimental language the vulgar reality that, as Wilson-Buterbaugh explains, adoption is
often a system in which "young fertile women are breeding for more powerful, moneyed, older people."

As this language, ideologically weighted toward adoptive parents, has
become the accepted standard, there is quite literally almost no neutral
way to discuss adoption, as the very words people use to discuss it shape

---

*Although a number of adoption reform advocates take issue with the name
"birthmother," preferring terms such as first mother or mother (or family) of
origin, the term has become so commonplace that discussing adoption without it is difficult. For the sake of clarity it is the term generally used in this
book.

and betray their perspective. Further, this type of language, prevalent in even secular discussions of adoption, goes into overdrive in the Christian adoption movement. "When people are talking about their very difficult road with infertility, and the adoption finally happens and it seems so right, that's when they start saying how it was very clear that God intended this child for us," said Jessica Pegis, an adoptive mother of a daughter from China who wrote the influential adoption blog O Solo Mama. "If you dissect that, that really means God picks some people far away to undergo a terrible tragedy: that God chose some people to live under the One Child policy, and it's all going to work out that you get your baby in the end; that some people suffer so that other people can be happy. That's a theology I wouldn't want any part of."

But that's the message that the Christian adoption community receives—and it comes from the top. Brian Luwis, founder of the Virginia-based evangelical adoption agency America World Adoption and a Christian Alliance for Orphans board member—the Alliance in fact shares his agency's McLean, Virginia, address—gave voice to this in an interview with the *Christian Post* about "God's Design for Adoption." "God knew there was going to be a Fall," Luwis said, explaining his belief that just as the sin of Adam and Eve was predestined, so is it predestined that some parents are infertile because God has a child for them "in another place." "It's part of His plan that other families raise other children, because he knew that this world was going to have sin."

"When we know that suffering is part of a loving God's plan," he continued on America World Adoption's website, "then we can understand that the existence of orphaned children is not an accident or failure of God's plan."

Many Christian adoption advocates not only accept this logic but take it to absurdist ends, using it to justify laying claim to children of poorer parents. For instance, one Christian prospective adoptive parent blogged about her plans to adopt a newborn Ethiopian girl she intended to name Bethlehem. As she wrote, it became clear that the child she was talking about as an orphan in need of rescue was as-yet unborn, indicating that she had requested an adoption agency to supply her with a baby as young as humanly possible, not an orphan already out in the world in need of parental care. "Somewhere there is a woman who is pregnant with a girl," wrote the blogger. "The woman will make a great sacrifice to give her life—either by her own death, or by handing the child who has kicked her womb for months to strangers with a desperate plea for them to care for her." After that mother gives birth, relinquishes the child, and the child is handed over to her, the blogger, then and only then, the woman wrote, would the future child "be an orphan no more."

This was a particularly baffling example, but not uncommon logic. Within this framing—the idea that some families' suffering is part of God's plan to complete other adoptive families—a child's first family is too easily pushed aside. "Children don't grow in cabbage patches, just waiting for us to find and rescue them," said Karen Dubinsky, author of *Babies without Borders*. "In order for the 'rescue' narrative to work, you really have to erase the families of origin."

Some Christian adoptive parents recognized the problem, however. The ubiquitous "rescue" narrative and what it means for the original families of "rescued orphans" disturbed one such mother, who writes the blog Our Little Tongginator. She protested that the biblical call in James 1:27 specifies caring for widows and orphans *together*. "It says to care for, not necessarily to adopt. Which, to me, reinforces the idea that family preservation"—the practice of supporting poor families to enable them to keep their children—"is God's top priority and that adoption is His second choice for a child." The Christians "pushing an adoption agenda with a zeal that makes me feel uncomfortable," she wrote, reminded her of the Bible's story of the Judgment of Solomon, when two women claimed the same baby as their own.

David Smolin, the Cumberland Law School professor as well as an adoptive parent and a conservative Christian himself, made an even stronger critique. Smolin and his wife, Desiree, are intimately familiar with the ugly side of adoption. In 1998, moved by stories of infanticide in India, they adopted two adolescent Indian girls whom Smolin describes as having been "kidnapped" from their mother: taken from the orphanage where their impoverished mother had put them temporarily and threatened by the orphanage and adoption agency staff so they would lie to US embassy officials. Smolin's own experience with adoption fraud has informed his numerous academic critiques of the international adoption industry, and in 2012 he reluctantly turned his attention to the movement growing among his fellow Christians.

Although Smolin comes from a similar theological background as many of the proponents of the Christian adoption movement, he leveled a stinging rebuke of both the theology and the aims of the movement in a paper published in the *Regent Journal of International Law*, "Of Orphans and Adoption, Parents and the Poor, Exploitation and Revenue: A Scriptural and Theological Critique of the Evangelical Christian Adoption and Orphan Care Movement." In it Smolin argued that the movement's theological claim—that American-style adoption reflects the Bible's story of salvation—was bad theology that misinterpreted and overemphasized the scriptural analogy of adoption.* More importantly he argued that this misinterpretation covers up a history of abusive adoption practices and in fact perpetuates more as Christians have signed onto an adoption industry that is rife with ethical problems, thus displaying what Smolin describes elsewhere as a "willful ignorance of what has come before them in the wider history and world of adoption."

A key aspect of that is such an exclusive focus on orphans that Christian adoption advocates overlook the exploitation of families from which the orphans originate. "Normatively, the orphan and widow are a unit in the Bible, but people can read those same passages and miss that because they're being taught to miss it," Smolin told me. "Because, you know, 'widows' are messy. Are you subsidizing them being lazy, and how do you do it? Children, well you just take them into your home. . . . They're dependent already. It's simple and cute."

A 2010 *Christianity Today* editorial on the movement, "210 Million Reasons to Adopt," seemed to underscore this point, literally making "widows" a parenthetical reference in their discussion of the biblical mandate to care for orphans. "The Book of James beckons every true follower of Christ to become involved in the lives of orphans (and widows)," they wrote.

Sometimes the treatment of birthmothers goes further than simply ignoring them but instead outright denigrates those families as inherently unworthy: the Bible's widow as Ronald Reagan's welfare queen. That perspective is hardly limited to Christian adoption advocates, though. The counterpart to positive adoption language is a lower hum of warning, portraying birthmothers as loose cannons, immoral, or manipulative, as liable to turn up on adoptive parents' doorsteps, looking for something. Such is their depiction in a 2012 reality TV show on TLC called *Birth Moms* that shows pregnant women who are considering adoption as drug addicted and sexually loose, clearly unworthy of a child that so many

---

*Theologically, Smolin said, in biblical times during the Roman Empire the concept of adoption functioned more as a sort of social promotion for adult males, where rich elites without male heirs sometimes chose a man outside their family to inherit their estate, "adopting" them as sons to leave them their wealth, not as the rescue of a child. Focusing on the latter, Smolin argues, shifts the intended meaning of the Bible's metaphor.

other parents want and better deserve. Even the popular MTV shows *16 and Pregnant* or *Teen Mom,* though not quite as condemning, still portray young, pregnant girls or single mothers as inept and immature.

These are reactionary portraits, but they find surprisingly little resistance. Wilson-Buterbaugh said she has reached out to both the National Organization for Women and the American Civil Liberties Union to discuss advocacy against adoption coercion, but she has received no response, leaving her and the rest of the Baby Scoop Era mothers a largely invisible constituency as well as suspicious that progressive activists and feminists who would normally object to such slanted depictions of women are unwilling to look too closely at an adoption field they may one day turn to themselves.

The mothers of the Baby Scoop Era are aging, and more than one shared the concern that Sandy Young articulated: "We're getting older, and we're terrified we're going to die . . . without getting some acknowledgement that a crime was committed against us . . . six million of us," she continued. "The industry's biggest fear is that someone's going to listen to us. We don't want this to happen to another generation."

ROE V. WADE is often recognized as the unofficial end to the Baby Scoop Era, as women with unplanned pregnancies gained greater access to legal abortion and, concurrently, societal norms began to liberalize, making single motherhood more acceptable. But within the *Roe* decision were the seeds of a new model of adoption pressure. With the backlash against legalized abortion, millions of apolitical evangelicals and Catholics were transformed into a mobilized religious right who developed an early wave of crisis pregnancy centers (CPCs), nonprofits set up by antiabortion groups to offer free pregnancy tests and dissuade pregnant women from having abortions.

Today CPCs have become a fixture of the antiabortion landscape, buttressed by millions of federal dollars from abstinence-only and marriage-promotion funds. The National Abortion Federation estimates that there are around four thousand CPCs operating in the United States—about twice the number of abortion providers in the country. Heartbeat International, a network of more than 1,100 CPCs, claims that its affiliates receive $125 million in donor support. Funding for the centers isn't limited to individuals and large Christian groups, though, but also includes many millions in state and federal grants. The federal government has been funding CPCs since 1996, when welfare reform made $50 million available to abstinence-only programs, which in some states included CPCs. CPCs receive funding from a pot of more than $100 million annually through allocations to "abortion alternatives" programs that are often matched by state grants, like Minnesota's 2005 Positive Alternatives Act, which distributed $5 million to nonprofits that encourage women to not have abortions, or Pennsylvania's 2004 budget allotment of $4.3 million to facilities that counsel against abortion. California even designated a portion of its tobacco tax to CPC support. Additionally, CPCs benefit from pro-life fundraising mechanisms such as the popular "Choose Life" license plates sold in twenty-eight states, the sale of which through state DMVs has helped support CPCs to the tune of $16 million nationwide over eleven years. But even in this program, which purports to fight abortion a few dollars at a time, there is evidence of adoption coercion. In Florida, the pioneer state for the "Choose Life" plate program, much of the money raised has languished in bank accounts because, by statute, the funds were restricted not to any woman "choosing life" but only those choosing adoption.

In addition to CPCs, affiliated maternity homes, like the one described above, have also made a comeback in recent years. According to Heartbeat International, there are at least three hundred homes in the United States today and likely a number of smaller, independently run houses that aren't counted.

In contrast to the warehouses of the Baby Scoop Era, modern-day maternity homes tend to be run on a smaller scale and incorporate life-skills training or educational opportunities. Some advertise having almost luxurious living facilities, as in the boast of one home run by the mammoth Texas adoption agency Gladney Center for Adoption, whose former president Michael McMahon told a British paper, "Here the birth mother is queen. If what she wants is at all possible, she gets it." Others still incorporate the isolationist tactics of decades past, keeping young women away from outsiders and limiting phone calls and contact with friends, family, and, especially, boyfriends.

In 2007 three teenage girls made headlines when they forced an escape from the New Hope Maternity Home in Kanab, Utah, where their parents had sent them and they were pressured to make adoption plans for their children. In desperation the girls assaulted home director Jana Moody with a frying pan, tied her up along with another pregnant resident, and stole the home's van to flee the state. One of the girls' mothers suspected that her daughter had escaped because she didn't want to relinquish her baby for adoption.

Even without draconian rules, though, the pressure for adoption can be subtle and strong. As one Ohio home, Harbor House, simply declares, "Single-parenting does not fit God's perfect plan for the family." Many homes reserve their beds strictly for women planning to relinquish their children for adoption or keep only a fraction for women who choose to parent. Although in some ways this may appear a straightforward market exchange of room and board for women providing the agency with an adoptable infant, these centers frequently advertise their services as free, church-based help for women in trouble and only begin the hard sell for adoption after a woman has moved in.

Other groups seamlessly blend advertised services of crisis pregnancy counseling with domestic and international adoption services, like Last Harvest Ministries, a Garland, Texas, crisis pregnancy center with ties to antiabortion extremist Flip Benham. At Last Harvest pregnant women are advised that adoption is "the only WIN-WIN solution a young teen mother can really make." On the flip side of their ministry, Christian couples are invited to list their family profile on a website, MayWeAdopt.com, "where birth mothers are going to find you and your dreams come true!"

This kind of situation is one that is "ripe for coercion," said Ann Fessler, who describes adoption coercion as much more subtle than that of the Baby Scoop Era but still prevalent. Women who encounter pressure from CPCs to relinquish can face a process that Fessler likens to stepping on a conveyor belt, funneled from CPCs to maternity home or host family situations to adoption agencies, urged to make "the right decision" and sometimtes subjected to both moralistic and financial intimidation if they waver. Sometimes women are warned that if they don't give up their babies, they'll have to repay the financial help or housing they have received. Women are routinely given a façade of legal representation in the form of a lawyer paid by the agency and the prospective adoptive parents in an obvious conflict of interest that the American Bar Association's ethics committee has explicitly condemned. Most information women receive comes from people with an agenda, said Fessler. "There's no uninterested party in adoption."

Although women may have more access to do their own research today, critics note, the drumbeat of information from maternity homes and adoption agencies amounts to propaganda, telling women that they will only feel a little sadness at relinquishing or that giving a child up to a wealthier family is the truly loving choice. "Part of the big picture for a young woman who's pregnant is that there are places to go, people holding out their hand, but the price of admission is giving up your child. If you decide to keep your child, it's as if you're lost in the system, whereas people fight over you if you're ready to surrender. There's an organization motivated by a cause and profit. But it's a pretty high price to pay: give away your first born and we'll take care of you for six months."

SUCH WAS THE CASE of a woman I'll call Carol Jordan, who became pregnant as a twenty-one-year-old living in South Carolina in 1999. She called Bethany Christian Services, the largest adoption agency in the country, which had advertised crisis pregnancy services in her local phone book. Within hours of calling Jordan received a call back offering her free boarding and medical care in a single mothers' home. After several counseling sessions she was instead convinced to go to one of Bethany's volunteer "shepherding families," where, away from the influence of her family or friends, she could decide what to do. Instead, she found herself isolated in the home of conservative, homeschooling evangelicals in Myrtle Beach, South Carolina, hundreds of miles from her home, where the only people she knew were agency staff that were pressuring her to relinquish to one of Bethany's hundreds of waiting prospective adoptive parents, who advertised their families through elaborate scrapbooks and birthmother letters. "I was never an 'expectant mother,' a 'mom-to-be,' or even 'Carol,'" said Jordan. "I was simply one of the agency's 'birthmothers,' although I hadn't signed a thing. I felt like a breeding dog . . . a walking uterus for the agency."

When Jordan went into labor, the room was crowded with people from Bethany, including the couple she had chosen, her shepherding mother, and Bethany's counselor. The couple was handed the baby—a girl—first, and when Jordan requested to keep her daughter in the room, the Bethany staff objected. The next day, as Jordan was having second thoughts, she asked the shepherding family if they would allow her to return to the house with her daughter or at least bring Jordan her savings from a local part-time job so she could get herself and the baby back to South Carolina. The shepherding father brusquely refused, telling her she was on her own if she kept the baby. The counselor called the prospective adoptive couple to warn them that Jordan was reconsidering, and they came to the hospital immediately, sobbing at Jordan's bedside. The counselor told her that she would end up homeless and that social services would take the baby anyway. "My options were to leave the hospital walking with no money—just enough saved to stay two nights in a hotel in Myrtle Beach in high season. Or there's a couple with Pottery

Barn furniture and a car seat already. You sacrifice yourself, not knowing it will leave an impact on you and your child for life."

The next morning a nurse who served as a notary public rushed Jordan through signing her relinquishment papers. As soon as she had signed, Jordan was told to hand over her daughter. The adoptive parents left quickly, and five days later Jordan used her last $50 to buy a bus ticket home. Back in South Carolina Jordan struggled for weeks to get in touch with a local Bethany postadoption counselor, as her milk came in and she rapidly lost more than fifty pounds in her grief. When she called Bethany's statewide headquarters to voice her hurt, she was surprised one night to hear her former shepherding mother working the hotline and shocked at the woman's cold response. "She told me, 'Carol, you're the one who spread your legs and got pregnant out of wedlock. You have no right to grieve for this baby.'"

CPCS HAVE frequently been accused of misleading women seeking abortions through deceptive advertising and clinic names; locating themselves in or near the same building as abortion clinics; luring patients in with offers of free help and an ultrasound, then inundating them with antiabortion literature and graphic videos of late-term terminations instead. Many have been accused of misinforming clients that abortion increases their risk of breast cancer, depression, and suicide— claims that are not accepted by the medical establishment. Other CPCs have been documented misleading women about when they can legally obtain an abortion or emergency contraception, withholding results of pregnancy tests while showing clients antiabortion literature or films, telling women to come back repeatedly for confirmation pregnancy tests, encouraging minors to hide pregnancies from their parents, and even lying about how far along in pregnancy a woman is—all stalling tactics employed in hopes that a woman will wait until it's too late to legally abort.

These tactics seem to be in the centers' DNA, passed down from the founder of the first CPC, Robert Pearson, who created his Hawaii facility in 1967 after the state abortion ban was lifted. Pearson authored the 1984 manual, "How to Start and Operate Your Own ProLife Outreach Crisis Pregnancy Center," which suggests that followers adopt some of the tactics he had found useful, such as using misleading but technically neutral names like "Abortion Advice" or "Pregnancy Problem Center." "Obviously, we're fighting Satan," he argued in a later speech, rationalizing giving women misinformation. "A killer, who in this case is the girl who wants to kill her baby, has no right to information that will help her kill her baby."

Pearson's blanket blessing on deception has led to a variety of confusion and intimidation tactics. On Crisis Pregnancy Center Watch, a pro-choice watchdog site that collects testimonials from women who encounter manipulative CPCs, some women claim that CPCs called their parents to tell them their daughters were sexually active or pregnant; one woman who had an abortion after going to a CPC said she received annual birthday cards spattered with red paint on what would have been her due date. Another described how a friend went to a CPC that allowed her to believe she had scheduled an appointment for an abortion and instead strung her along for several weeks, repeatedly rescheduling her appointments until she had passed the state's legal cutoff for elective abortions. She ended up having to carry the baby to term and relinquish it for adoption—a choice that left her with severe depression and guilt.

A 2006 congressional report requested by Representative Henry Waxman, a California Democrat, found that around 87 percent of CPCs that received federal funding provided false information about the long-term health effects of abortion. The report prompted both federal and local lawmakers to propose legislation to mandate truth-in-advertising standards for the centers. But four years later little had changed. A 2010 investigation conducted by NARAL Pro-Choice Virginia Foundation found that out of fifty-two clinics they visited or called, 67 percent still misrepresented the services they provide or gave false information about the safety and effectiveness of contraception and abortion, including one CPC that told a client that abortion would pull out her uterine lining.

Another legacy early CPCs left is their history of coercive adoption practices. Leslee Unruh is a key antiabortion campaigner who helped draft South Dakota's unenforceable 2006 abortion ban (which voters ultimately overturned) as well as the founder of Abstinence Clearinghouse, the most prominent abstinence-only sex education group in the country. In 1984 Unruh established a crisis pregnancy center called the Alpha Center in the basement of her South Dakota home. Three years later the state attorney's office investigated her over complaints that she had offered young women money to carry their pregnancies to term and then relinquish their babies for adoption.

"There were so many allegations about improper adoptions being made [against Unruh] and how teenage girls were being pressured to give up their children," then–State Attorney Tim Wilka told the *Argus Leader* in 2003, that "Gov. George Mickelson called me and asked me to take the case." The Alpha Center, which Unruh estimates offers counseling to more than five thousand women per year and was the first of fourteen sister CPCs around the country, pled no contest to five counts of unlicensed adoption and foster care practices. The center, which later called Wilka's allegations "baseless" and ideologically motivated, paid a $500 fine in a plea bargain to drop nineteen other charges, including four felonies, involving her alleged offer of payments to pregnant women. Unruh, however, was unrepentant, protesting in court, "If saving babies is against the law, then I'm guilty."

A decade after Unruh founded the Alpha Center, the *Village Voice's* Marc Cooper investigated several California CPCs under the umbrella CPC network Care Net—the largest CPC association in the country, with eleven hundred CPCs with ties to maternity homes, adoption agencies, and clinics—that were sued for coercively counseling pregnant women or new mothers. Among the accusations were allegations that CPC staff had held an infant under false pretenses while they hounded its unwed parents to relinquish, detained a woman in labor in the CPC offices for four hours in the same effort, pressured new mothers to sign unidentified papers while they were under heavy medication shortly after they gave birth, failed to provide legal counsel for surrendering parents, and badgered one young couple with pressure tactics that a psychiatrist compared in court testimony to brainwashing. Many of the children adopted went to born-again Christians who had donated to the CPC. The cases Cooper covered were among nearly twenty lawsuits brought against CPCs between 1983 to 1996 in nine different states.

Though the agency where the worst abuses occurred was closed, many others have taken up the tradition of frightening unmarried pregnant women with predictions of poverty, making a causative argument against single parenthood as though the mere fact of being unmarried creates poverty and not the backgrounds that many unmarried mothers are already coming from, in which systemic poverty and lack of support services are facts of life. Conservative politics reinforces these arguments as well. In February 2012 Wisconsin State Senator Glenn Grothman, a Republican, introduced legislation that would officially label single parenthood a risk factor for child abuse. In Grothman's brief on the legislation, he lamented that too few out-of-wedlock births had resulted in adoption and raised the specter of Reagan's "welfare queens"—unwed mothers allegedly having so many children on the public dime that married taxpayers have to restrict themselves to bearing just one or two kids, because they are so overburdened by paying for tax-funded public assistance that supports single moms.

Religious women are particularly susceptible to coercion like this, argues Mari Gallion, a thirty-nine-year-old single mother in Alaska and author of *The Single Woman's Guide to a Happy Pregnancy*. Gallion founded the support group SinglePregnancy.com after a CPC unsuccessfully pressured her to relinquish her child, despite the fact that she was college educated and a homeowner. Since then she's made it her calling to support women with unplanned pregnancies if they decide to parent alone, helping nearly three thousand women find the resources that are available to single mothers—resources that CPCs claim to offer but often fail to provide.

Through this experience Gallion has come to see CPCs as "adoption rings" with a multistep agenda: evangelize women and convince them not to choose abortion; hunt for and exploit women's insecurities about their age, education, finances, sexual past, or ability to parent alone; then hard sell adoption, portraying single parenting as a selfish, immature choice. "The women who are easier to coerce in these situations are those who subscribe to conservative Christian views," said Gallion, like Southern Baptists or Pentecostals. "They'll come in and be told that, 'You've done wrong, but God will forgive you if you do the right thing.'"

To the minds of some CPCs, not only is single parenthood not "God's plan for the family," it's so anathema as to render a child born to a single-parent home an automatic orphan. A flyer from Decisions, Choices & Options, a Christian crisis pregnancy ministry that does adoption-outreach programs in high schools and church youth groups, argues incredibly that, because the biblical definition of an orphan is a fatherless child, all children born to single mothers in the United States are orphans *by definition*, just barely better off than if they had never been born at all. If 43 percent of the six million babies born that year were born to unwed mothers, the ministry reasoned, "that means 2.6 million new orphans last year!"

"With over 2 million couples waiting to adopt and over 10 million wanting to adopt," the flyer continued, "every child aborted or born to an unmarried mother could have the stability and love of a father and a mother."

ALL OF THESE NUMBERS are arithmetic I've come across before. In 2010, at the sixth annual Christian Alliance for Orphans' Summit, held at the fifty-five hundred–member Grace Church in Eden Prairie, Minnesota, a man named Jim Wright announced that "There are ten million couples between twenty-two and sixty-four who would adopt if they could, if they had a supply." Wright, president of a Washington, D.C.-area ministry called Birthmothers, was speaking to an audience of around forty people gathered for an afternoon workshop on "Serving Birthmothers and Birth Families."

Noting the lack of women relinquishing babies for adoption, Wright said he would love to see that number come up, something he imagined would also lead to the closure of abortion clinics, gone bankrupt without clients, "and we never fired a shot." To that end, he said, "We employ ladies who will give the love of Christ to these women who don't feel it in their hearts. . . . If we could save millions of women, how many more babies would be available for adoption?"

Wright's personal story seemed surprising in the halls of Grace Church. A lifelong hemophiliac, Wright contracted HIV and Hepatitis C from infected blood supplies in the 1980s. In 1989 his wife, Tammy, contracted it as well through a tragic medical accident. The two were trying to get pregnant using a technique called sperm washing, which would allow the couple to conceive without risking infecting Tammy. However, one of her blood vessels was punctured during the procedure. It was then, said Wright, a tall man with a gaunt face and deep bags under his eyes, who still poses for pictures with the confident smile he relied on for years as a Beltway realtor— top broker four times in the '90s, he told me—that he began thinking about adoption and abortion and how the two were now connected in his mind. "That's how Birthmothers came to be: because we go to adopt, and we can't get anybody to do a homestudy"—that is, an agency evaluation of prospective adopters' fitness to parent—"because we had the plague. I couldn't pay enough money. . . . Out of that tragedy of hemophilia and HIV/AIDS," he continued, "Birthmothers was born. Then I was introduced to the concept of adoption and abortion, and I'm going, 'Wow, this is unbelievable.'"

The "concept of adoption and abortion" Wright means is the clash of two statistics a friend from the National Council for Adoption told him: that when he was seeking to adopt in the early '90s, there were an estimated 1.5 million abortions performed in the United States annually. "And then there are ten million couples seeking to adopt?" he asked incredulously.

For Wright, this tragedy presented a simple equation: many couples, like he and Tammy, wanted children but couldn't have them, whereas many pregnancies were being aborted. These two facts seemed like a natural match—the "win-win" situation that so many CPCs describe.

"How can you have all these people seeking to adopt and all these people aborting, and the two aren't meeting?"

In 1991 Wright and Tammy, who later died, were able to privately adopt their son, A. J., from a teenage mother in Virginia. Five years later Wright turned his experience into a ministry. Partnering with established CPCs like the Sanctity of Life or Care Net franchises, Birthmothers aims to provide a personal mentor, a "Birthmother Friend," who will be available to pregnant women on a long-term basis—after all, a woman who goes to a CPC might still walk out without having her mind changed, whereas a longer-lasting relationship could have more effect. The ministry has trained 151 "certified" Birthmother Friends—certified by Birthmothers, that is, after courses with adoption attorneys and other experts—who can then be matched with local pregnant women across the country and urge them first to "choose life" and then consider adoption.

When we spoke in 2011, Wright was on the cusp of what he described as a major fundraising push, hoping to raise $100 million in startup capital to hire marketing staff to visit churches across the country and develop Birthmothers chapters there as well as to place national TV spots that would lodge Birthmothers' name in the minds of teenage girls for years to come. The campaign has been slow going, but for now the ministry spreads the word in a more modest fashion, asking supporters to order and distribute their crisis pregnancy cards around their towns, leaving them with waitresses and cashiers, in dressing rooms, pay phones, and laundromats—"anywhere women may find them."

"The reason we use 'Birthmothers' as our name is because it connotes adoption," Wright said, even though, he admits, not one of the women they have worked with so far has chosen adoption. Out of one hundred women who have been partnered with a Birthmother Friend, Wright said there have been no abortions but also no adoptions, meaning the women Wright's ministry is serving are being labeled as birthmothers despite the fact that they have all gone on to parent their children. That makes the organization's name an aspirational title, to say the least, labeling mothers according to what Wright wishes they had done.

Wright's casual reflections clearly show that he thinks that more of these women should have relinquished for adoption. "Women want adoption because they're not able to care for their child, so they make a loving decision," he said, describing the claim of his own son's birthmother, that after seeing the babies of teen mothers around her fail to flourish, she had decided to relinquish her son.

In May 2011 I traveled to Wright's home church in Falls Church, Virginia, a wealthy and conservative suburb of Washington, D.C., for a special "birthmother's brunch." It was the Saturday before Mother's Day, a day recognized in the adoption community as "Birthmother's Day." In an open first-floor classroom about twenty people, mostly women, milled and sampled from a brunch buffet table of bagels, Mexican egg casserole, and Waldorf salad before the program began. Introduced by Wright's fiancée, Cindy Little, a nervous blonde in glasses, three birthmothers got up from a horseshoe arrangement of folding tables to tell their stories of relinquishing children. Two of the three described stories "back in the old days of adoption, where [my son] was sort of stolen from me"—a testimony of ambiguous value for Wright's mission.

The youngest of the three, a voluptuous brunette in her early forties with flowing dark hair and a canary yellow scarf, had relinquished her son in 1987, when she was a high school senior, to a couple she had met in a local Bible study. She had been suffering from depression and was stuck in a bad relationship. The couple directed her to a crisis pregnancy center for counseling, and there, the woman said, she learned that "there were sin patterns in my life that I refused to stop."

"I begged God to show me what His will was for the little one I was carrying. After much prayer, God began to show me that adoption was indeed His want. I confess that I struggled tremendously with this. I secretly hoped that He would say, 'You can keep your baby,' as any mother would. But I loved God more than I loved my baby." She quoted Ephesians 1:5: "He predestined us to be adopted as his sons through Jesus Christ, in accordance with his pleasure," and John 3:1: "How great is the love the father has lavished on us? That we should be called children of God and that is what we are?"

The small audience at the horseshoe tables was crying when she finished. Jim got up to take her place at the front. "Your story is everything this ministry is about—love, forgiveness, second chances, third chances," he said. "We think the church should have open arms to us sinners." He led the room in prayer—for more resources to reach more women, more men, and more families, and, "With the hope of Christ, hope of adoptions."

THE LARGER CONTEXT for Wright's disappointment with relinquishment rates and his push for more women to choose adoption is that since *Roe v. Wade* was decided in 1973, the number of women relinquishing children for adoption has not just fallen but dropped off a cliff. There are few reliable, current numbers on domestic infant adoptions, in part because states are not legally required to report how many babies are privately adopted within the United States. But among the figures that are tallied, there has been a drastic dropoff in infant relinquishments, from 19.2 percent of unmarried white mothers in 1972 to 1.7 percent in 1995 to around 1 percent ever since. Among never-married black women, the rate of relinquishing infants for adoption has been statistically zero for decades.

What that adds up to in real numbers is disputed. A 2010 report by Jessica Arons for the Center for American Progress found that annual domestic infant adoption rates have dropped so low that they are hard to track, but Department of Health and Human Services estimates have ranged from 7,000 to 23,000 in recent years, with an average of 14,000 per year. By comparison, 1.2 million women choose abortion, and 1.4 million decide to continue the pregnancy and parent their child. (The CAP report notes that abortion is not the cause of lower numbers, as both abortion and adoption rates have fallen while rates of unwed parenting have risen dramatically.) In a fretful 2009 feature, "Last Days of Adoption?" the conservative paper the *Washington Times* put the numbers at their lowest estimate, at 6,800 a year between 1996 to 2002, based on data compiled for the paper by the National Center for Health Statistics.

Whatever the exact figure, these private domestic infant adoptions, so common during the Baby Scoop Era, are now the least common form of adoption in America, falling behind adoptions from the foster care system, within families, or from overseas. But demand for adoptable infants has not decreased with this reduction in supply.

Many of the women who continue to place for adoption come from particularly vulnerable groups, including those from conservative religious backgrounds in which premarital sex is taboo, and marginalized groups like poor women, recent immigrants, and victims of domestic violence. Because of this, the CAP report concluded, "We should be wary of any programs that would propose increasing the number of infants available for adoption at the expense of pregnant women's interests."

Yet that's exactly what is happening, both as an economically driven response to high demand for adoptable children and large adoption agencies' demanding budgets as well as because promoting adoption has become a popular political compromise, a seeming third way out of the abortion debates. President Obama said as much in a 2009 speech at Notre Dame, during which he suggested lowering abortion rates by "mak[ing] adoption more available." In an online debate that same year, Slate columnist William Saletan and Beliefnet editor Steven Waldman made the tin-eared proposal to neutralize the abortion wars by offering unmarried pregnant women a nominal cash payment to choose adoption instead.*

The pressure to increase relinquishments can impact the services adoption agency counselors offer. In an unsigned post on a forum for birthmothers, a writer claiming to be a former birthparent and adoptive-parent counselor at Bethany Christian Services recalled her efforts to counsel women against the backdrop of a large nonprofit's financial needs.† "The type of work I do not miss are the staff meetings," the author wrote. "The review of the numbers of placements, adoptive families, prospective birth parents (who of course were not called 'prospective'). The reality of the revenue . . . the risk of job cuts 'if the budget' (read: placement #s) are not met."

Joan Aylor, the peer counseling director of A Woman's Touch CPC in Bellevue, Nebraska, gave me an illustration of what adoption-oriented counseling for pregnant women looks like. "We don't say, 'Give your baby up for adoption,' because that's negative right then and there," Aylor told me. "We present it as, 'Would you please think about making an adoption plan? We tell them that God will bless you if you consider adoption, and [that] she is a hero in our eyes."

---

* It's not always a means of reconciliation, though. During the 2012 presidential campaign Republican Congressman Tim Huelskamp, a white Kansan who has adopted four children of color, used adoption as a platform to attack abortion rights, using the old antiabortion canard that Planned Parenthood targets minorities for population control. "I am incensed that this president pays money to an entity that was created for the sole purpose of killing children that look like mine," Huelskamp said at the right-wing Values Voters Summit in September 2012.

†The numbers support the idea that adoption is big business even as most adoption agencies are nonprofits. A 2010 investigation by the *Atlanta Journal Constitution* found that $8.4 million out of Bethany's $9.1 million total annual budget went to management costs or fundraising, and only $694,000 to programs serving children directly.

The ubiquity of this line of argumentation affects even counselors trying to provide ethical services. "One of the hardest things about being a
counselor in this field these days is distinguishing oneself from the powerful forces of religiously and financially motivated 'counseling' that is so
blatantly biased and yet, understandably, so seductive to women in crisis,"
said Anne Moody, an adoption counselor who has been talking to women
about their options in an unplanned pregnancy for decades at the independent secular agency Adoption Connections in Washington. "It's hard
to explain when what you're dealing with on a personal level is some
really nice lady, who seems like she's doing this really nice thing as she
goes around and sees all her clients, but she's leaving all this devastation
in her wake, of girls who never should have given up their babies."

But biased counseling is exactly what some adoption advocates call on
CPCs to do. Despite the enthusiasm to transform CPCs into the means to
save domestic adoption, relatively few women make the choice. CPC directors commonly report that they have little success convincing women
to choose adoption. "They say, 'I would never do that to my child,' even as
you're explaining how adoption is an act of sacrificial love," lamented
Robin Marriott, head of Your Choice Pregnancy Resource Center, a CPC
in Kansas City, Kansas.

The fact that pregnant single women refuse to relinquish their babies
is a source of irritation for antiabortion advocates like Flip Benham, director of Operation Save America, an extremist protest group that broke
off from other extremists at Operation Rescue. "We could adopt a child in
a second. We have everything available. . . . But [the women] aren't going
to do that," Benham told me. "Because they're selfish."

Benham suggested there was an exception to the poor results CPCs
are having. Angela Michael, a fifty-seven-year old former registered
nurse and frustrated CPC volunteer in Illinois, has taken a different approach to crisis pregnancy work. Instead of directing women to a separate CPC, four days every week Michael parks herself—literally, in a
customized RV—in front of an abortion clinic in Granite City, Illinois, a
despairing strip of crumbling steel mills, prairie, and scrap yards a few
miles upriver from East St. Louis. As a result, she claims she's stopped
forty-two hundred women from having abortions and has facilitated
forty-two private adoptions in the last several years—a number that stag-
gers other CPCs—including two children she and her husband Dan have
adopted themselves.

Her approach is guided by the same principles as traditional CPCs,
but she is obstructionist in a way that many other centers are reluctant to

be, as many CPCs have official regulations prohibiting staff or volunteers from participating in so-called sidewalk counseling (what antiabortion protesters call their efforts to stop women from entering abortion clinics). But Michael draws no such lines, and when she stops women, she brings them into her RV, where she keeps two upper cabinets stuffed with nearly forty profiles of would-be adoptive families. Michael estimates that she saves adopting parents at least $30,000, as she's doing all the legwork, leaving only an approximately $3,000 fee for the adoption attorney. And she is so confident that she can find enough adoptable babies for prospective adoptive parents that she and Dan put advertisements in church bulletins and once even aired a TV commercial on local Saint Louis stations, showing Michael holding a baby "saved from abortion" and soliciting potential adopters.

DESPITE THE SMALL-SCALE success of Michael's on-the-ground ministry, few CPCs are likely to follow in the footsteps of such a high-commitment endeavor. For the others, there are more systematic efforts in place to increase adoption numbers.

In 1996 Frederica Mathewes-Green, a syndicated columnist, author, and veteran antiabortion advocate, wrote about the need for more adoptions in an essay for the Heritage Foundation, "Pro-Life Dilemma: Pregnancy Centers and the Welfare Trap." The "dilemma" at hand was the dearth of women among America's "seemingly endless supply of pregnancies to unwed mothers" who would relinquish those babies for adoption. Although CPCs had an honorable track record in helping women make "life-affirming" choices, wrote Mathewes-Green, the babies they were saving also deserved "a better life than welfare and single-parenting can offer. Pregnancy centers, which have already done so much to better the prospects of women and children, need to expand their vision one more time. They should do far more to encourage mothers to consider adoption."

Others in the antiabortion movement saw a similar problem, and four years later the right-wing Christian group Family Research Council (FRC) released its 2000 research paper, "The Missing Piece: Adoption Counseling in Pregnancy Resource Centers," which critics have described as the "CPC Bible." "The Missing Piece" was designed to address why less than 1 percent of women who entered larger CPCs were relinquishing for adoption. Its author was Curtis Young, a Maryland pastor who had directed the Christian Action Council, the CPC umbrella network that was later renamed Care Net. Young had also founded the Protestant "Sanctity of Human Life Day" in January, when many churches formally protest the anniversary of *Roe v. Wade*, and had previously written a market research report for the FRC on choosing the most appealing names for CPCs.

"The Missing Piece" was based on additional market research conducted by Charles T. Kenny, whose Tennessee marketing firm, Right Brain People, purports to study consumers' "subconscious emotional motivators" so that companies can "leverage their brands as never before." The brand that Kenny was trying to optimize in his research for "The Missing Piece" was adoption, or rather the idea of women relinquishing children for adoption. Kenny, himself a personal benefactor of the National Council for Adoption (NCFA), studied the emotional reactions of fifty-one women who had had unplanned pregnancies as well as twelve Christian CPC counselors to figure out why so few women relinquished. He found that the women largely resisted adoption because they worried it would be unbearably painful or that it constituted a form of abandoning their children.

Based on this research, Young suggested a new CPC communications strategy that would "chip away at those associations and establish new ones," presenting adoption as an expression of birthmothers' selfless love as well as a means of redemption—a way for mothers to "[defeat] selfishness, an 'evil' within themselves." Women who kept their children were described as immature and emotional, peevishly holding onto babies they didn't really want and whom they would later neglect or harm. Women who chose adoption, however, were described as expressing "a higher and less selfish form of love." Young suggested that counselors help women see relinquishment as a step in their own spiritual development, with a woman "proving her character by relinquishing her child." Young recommended a new national CPC strategy that would promote adoption as a "heroic," "courageous and loving" choice, "associating adoption with the grace of God, who gave his own Son for the life of the world." He suggested that CPCs get over any fears of appearing that they were engaging in "baby-selling" so they could create a streamlined path between their center and local adoption agencies.

In 2007 the FRC and the NCFA went beyond overlapping mandates to collaborate directly on the joint publication of a follow-up report, "Birthmother, Good Mother: Her Story of Heroic Redemption." Authored this time by Charles Kenny and intended to "deliver the message through birthmothers that sometimes choosing adoption is what it means to be a good mother," this publication targeted "potential birthmothers"—that is, women who weren't yet pregnant—so they would see adoption as a good option if they did become pregnant outside of marriage down the line. This seemed to contradict CPCs' abstinence focus, unless, as some adoption critics wryly suggest, the abstinence movement is indeed functioning properly to provide more women with unplanned pregnancies and, thus, potentially more babies available for adoption.

For "Birthmother, Good Mother," Kenny's team interviewed fifty-one women in Texas and Illinois who had relinquished children, including a number of mothers from the Baby Scoop Era. Drawing on the "bitter feelings" of those women whose relinquishments took place fifteen years or more earlier, the report sought to identify what had turned women away from adoption in the past, using Right Brain People's methodology of "visualization, relaxation and repetition." At least some women in the market research pools didn't know what the research was for when they were paid a small amount to participate in the study. For some, it felt like a second violation. "They had to find out what it was that made it ok for us to have surrendered," said Baby Scoop Era mother Sandy Young. "What came from that is teaching these mothers that they're heroes for surrendering. . . . It really burns the Baby Scoop Era mothers up, that they continue to use us to refine their strategies. The more we talk, the sharper they are."

But this wasn't the first time Baby Scoop Era mothers' experiences were used to figure out how to increase adoptions. Birthmother experiences were also tapped to develop the Infant Adoption Awareness Training Program, a Department of Health and Human Services initiative passed in 2000 to teach adoption education "best practice guidelines" to public and private employees who may come in contact with pregnant women. "Birthmother, Good Mother" author Kenny and other religious conservatives, including members of the National Council for Adoption, helped develop the program. Since 2002 the program has been used to train more than twenty thousand individuals—including staffers at schools and state health facilities as well as crisis pregnancy centers, domestic violence crisis centers, and immigration health centers—on how to present adoption as a positive option to women with unplanned pregnancies. The NCFA was picked to administer more than $6 million in federal grants to conduct the trainings for the first few years of the program's life. They frequently subcontracted out to partners like Bethany Christian Services and other adoption agencies, many of which were religious.

Unsurprisingly, the trainings were sometimes biased. The Guttmacher Institute, a pro-choice research group, charged that although the program stipulates "nondirective counseling" to help women explore their options without pressure, some attendees at the trainings still found them coercive: discouraging abortion, overpromoting adoption and suggesting "tips and techniques . . . about how to work against [women's] resistance, make them proud of their decision and convince them that adoption is a good choice"—words that could have come directly from the "CPC Bible."

SOME BIRTHMOTHERS think their experiences sparked yet another adoption industry innovation: the promise of open adoption. One of the strongest improvements adoption agencies cite when comparing today's adoption system to the "bad old days," open adoptions offer birthmothers some degree of ongoing contact with the adoptive family. In meetings with prospective birthmothers, this is often a key selling point: promising the woman that she will be able to choose the family that adopts her child, receive updates, and have continuing contact with the family and possibly regular visits with her child as he or she grows up. Some agencies even suggest that birthmothers will be able to name their child and effectively become a part of the adopting family themselves. A 2012 study found that 95 percent of all domestic infant adoptions in the United States are now, to some degree, "open."

Although advocates of open adoption point to many pairings that work out well, in which the adoptive and birth parents find a workable harmony in raising the child, at other times open adoption can turn out so poorly that birthmothers later regard it as a ploy that was used to secure their cooperation. A significant problem with open adoption is the fact of its unstable legal footing. In most states in the country open adoption is not legally enforceable and depends almost entirely on the continuing commitment of the adoptive parents, some of whom drift away or cut off contact abruptly and others who may have never knowingly agreed to such contact in the first place.

Karen Fetrow, a cheerful but shy forty-two-year-old Pennsylvania computer technician, used to be a firm supporter of adoption. A lifelong evangelical and pro-lifer, Fetrow said she briefly slipped from her family's conservative Christian principles and became pregnant at twenty-four with the man who would later become her husband. After a childhood of listening to Christian ministries, Fetrow knew that the answer to her situation was a Christian adoption agency. "For years, the seed had been planted in my head that unplanned pregnancy equals adoption," she said. "Before I even got the pregnancy test back, I thought, there are all these families out there that need my baby."

It was 1994, and Fetrow turned to the local Bethany Christian Services branch outside Harrisburg. Although Fetrow was in a committed relationship with the father, now her husband of nineteen years, who wanted the two of them to raise the child as a family, Bethany told her that women who sought to parent were on their own. Fetrow had been primed to believe that adoption was the only ethical option for an unwed mother, so she didn't argue.

After Fetrow relinquished her son, her experience with Bethany quickly soured. She received no postadoption counseling beyond one checkup phone call. Three months later, around the time her boyfriend proposed, Bethany called to notify her that her legal paperwork was en route but that she shouldn't read it or attend court for the adoption finalization because "the language was harsh" and she might find it painful. In reality, the adoption wasn't yet final, and if Fetrow had attended court, she could have changed her mind.

Although for thirteen years Fetrow couldn't look at an infant without crying and grappled with secondary infertility—a not-uncommon affliction for birthmothers who feel intense anxiety about getting pregnant again—she continued to support adoption and CPCs. However, when she later sought counseling—a staple of Bethany's advertised services—the director of her local office said he couldn't help. Incredibly, he said he couldn't think of any books she could read or counselors she could talk to or advisers he could refer. But Fetrow's harshest realization came when the adoptive family of her son stopped sending pictures or updates after he turned five. Fetrow had been led to believe that the adoptive parents would keep in touch until her son turned eighteen and could make contact with her himself. When she asked Bethany about it, they stalled for three years before admitting that the adoptive parents had only agreed to five years of contact, producing an unsigned document that Fetrow had no recollection of ever reading before.

In 2007 the local Bethany office attempted to host a service at Fetrow's church, "painting adoption as a Christian, pro-life thing." At a friend's urging, Fetrow told her pastor about her experience. The pastor hosted a three-way meeting with the Bethany director, who called Fetrow angry and bitter and implied that she was obsessive for bringing in documentation of her case. In a particularly insulting move, the director asked Fetrow's husband whether she could be trusted with pictures of their son, insinuating that Fetrow might use them to hunt the child down.

The pastor refused to let Bethany address the congregation. It was a minor victory for Fetrow, but she is still barred from seeing her child and feels that Bethany is at the root of the problem, having facilitated her adoption by telling both sides what they wanted to hear and leaving both with false impressions about the agreement. Bethany has an online forum, and Fetrow had started going there in 2002 to ask other women for help. In 2007, after the incident with the Bethany director, she logged on to vent, writing that she finally got it: adoption is all about the money. She was kicked out of the group.

Kris Faasse, director of adoption services at Bethany, said that although she was unaware of Fetrow's or Carol Jordan's particular stories, their accounts are painful for her to hear. "The fact that this happens to any mom grieves me and would not be how we wanted to handle it." She added that only 25 to 40 percent of women who come to Bethany choose adoption, a figure that, she said, "is so important, because we never want a woman to feel coerced into a plan."

Some adoption reform advocates see open adoption as the panicked reaction of the industry to dwindling adoption numbers, an effort to court potential birthmothers with promises that their experience will not resemble that of previous generations. Adding insult to injury, they also charge that open adoption was again the result of adoption agencies' research into the lives of Baby Scoop Era birthmothers, finding out what was worst about their experience—resoundingly they said it was not knowing if their children were okay—and coming up with a cosmetic fix. "They said your child will know who you are. What they didn't do was make any of it legally enforceable," said Young. "It's just a marketing ploy. As soon as they get the papers signed, a lot of adoptive parents will close the adoptions, 'in the best interest of the child.'"

Mirah Riben said that open adoption became necessary after changing public attitudes toward single motherhood made shame an ineffective recruitment tool. "Now they use open adoption: you can have your cake and eat it too. You can be a Sunday parent." New birthmothers are told that older mothers are embittered by the way things were back then and that today adoption is different, "a gentle and sweet loss." But that's not what happens, Riben said.

Riben argues that open adoption is, in a subtle way, a key aspect of coercion today, as agencies enmesh expectant mothers with prospective adopters from the early stages of their pregnancies through to the delivery room, and agency counselors progressively condition women to think of the fetus they are carrying as a child that belongs to the prospective adoptive parents (a sentiment taken literally by yet another 2012 reality TV show about women considering adoption, *I'm Having Their Baby*). "Their whole bonding experience is being corrupted," said Riben. "They're made to feel as if they're carrying this baby for them, as if they're a surrogate mother or a handmaid." As a result of the relationships many women are encouraged to build with prospective parents while pregnant, many new mothers feel unable to keep their babies after they've changed their minds.

After birth is when many open adoption plans falter. Although in some cases, agencies say, the birthmother is the one who drifts away, not the adoptive parents, many birthmother websites, blogs, and online forums are filled with testimonials of women who agreed to open adoptions and then lost contact, often after birthmothers expressed regret or the dynamics of the relationship proved too complicated or painful, spooking adoptive parents into cutting off contact. That threat, thinks Riben, makes other birthmothers reluctant to complain. "If their adoption is remaining open, they need to be compliant, good birthmothers and toe the line. They can't afford to be angry or bitter, because if they are, the door will close and they won't see the kid."

Shari Levine, from Open Adoption & Family Services, is such an avid supporter of open adoption that she featured the practice in her agency's name. But she has seen the promise of open adoption used in manipulative ways so often that their website has a list that warns potential birthmothers of what to look for—and to learn what to avoid—in any adoption agency they consider. Some independent adoption attorneys advertise open adoptions, Levine said, but in practice may only offer a birthmother the chance to view her child once from afar. Others coach prospective adoptive parents to sell themselves to expectant moms in dishonest or emotionally manipulative ways, including one woman who was urged to change her name from "Ann" to "Annie," to appear homier. To Levine, such deceptions contradict the very nature of honest open adoptions, meant to be based on building clearly defined relationships that will withstand extreme emotions. "If you don't have an agency that has a philosophy about relationship building, then you have pretty empty open adoptions that end up not being open at all," she said. "That's when open adoption becomes a ploy to get moms on board."

That outcome—an open adoption suddenly closed—can be the worst for birthmothers. The Center for American Progress found that "the poorest grief resolution occurred when adoptive parents did not honor agreements for ongoing information." This was evident in the story told to me by one Texas mother who relinquished in 2006, only to have the adoptive parents close the adoption. "They had to put me on pills," said the woman, who declined to use her name in the hopes that the adoptive parents might change their minds. "If I hear a baby crying, I need to cover my ears. I can't watch movies with kids of a certain age. My heart hurts, like a constricting pain. I'm not moving on with my life, that's for sure. . . . I have a good friend who went through a situation like me, and she said, if I don't get my child, I'm going to commit suicide. I said I'm right there with you. . . . Life is nothing without your children. You're walking among the dead."

UTAH MIGHT PROVIDE the best example of what domestic adoption would look like if some of the advocates seeking to raise numbers had their way. Although women have made many reproductive gains since the Baby Scoop Era, surprisingly many state adoption laws have become less favorable for birthmothers, drastically reducing the time after birth when a mother can relinquish, varying from several weeks to within twenty-four hours in some states, all far short of the six weeks that is standard in most European countries and in some cases cutting the period to revoke consent completely. Adoption organizations publish comparative lists of state laws almost as a catalogue for prospective adopters seeking states friendliest for adoption, usually meaning those most restrictive of birthparent rights. Among the worst is Utah, roundly recognized as the most "pro-adoption" state in the country, earning it the nickname the "baby warehouse."

Utah adoption agencies are a vital presence in the Christian adoption community, particularly the Mormon Church's LDS Family Services, which has sixty-nine offices worldwide and, critics say, has influenced many of Utah's adoption laws.* Although many Americans still consider the Mormon Church exotic, it is an increasingly important actor in conservative activism. In recent years Mormons have become a vital partner to the traditional religious right, with LDS donors and scholars pairing with Protestant evangelicals and conservative Catholics to advance conservative goals. Adoption politics seems not just another aspect of this shared agenda but rather an arena in which Mormons are leading the pack.

In 2005 LDS Family Services was inducted into the NCFA's "Adoption Hall of Fame." On the occasion then-NCFA President Thomas Atwood

---

*LDS Family Services is one of the largest donors to the National Council for Adoption, and NCFA officials have reciprocated the support, with board members donating millions to the LDS "Temple Fund."

lauded Utah and LDS Family Services for providing a national model for advancing the "best interests of children." But for Mormon women facing an unplanned pregnancy, life in Utah is a virtual reenactment of the Baby Scoop Era. Mormon church policy encourages and sometimes demands that unmarried pregnant women surrender babies for adoption, "preferably through LDS Social Services," as repentance for their sin. For Mormon adoptive parents, adoption costs through LDS Family Services are significantly lower than nationwide averages, at approximately $4,000 to $10,000 per adoption, due to heavy church subsidies. (Together with federal adoption tax credits, this would render an adoption effectively free.) A number of women have alleged severe pressure from local clergy to relinquish children in exchange for good standing in the church, and some claim they were threatened with excommunication if they didn't. One Mormon woman in Massachusetts, Peggie Hayes, who became pregnant out of wedlock in 1983 said that her ward bishop, future 2012 presidential candidate Mitt Romney, for whom she had babysat, "pressured" her to relinquish her son to LDS Social Services. "He told me he was a representative of the church and by refusing, I was failing to comply with the church's wishes and I could be excommunicated," Hayes told the *Boston Globe*. Though Romney has denied that he threatened her with excommunication, Hayes said the message she received was that she had a choice between keeping her child or keeping her standing with God. "This is not like 'You don't get to take Communion,'" she explained. "This is like 'You will not be saved. You will never see the face of God.'"

But Utah's pressure to adopt reaches beyond church influence or state borders. Jo Anne Swanson, a court-appointed adoption intermediary and independent researcher, has studied a number of cases of pregnant women lured out of their home states to give birth and relinquish babies under Utah's lax laws. By bringing women into Utah while they were still pregnant, agencies could avoid having to deal with the Interstate Compact on the Placement of Children (ICPC), federal regulations that govern the adoption of children between states. Some women were recruited by 800 numbers listed halfway across the country, dialing what they assumed was a local number that instead rolled through to Utah.

The reason agencies want to get women to Utah is because there mothers can relinquish their babies twenty-four hours after birth, and relinquishments are irrevocable from the moment they are signed. The state allows relinquishments to occur with only two witnesses, and numerous mothers who have been flown in from out of state have relinquished their children in locations as haphazard as hotels and parks. Some agencies even give birthmothers small payments—something considered a deeply unethical practice. Women who reconsidered the relinquishment once they were in Utah have had agencies threaten to refuse airfare home.

In 2005 a prospective adoptive couple in Utah, Steve and Carolyn Mintz, recounted to the *Salt Lake Tribune* how they witnessed the director of their adoption agency, A Cherished Child, fly into a rage at an out-of-state woman in labor who backed out of their adoption. "She started screaming at [the mother] saying, 'You can't do this. You made a deal.' She was intimidating this girl right as she was about to have this baby," Steve told the *Tribune*. But then several weeks later the story got worse when the couple saw the same birthmother and her newborn daughter on a local TV news story about crowded homeless shelters. Both mother and child had been stranded in the state after she refused to relinquish.

Women aren't the only ones who get hurt in Utah. A number of complaints have been lodged by birthfathers who sought to parent their children but Utah's complicated system of registering paternity shut them out. The confusion, many fathers contend, is deliberate, and Utah again is at the forefront of "adoption-friendly" states in bending the rules to assist its agencies. For a father to contest an adoption happening in Utah, he must register with Utah's putative father registry within twenty to thirty days of receiving notice not necessarily that the mother is planning on adoption but just that she may be visiting Utah—a vague statement that few would understand as a declaration of intent to relinquish but that under Utah law has often been considered forewarning enough.

Utah's law on paternity was changed to accommodate more adoptions in 1995, stating that "by virtue of the fact that he has engaged in a sexual relationship with a woman," an unmarried man is considered "on notice" that an adoption may occur and the burden of protecting his parental rights is entirely on him, relieving agencies of the need to seek consent.

Adoption attorney Larry Jenkins, who has defended adoptive parents in many lawsuits over contested paternity rights, explained that under the registry law, "Our statute puts the burden on him to take affirmative steps to protect his rights. And he doesn't have any rights at all unless he takes those steps before she signs."

Following this move, nonkinship adoptions in the state doubled between 1996 and 2002. The increase included cases like that of Robert Manzanares, a Colorado birthfather who fought LDS Family Services for four years for custody of his biological daughter after his former girlfriend tried to relinquish her for adoption in Utah. In an interview with New Mexico's *KOB Eyewitness News,* Manzanares alleged that a Mormon bishop told the girlfriend that, unless she placed her child for adoption with a Mormon family, she would not get to the highest level of heaven. At eight months pregnant, the girlfriend wrote Manzanares an e-mail claiming she was going to visit her sick father in Utah, thereby setting a clock for Manzanares to challenge an adoption he didn't know was occurring.

Or there is the case of Mario Beltran, a California father whose pregnant girlfriend planned an adoption through an LDS Social Services office that relocated her to Provo, Utah. Attempting to stop the adoption, Beltran wrote a letter to the agency clearly indicating his desire to parent, but because he didn't also contact Utah's putative father registry, he lost his claim. When the case went to court, an adoption attorney successfully argued that Utah law does not obligate agencies to inform unwed fathers of how they must register their rights.

In 2011 the *Deseret News* reported that 71 of 320 pending and completed adoptions—almost a quarter—were for mothers who had traveled from out of state to relinquish. Among those 71 cases, only 7 fathers asserted their rights, something adoption advocates in Utah claim is due to lack of interest but critics say should be attributed to Utah's labyrinthine legal process and adoption agencies' deception. Some agencies brazenly admit to the deception, as one advertised an available infant with the notice: "Agency will not be getting a consent from the birth father. The Utah Birthfather Registry can be used specifically for families finalizing the adoption in Utah."

The mounting number of controversies that have arisen in recent years led a Utah state lawmaker, Democratic Representative Christine Watkins, to propose two bills in 2012, providing that pregnant women or recent mothers intending to relinquish infants younger than six months old must give explicit notice to the expectant fathers and that adoption agencies that make fraudulent representations related to adoption be sanctioned.

Utah, however, isn't the only state that tries to disenfranchise birthfathers. At the tail end of 2000 a Midwestern nurse and grandmother who asked to be identified as "Ann Gregory" (not her real name) fought doggedly for her son, "Colin," a Navy enlistee, to retain parental rights over the baby boy he had had with his girlfriend, "Kara," the daughter of conservative evangelical parents. When Kara became pregnant her parents brought her to a local CPC affiliated with their megachurch and tightly connected to an adoption agency. The agency told Kara not to talk to the Gregory family or Colin, that they would handle them. That they did, contacting Colin, who was splitting his time between home and boot camp, and pressuring him to "be supportive" of his girlfriend by signing adoption papers and to make out extensive budgets to demonstrate his inability to support a family. "They said if he didn't sign papers to give the baby up for adoption," Gregory remembered, "it would mean that he wasn't being supportive of [Kara]. They said they'd fight him in court, and made him feel this was cruel to [his girlfriend]."

Documents on the agency's website, which Gregory has asked I not name to protect the privacy of her grandson, explain its status as a long-time "sister organization" to the CPC Kara visited, partnering directly with them for eighteen years before becoming an independent agency. At the time the CPC was in the same office as the adoption agency, sharing an address but with two separate phone numbers. It offered its services to help "work with" women whose partners were not supportive of adoption, and it provided free legal counsel to women who relinquish for adoption through the agency's lawyer.

Gregory was surprised that the agency's budget worksheets didn't account for possible family help and was wary when they called her and her ex-husband, Colin's father, to say that the young parents were "angels" for relinquishing their child to make another family happy, quoting scripture about how "we're all adopted children of Jesus Christ." Gregory told her son, "It's not your job to be some stranger's angel." She then promised both the couple and Kara's parents that she would provide child care so neither of the young parents would miss out on college or normal life. "We weren't thrilled about the pregnancy," said Gregory, "but in our family you express your anger for fifteen minutes if you need to, then pick up the pieces and move on. We didn't see it as a disaster."

What followed instead, Gregory said, was "six weeks of pure hell," as she watched her son and his girlfriend being "brainwashed" into adoption as the agency simultaneously sought to shut the Gregory family out of the decision-making process. "It felt like we were being robbed," she said. Gregory began researching coercive adoption practices online, corresponding with birthmothers who had encountered similar CPC tactics in the past. "I had these fifty mothers who'd lost children to adoption saying, don't let them do it." After hearing the mothers' stories, she and her ex-husband retained a lawyer for their son; the lawyer told them that she received multiple calls each week about exactly these sorts of stories.

When Kara delivered, during a week Colin was in Chicago, the attorney had Gregory notify a hospital social worker that parental rights were being contested to keep the baby from being relinquished, because in adoption, as critics point out, possession often ends up being nine-tenths of the law. Two days later, as the adoption agency was en route to take custody, Gregory filed an emergency restraining order. The matter had to be settled in court. The legal bill for two weeks came to $9,000—an impossible amount for many birthparents.

Kara went to college, and though she and Colin's relationship didn't weather the strain of the dispute, Gregory praises their cooperation in jointly raising their son, now eleven years old. But Gregory is still shaken by the experience and what it took to prevail. "You've got to get on it before the child is born, and you'd better have around $10,000 sitting around."

"They brainwash these kids. Other than their age and the fact that they weren't settled, there was no reason that these kids had to lose their child. They had resources and weren't going to fall through the cracks," said Gregory. "I can't even imagine how they treat those in a worse position than us. . . . They say they want to help people in a crisis pregnancy, but really, they want to help themselves to a baby."

FOR CLOSE TO A DECADE Reanne Mosley's mother avoided conversations about New Beginnings, motivated, Reanne thinks, both by regret over her involvement in sending Reanne there in the first place and pain over the loss of her grandson Jason. In November 2009, however, Reanne's mother attempted to contact the Butlers to get news about Jason, but after being quizzed on her beliefs about the biblical basis for adoption, Reanne said they shut her out too.

For their part the Butlers' deepening commitment to adoption led them overseas to Ethiopia, where three of their seven adoptees (among nine children in total) were born. Reanne said the children are home-schooled, and she has found pictures of them online among Jeff Butler's frequent writings on adoption, standing in large groups and holding signs that declare a theological message: "We are all adopted."

The Butlers' large family and escalating enthusiasm for adoption fit a pattern. After Reanne's time at New Beginnings the founders of the maternity home, Miles and Debi Musick, created a partner organization, Youth With A Mission's Adoption Ministry. Through its "Ethiopia project" YWAM collaborates with four orphanages and a US adoption agency to provide Ethiopian children for US Christian adoptive parents and chronicles its work on a ministry blog titled "That We Might Be Adopted." Joy Casey, the wife of Dennis Casey, the attorney who facilitated Reanne's adoption, is ministry director for the Ethiopia project and, in 2012, called for missionaries to travel to Ethiopia and conduct "intercessory prayer" on behalf of Ethiopian adoptions. Jeff Butler himself became program director for yet another spinoff organization, YWAM's Adoption Ministry 1:27, an offshoot that, ironically, augments YWAM's adoption focus by supporting local Ethiopian families so they aren't compelled to give up their children for adoption.

Jeff Butler's involvement in such an organization seemed like a dramatic philosophical shift from the model of adoption that had separated Reanne from her son. Reanne herself doesn't know what to make of it, whether "they're doing this, keeping families together, as some kind of atonement." In the meantime the Adoption Ministry has also recently begun Ethiopia's first and only crisis pregnancy center and maternity home, Living Hope, to help begin an antiabortion movement in the country and, likely, more adoptions to come.

Although Reanne was a new Christian during her time at New Beginnings, her faith deepened over the years, and despite the fact that religion was once used to convince her to relinquish her child, she has also found in it a justification for her continuing fight. Once, when her daughter, Reanne's first child with her husband, was young, the family went to a revival meeting held by an evangelist who does prophesy: "hearing a word" from God about people in his audience. Reanne's daughter was invited on stage, then the evangelist called for her mother. Reanne walked up and the man asked her, in front of a crowd of hundreds, whether she had lost a child before. On a CD recording of the event that she played for me in her driveway in Temecula, looking past the streets stacked with development houses to the Santa Ana Mountains rising like a distant blue wall, a barely audible Reanne whispered something about adoption.

"So you're the one God is speaking about tonight," said the evangelist. "Well, you're going to leave this building tonight and you're going to lose something: you're going to lose that guilt, that lie from the devil. That child was taken from you." Reanne started to cry heavily on stage. The prophet continued, "They said you weren't good enough. This is what religion has done over and over. But this is what I hear from God: you are a qualified supermother. And you and your children shall chase, chase, till the point where the law will change."

CHAPTER 4

Inside the Boom

Youth With A Mission and the Butlers weren't the only ones who had come to Ethiopia to adopt. In 2007, in a rural hamlet outside Ethiopia's southern Kembata region, an American woman named Michelle Gardner led a mass interview with village families, announcing through an interpreter that those who wanted their children to go to America should stand to one side. "If you want your children to be adopted by a family in America, you may stay," said Gardner, a middle-aged woman with glasses and short blonde hair, to a crowded circle of Ethiopian families. "If you do not want your child to go to America, you should take your child away."

Gardner, a Washington mother of twelve, including nine adoptees— six from Ethiopia—is founder of a Christian adoption grant-making group called Kingdom Kids Adoption Ministries. But that day she was working on behalf of a US adoption agency, Christian World Adoption (CWA), which proclaims in its slogan, "We believe that God is in control of our agency & your adoption." The interview process was filmed as part of a larger "DVD catalogue" of potential adoptees that the agency would send to prospective US adoptive parents. In the video Gardner sits with family after family, coaxing toddlers sitting on their mothers' laps into smiles and describing in English the children's medical and family situations while the Ethiopian adults wait silently in smiling incomprehension.

The video became infamous in 2009, when it was incorporated into an Australian Broadcasting Corporation exposé, *Fly Away Children*, that accused CWA of engaging in what some government officials and child protection experts in Ethiopia have come to call "child harvesting." It's an unsettling term for adoption agencies' common practice of recruiting children for intercountry adoption from intact families, often in rural areas and sometimes by exploiting parents' lack of familiarity with adoption.

The videos were a common practice at CWA, which regularly had its visiting staff record footage of older children to share with potential clients online. Although critics disparaged the practice as a "cattle call," crassly marketing children as merchandise, agencies responded that it was the only way they could process the many children in need and the only way Western adopters could meet a particular child, fall in love, and bring them home.

AMONG THE VIDEOS CWA made was one of a seven-year-old girl named Tarikuwa Lemma, and her two sisters, six-year old Meya (originally named Yemisrach) and four-year-old Maree (formerly Tseganesh). The sisters grew up in Wolaita Sodo, or Sodo, one of the larger towns in Ethiopia's Southern Nations, Nationalities and People's Region (SNNPR), a lush agricultural state bisected by the Rift Valley where a large proportion of Ethiopian adoptees come from.

In the video, narrated by Gardner, the girls sit on a couch covered in striped cloth at Children's Cross Connection (CCC), a Christian organization that ran an orphanage in Sodo that partnered exclusively with CWA, meaning that CWA supported CCC, and CCC provided the agency with adoptable children like the Lemma girls. From the striped couch, Tarikuwa, in a faded turquoise shirt, looks at the camera with a slightly confused but willing smile. Next to her is Maree, tiny in a dusty pink jacket, and at the far end of the couch, Meya, smiling with braids coiled on her head. The girls look around as they're filmed, responding to cues off camera, singing when prompted.

In 2006 a US military couple in New Mexico, Katie and Calvin Bradshaw, watched the video. They say they were told that the sisters' mother had died of AIDS, that their widower father was also HIV-positive and dying, and that they had no other siblings save an older brother who could not care for them. Unless they were adopted, the video warned, "a life of prostitution is all but assured."

In reality, although the girls' mother had died in childbirth years earlier, their father, Lemma Debissa (in Ethiopia, a father's first name becomes his children's surname) was completely healthy and employed as a government clerk, and the sisters had four older siblings, variously working as teachers or still attending high school and college. Additionally, the girls were nowhere near as young as CWA had claimed. Tarikuwa, who had been described as either seven or nine, was actually thirteen; six-year-old Meya was really eleven; and four-year-old Maree was six.

The girls were videotaped receiving gifts and photos from the Bradshaws, their future adoptive family, although they didn't understand that at the time. "There's a picture of us looking at Katie and Calvin," Tarikuwa later told me. "Someone shouted smile and took a picture of us. They didn't tell us who the people were or that they were going to be our new adoptive parents." Instead, the girls say, they and their family were told that after they completed an education in the United States, they could return to Ethiopia—perhaps in just a few years.

A few weeks later the girls were transferred to the agency's home in Addis Ababa, where they were unknowingly awaiting the finalization of their adoption. For three days, Tarikuwa remembers, a woman came to the gate crying. The guards wouldn't explain to the children why she was there, but Tarikuwa said that among the kids in the home was the woman's young son, who watched, stricken, as the guards yelled at the woman, telling her that it was too late to get her child back.

In mid-August 2006 they were taken to the Addis Ababa Hilton Hotel to meet Katie Bradshaw, and they were surprised when Katie told them they had new names: Maree, Meya, and Journee (for Tarikuwa, who has since reverted to her Ethiopian name). After they flew to America they were surprised again when Katie introduced the girls to her husband, Calvin, and told them to call him "Dad." Several weeks later, when Tarikuwa asked when they would be going back to Ethiopia, the Bradshaws sat them down to explain that they wouldn't, that adoption was forever.

MANY ADOPTIVE PARENTS flocking to international adoption were responding to the crowded field of US domestic infant adoption, with more prospective parents than relinquishing mothers. The depressing ratio of would-be parents to available infants drove some parents. In the late 1980s the National Committee for Adoption (which would become the National Council for Adoption) estimated that there was a hundred-to-one ratio of parents who wished to adopt and healthy children available for them. Some were repelled by the growth of open adoption, where they had to advertise themselves to potential birthmothers, were left vulnerable to mothers changing their minds, and often had to promise more ongoing contact than they preferred. By comparison, in international adoption the chance of birthparents reappearing was virtually nil. And adopting a child from a third world country made adoption seem like more than just a way to build a family; it was also a humanitarian cause.

As demand rose for overseas adoptions, a number of popular "sending countries" or "source countries" emerged, and in waves hundreds of children began to arrive from South Korea, Romania, Russia, China, Vietnam, and Guatemala. Many countries' adoption programs ballooned quickly, rising in just a few years from a handful of annual adoptions to hundreds or even thousands—sudden increases often indicative of behind-the-scenes corruption. International adoptions are often slightly more expensive than domestic adoptions, and although the sums aren't delivered directly to any one orphanage, the cut that does go to various middlemen is worth far more in developing nations than it is to the adoptive parents writing the check, creating a powerful incentive for adoption workers to find children who match the desires of Western families: most often babies or small children, with a high premium on girls. When a country emerges that can supply numerous healthy, young children through a relatively quick and uncomplicated process, an influx of adoption agencies is usually close behind. As a result, in recent years international adoption has become an ever-quickening boom-bust spiral. "Corruption skips from one unprepared country to the another—until that country gets wise, changes its laws, and corrupt adoptions shift to the next unprepared nation," wrote journalist E. J. Graff, who researched international adoption corruption for several years at the Schuster Institute for Investigative Journalism at Brandeis University. The corruption goes unnoticed, Graff continued, because "American perception and policy about orphans have been distorted by a fundamental myth"—that is, the myth of the orphan crisis. The belief that developing nations are full of healthy babies waiting for Western homes also assures aspiring American parents that their desire for a family is likewise an act of charity.

When these prospective adoptive couples then approach adoption agencies, their initial application paperwork includes a checklist asking them to indicate the sort of child they are willing to accept, specifying age, gender, and levels of illness or disability. These checklists, made by individual parents assessing their own desires and capacities, became, in effect, "wish lists." Collectively, they form a wave of demand, most often for healthy baby girls. Although adoptive parents' role in this market chain is rarely intentional—as one adoptive mother reflected, "Everyone has their own personal reasons why they need an infant girl under two"—on the other side of the world those wish lists can read like a stack of orders, which adoption brokers emerge to fill.

A lot of times adoption demand creates an adoption underworld, where children are procured from parents, sometimes with small payments and sometimes through coercion or deception. In Vietnam, for instance, adoption facilitators reportedly used poor families' hospital bills as leverage to get new parents, many of them illiterate, to sign over their babies; often these parents did not understand that they wouldn't see their child again. In Cambodia, after adoptions were suspended, the number of infants in orphanages plummeted almost immediately: an indication to adoption reformers that the international adoption system and the revenue it generated was the only reason many babies had been placed in institutions. Yet Western parents continue to display an incredible willingness to believe the stories of their children's provenance, despite the fact that so many read as remarkably the same: hundreds of children allegedly left on police station doorsteps, swaddled in blankets and waiting to be found—a modern-day version of Moses's basket among the reeds. In reality, the abandonment of babies is not such a common occurrence. But among Christian adopters lining up, the stories usually go unchallenged.

In other cases the coercion is less a matter of payments than brokers fostering false impressions. The Western understanding of adoption, as a total transfer of parental rights, is not a universal concept, and in many developing nations the closest analogues are traditional systems of temporary care, in which children stay with family members after a parent dies or are sent to richer acquaintances as a means of furthering their education and prospects. When international adopters come to regions that have only ever experienced these traditional forms of adoption, relinquishing parents often mistake the new adoption process for a chance for their children to get educated abroad and return better able to help the family or as a way for the family to make a connection with potential financial sponsors in the United States.

In some of the worst cases there has been outright kidnapping. Guatemala became one of the most notorious examples of adoption corruption, leading the country to close its adoption program in 2008 after a diverse array of abuses that included reports of missing children. Guatemala had a uniquely privatized system, run by unregulated independent adoption lawyers working for some two hundred US agencies. At the height of Guatemalan adoptions, in 2007, nearly 5,000 children came to the United States—up from 257 in 1990 and amounting to nearly 1 in every 100 children born being sent to America. Most were infants. Among the adoptions were some in which mothers were paid for their babies—creating a system in which some poor women became pregnant explicitly to relinquish—and others in which mothers had been pressured socially or financially. As journalist Erin Siegal painstakingly documented in her 2011 book, *Finding Fernanda: Two Mothers, One Child, and a Cross-Border Search for Truth,* some baby brokers even employed violence and kidnapping to protect what had become, in very real ways, their business.

The tactics grew so abusive that they amounted to what historian Karen Dubinsky calls "a culture of 'missingness,'" in which the local population sometimes imagined the worst, spreading a macabre rumor frequently repeated in other adoption-boom countries: that adopted children were really being sold to organ harvesters. The rate of children leaving the country inspired a violent backlash, with residents in remote villages twice attacking outsiders who were suspected of or mistakenly thought to be recruiting children for adoption. All the while adoption lawyers and advocates defended the system as rescuing children from near-certain death, and adoptive parents continued signing up by the thousands, even after the US Embassy warned that the program was imploding.

In 2008 Guatemala's adoption boom went bust, and the country closed to address systemic adoption corruption and implement the Hague Convention on Intercountry Adoption. But soon enough, adoption scholars say, a new market was found, in Ethiopia, which agencies suddenly began to trumpet as home to five or six million orphans in need.

WHEN ADOPTION BEGAN to pick up in Ethiopia, it was not party to the Hague Convention either. In spite of this—or perhaps because of it—adoption rates rose from 82 children adopted to the United States in 1997 to 2,511 in 2010—nearly a quarter of all US international adoptions that year. And Americans weren't the only ones adopting. Ethiopia sent a total of around 4,500 children abroad each year in both 2009 and 2010. It was so rapid a rise that some locals, like radio host Ellene Moria, lamented that children were "becoming the new export industry for our country." By 2010 adoption advocates began to predict that Ethiopia would overtake China as the top sending country in the world.

"There were many factors to having such a surge in such a short time," said Mehari Maru, an Ethiopian human rights lawyer whom the Ethiopian government invited to craft an institutional adoption framework. Ethiopia did have large numbers of children who had lost a parent to HIV/AIDS as well as a significant population of street children. Further, its popularity rose as traditional source countries like Guatemala, China, Romania, and Russia were all slowing or shutting down. Another factor, Maru said, was the wide range of actors involved in the local adoption support industry—from those caring for the child at the local level to hotels catering to adoptive parents, and taxi drivers hired to guide them—who began to find a steady stream of income related to adoption.

The exponential growth in Ethiopia corresponded almost perfectly with the closure of Guatemala, said Karen Smith Rotabi, an intercountry adoption scholar at the Virginia Commonwealth University. In fact, some agencies accused of deeply unethical behavior in Guatemala are widely thought to have moved their operations to Ethiopia. For some of these agencies, which were dependent on new adoption fees to stay afloat, Smith Rotabi wrote, "a shift to Ethiopia was the only way for the agency to remain fiscally solvent." For other agencies denied Hague accreditation—a prerequisite for those that conduct adoptions from any Hague-approved country—the fact that Ethiopia wasn't a Hague signatory meant it was on the shrinking list of countries where the agencies could still do business. These factors, together with Ethiopia's easy regulations and high availability of young children, conspired to create what Smith Rotabi calls "a perfect storm for an emerging adoption industry."

Agencies weren't the only ones benefiting. In addition to agency support of orphanages and the trickle-down business for industries serving adoptive parents while they were in the country, the Ethiopian government mandated that adoption agencies make humanitarian aid commitments as a price for doing business, meaning that any agencies performing adoption services for Ethiopian children must also make a separate charitable contribution to the nation, often by supporting the construction of new infrastructure or institutions such as hospitals or schools. A 2010 survey by the adoption reform group Ethica estimated that US agencies licensed in Ethiopia were sending the country approximately $3.7 million in annual humanitarian aid.

With so many incentives to support the adoption business, what followed was predictable. Adoption agencies entered en masse with a seemingly unlimited amount of money, and they started working with existing orphanages or new start-ups to identify children who could go overseas for adoption.

"When Ethiopia started getting popular and opening orphanages and making deals with adoption agencies," America World Adoption head Brian Luwis told me, a class of child finders rose up to work on a per-child basis. "A lot of people said, 'If you give me $5,000, I'll get you a child.' So [agencies] paid a fixed fee [to adoption facilitators], and there was no staff maintained. Unfortunately, with that kind of system, when supply gets low, they have tended to go get children."

What that leads to, said Niels Hoogeveen, spokesperson for the adoption watchdog website Pound Pup Legacy, is nearly automatic corruption. "Imagine what that sum of money does in a country like Ethiopia, where people make $300 to $500 a year. All of a sudden, someone receives $5,000. That's ten annual incomes. Nearly everyone is corrupt for ten incomes."

Added to these incentives for corruption, Ethiopia's legal system simply wasn't up to the task of regulating the new influx of adoption cases. This has been the case in most countries where international adoption takes off, given that countries where parents can't afford to care for their children are often also countries that can't afford to run a comprehensive legal system. "My thesis is simple," Maru said. "Adoption increases partly because you have an institutional framework that allows for the proliferation of agencies without any strict oversight." By 2011 Ethiopia had accredited twenty-two US agencies to work in the country. But thanks to an "umbrella" process, in which agencies that had accreditation processed adoptions for those that did not, there were in fact more than seventy agencies in total performing Ethiopian adoptions.

It wasn't just Ethiopia. From 2003 to 2010, a report from the African Child Policy Forum found, adoptions from Africa increased threefold; around 33,500 children were adopted from various African countries between 2004 and 2010. "Commercial interests have superseded altruism, turning children into commodities," the ACPF wrote as they introduced their 2012 report, "Africa: The New Frontier for Intercountry Adoption."

But Ethiopia became the chief country of interest, with twenty-two thousand of that 33,500 coming from Ethiopia alone. There were a lot of reasons for that, from Angelina Jolie's high-profile 2005 adoption of her Ethiopian daughter, Zahara, to Melissa Fay Greene's 2006 best-seller about the country, *There Is No Me Without You: One Woman's Odyssey to Rescue Africa's Children,** and the fact that in 2010 thousands of parents eager to adopt from Haiti were diverted to Ethiopia instead. Some attributed the popularity of the country in part to unacknowledged colorism, a

---

*The book's subtitle was slightly changed for publication of the paperback to *One Woman's Odyssey to Rescue Her Country's Children.*

preference for lighter-skinned black children from a country that has sometimes held itself separate from the rest of Africa.

Adoption champion Senator Mary Landrieu had a simpler explanation, crowing to an audience at an Ethiopian orphanage in September 2010 that "people in America are falling in love with Ethiopian children. . . . They love them. It's very simple. They think they're beautiful and smart." And with demand so high, even older children were recruited for export.

KATIE AND CALVIN BRADSHAW had always wanted a large family, but after giving birth to their first two children, Katie suffered pregnancy complications. They were already an interracial family—Katie is white, Calvin is black—so they decided to look at Ethiopia, where adoption agencies said there were millions of orphans in need of homes. Because they had already raised their biological children from infancy and knew that children over five are less likely to be adopted, they said they were open to adopting older kids.

Michelle Gardner, acting as case manager for Christian World Adoption, returned with a referral for the Lemma girls, highlighting the fact that adoption fees at CWA are discounted for children over four and for adopting multiple children at once. The Bradshaws accepted the referral within twenty-four hours.

Katie was only twenty-six at the time, and although she had only parented children up to the age of three, adding an oldest daughter of seven—and not the thirteen that Tarikuwa really was—had seemed feasible. "I kept looking at the pictures thinking, you know, they look older. And so I would call Michelle Gardner and she would say, 'Oh no, Katie, I've met them several times . . . and she can't be older than nine.' She said the pictures are deceiving, and she's really a very, very small girl."

Gardner wasn't just any case manager. In addition to her adoption fundraising ministry, Kingdom Kids, she was one of the earliest leaders in the Christian adoption movement. In 2003 she had published her book, *Adoption as a Ministry, Adoption as a Blessing*, in which she described how she and her husband, longtime missionaries in Taiwan, began adopting special-needs children from China, India, and Russia in the 1990s, using CWA's services for at least one of the adoptions. She promoted adoption as "a ministry that has been largely overlooked by the body of Christ" and made early recommendations for ideas like church-based loans for adopting families. Like movement leaders who would come later, Gardner warned that merely sponsoring a child living in poverty wouldn't help his spiritual needs. "We have the opportunity to introduce children from other countries to the truth of the Gospel," she wrote, and she described how she hoped her own internationally adopted children would return to their home countries as adults to evangelize.

Interestingly, Gardner's book also predicted some of the pitfalls of the movement and warned parents not to approach the children they were adopting as though they were rescuing them. "No one, least of all a vulnerable child, wants to feel like he is being rescued." But Gardner's approach seems to have changed by the time she began working for CWA, and the video child-listings that Gardner created in Ethiopia were crafted to tug on parents' heartstrings. In 2004 she adopted her first two children from Ethiopia, and then helped CWA become licensed to conduct adoptions from Ethiopia's southern states. For two and a half years Gardner was the agency's coordinator for older-child adoptions, during which time she interviewed children for the videos. "I think the Christian church kind of encourages this behavior that's like a savior complex, and I think that this is one way of filling that—that need to be a savior," said Katie today.

In mid-August 2006, half a year after getting the referral, Katie was scheduled to travel to Ethiopia to pick up the Lemma girls. She would be traveling at the same time as Michelle Gardner, who was adopting three more Ethiopian children herself. A week before the trip Katie went to Spokane, Washington, to participate in CWA's mandatory older-child adoption training, conducted through Gardner's Kingdom Kids. While she was there Gardner handed her paperwork stating a different cause of death for the girls' mother, explaining she had died in childbirth, not from AIDS as they had originally been told.

The Bradshaws were confused. A month earlier she said they had been informed that the children were now legally their responsibility, and if they didn't pick them up in Ethiopia, they would be liable for child support until the children turned eighteen. Katie and Calvin told themselves that the paperwork was mistaken—possibly a misprint, because so many other details, like the spellings of names, also kept changing. Katie went to Ethiopia, and a week later was standing with Michelle Gardner and Gardner's husband in the lobby of the very Western Addis Ababa Hilton Hotel when a CWA agency worker brought her new daughters in. "I was in shock," said Katie, "because they were so big. They were so much older than I was prepared for." At thirteen, Tarikuwa was half Katie's age—a child she barely could have given birth to herself. The girls seemed uncomfortable but were polite and affectionate. They hugged her, called her mom, and told her they loved her—all things they had been told to do. "It was this very rehearsed exchange of pretend emotions," said Katie.

Katie brought them upstairs to change into the new clothes that CWA had suggested she bring as a treat, and she was surprised that the girls, allegedly destitute, came with their own backpacks of extra shoes and outfits (which an agency worker told Katie to give to him). The girls, meanwhile, repeated one of the only words they knew in English, "Photos, photos" while pointing to the TV. Also in the backpacks was a photo album and a videocassette, showing the girls amid a crowded house of family and friends. "That's when reality hit me," said Katie. "They have this huge family. It had to be over a hundred people: godmothers, aunts. That's when I realized that we had gotten scammed and that they weren't orphans." There had been earlier signs that all wasn't right, Katie said, but this was the moment she began to realize she had, from the beginning, been a victim of what she's come to call "faith manipulation."

Katie went to Gardner's room to ask what was going on, and she said Gardner responded by offering to "hold on to the photo album for me." In shock, Katie handed it over. Later that night Katie went and got the album back and tried to figure out what to do—alone and young in a foreign city, with children she thought should go home to their family but whom she had been warned were now her legal charge. When she spoke to another CWA employee who said he was a friend of the girls' father, Lemma Debissa, he became offended when Katie mentioned Debissa's alleged HIV status, accusing her of slandering an honorable man.

Today, she believes she should have hired a driver to make the six-hour trip to Sodo to find Debissa and straighten things out. But at the time she was cowed by CWA's and Gardner's forceful warnings that such a meeting could cause problems for future adoptive parents and could traumatize the girls, who had already said their goodbyes.

When Bradshaw and the girls got to the United States, an Ethiopian friend of the family helped Katie and Calvin call Debissa to find out the truth. He emphatically denied he was HIV-positive and told the couple he had sent his girls to America to get an education. "That's when we found out what this was. He was told that it was basically a foreign-exchange program. And he wasn't sick. And we had just mortgaged our house and cashed out our IRAs to give his kids an education," said Bradshaw. "I felt like such a fool. I had told everyone they're HIV orphans. How was I going to explain that this wasn't even a legitimate adoption?"

What was worse was the girls' reaction to the news. Meya charged that CWA had "bought" them from their father. Tarikuwa exploded, saying she had been told she was coming to the United States for an education and demanded to be taken back home. When lawyers told the Bradshaws that that couldn't be done, thirteen-year-old Tarikuwa—who, on top of everything, was enrolled in the fourth grade because her paperwork made her legally only nine—fell into a grief that didn't recede. "Her meltdowns were so aggressive and powerful," Katie recalls. "She was grieving so painfully and so deeply, we didn't know if she was going to survive."

The Bradshaws' confrontation with CWA was almost as upsetting. When the Bradshaws told the agency that they thought the adoption should be canceled and the girls returned home to their Ethiopian family, CWA responded with surprising disregard. When Katie requested help from CWA's postadoption support services when Tarikuwa was going through a crisis, she went days without hearing back from a counselor; when she finally did, she was told she needed to pray and give her burdens over to God. When Katie posted her complaints to a private web forum for CWA clients shortly after she returned from Ethiopia, warning other clients not to believe the stories they were told, she was kicked off for bad behavior and said the Gardners called to yell at her.

In October 2006 CWA's Complaint Review Committee chairperson, Carol Nelson, responded to Katie with palpable condescension, writing, "Bottom line, you seem to be extremely unhappy and angry about the choices you made, and I honestly do not know how an apology can change that."

Nelson continued disdainfully, "From your letter it clearly sounds as though you were hoping for children from dirt floor, straw-roof-hut and were angry to learn this was not the case at all. You state it is not the father's fault. Please remember it is not your children's fault that they do not fit the image you created for them in your mind." She closed with a word of advice: "If you truly trust God and know that He led you to adopt, it is safe to believe He has a greater plan for you than what you currently can see." In a brief letter the next month CWA's founder and CFO Robert Harding told her that the case details didn't support Katie's complaints and wrote, "May God help you find peace."

Katie's continued calls to CWA were never returned. (CWA did not agree to my requests for an interview either and cited legal restrictions on their ability to discuss individual adoptions.) So in May 2007 Katie reported them to the Better Business Bureau of Western North Carolina, where CWA is based. In CWA's response to the Bureau that month, written by then-Assistant Executive Director Anita Thomas—now the agency's CEO—the agency maintained that they had not intentionally been dishonest and that the age discrepancy was solely a product of Ethiopians not having any idea what their birthdays are, as "This information is not relevant to them as a society." They further argued that they could not find any record of CWA telling the Bradshaws that Lemma Debissa was HIV-positive and dismissed her concerns that the family was intact by stating that the father's Ethiopian salary of $58 per month was "well below any acceptable standard of living here in the U.S."

Thomas concluded her letter to the Better Business Bureau with the notice that CWA was reporting the Bradshaws to their social worker and New Mexico's child protective services, advising them to look into the safety of all the Bradshaws' children, including their biological toddlers, "as we are concerned as to their well being as it is obvious there is no attachment on the part of Mrs. Bradshaw to her children."

It wasn't the first time that adoption agencies have responded to criticism by reporting complaining adoptive parents to CPS, but the Bradshaws were horrified, and Katie considered fleeing to Mexico with her biological children. "The night I got that in the mail was the most horrible moment of my life," she said. "We tried to help some kids and in return I could have my children taken away."

The Bradshaws' social worker was understanding, said Katie, and explained to the CPS department that the family's adoption agency was acting in retaliation. But the experience left the Bradshaws extremely anxious about how far the agency would go to protect their own side of the story. After *CBS News* began to investigate CWA and the Bradshaws' story in 2010, the family received a suspicious letter from Lemma Debissa, denying that he had ever received money for the children and telling them, "[the] children are yours." The letter was typed while all his previous letters had been handwritten, had unusually poor grammar, and even spelled his own name wrong. The Bradshaws and the girls all suspected that the letter was written by or under the influence of CWA associates in Sodo.

After the 2009 airing of the Australian exposé *Fly Away Children* showed Michelle Gardner recruiting children near Kembata, CWA attempted to distance themselves from her, claiming she was not a CWA employee. However, Gardner herself said she was in a public statement, and her name was listed on all of the Bradshaws' agency paperwork.

After the follow-up *CBS News* story came out in 2010, introducing the Bradshaws' experience, CWA responded by denying that the agency had ever had any contact with Debissa. They further argued that the process of relinquishment in Ethiopian law—that children must be vetted at three levels of government—would not allow any fraudulent cases to slip through. However, many experts on Ethiopia's adoption system contend that most fraud and corruption occurs at the local level, when false paperwork is first created. After *Fly Away Children* was released, CWA suggested that they were being targeted for their Christian faith, as "The entire film had a very anti-Christian stance," and that foreign countries only opposed international adoption out of a sense of misplaced nationalism and their embarrassment at being unable to provide for their own children. Finally, CWA lashed out against parents who had gone to the media, accusing them of risking the lives of Ethiopian street children who now might die before they were adopted. "This desperate country has an estimated 6,000,000 orphans of whom only .03% per year will be adopted into the United States. This means that for every child chosen for adoption there is a pool of approximately 3,000 legitimate candidates from whom to choose," a CWA statement protested. "There is never a justification for paying a parent to surrender a child, but in Ethiopia there is also no motive to do so. The sad fact is there is no lack of children in Ethiopia needing homes, and no motive to 'buy' them."

Nonetheless, the stories had their impact. In Australia the news helped lead to a temporary suspension of adoptions from Ethiopia, as the attorney general worried that corruption in Ethiopia ran counter to Australia's Hague Convention obligations. In 2012 Australia's government stopped allowing Ethiopian adoptions altogether, stating that an environment of "increased competition" between adoption agencies jostling to get more child referrals "makes it difficult for Australia's Program to continue to operate in a sustainable and ethical manner."

Conversely, in the United States the adoption lobby group the Joint Council of International Children's Services (JCICS) launched a probe of Ethiopian adoptions after the bad press on CWA but later refused to release its findings. CWA was a long-standing member of JCICS, and the agency's then-executive director, Tomilee Harding, was JCICS's onetime president.

Gardner, who resigned from CWA in 2007, before the videos ever became news, complained in an open letter posted online that she felt she had been made a scapegoat. She denied that it had been her responsibility to check children's backgrounds or medical conditions and wrote that "I also tried to be very clear with any relatives or guardians of the children that adoption is permanent, that the children would join a new family and have new parents, that the children would become American citizens and therefore would probably spend their lives in America. I told them that if they made a decision for a child to be adopted they would probably never see that child again."

Yet to *CBS News,* she acknowledged, "I was aware of a number of times when things were problematic. . . . And several families where children came over and the children didn't understand that the adoption was permanent."

NEITHER TARIKUWA, her sisters, nor their family understood what adoption was, said Aynelum Lemma, the girls' older sister, when I met her in Sodo in 2011. At the time Aynelum, a teacher in a local school, lived in the home they all grew up in with one of her remaining two sisters and their brother, a gracious group of young adults keeping the house together while their father's government job took him to a neighboring town for weeks at a time.

The city of Sodo, nestled below the fog-covered hills of the SNNPR, is wide and flat, with low buildings spreading out from a central lot where buses wait, puffing fumes, and throngs of pedestrians and donkeys, burdened with goods, contend with cars on downtown streets. Street children wander, peddling carved wooden sticks sold as toothpicks, sometimes giving a coy smile before shouting *ferengi,* or foreigner—a word that can feel like an endearment or a curse—and unrolling a graceful middle finger.

Tarikuwa and her sisters grew up there, going door to door to sing for neighbors and walking to school. Among the pictures she brought with her to the United States are shots of her and her classmates after choir practice: a group of ten preteen girls, smiling in modern clothes—jeans, T-shirts, capris, and skirts. "We wore the same things there!" Tarikuwa told me defiantly. Many American high schoolers she's encountered, whose only knowledge of Ethiopia was its mid-eighties famine, assume she played with lions and had never seen a car. In two pictures Tarikuwa has, one of Tarikuwa in the United States and one of Aynelum in Sodo, the sisters are unintentionally dressed identically, in gray Aéropostale hoodies with red bandanas over their hair. It's the sort of evidence of modernity that Tarikuwa holds up in the face of the adoption agency claim that Ethiopians don't know their children's ages or their birthdates. Whereas CWA claimed to the Bradshaws that they had had to guess the girls' ages, Tarikuwa said her father had brought their birth certificates the first time they visited the agency.

Indeed, when I met Aynelum at the coffee shop of a small Sodo hotel one day while her father was out of town at work, she knew her sisters' ages well. Aynelum was then twenty-two, a young woman in a green sweatshirt, with neat braids and a delicately pretty but worried face, and an air of seriousness that made her seem far older. She had already been teaching professionally since she was sixteen, and as the oldest daughter in a family where the mother had died, she was the woman of the house. She approached the hotel parking lot from the city street with nervous determination, steeled, she later told my translator, for bad news about Tarikuwa, whom she knew had caused problems in the past.

Staring at her hands as she sat at the table, with a tightly controlled expression, Aynelum explained that, before the adoptions, the family of seven children had been struggling somewhat in the wake of their mother's death. As a government employee, Lemma Debissa was relatively middle class by Ethiopian standards but still not making much. One day the family saw a presentation from Children's Cross Connection, the orphanage organization that partners with CWA, at the local Kale Hiwot, or Word of Life Church. The church worked frequently with CCC, and that day a representative spoke to the congregation about "an opportunity to go abroad for adoption" that was open to children in the region. Seeing it as a great chance for the youngest three daughters, the Lemmas contacted CCC.

Following that, a friend of Debissa's who seemed to be affiliated with CCC started coming to the house. He was rumored to have already put one child in his care up for adoption and to have written the girl demanding she send money from America. Tarikuwa thinks she remembers him talking about how CWA could help their single father with clothing and food. Meya insisted that she saw the friend give her father money—something Aynelum hotly denies. "We didn't receive anything from the organization CCC or any other," she told me. "The church people from CCC would come to Kale Hiwot and share this idea about adoption. We didn't know, and my father didn't know that it was for good. The organization told us that they will come back after getting a good education and a decent life—that even after only three years they might come back."

After the girls left, the phone calls home made it clear what had happened. Aynelum said, "Finally it came to our attention that it was final, that adoption was for good." Her eyes teared and her expression tensed as she recalled how the family learned what adoption really means. "We were very angry, very angry, when we learned that they did this thing against us. We believed it was a good opportunity for the children, not for disclaiming our blood relationship. They are still our sisters, our family members, so when we heard these things, we were really terribly sorry and father was disappointed. If we knew that it was for good, we would not have let them leave this country or our family."

The family is now resigned, Aynelum said, to the permanency of their sisters' adoption, and they're grateful for the Bradshaws, whom Aynelum describes as part of the family. In the Lemmas' house outside the town center—a respectable compound of several small buildings, built in traditional style from wood branches packed with mud, then painted mint green—a corner of the living room wall is dedicated to framed photos of the Lemma sisters and their new family, whom the Lemmas all know by name. "The Bradshaw family is like our family," she said. "They informed us that we are like one family."

Still, when the sisters call from the United States, they can no longer speak the national language of Amharic, and although the families hope the sisters can one day visit, they can't imagine them readjusting to Ethiopian life. "We know it is difficult to live here after being educated in the US," Aynelum said.

Inside their house Aynelum showed me the family's new furniture: a couch and a table, an elaborate Ethiopian coffee service set up on the floor. She hastened to add that they hadn't had all that when the sisters were there, conscious that their lifestyle could be taken the wrong way. She knows that the Bradshaws' adoption caused significant problems, as the family had written CWA to demand how they could separate a family that was happy and had a decent life. And she knows that any indication that the Lemmas are doing well could be taken as proof that they were given money for the girls to be adopted. Once, when a friend of the Bradshaws who frequently visits Ethiopia came to Sodo, the friend reported back that the Lemmas were living a middle-class lifestyle and didn't need any help, causing what the Lemmas feel was "a gap between the two families."

Aynelum said that although some other families in the area that relinquished children for adoption have received gifts and donations from the people who adopted their children, they don't have that kind of relationship with the Bradshaws. "We didn't receive anything small or big," she said, her voice rising slightly, a rare sign of anger in a culture that prizes deference, particularly from women. "The Bradshaws sent us some small things: T-shirts, hair combs, toothpaste, and we are thankful for that." There are other families "who have nothing," she added, "no contact with [the adoptive] parents. They are very angry and disappointed; they are terribly sorry."

Still, the Lemmas' financial situation did cause conflict. After the girls were adopted the Bradshaws began to receive letters from Debissa, asking for financial assistance. They had received his bank routing number previously, when the adoption was finalized, seemingly an indication that he had been told financial support would be forthcoming. Aynelum allows that on one occasion her father had written to the Bradshaws that he was facing government downsizing and asked for financial support, as his children weren't coming back. At the time, she recalls, the Bradshaws responded strongly, explaining that wasn't what adoption is about.

Today, Katie Bradshaw said she no longer finds the requests insulting but rather proof that the family was misled. "I think it's not that he was so desperate that he couldn't provide. But here came CWA, harvesting kids, and offering this promise of America. They were telling him the girls will be able to go to college and send money back and take care of the whole family, and the people in America will help you. I believe in his mind, it was this amazing opportunity."

On the American side, she added, "I think the damage from harvesting is so much greater than the help that's happening. The degree of damage this does to these kids is so severe. There's this mindset that life in America will be better and that they will be happy. But the truth is that nothing replaces family. And their family is in Ethiopia."

"WE CAN'T COMPARE first world families with third world families," Stephne Bowers told me in June 2011. Bowers was then CWA's local associate in Sodo, running three Children's Cross Connection (CCC) orphanages in the SNNPR and living across town from the Lemmas' home in a cottage on the grounds of the Sodo Christian Hospital. She explained that although she cries over the mothers who come to relinquish their babies, her Ethiopian staff assures her the mothers are too broken by poverty to care. "It's not as we understand families," Bowers assured me.

A midforties blonde from South Africa who had lived for years in Zimbabwe, Bowers came to Sodo when her American husband, Harry, was stationed as a medical missionary at in Sodo. Like Michelle Gardner, Bowers and her husband were adoptive parents who had used CWA for their own adoptions from Russia years before. A few short weeks after they arrived in Ethiopia, they spoke with CWA's founders, Robert and Tomilee Harding, and Stephne agreed to oversee their local orphanages, building bridges between CCC's orphanages, CWA, and the local government and community.

She also helped with CWA's PR work, appearing in a 2009 online video with Tomilee Harding to address adoptive parents' complaints that the stories their children told them after they came to the United States were different from the background information CWA had supplied. "We must understand that when children are on that side and on that continent, they are busy surviving," Bowers told a nodding Harding. "They are going to withhold things and hide things that will give them the best opportunities, because that is what you do when you survive, to live, just to stay alive." It's not until children get to the warmth and unconditional love of their adoptive parents' home that they open up and tell different stories, Bowers continued.

"And that's when our phone starts ringing," Harding chimed in. Bowers went on to discount children's claims of having surviving family by arguing that Ethiopians call everyone "brother" and "mother" and that CWA and CCC will nonetheless "triple check, quadruple check" family backgrounds. However, in the same video conversation she also said it was sometimes too dangerous for CWA staff to verify facts about children from rural villages, where "They're not used to white faces."

"There are times that I don't take [my own children] outside the hospital gate because they are thrown with rocks [sic] and I often get yelled at and screamed at and pulled and pushed and pinched," Bowers told Harding. "It's normal for them, they see us as threatening, because here we come in from America, and you know the media has projected America as the saving place, heaven on earth."

In fact, Bowers was coming from South Africa's Afrikaans community, where she was raised before marrying Harry in 1991. And at times it seemed like her Afrikaner roots were showing in some of her assessments of the people CWA served, whom she described as having "low understanding, low education, and low intellect," with some street children "as wild as a little animal" and many mothers allegedly detached from their children: not naming babies immediately after birth or nursing them at arm's length as a self-defense mechanism against high infant mortality. "There's not this snuggly, motherly comforting," she said to me. "That's a taught behavior." Although the last may be a cultural custom, Bowers extrapolated from it a larger picture of poor mothers' lack of attachment to their children. "Survival is in a very different place [here]. I don't think we can in a first world environment understand the concept of survival in this environment because it's so extreme," she continued to me, noting that two women had offered her their children on the street just the day before. "A part of me feels, how is it possible that women can conceive so easily here, when there's such a fertility problem in the US? What I really sense [in Ethiopia] is the lack of understanding the value of children."

By comparison, Bowers finds the adoptive parents who come "such special people. They are tender and soft and understanding, and they come here and it's almost as though the seed was planted and they come and walk in the land and it gets roots. They get the connection of what they're doing and that it has eternal value."

In the five years Bowers worked in Sodo, CCC and CWA had begun a wealth of community outreach programs, from feeding programs administered through local evangelical churches, which give food aid to people who attend a worship service, to medical work, to sponsoring a couple of promising young evangelists at a local Bible college to spread the word about CCC's approach to child care.

"Oh, and by the way, there's adoption," joked Bowers, as she gave me a tour of CWA's temporary Sodo orphanage, a cramped but clean rental facility set among houses on a dirt road but protected by strong concrete walls topped with shattered glass bottles. In rooms divided by age, young women dressed in blue uniforms sat with groups of infants, surrounded by reminders of US supporters: bins stacked high with donated toys, toiletries, and clothes, and a soccer ball sent by one adoptive family, meticulously covered in handwritten scripture verses.

The home housed approximately thirty children, ranging from a few weeks to five years old, all bound for adoption, mostly to the Untied States. But not just then. When I visited in 2011 the SNNPR had been under an administrative freeze on adoption-intake documentation—the process that allows children to be listed as available for adoption—for seven months while the government conducted investigations of all orphanages in the area. Later that year the government shut down a number of orphanages in the region that were said to exist for the purpose of adoption alone—not serving children who would stay in the country—as part of its efforts to regain control of the runaway adoption boom. Although CCC's orphanages were not directly affected, the government's newly assertive role had touched many aspects of life. As I arrived, Bowers told me, Sodo's most local level of bureaucracy, the *kebele*, had just undergone a major turnover "as a result of the tensions and stresses around adoption."

But still, she stressed, adoption wasn't what the organization was about. "Adoption has never been the real motivation for CCC. It has always been community development and care." After the orphanage tour she fed me and my companions a snack of tea and pancakes made from a high-nutrient grain mixture, mitten, which CCC staff produce to feed the children and generate outside income. She said she and other CWA personnel took the media accusations about "child harvesting" deeply to heart for being so misrepresentative of their work.

Bowers claimed that she had never seen the video of Michelle Gardner recruiting children, and that Gardner wasn't CWA staff anyway. There was trafficking among other agencies, Bowers said, though she maintained that her Ethiopian colleagues in CCC deliberately shielded her from knowing too much. "We heard the vehicles go and bring children at night. The staff are so careful with me. . . . I would ask them, is that vehicle doing the right thing, and they would say, 'There are so many children' and draw my attention to something else." Bowers believed her staff downplayed the trafficking out of safety concerns or embarrassment about fellow Ethiopians' choices. But she also sympathized with other agencies' behavior. "We know there were social workers from other agencies who went out into the community and asked if there were children who were orphans. And the government saw that as child harvesting. At the time it was not intended like that. When adoption just boomed, and it became this almost lucrative thing, everyone, all potential social workers, were just absorbed into orphanages," she said. "The social workers hear these numbers: three million, six million, four, five million. Everybody is confused: is this true? Where are these children?"

The whole "adoption thing," she imagines, caught Ethiopia off guard, becoming an embarrassment when people approached it as a way to make money. But the corruption Bowers acknowledged was strictly on the local level—not from the foreign agencies bringing the business to town, but local government officials pressuring her for kickbacks in return for inspecting her orphanages.

Whatever the cause, some adoptions have gone wrong. Biological family members of the children have shown up at the gates of CWA's orphanages crying, Bowers said, upset because they haven't received word from the children who were sent to the United States and looking for "the next letter, photo, birr" (Ethiopian currency). CWA responded by asking adoptive families to stop traveling to the villages their children came from because of the confusion it caused among parents, who gained stature among neighbors from a visit or gifts bestowed by adoptive parents. The impact of those gifts—ranging from token presents to new roofs or money—Bowers said, led other families to place their children for adoption as well, creating a minifad among families who were unaware of adoption's permanence, as was the case when three mothers from the same small community showed up at a CCC orphanage at once, all seeking to relinquish together.

But in 2011 Bowers was focused on moving forward. From her desk at CCC's cramped office, she could see over the compound's walls and shattered glass to the top of a nearby hillside, where CCC and CWA were building a new multipurpose, six thousand–square meter compound, Wolaita Village. Once finished, it would house all of CCC's programs and could potentially separate funding for orphanage work from adoption revenue. "When I sat down here, I felt like Moses, because there is the Promised Land," Bowers said, gazing up at the future construction site, which overlooks all of Sodo. At Wolaita Village a large children's home would be surrounded by money-making ventures: a guest home for adoptive parents or short-term missionaries, a multipurpose conference facility, a factory making mitten, a café serving mitten pancakes and other mitten goods, and a central plaza with a well where community members could wait to be ministered to by CCC staff, just as Jesus ministered to the woman at the well. There would also be a newly constructed manager's home for the Bowers to live in, as they were shortly facing a move off hospital grounds.

But two years after the child harvesting scandal the future of Ethiopian adoption was uncertain. "We don't know the face of adoption. . . . If the support or funding dries up, what then?" she wondered to me.

By late 2011 it was no longer her concern. Bowers and her husband moved to Germany to work as dorm parents in a Christian boarding school. By the time they had to vacate their mission hospital quarters to make room for more doctors, their manager's house had not yet been built, and the plans for Wolaita Village remained stalled.

THE LEMMAS and the Bradshaws were far from the only ones who experienced the ugly side of Ethiopian adoptions. Adoptive parents in the United States registered complaints with the US government and in the media that, when their children learned enough English to communicate with them, they told their adoptive parents that the birth parents whom adoption agencies had said were dead were actually alive, that there were more siblings than the agency had claimed, that mothers said to have conceived from stranger rapes were in fact married to their children's fathers.

Further, mothers in Ethiopia began coming to orphanages or government offices to seek news about their children. Adoptive parents shared stories on online forums about visiting the villages their children were from—sometimes hours away from the orphanages that had helped shepherd their adoptions, indicating that orphanage staff with access to vehicles had likely sought out the families, rather than the reverse. There, the adoptive parents were greeted by numerous families whose children had been adopted, families who were desperate to get word about how the children were doing. Some adoptive parents sought more information about how their children had actually been relinquished, including one woman who found her child's birth family by driving into their town and literally calling out their name. When they found birth families, they often learned that the stories agencies had provided didn't match up with what their children's birth families told them. "It feels terrible," one adoptive mother told me. "Like you stepped on something solid and it turned to quicksand." Another explained, "When you go to adopt, the last thing you imagine is going into some developing country and stealing someone's child."

In videos that agencies supplied to adoptive parents, birthmothers were filmed proudly handing over children they had raised nearly to adolescence, smiling at the camera in a way that made US adopters suspicious that the mothers didn't know what they were doing. One prospective adoptive mother received such a video from her adoption agency, and when she hired a translator to interpret the Amharic conversation the agency had with the mothers of two unrelated children she wanted to adopt, the translator implored the woman not to proceed. "She said 'Please, I beg you, do not go forward with this adoption. The mothers do not understand anything.'" In the video one of the mothers was asked whether she understood what adoption was. She replied no, and the footage stopped. When it came back on, the mother said yes, she understood, and could they excuse her to return to her baking? The US mother withdrew from the adoption but soon after learned that the children were given to another US family instead.

Some adoptive parents who connected with their children's birth family, either to ensure that their adoptions were ethical or so their children retained ties to their homeland and kin, ended up being approached by those families to adopt another child. Such was the case for one family who adopted two biological siblings from the country under what they came to learn were unethical circumstances. Several years later the children's Ethiopian father offered the adoptive parents his two remaining children, placing the US family in the fraught position of either proceeding with an adoption they suspected would be unethical and that they knew was not a case of saving orphans, or letting the children be adopted to another family and thereby miss this second chance to grow up with their US brother and sister.

In a way this no-win situation is the predictable result of the confused idea of the orphan crisis that UNICEF's Susan Bissell described: a complex and persistent development and poverty crisis has been transformed into a crisis solely about the poor's vulnerable or orphaned children. This created a system on both the US and Ethiopian sides that treats adoption as the go-to solution for family crises. Although the Christian movement pledges to bring the "end of orphans in the world," making adoption the answer seems to ensure that the root causes that create "orphans" will go unchanged and that the poor—or at least their children—will always be with us, as families mired in a cycle of devastating poverty, and in the absence of a working child welfare system, continue to relinquish children they still have inadequate means to provide for.

On adoptees' paperwork birth parents were sometimes simultaneously declared dead and unknown—a logical gap that usually went unchallenged as the papers wound their way through Ethiopia's elaborate infrastructure for processing adoptions. This system involved various levels of Ethiopian government required to sign off on different aspects of each case, including federal and regional branches of the Ministry of Women, Children and Youth Affairs (MOWA), the Ministry of Justice, and a Charities and Societies Agency that oversees accreditation for all NGOs, including adoption agencies. "You couldn't design it in a more complicated way if you tried," said Doug Webb, then-chief of section for Adolescent Development, Protection, and HIV/AIDS at UNICEF Ethiopia. But instead of the complex process making the system clearer, in some ways it has compounded the problem, creating new ways for corruption to flourish and fraudulent claims to be rubber stamped and made official long before they ever reach federal courts. "A lot of the arrangements and paperwork that makes things appear differently than they are happens at the local level, out there in the bush with brokers, agents, officials, and policemen," said Webb. "Once the paperwork reaches the federal level, in some cases the opportunity for abuse may have already been taken."

Judge Rahila Abbas, Ethiopia's federal judge in charge of all the country's adoption cases, told Peter Heinlein of *Voice of America* that the court has limited power to tackle corruption when presented with falsified documents that were certified at an earlier stage of the process, leaving the higher branches of government impotent to challenge documents they suspect to be false.

Worse yet, adoptive parents began to hear rumors from contacts in country of "birthing centers," where women were paid to relinquish infants for adoption—catering to parents who want "as tiny a baby as possible," as one hopeful prospective adopter put it on her blog—or that women had relinquished children for adoption in exchange for the promise of work, sometimes at the very child care centers where their babies were being offered for adoption. Some parents who traveled to Ethiopia saw their donated clothes, toys, and diapers sold on the street for profit. In some orphanages, evidence emerged of unqualified staff who were accused of allowing physical and sexual abuse of their children. Other orphanages gave visitors a distinct impression that something wasn't right. One adoptive mother from Virginia told me that when she went to visit an orphanage—later closed amidst allegations that its director had promised birth families that adopters would pay them—the children had stood up and chanted in unison, in English, "We are all fine here."

Around 2008 things started to change, said JoAnna Luks, an adoptive mother with two older Ethiopian children who runs a Yahoo discussion group for parents adopting from Ethiopia. "Some of the agencies were threatening clients who were questioning what was going on, like 'Why is this child you referred to me still living with her birth mother?' Then the agency threatened to take the referral away and give it to someone else. One of my friends had her agency try to make her take a psychological evaluation."

Then, said Luks, came the rules. "There was a new rule that [adoptive parents] weren't allowed to be seen in public with adopted children. There was starting to be an upswell of discontent about how many children were leaving the country. People started to tell stories of having rocks thrown at them or names called. The Hilton and Sheraton started to get reputations as baby hotels, full of white couples with Ethiopian babies."

A number of adoption agencies began requiring adoptive parents to sign waivers acknowledging that the information they received about their children might be inaccurate. Some agencies began requesting that adoptive parents keep an increasingly lower profile: to not travel the country with their newly adopted children and to avoid the Hilton and Sheraton and instead stay in guest houses catering exclusively to adoptive parents.

Bit by bit the stories added up to a compelling body of evidence, and American officials started to put the brakes on Ethiopian adoptions. In March 2010 the US State Department, the body that investigates whether or not children are actually eligible for adoption to the United States as orphans, announced through its embassy in Addis Ababa that it was placing extra reviews on adoptions originating at a particular problem orphanage that fed children into the adoption programs for three top agencies: Bethany Christian Services, Christian World Adoption, and America World Adoption. The US embassy in Addis Ababa had begun looking for patterns in the cases that were coming across their desks: the same social workers or police officers in case after case "finding" children said to be abandoned, or multiple children from a single agency who had similar background stories. It was the only tactic the State Department had at their disposal, as they can only control international adoption corruption by denying entrance visas to the adoptees.

The next month brought word that Ethiopia's government was closing nine orphanages for providing inadequate child care and sending too many children abroad for adoption. By the end of that year Ethiopia announced plans to shutter nearly fifty orphanages and revoke the accreditation of some foreign adoption agencies, and the State Department warned prospective adoptive parents to expect delays and potentially additional requests for proof that their child was an orphan.

ON LISTSERVS dedicated to adopting from Ethiopia, a culture war of its own cropped up in recurring fights between two groups: prospective adoptive parents still in the adoption process, often known by the acronym PAPs, and adoptive parents whose children had already come home—often parents who had encountered signs of corruption. PAPs would enter the listserv asking for advice on what agency they should use and be met with a barrage of warnings from seasoned adoptive parents who advised them to stay away from Ethiopia, which they described as an ethical Russian roulette. They told PAPs that if they were trying to adopt a healthy, infant daughter, they were contributing to trafficking. They asked in frustration how many stories of corruption would it take for PAPs to stop burying their heads in the sand. Some PAPs responded that the older adoptive parents were embittered and had an agenda to stop adoption after they had gotten theirs, charging that the proliferation of stories about corruption would itself shut Ethiopia down.

Other PAPs responded with bewilderment, asking why should all this corruption be happening when there were millions of orphans in need? One adoptive father and blogger, Dan Carroll, insisted in 2012, after facing delays in his adoption, that "Ethiopia has millions of orphans, so the incentive to purchase or kidnap children is non-existent. A simple supply and demand model shows that the supply of children far exceeds the demand, pushing the price to zero. They can't give the children away."

But this ignored not only the complicated reality of orphan crisis statistics but also a basic, accepted fact of intercountry adoption: that, as UNICEF's Doug Webb said, "If you build an orphanage, it will be filled with kids." That is, when orphanages are created in places that didn't have them before, suddenly that region will have more "orphans," as poor parents see the institutions as a way to ease their burden and give their children an opportunity for better food, shelter, and education. Children who were not homeless or unparented before end up becoming institutionalized as a direct result of orphanages setting up shop in poor areas. Then adoption advocates point to the increased rates of institutionalization as evidence of the need for adoption. It's what some have come to call "a culture of adoption," functioning like a self-fulfilling prophecy.

Many—though not all—of Ethiopia's orphanages, Webb continued, were established because of the readiness of Western donors to support the institutions even though the orphanage model has long since been discredited in developed nations—widely understood to be harmful to children's development. Despite that accepted assessment, the potential for profit led to an exponential leap in the number of orphanages operating in Ethiopia, with a government study Webb saw finding that many of the homes were financed from outside the country. "An estimated 40 percent of institutions here are paid for by adoption agencies, so 40 percent of institutions are here because of the interest in intercountry adoption," he said, "leading one to argue that if there wasn't intercountry adoption, there would probably be 40 percent fewer children in institutions."

As Jedd Medefind of the Christian Alliance for Orphans admits, too often the children who end up in the pipeline for international adoption—which starts at orphanages—are not the same children advertised as composing the orphan crisis. The throngs of street children walking through Addis Ababa and approaching cars for spare change are almost categorically ineligible for adoption in a country where adoptees must come from orphanages that accept limited categories of children directly from their families or government authorities. Children without documentation can rarely be processed for adoption. It's a complication that makes reaching the goal—a system in which the right children, who actually have no one to care for them, find families—something Medefind calls "the million dollar question."

"The fundamental issue in Ethiopia is extreme poverty, and that the birth family's idea of adoption is different than ours," said adoption scholar Karen Smith Rotabi. "You have a very sophisticated, legalistic society communicating with a very poor, traditional one." Misperceptions about possible benefits from relinquishing children for adoption can take over a village quickly, she said. "It's very dangerous stuff, playing with people's poverty, emotions, and needs in a way that's really quite profound."

And it's dangerous in other ways too. Smith Rotabi warned that Ethiopia must learn from other countries that have seen sharp rises in adoption, like Guatemala, where adoption corruption eventually came to have what she calls "hidden structures of organized crime" and critics faced so much intimidation that many hired bodyguards or, in one case, disappeared.

IN 2008 A THIRTY-FIVE-YEAR-OLD Oklahoma nurse whom I'll call Kelly adopted a seven-year-old girl, "Mary," from Ethiopia. It was the second adoption for Kelly, following one from Guatemala. Kelly had turned to Ethiopia in the hopes of avoiding some of the ethical problems she had witnessed in Guatemala. But even after using a reputable agency, Kelly has come to believe that Mary never should have been placed for adoption. Kelly came to this determination after hiring what's known as an adoption searcher—a specialized independent researcher who works in a unique field that few outside the community of adoptive parents even know exists, tracking down adopted children's birth families. "Her entire paperwork, except for a couple of names, was completely falsified," Kelly said. Mary's paperwork listed her as two years younger than she was, it said she had one older sister when she in fact had two younger sisters, and, most importantly, it said her mother had died years ago. "One day I said to Mary, 'You know how your paperwork says you were five and you're really seven?'" Kelly recalled. "'It also says that your mom's dead.' And Mary goes, 'My mom's not dead.' She was adamant that her mother wasn't dead, and in fact she wasn't. Her mom is alive, and it took our searcher just two days to find her."

Kelly hired a searcher through a friend who had also adopted from Ethiopia. She sent copies of all her paperwork and $900 and waited for him to make the nine-hour drive from the capital, Addis Ababa, to the northern region from which Mary had been adopted. "I wanted to verify that she hadn't been stolen. I searched with the intention of sending her back to Ethiopia if I found out she'd been stolen," said Kelly.

The searcher determined Mary's real birth date and that, though her birth family and mother hadn't understood about the adoption, they were okay with Mary being in the United States now. "I can't imagine the weight that was on her," Kelly said of Mary. "After I told her the paperwork said her mom was dead, she thought maybe she was dead and nobody told her. So it was huge for her to know she was right, that her mother was alive. I was lucky she remembered and was strong enough to stick with her story."

IN THE PAST SEVERAL YEARS connecting with a searcher like the one Kelly used has become increasingly difficult. Although the information searchers bring back is often innocuous, a window into the world your child came from, searchers are also implicitly tasked with determining whether an adopted child is a "manufactured orphan"—a child with a family made to look parentless on paper. The contradictions searchers have unearthed in recent years have damaged the reputations of adoption agencies in Ethiopia. Agencies, some adoptive parents claim, have retaliated against searchers with legal action, jail time, and even death threats. In response, for a time Ethiopia's adoption searchers went underground. Finding adoptive families willing to share the name or contact information of searchers they had used took months and, for me, months more to convince a young Ethiopian searcher I'll call Samuel to meet with me.

For several years Samuel, a tall, soft-spoken filmmaker from Addis Ababa in his midtwenties, has traveled across Ethiopia to locate the remaining parents, brothers, sisters, and neighbors of Ethiopian children adopted to North America and Europe. For a moderate fee—around $600, plus travel and lodging for a two- or three-person crew—he creates a DVD of interviews with family members and a brief glimpse of the area the child is from. For Samuel, it's a living as well as a source of personal fulfillment. He lost his own father at seven, and his mother, who had not had a lasting relationship with the father, could tell Samuel little more than that he had been tall. Like many others in Ethiopia, Samuel worries that adopted children who don't know their background will face an identity crisis down the line.

Samuel started making the DVDs for a prominent US adoption agency, then later moved on to independent production, working from a script of sixty to seventy questions to ask of whatever closest relative or neighbor can be found. The questions ranged from the specific, about how each child was relinquished, to broader cultural queries about wedding ceremonies and cultural observances in the region the child came from.

The first several times I e-mailed or called Samuel he responded with trepidation, confirming with me repeatedly that I was not associated with any adoption agencies working in Ethiopia and that I wouldn't pass on his name or information to any of them. He had good reason to be cautious. In August 2010 Samuel was jailed for forty-one days in the northern Ethiopian province of Tigray, which shares a hostile border with neighboring Eritrea. He had traveled to the region to film two birth-family interviews, one of which Samuel said he did pro bono out of his respect for the family, which had adopted an HIV-positive child. When Samuel met the birth sister of one of the children whose story he was tracking, the local director of a US adoption agency came along and began accusing Samuel of giving the agency a bad name. (Out of fear of further repercussions, Samuel requested that the agency not be named either.) Shortly thereafter Samuel and his crew were arrested. While in jail he was told that the arrest was made at the request of the agency, which had accused him of performing illegal adoptions and filming the "bad side" of Ethiopia to sell to the Eritrean government. An employee of the agency was also arrested—it's still not clear why—as well as three of Samuel's friends and a translator. When a local man brought Samuel food and water, he was arrested as well.

Although his jailers treated him as a serious criminal, in time, with the help of US adoptive families, Samuel's case reached the attention of the United States and federal Ethiopian governments. Families who had adopted through the agency raised thousands of dollars for bail and led a letter-writing campaign that spurred the Ethiopian ambassador to the United States, at the consulate in Los Angeles, to get involved. Eventually Samuel was released.

Samuel's story is not the only example of agencies using local clout to silence critics. In 2009 Arun Dohle, a researcher for the adoption reform nonprofit Against Child Trafficking (ACT), traveled to Ethiopia to investigate twenty-five adoptions handled by the Dutch agency Wereldkinderen Child Welfare Association. The agency commissioned the research, but when Dohle's findings led to him being "put out" of the country, ACT published the report independently under the title "Fruits of Ethiopia, Intercountry Adoption: The Rights of the Child, or the 'Harvesting' of Children?"

"We were seriously threatened by the orphanage directors and by the local representative of the agency we were working with as well," Dohle told me. "We got a letter from Ethiopian orphanages saying we were involved in illegal adoptions. . . . The social worker [I was working with] was accused of damaging the image of Ethiopia. . . . It proves you can't do independent research." He added, "Of course [the research] was actually legal, but they were dropping high-up names of politicians."

In his research Dohle found that a majority of the twenty-five cases involved clear ethical concerns. These included living and easily identified parents listed as dead or unknown, agency or orphanage representatives giving false information on court documents, parents relinquishing children in the stated hopes of receiving support from adoptive families, and orphanages recruiting children directly from intact families. He recorded testimony stating that some child recruiters are salaried employees of orphanages and work to collect children from villages, health centers, and other places families visit. Overall he found that Ethiopian families don't have the same understanding of adoption that Western agencies do. The report explains that Dohle's research came "to an abrupt end" when a local representative of the agency "threatened to report the researcher to the Ethiopian Immigration or Police."

Officials from two orphanages that Dohle had identified as problematic (both of which the Ethiopian government has since closed), Bethzatha Children's Home Association and Gelgela Integrated Orphans and Destitute Family Support Association, sent a letter to Wereldkinderen accusing Dohle of engaging in illegal adoptions; of "terrorizing the families of the children who have been placed in the Netherlands" by claiming that the children are being sold for compensation, for organ harvesting, or for experimental HIV medication testing (his report made none of these claims); and of taking "persons"—presumably the birth families Dohle was researching—hostage during interviews. "These situations have proven to be rather problematic to our operations," the letter stated. It demanded that all adoptions to the Netherlands be investigated, claiming that Dohle's research impugned not only the orphanages in question but the government of Ethiopia as well.

ALTHOUGH SAMUEL typically finds little more than discrepancies in the children's ages—younger children are more attractive to adoptive parents, Samuel imagines, because they are like "empty papers," with no past and no history—sometimes he finds that birth families are alive when they were said to be dead. Sometimes the birth families received no word about their children despite agency promises for updates. One birth family was not even aware their child had been sent to America. Sometimes, Samuel said, birth families are complicit in these falsehoods, making stories they think are more conducive to getting their children adopted. "People are promoting adoption to foreigners, and the birth families were fooled by some adoption advocates," Samuel said. "They got the wrong information about adoption: that if you send this child, you will get some money from the adoptive parents and you'll be someone great."

In 2011 I accompanied Samuel on a birth-family interview: a trek deep into the rural countryside outside Sodo to locate the family of a toddler girl adopted and living in Canada. We took a twelve-mile drive through rural roads so pitted it took more than an hour: first over dirt throughways cutting across wide expanses of grazing land; then off road toward a hamlet so small and remote, with just a few houses and an HIV clinic, it might have been impossible to find without a guide; then even further, on overgrown backcountry paths where our Land Rover got stuck in deep trenches of mud. There, a handful of local children emerged shyly from bordering fields to lead us the last half mile on foot until we reached a solitary rectangular house, mud-walled with a skeletal wood-branch fence and surrounded by lush gardens of cassava, mango, and coffee trees.

We came unannounced, as there was no way to contact the family ahead of time, and found only a toddler boy standing in the front yard in a long-sleeved jersey and naked from the waist down. The boy stared as Samuel's crew filed into the yard: Samuel's "journalist," a stocky man in a florid button-down who conducts the birth-family interview, and Semayat, a social worker from the adoption agency, Kingdom Vision, which facilitated this child's placement. There was also me, my translator, Yosef, and a photographer traveling with us.

We walked up to the house, which had three shuttered windows and unpainted mud walls decorated with a trim of shiny blue and silver streamers extending in a crisscross pattern along its front wall. Above the doorway, in the spaces around the trim, was taped a child's graded chemistry test, a miniature Ethiopian flag, a political poster instructing people to vote for the ruling party, and a banner, handwritten in Amharic, reading, "You can love 1,000 people and you go a long way to do this, but there is only one person who can love you, and it's me."

Semayat, the social worker from Kingdom Vision, explained that the family's father had died, leaving them vulnerable in a region periodically struck by "green famine," when the crops are still growing or are in between plantings and there isn't ripe produce to eat. Though he hadn't worked on this adoption, Semayat said the family would have approached their local *kebele,* which would have instructed the agency to investigate whether they were candidates for relinquishing a child: assessing the family's available resources, livestock, and land. In what seemed like no time the spectacle of out-of-town visitors carrying camera equipment drew nearly thirty neighboring children and adults, who leaned against trees and watched solemnly in jeans, T-shirts, and tracksuits while Samuel framed shots of the exterior of the house.

The birthmother Samuel sought to interview, a widow in her early forties with six other children, five of whom still lived at home, was called from a neighbor's house to host her unexpected guests. She smiled obligingly, without question, when Samuel and his colleagues explained that they had come to film for several hours at the request of her daughter's new adoptive parents. Her response was a testament to the rural setting—unexpected guests may be interrupting work but are unlikely to be interrupting appointments—as well as the privileged position of wealthier, more urban people arriving suddenly at the doorstep of the country poor.

Given what a production our visit became, it was easy to understand why adoption scholars remark that the very fact of adoptive families visiting birth families in Ethiopia's rural villages can become an aspect of adoption coercion, convincing other parents to relinquish too. As Smith Rotabi wrote, "The activity itself may well be a mechanism for recruitment of other families and the result may be the identification of children who were, prior to the practice of village visiting, well-cared for in a family system." The mother at this house, unnamed at Samuel's request, had relinquished her daughter after two neighboring families had done the same.

Samuel and his team found a place to interview the mother: behind the house, following a diagonal path of rich red earth through a backyard garden, into a lane of cleared grass bordering several fields of greens, corn, and "false banana." Down a sloping hill several goats grazed, tied to wooden stakes in the ground, with gentle hills rolling into mountain peaks in the distance.

Sitting in a chair in the fields behind her house, her fingertips pressed together and her eyes cast down, the mother solemnly answered dozens of questions about her background, her remaining children—all looking healthy and well clothed—and the circumstances of her husband's death, which had prompted the adoption. She answered as though she were complying with an official request, without emotion and with clipped answers of one or two words. It was nonetheless a lengthy process, as each question had four parts: Samuel's journalist asking questions in Amharic, Semayat translating them into the local language of Wolaita, the mother answering, then Semayat translating back into Amharic. The team would translate the conversation to English later, back in Addis.

After the interview Samuel took b-roll footage of the house and the neighbors. Several of the men who came by from nearby houses, crafted in the traditional roundhouse, thatched-roof style, brought a steer into the mother's front yard to pull a wooden hoe across the red dirt and grass, demonstrating for the camera Ethiopian agricultural chores: a simulacrum of rural living for a child who will grow up in Canada to watch and rewatch a handful of images from Ethiopia, as foreign to her as pictures in *National Geographic*.

Among the crowd of neighbors was a twenty-two-year-old woman named Adanech who explained the local understanding of adoption by citing *gudifecha*. That's the Ethiopian custom of informal adoption, when another family raises a child temporarily but always with the understanding of who the child's parents are. "They believe the children will come back and be part of the family," my translator, Yosef, told me.

This cultural difference in the term "adoption" is a misunderstanding that some agencies seem to perpetuate, equivocating on whether children will come back, although very few children adopted to the United States ever return to their countries of origin for more than a one-time visit, if at all. As Semayat told Yosef, "Until age eighteen the child could stay in the adoptive parents' home. After that the adoptive child has every right to decide whether to live here or to stay there. The family knows the blood relationship is always there, so wherever the child is, it belongs to them."

In a way this points to the larger question of how adoption is functioning in traditional societies facing rapid modernization. Adanech, who attended school until the tenth grade, said that while there's generally enough food in the area, there's usually no money to buy things that can't be grown or processed on the land—no oil, no sugar, often no shoes. Although these items weren't components of life in the past, they've become customary, even in remote areas, and families now see their absence as a deprivation. They grow ashamed of their circumstances, suggests Yosef, and seek for their children to do better. "They'll think they're not in civilization, and the whole concept of their humanity will be in question, and they'll wish for their children to go anywhere—not only to the US but also [Ethiopian cities like] Awassa, Wolaita, Addis Ababa," Yosef told me. He pointed out that the whole village had assembled on the mother's yard because they believe we—

and me in particular—had come not just to make the video or to report but rather to pick out another child "and maybe give an opportunity for another family." "This is going to be a celebration," he said. "Coffee is going to be prepared and served."

And it was, in an elaborate ceremony in keeping with Ethiopian tradition, with coffee beans roasted, hand ground, and brewed strong, then served to us guests as we sat on a log in the front yard. A circle formed among the children, and the girls shook their shoulders in the traditional Wolaita dance I would later see adult women perform at a local nightclub, where the DJ alternated between regional songs and Bob Marley. At the end Samuel presented the mother and her children with a stack of pictures from Canada. They sat on a bed inside the house carefully shuffling the photos as Samuel filmed and a dozen neighbors watched from the corner, under a poster of two doves taped to the wall, reading in English, "love is enough." When Samuel was done the mother looked up at me, the only white person in the house, and smiled as she pointed to a picture of her daughter's adoptive mom, asking if that was me.

IN 2009 A GLUT OF ABANDONMENT cases from orphanages in Addis Ababa prompted Ethiopia's First Instance Court, responsible for approving all international adoptions, to announce it was temporarily suspending hearing abandonment cases that originated in the capital while it investigated the reason for the surge. The court continued to hear adoption cases for children abandoned in other parts of Ethiopia, however.

Following this announcement, a van from Addis carrying seven children and babies was stopped as it was driving outside the rural town of Shashemene, in central Ethiopia. The children in the van were wards of Better Future Adoption Services (BFAS) and had been declared abandoned in Addis Ababa. Police outside Shashemene stopped the van, and seven adults were arrested, including five BFAS employees. The adults were accused of trying to process the children as abandoned in another region so their adoptions could proceed without delay.

One of the children transported to Shashemene would later be adopted by a Christian couple just outside Nashville, Tennessee: thirty-one-year-old Jessie Hawkins, a health and wellness author, and her thirty-eight-year-old husband, Matthew, a marketing executive. The Hawkinses had chosen BFAS as a protection against corrupt adoptions, assuming that because an Ethiopian woman living in the United States, Agitu Wodajo, ran it, the agency would operate more ethically than agencies without a local connection. Wodajo's public professions of Christian faith were reassuring as well.

Before the children were transported to Shashemene, BFAS notified Hawkins and the adoptive families for the other six children that they were moving the children to an orphanage that was cleaner and safer. (Wodajo later told me the improbable story that the children were moved not to change their abandonment paperwork but because a colleague of a BFAS staffer wanted to set up his own orphanage in the region and had asked to "borrow" BFAS children to pose as his wards when inspectors came to check.) The families didn't learn until much later that the party had actually been arrested.

A July 8 e-mail from BFAS to US adoptive families said that the agency was trying to locate children's birth families in case they couldn't be processed as abandonments. "If [the birth families] are willing, your children will be filed for court as a family member relinquishment and not as an abandonment," the letter read. "So, BFAS is waiting for one of two things. 1) For the court to open their doors to new abandonment cases or 2) For birth families to relinquish the children so we can file immediately." This e-mail seemed like an acknowledgement that the information on the children's paperwork was fluid and that the agency would pursue whatever avenue seemed quickest.

Hawkins herself was told different stories about the daughter she had committed to adopt, a four-year-old girl who had been declared abandoned and whose mother BFAS now said they were trying to locate. "This is when I started to get suspicious," she said. "I thought, if you're so confident she was abandoned, why are you trying to find her birthmother now?" But, she continued, "You get attached to this child and you're basically at their mercy at this point. You believe these children are abandoned, orphaned, and you're willing to do whatever or you'll lose this child and they'll live there forever."

In the weeks that passed, while the children were said to be on the road, Hawkins and the other families grew close, comparing stories they had been told. Some parents heard that many of the nannies working at BFAS were in fact the mothers of the children being relinquished for adoption, with the agency operating as a sort of de facto maternity home for poor women who had been offered a job in exchange for their infants—something Wodajo later denied. But as rumors spread that their adoptions would be terminated or libel lawsuits filed if they pushed too hard, a hush fell over the group.

When Hawkins was finally called to Ethiopia to finalize her adoption, the BFAS staff there reassured her that her daughter had indeed been abandoned. But after the girl came to the United States she began acting out, behaving violently toward a set of baby dolls she had gotten for Christmas and systematically shattering glasses she found in the kitchen. A few months later, when she had learned some English, the daughter pointed to a picture of the orphanage that Hawkins had taped to her bedroom wall and told her, "When I lived there, I missed my mom."

Hawkins responded, "'Honey, that's nice of you, but you didn't know me then.' And then she kind of looks at me like she's afraid she was going to be in trouble, and you could see her really choosing her words with the little bit of English she had. And she said, 'You know, I have another mom.'"

"I can't even begin to put into words what that feels like," Hawkins told me. "Finding out that you have someone else's child simply because you happen to have been born in a country where you're more privileged than they are? You want to throw up, you don't know what to do."

When Hawkins called BFAS to present this information, she reached Agitu Wodajo directly. Despite the many reassurances Hawkins had received in the past that the girl was abandoned, she said Wodajo replied without hesitation that yes, she had met the girl's mother herself.

Hawkins hired several searchers to try to find the mother and even tried bribing one of the BFAS nannies, but she didn't have enough information for the searchers to go on. When she's reached out to other former nannies, eventually they stop talking. As more information about how BFAS operated came to light, Hawkins had difficulty absorbing it all. The first time she read the word "trafficking" in relation to the agency, she had to sit down. "When my daughter cries herself to sleep that she misses her birthmother, having given birth before, I know that there's someone else on the other side of the world doing the same thing. And I have her daughter. I love my daughter, and selfishly, I want to keep her forever. I want there to be this great story behind it about a child who needed a home and got one. But a lot of times I feel like we've done something wrong."

IN AUGUST 2010 an Ethiopian newspaper called *Sendek*, edited by journalist Fanuel Kinfu, published an interview with BFAS's former deputy country director, Abebe Tigabu (a college friend of Kinfu's). Tigabu had recently been let go from his job, and he denounced the agency in *Sendek,* accusing Wodajo of participating in numerous unethical adoption practices.

I met Tigabu and Kinfu in 2011 in Addis Ababa. Tigabu, an attorney, told me he had started working for BFAS after he consulted on the Shashemene case. He claimed he helped get the charges against BFAS employees dismissed by paying bribes of laptops and cash to those involved in the cases's prosecution. All of the Shashemene children, like Hawkins's daughter, went on to be adopted to the United States, and Tigabu claims that Wodajo was so pleased with this result that she offered him a full-time job. As country director, Tigabu claims, he witnessed children's records changed so that they were adopted under false last names, thereby destroying their ability to track their heritage later. Further, he said female employees of the agency were heavily pressured to give their own children up for adoption—children who were later declared "abandoned."

Tigabu charged that Wodajo found other ways to obtain children for adoption, such as giving small payments to pregnant women to relinquish their children directly, in order to avoid paying larger donations to orphanages, thereby maximizing profits. "She always wanted to work out of the law," Tigabu told me. "She collected children out of their reality, especially a number of children who had their own natural parents." Children who had parents, he claimed, were recruited with promises to the birth parents that adoptive parents would give them gifts or payments "and change your life even" if they formally relinquished custody in court. When that didn't work, the children's paperwork was changed to allege they had been abandoned at an orphanage in another town. In that way, he said, "the adoption process is finalized in an easy way. There is no need for the family to appear at the court. They say . . . the parents are dead or that they abandoned the child and left the area."

The birth families of the Shashemene children would later complain to the government that their children had gone on to the United States without the birth parents' appearance in court to relinquish them, and they asked how that had occurred without their permission. "There is no answer to their question," Tigabu said, " . . . because the children went in the name of abandonment."

After the *Sendek* accusations came out, Wodajo promptly responded by denouncing Tigabu as a disgruntled former employee who had been fired for embezzling agency funds. "Because of our Faith, ethical and professional background," Wodajo wrote in a statement, "we had [sic] and will never ever be engaged in exploitation or use of children for exploitation under any circumstances."

In a contentious phone interview in 2012, a recalcitrant Wodajo expanded on her defense to me, arguing simply, "What happened was we hired the wrong person" and claiming that Tigabu had coached birth parents to lie to the government in retaliation for being fired. She denied that BFAS had ever taken in pregnant women to relinquish their newborns and argued that when things had gone wrong on her watch, it was because she had been out of the country. In the case of one BFAS employee whose children had been processed for adoption as abandoned, Wodajo placed the blame on the mother, whom she claimed had her friend relinquish for her; further, Wodajo at first denied the woman had been a BFAS employee, repeatedly saying that she "wasn't on the payroll," before finally admitting that, payroll or not, the woman had in fact worked there part time. In any case, Wodajo argued, Tigabu had presided over that case. But she fell mute when I asked whether that meant he had processed an unethical adoption.

"Nobody pressured nobody," she said. "You know that there are over four million orphans in Ethiopia? You don't need to go any wrong way to get a child." She paused, then continued. "I know it is not a clean business. I know that very well."

In December 2010 Ethiopia's Charities and Societies Agency revoked Better Future's license, citing involvement in child trafficking and falsifying documents. A printed notice was posted outside the CSA offices in downtown Addis Ababa, reading that BFAS had been closed and its property confiscated. Hawkins and the other families were thrilled.

AROUND THE SAME TIME that BFAS lost its license, the Ethiopian government vowed to clean up its system and close orphanages that existed only to feed into the adoption pipeline. In January 2011 the US State Department hosted a conference to address allegations of corruption and coercion in Ethiopian adoptions, offering the startling statistic that 90 percent of adoption cases that went through the embassy required further investigation or clarification, often regarding misrepresentations or concealment of facts intended to expedite approval.

In March 2011 came news of a system-wide slowdown, as the Ethiopian government announced that it was reducing by 60 to 90 percent the rate at which it processed children's adoption paperwork, from approximately fifty cases per day to five. The State Department moved quickly to urge Ethiopia's government to reconsider, offering them technical assistance to keep the process moving more quickly. Meanwhile US adoption lobby groups, agencies, and evangelical ministries howled with outrage. One prominent advocate, Dr. Jane Aronson, the "orphan doctor" to some ten thousand adopted children, called the move "a hostage situation" in an open letter appeal to former President Bill Clinton.

The US Citizenship and Immigration Services (USCIS) explained that although most Ethiopian children being adopted did fit the loose US definition of an orphan, there were troubling patterns in the statistics when they and the State Department conducted a joint visit to observe the country's adoption program: that 51 percent of children in the cases they reviewed were under two years old and that there were too many exclusive relationships between agencies supporting orphanages and orphanages supplying children.

Ambassador Susan Jacobs, the State Department's special adviser for children's issues, emphasized to me at the time that the embassies had not found explicit evidence of corruption or fraudulent adoptions but rather problems in how agencies' paperwork presented information. She said what they really wanted was for MOWA "to do some real research into these cases before they're presented to us. We don't want to hold up the family."

The reason for Jacobs's hesitancy seemed clear. Prospective parents who face delays in their adoptions are very vocal, and their cause frequently becomes political. When USCIS implemented stricter approval procedures for Ethiopian orphan visas in late 2011, the *Christian Post* accused them of having "tampered with evidence, falsified information and badgered witnesses in apparent attempts to justify not approving an adopted child's visa application."

But the Ethiopian government seemed intent on reforming its program. "We were treating roughly fifty cases a day," Abiy Ephrem, a communications officer at MOWA, told me. "There were a few groups with an interest to make a profit in a short period of time. In the long term they can harvest a lot of things."

UNICEF's Doug Webb said that the media coverage of both CWA and BFAS had a serious impact, leading to changes of personnel in government and even the language MOWA used to discuss adoption. "They started talking to us about trafficking," Webb said. "They started talking in terms of business, supply chain."

After such extensive focus on adoptions from Ethiopia, Ephrem said the Ethiopian government wanted to shift the focus to the larger problems at hand. The four to five thousand children per year adopted out of the country were only ever a small fraction of the total number of vulnerable children, and the government sought to focus instead on getting the larger number of children who never would be adopted into family settings within Ethiopia.

In July 2011, with technical advice from UNICEF and underwritten by a $100 million grant from USAID, Ethiopia's government began implementing a massive "deinstitutionalization" plan. This plan would close a third of the nation's orphanages, shuttering children's homes that functioned as mere transit points for the adoption industry, and trying to establish a more holistic child welfare system that would promote Ethiopian foster care, reunification of children with their natural families, and domestic adoption by Ethiopian parents ahead of international adoption.

The program started by closing 46 of the country's 149 registered institutional care facilities, including 20 orphanages in the area around one city alone and dozens in the SNNPR. UNICEF's preliminary research in the region, conducted in partnership with MOWA, found that 75 percent of children in orphanages could be reintegrated with their parents or extended families. "The long-term vision is that the weaker institutions are fundamentally going to be closed, and the ones that will remain after all this is finished will be the very good ones," said Webb. "There are people in government who are very concerned about this, but we've turned a big corner here. The situation is over where alleged abuses were ignored, swept under the carpet; where nobody was listening and there was too much money involved."

Industry observers said that agencies were feeling the pressure, as staff were being laid off and organizations were considering closing—although a UNICEF analysis of Ethiopian court data in late 2011 indicated that the slowdown had already begun to reverse and that adoption processing rates were returning to normal levels. Meanwhile adoption advocates charged that deinstitutionalized children were returning to families who still couldn't afford to care for them.

Nonetheless, Webb said that those in the adoption business were becoming concerned that the shifts would put them out of business. "Now the people doing adoption for the wrong reasons are very nervous. They need to change their focus and change them fast to keep in line with new priorities. The future lies in management of fostering and prevention work. The primary focus should be making sure families don't fall apart in the first place. . . . If you don't provide an alternative for staff working in the agencies, goodness knows what they might end up doing." Some at UNICEF feared that the bad actors, newly unemployed, could contribute to child trafficking from Ethiopia to neighboring countries. "These guys are business people," Webb continued. "They know how to shift with demand."

Although these shifts might have fallout on many in Ethiopia's adoption economy, some "industry jobs"—like those searchers do—likely won't end any time soon. With thousands of children adopted out to the United States and Europe in the last decade, the searcher Samuel foresees a large, new market: children who will grow up to learn of the circumstances around adoption from Ethiopia in the 2000s and will be in need of information about their background that bankrupted agencies can't provide. Whereas Oklahoma adoptive mother Kelly paid $900 for her searcher in 2009, she has since heard that he increased his rates to as much as $3,000 to $4,000 per search. Samuel had plans in 2011 to integrate his business with the agency Kingdom Vision in order to provide DVDs for all their clients. When rising demand made adoption an important source of revenue in a country that had little of it, even investigators who found themselves at odds with agencies seemed to find a place in the adoption economy.

But on the other side of the equation, in Ethiopia little infrastructure was left in some areas to provide families with information about the children they had relinquished. In the communities around some orphanages that were closed, such as the Gelgela orphanage in Durame, in the SNNPR, Ethiopian families who had been receiving regular updates about their children through the orphanage—sent by adoptive parents in the United States or Europe—were suddenly left without any word, said Karin Schuff, an adoptive mother who had adopted a child from the home. When Schuff was in the area in August 2012 to help establish a sponsorship program for local families, within a matter of hours she was approached by four families "who begged us to find their children's adoptive families for them, one way or another."

Ideally, Webb hopes, some of those who had been involved in the country's orphanage and adoption sector can instead become childcare advocates with a larger vision of child protective services than simply adoption, instead trying to ensure families don't fall apart in the first place. "We're moving away from this 'orphan' labeling and targeting," said Webb. "The 'orphan crisis' is a term that's been used to raise money from people who really want to do something useful, but it's actually unethical. For me this is not about orphans but about kids who find themselves outside of family care, and poverty is a major determinant of that. Two-thirds of the children in this country live below the poverty line. The adoption discussion is an entry point, but it's not the issue. It never has been. It has become the issue though. Because many Westerners care deeply about it."

Whether the Christian adoption movement takes these lessons to heart remains to be seen. What happened in Ethiopia followed neatly in what Parents for Ethical Adoption Reform Vice President Gina Pollock describes as the five-stage process of adoption-boom countries. The first stage begins with a legitimate need for large numbers of children facing a particular crisis. In the second most of the original children have been placed, but adoption demand has grown as a result of pro-adoption advocacy that recruited potential parents. As a result, paid "child finders" enter the scene. In the third stage pressure to find children increases to keep pace with demand, and bad players begin to appear, along with suppressed stories of kidnapping or "baby farms." "At this point," Pollock said, "stories begin to emerge of adopting families experiencing severe issues with traumatized children for the reasons stated above, with increases in numbers of children grieving for their original family." In the fourth stage adoptive parents begin to come forward with their experiences of corruption or fraud, and governments and adoption agencies begin to respond, while international organizations like UNICEF get blamed. In the last stage there are few young, healthy children available for adoption, special-needs adoptions rise, and governments may shut down the program. It's a cycle that repeats year after year, in country after country.

True to form, as Ethiopia began to close, other potential hotspot countries began to emerge, and online chatter grew about adopting from Uganda, Rwanda, or the Democratic Republic of Congo (DRC). In 2012 stories began to emerge of abuses, bribes, and corruption in DRC. For seasoned observers, it wasn't even close to a surprise. "If the demand is blocked by the system, how will it be satisfied elsewhere?" Webb asked. "History has shown us that, when you push one country, another one pops up."

IN 2007, LESS THAN A YEAR into their adoption, Katie and Calvin Bradshaw sent Tarikuwa, who was still grieving heavily, to live with her adoptive grandparents, Mike and Mary Nelson, Katie's mother and father, in Iowa Falls, Iowa. The Bradshaws told Tarikuwa she needed a break from the stress of adjusting to life in their house: there had been conflicts over using their Ethiopian names, over the girls continuing to speak in Amharic instead of English, over Tarikuwa's continuing demands to be sent home to Ethiopia. When Tarikuwa asked her adoptive grandparents when she was going to return to the Bradshaws, the Nelsons told her she was going to stay with them instead. For Tarikuwa, it was the second time she was put on a plane, expecting to return, only to find out after she had arrived that it was permanent.

The Nelsons, whose children were adults, adopted Tarikuwa themselves and tried to help her heal. Mary Nelson would cry with her and say she wished that they could help her go home, but they had been told it was illegal. The Nelsons were legal guardians to another girl from Ethiopia, an adopted teenager who had also gone through a fraudulent adoption and had since been bounced between three other families before landing in Iowa—a story that hints at the world of failed adoptions that has grown in the wake of the boom.

As Tarikuwa grew older and neared eighteen, she began to talk increasingly about using her independence to return to Ethiopia and make a life out of activism around international adoption fraud. Her focus on it seemed to make the Nelsons and the Bradshaws somewhat uneasy; both families said they had had their share of the spotlight. Then, in January 2012, what began as a routine family fight over unfinished chores turned into a break. Mary Nelson challenged Tarikuwa that if she didn't like living under their rules, she was free to leave. Tarikuwa took what is a familiar ultimatum for US teenagers literally and moved out.

After a few weeks of staying with friends she moved to Maine, to the home of Nate Day and Lisa Veleff-Day, Portland-area parents to two Ethiopian siblings and among the community of adoptive parents who had lobbied to liberate the searcher Samuel after he was imprisoned in Ethiopia. Although Veleff-Day hadn't employed Samuel herself, she had used the same agency that had helped jail him and had come to doubt their ethics. Her adopted children told her stories of agency staff coming to their family's house prior to their relinquishment—seemingly a story of coercion—and when the Days had arrived in Ethiopia to finalize the adoption, the agency's in-country staff pressured them to tell the US embassy that the birthparents were dead, threatening that they might not get their children if they refused. "Right before we went into the embassy, we were told that there were certain things we needed to say. We were being coached. They were telling us to lie," said Veleff-Day. "We really felt like we were over a barrel, so we did what they said. I'm not proud of that, but they waited this long to coach us, because otherwise we wouldn't have felt as compelled to do what they said."

It was no coincidence that Tarikuwa came to know them; the world of adoption reform advocates is a small one, and Tarikuwa had stayed with Veleff-Day and her husband the previous month when she had flown there by herself to look at colleges in Maine. But the trip had caused tensions back home in Iowa. When Tarikuwa moved there after the family fight, the Nelsons and the Bradshaws reacted with alarm, accusing Veleff-Day of wooing Tarikuwa away in the midst of a domestic crisis.

Katie Bradshaw didn't want to discuss what she called a private family matter. Mary Nelson wrote to me to describe her sense that a small conflict had escalated into a breakup because of outside adults' interference. "This is not a failed adoption," she wrote. "It is a family situation between parents and an adult daughter that outsiders intruded into."

For their part the Days say they just told Tarikuwa, after she had moved out, that she had a place to stay if she needed one. They had witnessed their own children struggle for many months with the aftermath of adoption; now they just wanted to offer Tarikuwa a fresh start to finish high school and get on with her life. Tarikuwa gets along well with their children, biological siblings aged five and eight years old, who pile on top of her to cuddle and trail her around their house.

On the whole the conflict seems an illustration of what David and Desiree Smolin, the adoption reform advocates whose Indian daughters were fraudulently taken from their mother, call the long fallout of "abusive adoption practices." The lies and coercion of corrupt adoptions, wrote the Smolins in a 2012 presentation for the Joint Council on International Children's Services, can have repercussions for everyone impacted by the adoption, affecting adoptees, birth parents, adoptive parents, extended families, and even larger communities. Many are left with severe emotional wounds and little means of resolution, unable to trust in the foundational relationships of their lives or whether anything they're told can be believed.

"The problem with lies," the Smolins wrote, "is that they cast doubts on all that follows. One never again knows with certainty whether one is dealing with lies or truth." In an adoption industry in which false information has become so routine that prospective adopters must contractually agree to accept that their agency may be telling them lies, those affected by corrupt adoptions can end up feeling "it is no longer possible to know anything at all with certainty."

WHEN I VISITED TARIKUWA in Maine in 2012, at Lisa Veleff-Day and Nate Day's comfortable rural home, she hefted a pile of photos and letters onto the bed of her new roommate, the Days' five-year-old daughter. It was the third home Tarikuwa has had in America, and she has collected more photos with every stop.

For Tarikuwa, at least for the time, this one felt like a relief. Arriving as an adult, even if one still in high school, she said she didn't feel pressured to be a full part of the Day family—something she finds difficult while still mourning her lost life in Ethiopia—or to feel grateful for an adoption that she feels destroyed her own.

She looks at her photos of Ethiopia with incredible wistfulness. In her mind the country she was torn from has become everything the United States is not, such a paradise that the adults in her life fear that the reality will be a disappointment when Tarikuwa finally returns to visit, as she plans to do after high school.

Mary Hatlevig, Tarikuwa's former teacher and longtime mentor in Iowa, is afraid that when Tarikuwa makes it back, "Ethiopia won't be as wonderful as she remembers. We've talked about that, about how things we remember aren't exactly as we [recall] them to be." Everyday life will be poorer and tougher than in Tarikuwa's memories, and the technology and luxuries she's come to take for granted will be absent there.

Tarikuwa's sisters Meya and Maree, with whom she talks occasionally—though the family tensions have strained those bonds too—themselves returned to Ethiopia in the fall of 2012: Maree for several months and Meya for perhaps as long as two years to work with local missionaries. Katie Bradshaw said she tried to prepare the sisters to be confronted by relatives and friends who will ask them for money, assuming they've come back rich from their "trip" to America. Tarikuwa already has been asked; after once sending $20 to a sister who was in nursing school, she has denied other requests, so that her family understands "adoption isn't about sending money home; it's about losing your parental rights."

"What we hope for the girls," said Bradshaw, "is that eventually we'll reach a place where they can find some peace with what happened. Not to be happy about it, but to find peace with it and in their life. Whatever that means—going home, or establishing a different life, or being with us—we are willing to accept it."

In May 2012 Tarikuwa finalized the legal change of her name from Journee Bradshaw back to Tarikuwa Lemma in "two very happy minutes" at a Portland court. At 3:30 that afternoon in Maine she called her family in Sodo via Skype, a month before Ethiopia's authoritarian government announced a ban on Internet calling programs, to tell them the news. Across the country, while I sat at Saddleback Church at the Christian Alliance for Orphans conference, I received a text from Lisa Veleff-Day. "I am listening to the ululations of the Lemma family," she wrote, "as they celebrate Tarikuwa's return to her real name."

CHAPTER 5

A Little War

A s traumatizing as a corrupt or wrongful adoption can be, it's not yet the worst outcome for adoptees whose best interests haven't been taken into account.

In the fall of 2005 Sam Allison, a housepainter in his thirties from Tennessee, arrived at Daniel Hoover Children's Village, an orphanage housing more than four hundred children outside Monrovia, Liberia. Allison had come to adopt three children. He ended up with four: a five-year-old girl, to be renamed Cherish; her nine-year-old brother, Isaiah; their thirteen-year-old sister*, CeCe, who had taken care of her siblings for years; and a sickly infant from another orphanage named Engedi, whom Sam said he and representatives from the second orphanage had found when they'd gone "deep into the bush."

The older children were happy to go. The orphanage was run by African Christians Fellowship International (ACFI), a "church planting" ministry that often had food shortages and rarely had school. For years Isaiah had been sexually abused there by an older ward. Once, during Liberia's civil war, a twelve-year-old boy held a gun to Isaiah's head. In 2003 rebels attacked the orphanage and the children all fled, with CeCe carrying Cherish and pulling Isaiah by the hand as she ran, guns firing behind them. Liberian kids called America "heaven," and adoption, in a way, seemed like a ticket home for citizens of a country settled in part by

---

*On her adoption paperwork, CeCe (whom the Allisons named Selah) says she was incorrectly listed as fourteen, a year older than she really was.

freed American slaves, a nation that still sees itself as a fifty-first state, or at least an abandoned colony.

In Tennessee Sam and the four adoptees joined Sam's wife, Serene, a thin brunette in her late twenties who had attempted a career in the Christian music industry, and the couple's four biological children. Together the family moved to an off-the-grid log cabin Sam was building in Primm Springs, a rural hamlet outside Nashville, nestled in the hills around Tennessee's Amish country. During their first days in Primm Springs Serene welcomed the children with familiar foods—rice, stew, sardines—and they were photographed in clean American clothes, smiling and laughing, happy to have arrived.

The Allisons' cabin was on or next to a compound owned by Serene's parents, Colin and Nancy Campbell, where Serene's two sisters and their families also live. Colin pastored a small church, and Nancy, author of anticontraception books like *Be Fruitful and Multiply*, is a fundamentalist Christian women's leader with a large following among homeschoolers. Her free magazine, *Above Rubies*, is a thirty-five-year-old institution that focuses on Christian wifehood and the imperative to bear many children. With a circulation of 130,000 across more than one hundred countries, the magazine has spawned a circuit of local Above Rubies ladies' retreats in the United States, Canada, and Australia. Her followers are mostly large families, with eight, ten, or twelve children, who eschew contraception and adhere to rigid gender roles, in which husbands are spiritual leaders of the home, and wives their submissive "helpmeets."

Although Nancy's followers include many women who look the part, in floor-length denim jumpers and modest homemade dresses, the Campbell clan can seem like a new age Christian avant garde, tracing a thin line between Plain People austerity and back-to-the-land granola. In *Above Rubies'* Facebook album Nancy, well known for her cooing accent—the entire family emigrated from New Zealand by way of Australia—twirls in a tie-dyed peasant skirt, her eyes closed in a beatific smile. Serene and her sisters—two of the three have had ten children or more—are fixtures of the magazine. They are striking women, in form-fitting T-shirts, jeans, and cargo pants, with waist-length hair. They sell motherhood-themed CDs ("Peace All Over Me") and raw-food lifestyle cookbooks (*Trim Healthy Mama*), and they contribute cheerful essays to their mother's magazine about raising children in half-built homes without running water. In Nashville two of their three brothers have helped manage Australian Christian rock band the Newsboys. It's a family that thousands of homeschooling mothers know nearly as well as their own.

In 2005 Campbell turned her attention to international adoption, specifically from Liberia, then just emerging from a fourteen-year civil war, and specifically through a handful of Christian adoption facilitators with ambiguous legal standing. As early as 2002 *Above Rubies* began pushing independent international adoptions—meaning those arranged independently of licensed agencies, with parents using private brokers known as facilitators—as an economical way for Christians to conduct "missions under our very own roof!"

Three years later, in 2005, Campbell wrote about her own mission trip to Liberia, where she had spent a week visiting three orphanages, including the Daniel Hoover and Acres of Hope homes, and had come "home with piles of letters addressed 'To any Mom and Dad.'" She touted the cost effectiveness of adopting from Liberia—"one of the cheapest international adoptions." She also offered spurious statistics to urge readers to action: that one million Liberian infants—what would have then been a full third of the country's population—died every year and, as she later claimed, that they were among "a billion orphans in the world today."

She promoted three Christian adoption facilitators: Acres of Hope; West African Children's Support Network (WACSN); and one, Children Concerned, that an *Above Rubies* family started in order to manage adoptions from Daniel Hoover and other ACFI orphanages (and which was later renamed as Amazing Grace Africa Ministries). At the time the United States licensed none of them as adoption agencies, but all nonetheless conducted adoptions out of Liberia for between $3,000 and $8,000—a fraction of the $20,000 to $35,000 that most international adoptions cost.

The fire caught. After reading *Above Rubies,* members of a group on Yahoo wrote that God had laid Liberian adoptions "heavy on [their] heart." They asked whether there was a discount for taking more than one child. They compared notes on passing their home study, as religious convictions about corporal punishment, for example, might cause a family to fail.

"These families lined up by the droves," said Johanna, a nurse and adoptive mother who used to read *Above Rubies* and who requested I use her first name only. "They were going to Liberia and literally saying, 'This is how much I have, give me as many as you can.'" In July 2005 Campbell wrote that seventy children were in the process of being adopted through ACFI, most to large families; some of these families were taking as many as five children. Several months earlier, Campbell described how she had helped one adoptive father navigate the Washington Dulles airport with his new Liberian triplets on his way to meet his wife. One of the children, Grace, a wide-eyed infant with bow lips and a Peter Pan collar, was pictured on the cover of the magazine.

Campbell also published a lengthy testimonial from Acres of Hope cofounder Patty Anglin, her personal friend and a Wisconsin mother to eighteen, including eleven adoptees. She printed another from the Ahlers family of Kentucky, who would adopt five children from Liberia. The Ahlers marveled at the helpfulness of the older girls, who learned to make thirty loaves of bread for the family on "bread day" and had taken over laundry duties. Between 2005 and 2008 *Above Rubies* published nearly twenty articles touching on what came to be shorthanded as simply "Liberian adoption."

From 2003, when the first facilitators arrived in Liberia, until 2008, the State Department counted more than twelve hundred Liberian adoptees entering the United States; almost eleven hundred of them arrived during the years *Above Rubies* was heavily promoting the cause. More were adopted to Canada, and others likely bypassed official channels. "From my article in *Above Rubies* about the children in Liberia there must have been up to a thousand children adopted," Campbell estimated in an e-mail to me, "and most have been a blessing." Almost an entire children's chorus from ACFI, known as the Liberian A Capella Boys Choir, had been adopted into families outside Charlotte, North Carolina, two years before Campbell's campaign, when the orphanage had been attacked in 2003. Over the next few years nearly forty more Liberian children came to greater Charlotte, a phenomenon featured in a photo spread on the "Hallelujah Chorus" in Oprah Winfrey's *O* magazine.

In September or October 2005 Sam Allison arrived home with his and Serene's four adoptees, and the newly expanded family was featured in *Above Rubies*. In the photograph Sam sat on one end of a couch, his hair in microbraids, and Serene on the other, with a line of eight grinning children between them.

The next year I happened to visit Nancy Campbell at her home to interview her about her teachings on large families and contraception. At the end of a long driveway I was greeted by three dogs and two towheaded toddlers, who wordlessly guided me from my car to the living room. Nancy told me that she was adopting three Liberian children, whom she hoped would arrive by Christmas, as part of what she would describe in *Above Rubies* as her "vision of finding families for the children in this nation of orphans." She ended up adopting four; Serene took a total of six. "If God is putting it on your heart to adopt, start the process!" Campbell wrote in 2005, promising that the necessary funds would follow readers' leaps of faith. "When we welcome a child into our heart and into our home, we actually welcome Jesus Himself."

ALTHOUGH LIBERIAN adoption gained a viral popularity among *Above Rubies* followers, in Monrovia the process was operating in a state of near lawlessness. The country was just two years out of a war that had touched nearly everyone who had survived it and left its infrastructure shattered. Nearly a decade later, buildings around Monrovia are still pocked from wartime gunfire.

For Acres of Hope's Anglin, the impact of *Above Rubies*'s promotion was jarring. "So many people responded, and they were responding at an alarming rate. Adoptions started to boom instead of growing slowly and naturally," she said, pointing to what she considers Campbell's regrettable characterization of Liberian adoptions as "cheap, easy and fast." But the characterization was true. Acres of Hope's adoption fees cost from $3,000 to $6,000, and they ended up brokering more than six hundred adoptions from the time Anglin arrived in Liberia, just days after the 2003 ceasefire, until the program shut down in early 2009.

In Liberia the adoption fees represented a potential windfall, and local operators emerged to supply children. The number of orphanages jumped from around 10 before the war to between 114 and 120 after, and they began to find children to match adoptive parents' desired gender and ages. In 2006 Liberia, which then had only three million people, became the eighth-highest adoption-sending country in the world.

As in Ethiopia, Liberian parents began to complain that adoption had been represented to them as a temporary education program, similar to the country's traditional "ward system." Some said their children had been adopted without their consent. Meanwhile, a local WACSN staffer seemed to reinforce the misunderstanding by reportedly announcing that two of his own biological children had been adopted and were now "benefiting from the program."

The postwar government, functioning without reliable electricity and Internet, let alone sufficient numbers of trained staff, was unable to monitor children leaving the country. Lydia Sherman, Senior Coordinator for Liberia's Ministry of Health and Social Welfare, told me that the high level of adoption "was understandable during the heat of war, but it continued. Children were being sent out of here six, seven at a time." Adoptions that would take most of a year in other countries could happen in weeks or days in Liberia.

Cheryl Carter-Shotts, founder and managing director of Americans for African Adoptions, one of the few licensed agencies operating in Liberia at the time, said that the government wasn't able to distinguish licensed American adoption agencies from groups that merely had US nonprofit status. When nonprofit facilitators like WACSN were caught acting as agencies, "They would say, 'We're doing a private adoption,'" meaning they claimed they were only assisting families through an independent process. Bribery was also rampant. Carter-Shotts told me that the founder of WACSN, Maria Luyken, a Liberian-born Minnesotan who did not respond to my interview requests, advised her to "stick a couple of hundred-dollar bills" in her letter when she met with a government ministry—a charge confirmed by Dirk Helmling, a North Carolina pastor and adoptive parent to four Liberian children whose wife would later take over WACSN's US operations. "She had to pay people off to get the paperwork done," Helmling told me. "What we were told is that everybody was doing the same thing. In order to get kids out, you had to pay these bribes."

In 2006 Liberia's National Legislature called a hearing on allegations of child trafficking. A 2007 joint report by UNICEF and Holt International Children's Services found that children were entering the adoption system through "fraudulent means" and "false promises" to parents. But the facilitators continued to flourish with the help of *Above Rubies* readers. WACSN, which had been a children's relief group during the war, seemed to tailor its operations to Campbell's followers, working with a volunteer stateside representative named Pam Gremillion, a Memphis woman on the edge of the Mennonite community who dressed herself and her three Liberian daughters in Amish- or Mennonite-style bonnets and layered dresses. Under the stewardship of "Sister Pam," WACSN promised that Liberian adoptions were "uncommonly uncomplicated" and "uncommonly affordable," and it declared that the organization would work only with biblical literalists. Their initial application materials focused largely on prospective parents' relationship with Jesus and how God had led them to adopt.

In 2009, as "Liberian adoption" reached its climax, WACSN drew a stage full of US preachers to Monrovia for a crusade called "How Big Is God?" One of the organizers of the three-day revival had blogged that readers at home could get involved by adopting through WACSN. "If you are interested in this vision, even if you have the least bit of interest, please contact me," one wrote. "Heck, even if you HATE the vision and think it's a stupid idea, contact me and at least give me a chance to talk you into it."

"EVERYTHING WAS good for a month," CeCe, the Allisons' oldest adoptee, told me about life in Primm Springs. She is now a twenty-one-year-old woman with a maternal face and a family of her own. "We got to the next month, and things started to get a little weird."

Serene's raw-food prescriptions, like green-leaf smoothies or kefir, were unfamiliar to the children, and if they balked at eating her food, some of the children say Sam would hit them. Other cultural differences emerged, such as the children's use of Liberian English or the Liberian prohibition on children looking adults in the eye. "They'd say, 'You are so rude. I'm talking to you, you should look me in the eye,'" CeCe remembered when I first spoke to her in 2010. "My mom started complaining a lot to my dad. They expected us to adapt to things in a heartbeat."

In October 2006, a year after their first adoptions, the Allisons adopted two more Liberian teenagers, Kula, thirteen, and her fifteen-year-old brother, Alfred,* whose parents had put them in the Daniel Hoover orphanage during the war to keep them safe. They had been at the orphanage at the same time as CeCe, and under the Allisons' supervision, CeCe had called Kula to entice her with stories of American life. The children arrived at night, and the darkness of rural Tennessee surprised Kula. "In Africa we thought America was heaven. I thought there were money trees," said Kula. Now a nineteen-year-old woman with olive-shaped eyes and soft, shoulder-length curls, Kula recalled her confusion when she woke the next day and found her surroundings at odds with her expectations. It was "like a dream, not what I expected, not what they said it was." After a little while, though, she thought that the Allisons' lifestyle must be how everyone in America lives.

Shortly after Kula arrived she said she and CeCe were told to sew traditional African dresses: matching tops, long skirts, and head wraps in the style of West African formalwear, something that felt like a costume to the girls after growing up in shorts and T-shirts at the orphanage. They would

---

*These ages, given by Kula and Alfred, are different from those reported by *Above Rubies*, which listed Kula as fourteen and Alfred (whom the Allisons renamed Jabin) as thirteen.

wear the outfits in public. At Colin Campbell's church they sang while the congregation passed the collection basket, soliciting donations "for African children." An *Above Rubies* photographer took pictures of the boys racing go-karts and the girls experimenting in the kitchen. CeCe sometimes traveled with Nancy Campbell to sing at Above Rubies retreats around the country.

Off-camera the children helped work on the new cabin on the Primm Springs compound. As in Liberia, which still hasn't restored a reliable power grid, the new house had only a generator, no air conditioning in the hot summer, and only a smoking woodstove in winter. The lack of running water meant showers were infrequent and toilets were flushed with a bucket of water. The children said they were hungry so often that a few times CeCe killed and dressed geese or turkeys they caught on the land. "We went from Africa to Africa," she said.

During this time Serene had become pregnant again. Instead of going to school, Isaiah and Alfred helped Sam in his house-painting business or worked in Campbell's immense vegetable garden. Meanwhile CeCe, Kula, and Cherish were put to work cleaning, cooking, and tending a growing number of young children. The "African children," as they referred to themselves, got up at six, as Sam prepared for work and Serene slept in with her younger kids. Both boys and girls carried five-gallon buckets of water up a hill from a creek behind the house or, in drought, on a long trek through the wooded property to the homes of Nancy Campbell or Sam's mother, also living nearby, to fill a reservoir tank on their roof.

Homeschooling for the Allisons consisted mostly of Serene reading to the younger children and an occasional worksheet. In Liberia schooling was not free, and the children wanted to learn. They watched a school bus drive the country road that borders the Campbells' property and asked why they couldn't go too. Alfred was told that school wasn't good for him, Isaiah that he would find it too hard, CeCe that they would be made fun of, and Kula that "black people don't go to school in America."

"Most days," said Isaiah, now a compact, muscley sixteen-year old, "I'd go to work with Sam, painting, going on roofs. He told me, 'If anyone asks you, tell them we're doing homeschooling.'"

CeCe hadn't yet learned to read when Serene gave her a book on mid-wifery in order to learn how to deliver the Allisons' future babies. Cherish, who was the same age as one of the Allisons' biological daughters, was charged with changing baby diapers and carrying the baby up and down the stairs. When CeCe asked why only Cherish had to work, she claims Serene told her, "'I heard that you guys work hard in Africa so you're strong.'"

"They treated us pretty much like slaves," CeCe said. It's a particularly provocative accusation coming from Liberian children, but it is one that Kula and Isaiah—as well as two neighbors and a children's welfare worker—all repeated.

There were clues in the magazine about the life the children were living: mentions of the boys working with Sam painting houses and the girls tending house while Serene went into early labor. The Campbells' four adoptees came in spring 2007, teenagers they renamed Sapphire, Mercy, Psalmody, and John. John was pictured in one editor's note, shovel in hand, watching Colin Campbell dig a precise hole in the garden.

Rachel Johnston, a twenty-eight-year old from Louisiana, also came to Primm Springs in March 2007 as an *Above Rubies* volunteer intern, one of many "Rubies girls" who came to help after graduating from homeschool. Her mother was an avid *Above Rubies* reader, but when Rachel arrived she was distressed at the dissonance between the image of large-family living presented in the magazine and the reality in Primm Springs. "I had only been there about a day when I realized that things weren't really right," Johnston said. Walking through the woods on the property, she came across a naked toddler, one of dozens of children living on the property, wandering on his own. Shocked, she picked him up and brought him to Nancy, who didn't understand why Rachel was upset.

In the middle of Rachel's internship Colin Campbell brought home three of the four adoptees. "They were so full of hope and excited to be starting a new chapter in their lives," Johnston recalls. The next morning at dawn Rachel found Nancy teaching them how to make bread—apparently to be their job from then on—and Nancy gushing "about the big garden she would have that year because all her new children would work in it."

Discipline in the Allisons' household was harsh and included being hit with rubber hosing or a sort of stick and was used to the point of drawing blood. These instruments could fall for disrespecting Serene or not wanting to eat her raw-food meals, for spilling a glass of juice or failing to fill the water reservoir. Another common punishment was being put out of the house for days at a time to sleep on the porch or in the car without blankets until the children apologized.

In the case of Engedi, the toddler, discipline came because of her attachment to CeCe, who was around the same age Engedi's own mother had been. Engedi was adopted at nearly two years old but had been so malnourished she looked like she was six months. "I remember holding her like she was going to break," said Isaiah.

To make her bond with Serene, the Allisons would place the child on the floor between them and CeCe and call her to come. If she went to CeCe, CeCe, Kula and Isaiah all remember, the Allisons would spank her until she wet herself. "They would beat that little girl, and you would see bruises on her and she would pee and she wouldn't even be able to breathe. It used to make me so sad," said CeCe.

The Allisons broke the bond not only between Engedi and CeCe but also her other siblings as well, forbidding CeCe from braiding Cherish's hair, as she had since they were young. "In Africa I was their everything, I was their mom and their dad. I always took care of them. . . . That was something special that she stole from me."

In March 2007 Serene gave birth to her fifth biological child. After she returned from the hospital Serene began demanding to know whether the children had been sexually abused in Liberia. In the larger world of Liberian adoptions, this was becoming a panicked theme, as sexual activity and abuse in some of the orphanages was coming to light. She began accusing CeCe of being sexually interested in Sam and took her for a gynecologist's exam—the only doctor's appointment CeCe recalls having had in Primm Springs. Serene criticized CeCe's developing body and accused her of dressing like a prostitute, and Nancy Campbell called a family friend and told her the family was worried because Sam had been seen walking with CeCe, holding her hand like a lover. In turn, Isaiah claims that Serene began to flirt with him, kissing him on the lips in a way that she didn't kiss any of the other children, calling him sexy, and asking him to massage her. CeCe felt that life at the Allisons' was worse than the orphanage, but she worried about Cherish and Isaiah, whom she had promised her mother to always look after.

In September 2007 Serene wrote a cryptic essay for *Above Rubies*, saying that her "mothering was challenged beyond anything I could have imagined." She wrote vaguely about "situations that seem out of your control or even out of your children's control" that other adoptive mothers might face.

From then on *Above Rubies*, which had begun to resemble a doting grandmother's scrapbook, mentioned the Liberian children with decreasing regularity. But between the lines they were there, as Campbell wrote about the need for strict discipline and training of children to bring about harmony in the home. "If you have to have a little war before you have peace," Campbell wrote, "don't be afraid."

When the Campbells first said they had adopted from Africa, their next-door neighbors, the Bufords, who are African American, thought it was a wonderful thing. Carolyn Buford, a sixty-four-year-old retired foster parent, saw the children on the Campbells' property and occasionally walking or riding a bike down their long country road. One of Buford's fellow church members told her she had stopped by the Campbells' compound when she noticed the children's hair wasn't properly combed to ask the two sets of adoptive parents if she could help, but was politely turned away. Buford spoke to the children when they passed in the street, but she noticed they were often abruptly called home.

One day two of Buford's foster sons saw Alfred and John out in the yard and asked if they could go make friends. They came back quickly and told Buford that something wasn't right—the boys were working hard and the Campbells had told them to leave.

Buford wasn't the only neighbor who was increasingly bothered by the goings-on at the compound. Carl Graham, a fifty-seven-year-old veteran police officer, had been Hickman County's first black cop, working in various departments for thirty years; its first black elected official; and one of its first successful black business owners, running a heating and air conditioning repair shop. Graham lives on a property adjacent to the Campbells, and when he first saw the children they were walking down the road in traditional African dress. He didn't see them again until Colin Campbell contacted him one scorching summer day, asking him to repair his AC. When Graham entered the Campbells' house, he said a thirteen- or fourteen-year-old girl he had never seen before stood up, walked across the room, and put her arms around him.

"She looked at me like, 'you're here.' That look sent chills through me, and it bothers me to this day," he told me. Graham and his partner returned to complete the job several days later, and while they were working in the Campbells' basement, he said they heard "blood-curdling screams." Graham stepped outside and saw Colin Campbell leading the same girl, Jennice (whom the Campbells had named Psalmody), by the arm and neck to a metal tool shed behind the house. Graham said his partner, who is not African American, told him he had no dog in this fight. The screaming lasted fifteen or twenty minutes. Before they left, Colin Campbell came in to say he hadn't whipped the child but just isolated her to calm her down. "He said these children are programmed and taught to lie," Graham said. "That in their native country, when they get old enough to speak, they teach them how to deceive and lie and cheat, and that's what we're trying to get out of them."

In the fall of 2009 Graham said that Colin Campbell knocked on his door on one of the first freezing mornings of the year and asked if he had seen Jennice, because she had left sometime in the night. Buford said Nancy Campbell had come to ask her the same thing. Graham said he would organize a search party and went to the Campbells' house. There, Nancy Campbell told him she had just found Jennice (who did not answer my requests for an interview) out back. Graham went to look, and said that he found her in a crawl space below the porch, dressed in summer clothes and open shoes. "She was shivering like nothing I had ever seen and crying uncontrollably."

Graham said Nancy Campbell told him that Jennice had been disobedient and couldn't come in until she apologized. It was then Graham thought he understood what had really happened. "She had been out all night in the freeze. They had put her out," he said. "If you want my opinion, they were building an alibi." Graham told Campbell she could let the girl in the house or he would take her home with him; Campbell grudgingly let them enter. "I got her warmed up enough that she got herself composed. And I whispered in her ear, I am going to get you out of here, but I need you to apologize and just be here until I can."

Later that day, Buford said, the girl came to her house and asked for help. Buford said she took her to an unresponsive Hickman County DCS. "They said there wasn't any abuse going on up there." Together with a Nashville woman, whom Buford said had taken in another of the Campbell's adoptees after she left the household, they appealed to other local leaders, whose influence allowed them to get Jennice out of the home.

In January 2011 Buford said the Campbells' son John, who also did not respond to interview requests, came to her as well. Buford and Graham had often seen him working long hours in the Campbells' vegetable garden, from ten in the morning until four in the afternoon in both the cold of winter and the heat of high summer, when Graham said even Tennessee guard dogs are brought inside. When John appealed to Buford, he was already eighteen and beyond the Department of Children's Services' mandate. Buford, who was leaving town for her sister's funeral, took him to the homeless mission in Nashville, but she said that John, whose only experience of life in America had been in Primm Springs, returned to the Campbells within hours. "They were going to help him, but this boy is so illiterate and frightened," said Buford. "He'd been there pretty much all his life and kept in the dark, and now he's afraid of everything." Buford later received a letter from John (who had at least basic writing skills)—in his handwriting but not using his normal vocabulary—saying it was all a mistake and the Campbells were good to him. From there he was sent to Kentucky, then returned for a period before leaving again.

Graham exhausted the possibilities of agencies he thought could help: the county sheriff, DCS, the state Department of Health, the Tennessee Bureau of Investigation. He never heard back from anyone—something that was not a surprise to another Tennessee children's welfare worker, speaking on condition of anonymity, who said that Hickman County has a reputation for not wanting to rock the boat with religious conservatives in the Primm Springs area. In frustration Graham and Buford called a local news channel, but when producers showed up at the Allisons' home, the children refused to talk. ("We didn't know who they were," Kula remembers.)

"Slavery is alive and well. There's no doubt in my mind," Graham told me in 2011. "I couldn't get anybody to do anything for those kids. I am strictly bitter over that, and I will always remain bitter."

ONE COLD SPRING MORNING in 2008 CeCe said Serene woke her up and demanded that she wash the dishes immediately. CeCe lagged, saying that she needed to get dressed, but Serene was adamant. She called Sam and told him that CeCe had declared she was sick of the family and was leaving the house. Though CeCe denied that she said that, she decided she agreed and went upstairs to pack a suitcase. "I told her I'm sick of everything that you guys have been doing to us. You don't send us to school, you don't feed us the right food." CeCe took her suitcase and hid in the woods until nightfall, at which time Serene called the police to report that CeCe had run away. CeCe sat among the trees and watched the police look for her.

That night CeCe decided she couldn't leave without Isaiah and Cherish, so she returned to the cabin. She said she could see the Allisons inside and banged on the door, but they ignored her. She banged harder, and Sam came out and pushed her; she fell hard on her back and said Sam then sat over her and hit her. CeCe kneeled in front of the house and wailed until the Allisons called the police. When they came CeCe said the police told her she had the option to obey her parents or go to jail.

Sam then took CeCe and Kula, who claimed the day before she had been beaten to the point of bleeding, to the home of "Sis Sherena," a black woman who knew the Allisons from a church in nearby Franklin, which they attended in addition to Colin Campbell's small congregation. The next morning CeCe awoke in pain and she said that Sherena took her to the hospital. According to CeCe, Sherena helped them call CPS and later accompanied them to court when they said they didn't want to return to the Allisons.

The children said the Allisons complained bitterly that Sherena had betrayed them, goading the girls into lies. When they saw her at the courthouse, CeCe said, they told Sherena to leave, then they took CeCe and Kula to Sam's mother's house until they figured out another place to send them. That day, while Buford was sitting on her porch with a visiting social worker, she saw CeCe walking up the road dragging a suitcase. When she asked CeCe what she was doing, CeCe replied that she was just exercising and would soon go home. The next morning, during a rainstorm, Buford awoke to the sound of the doorbell. CeCe and Kula were standing outside, drenched. They had left their grandmother's house in the morning, unsure where they would be taken next.

"Kula asked, 'Lady, can you help us?'" Buford said she would take them to the Department of Children's Services, but the girls told her that the agency had already been to the house and done nothing. Buford persisted, going to the Hickman County DCS. The agency, which would not comment for this story except to acknowledge that a case had existed regarding the Allisons, eventually allowed Buford to take the girls home with her that day, where they stayed for some weeks until a custody hearing was held. Kula had an uncle living in Eastern Tennessee who became her guardian. Her brother Alfred left with her. CeCe was sent first to Sam Allison's sister in nearby Franklin and eventually to the North Carolina home of the director of the Daniel Hoover orphanage. "[I felt] homeless, no parents," she said, "like a street dog that nobody cared about."

IN NOVEMBER 2008 the Allisons sent CeCe from North Carolina to Atlanta, where she stayed with Kate and Roger Thompson, wealthy family friends of the Campbells. The Allisons meant to keep her there temporarily, en route to a home for wayward girls. Kate Thompson has known the Campbells for decades, since they had appealed to the Thompsons—fellow Australians and Christians—to watch Serene and another sister while they went on a mission trip to Florida. After the Allisons adopted the Liberian children, Serene had gotten in touch with Kate to ask her advice about Engedi, who was slow in learning to talk. The Allisons had been hitting her to get her to speak, without results. Kate gave Serene speech exercises to try instead. Later the Thompsons gave the Allisons a gift of $5,000 to drill themselves a new well.

On paper Kate seems to fit the profile of an *Above Rubies* devotee: a Christian singer-songwriter with an album about adoption called "Broken Hearts and Broken Wings," she has fourteen children, eight of whom were adopted through foster care. But, she said, "We are not the Duggars," referencing the nineteen-child reality TV family admired by many *Above Rubies* fans. They hadn't set out to have so many children, Roger explained, but years of working with the local foster care system—they estimate that between forty and fifty children have passed through their house—left them with multiple sets of siblings the state hoped to keep together.

The Thompsons didn't feel that they understood the Allisons. Roger took Sam for a dreamer with half-baked ideas—to build a boat and start a family-run shipping company—but the Thompsons had believed that the Allisons' intentions were good. "I felt sorry for her. She was barely in her thirties, trying to deal with teenage kids coming from traumatic backgrounds," said Kate. "Serene always did wildly impulsive things."

Then in spring of 2009, several months after the Thompsons took in CeCe, Serene called to say that they were sending Isaiah back to Liberia. After the three oldest children left the compound Isaiah felt alone in navigating life at the Allisons; Sam had told him not to talk to his sister again. At an earlier point, Isaiah admitted to touching one of the Allisons' biological daughters, four years his junior, whom he said he kissed and lay on top of while she was in bed. Isaiah told the Allisons about the kiss, and a report of sex abuse between the children was filed by the Department of Child Services, which instructed the family to keep the boys in a separate bedroom. Now, Serene told the Thompsons, she had caught him watching her in the shower.

CeCe was beside herself. The Thompsons begged the Allisons to send Isaiah instead to counseling or at least to let CeCe see him; they warned them that it was illegal to send Isaiah back to Liberia. CeCe called the Allisons daily, but they hung up on her. The Thompsons called the local DCS and were told that the Allisons had been warned not to repatriate their son.

In Primm Springs the Allisons told Isaiah he would be in worse trouble if he stayed. "They told me, if we told people about what you did, they'd put you in jail, so the best thing to do is to send you to Africa," said Isaiah. "I felt so bad, I didn't even care."

He was sent first to a series of other homes: to stay with a young man from church; then on a bus by himself to the home of a Liberian pastor in St. Louis, who couldn't understand Isaiah's willingness to return to their struggling country and warned, "'Boy, you're going to die if you go back there'"; then into the Missouri countryside to the man who would escort him back.

CeCe and Kate spoke to him by phone, imploring him to let them come get him. "He said, 'Yes, CeCe, I did kiss Serene, I did kiss [the girl],'" Kate remembers. "'I'm a bad boy. I've got to go back to Africa.'"

Just before he left, Isaiah told Sam that an older boy had raped him for years in Daniel Hoover; the admission, however, made no difference. When they arrived in Monrovia Isaiah's escort found the orphanage closed and left him with another pastor who cared for street children. "When he was about to leave, I was scared and said, 'Please don't leave,'" said Isaiah. "I thought, oh my gosh, I'm so dead. Back here again?"

When Isaiah was dropped in Liberia he had only a backpack of clothes and forty dollars he had earned working with Sam. His passport had been brought back to the Allisons; his green card would expire after he was away from the United States for six months. He stayed with the pastor and scavenged for food for three weeks until his grandmother learned, through Liberia's finely tuned rumor mill, that he was back. She brought him to her home in River Cess, a desolate coastal outpost in the country's interior where, though Isaiah could no longer understand the Kru language his cousins spoke, he felt safe for the first time in months.

Food was scarce—a bowl of rice a day supplemented by coconuts, mangos, or what fish the older children caught—and disease was harsh. Isaiah slept much of the day to block out his hunger and picked up a foot parasite that burrowed under his skin and had to be dug out with sharpened bamboo. Then he contracted malaria along with a five-year-old cousin, who died one night asleep at his side after weeks of frothing and spasms. Isaiah lay in terrified silence beside her, afraid that her spirit would enter his body. He didn't know how long he was there; with the Allisons he hadn't fully learned how to measure time into weeks or months, and to him, it felt like forever. "I remember crying by myself all the time," said Isaiah. "To stop myself from crying, I would think that what I did"— with the Allisons' daughter—"was really bad and this is the least I can do for them."

ALL BUT THREE of the Campbells' and Allisons' original ten adoptions failed in one way or another, formally or informally, leaving only the Campbells' daughter Mercy and the Allisons' Cherish and Engedi living at home. Campbell purged her website of all mention of the other children and rumors began to circulate among *Above Rubies* readers about what had happened to the children. In an online video recorded in January 2009, Serene claimed that the missing children were off at school. Campbell's own biography was amended to say she had adopted "some" Liberian children.

Campbell refused to answer specific questions for this story and refused on behalf of the Allisons as well. In an e-mail she admitted there were difficult situations with the older Liberian children, who "came as adults with no interest in becoming part of a family." Serene, Campbell told me (as she would also claim to readers who asked), "did have some problems with her older children (who were adults) and wanted their independence immediately. . . . She embraced these children as though they were from her womb and it was terribly painful for her to be rejected by them."

· What happened in the Allisons' home was extreme but not isolated. In the years after the Liberian adoption boom there came a new wave of reports of troubled adoptions, disruptions, and abuse. Most cases arose from adoptions facilitated by the Christian brokers that Campbell and *Above Rubies* had endorsed.

In 2008, in Washington, Kimberly Forder, whose adopted daughter, Grace, had been pictured on the cover of *Above Rubies'* first Liberian adoption issue, pled guilty to manslaughter. WACSN had facilitated Forder's adoption of triplets despite the fact that a previous adoptee, an eight-year-old boy named Christopher, had died of pneumonia in her care in 2002. Forder moved to Monrovia and lived on the WACSN compound after an investigation into that death was opened in 2006, when another of her children alleged that Christopher had died because of their mother's abuse, beating the child, restricting his access to food and water, making him sleep in the basement and punishing him by dunking his head repeatedly in a bucket of dirty water.

In December 2010 an Oklahoma court stripped a Mennonite Brethren family in Fairview—where WACSN's "How Big Is God" Monrovia crusade was conceived—of custody of five sisters adopted from Liberia. Penny and Ardee Tyler were charged with felony child abuse as well as their adult son of rape by instrumentation, which revolved around their sense that one daughter was filled with "bad spirits." The couple, who adopted through WACSN, was accused by one of the daughters of hitting her with a rake, tying her to a bedpost, making her "fast" for up to twelve days, sleep outside, and attempting to commit her to a mental institution.

Also in 2010 a homeschooling couple in Paradise, California, who had adopted through Acres of Hope, Kevin and Elizabeth Schatz, beat one of their three adopted Liberian children, seven-year-old Lydia, to death over the course of several hours, breaking down her muscle tissue and causing kidney failure. In their home was found a book, *To Train Up A Child*, written by Michael Pearl, a fundamentalist preacher who lives near Primm Springs, and his wife Debi.

The Pearls' book has sold nearly seven hundred thousand copies, largely to conservative Christian homeschooling families. It received extensive media coverage after being found in the homes of several families whose adopted children died after severe beatings or neglect, including, in 2011, Hana Williams, an Ethiopian adoptee whose parents were charged with her death by hypothermia after they had put her outside as a form of punishment.*

Michael Pearl's methods of "biblical chastisement," though sometimes misrepresented in the media, champion strict physical discipline starting when children are less than a year old. Perhaps most famously, Pearl recommends flexible plumbing supply line as a spanking instrument and compares proper child rearing to training a mule. Pearl vehemently denies that those deaths followed from his teachings and has defended his book instead as corrective training for abusive parents, who hit out of anger instead of the impassive self-discipline he prescribes. "You must know that they did not kill their children with the little switches that we advocate using," Pearl told me. "[They were] locking them outdoors, giving them cold baths, denying them food and beating them mercilessly. There's nothing in our literature that would suggest anything like that."

---

*Williams' death led to the establishment of a Washington state panel called the Severe Abuse of Adopted Children Committee, which released a 2012 study on fifteen abuse or neglect cases in the state in 2010 and 2011. In 2012, Ethiopia's Ministry of Women's Affairs, the entity in charge of international adoptions from the country, temporarily suspended the licenses of two more US agencies, International Adoption Guides and Adoption Advocates International, the latter of which had conducted Hana Williams' adoption, over concerns about abuse of adopted children. (In December 2012, the suspension on the other agency, IAG, was lifted.)

What is in the book, though, is a constant promise that "the rod" will bring harmony to a family in chaos, creating "whineless" children who have learned to submit. "Somehow, after eight or ten licks, the poison is transformed into gushing love and contentment," Pearl wrote of a sullen child who is given a spanking. "The world becomes a beautiful place. A brand new child emerges. It makes an adult stare at the rod in wonder, trying to see what magic is contained therein."

Nancy Campbell's own teachings echo this. "It is amazing how peaceful and happy a child can be after they have received a good spanking," she wrote in one column. A guest essay further argues that children are "little bundles of depravity" that need spanking to drive out original sin.

In a community where the appearance of orderly family life may be the highest status marker, the stakes for extracting children's obedience are serious. But even Pearl has said that his "conditioning" methods, meant to instill complete obedience from infancy on, are not suited for older children or adoptees from other cultures. "If you haven't trained a child and won their heart by the time they're eight or nine, then you're basically living with an adversary," Pearl told me. "If you spank them then, it's not going to reap positive results."

PEARL'S MINISTRY, No Greater Joy, began to receive letters, said ministry representative Chuck Joyner, from some of the hundreds of *Above Rubies* families that adopted from Liberia, a number of whom lived along the forty miles between Campbell and Pearl. "Many if not the majority of the families encountered problems so severe that they had to give up the children," Joyner told me. Pearl published a warning about some Liberian children adopted by his followers in an advice column for parents. "Right here in our own community a family adopted three children from Liberia. We warned them, but they were so caught up with good feelings about how they were sacrificing their lives to save poor starving children from orphanages that they danced their way into tragedy. They have several children younger than the three adopted kids, who, unknowing to them, were well-versed in all the dark arts of eroticism and ghastly perversion." Pearl continued that he had received many letters from families who adopted from Liberia, "and nearly every one of them—if not all—told sad stories of the fall of their natural children into sexual deviance."

"You could see the sexualness in all four of them," Pearl elaborated to me. "The predatorness."

Pearl's accusation resonated with many parents whose adopted children had been sexually abused while in the orphanages and who had acted out sexually after adoption—and this fed the imaginations of other adopters. A 2008 letter from Acres of Hope explained that ministry staff had discovered children "engaging in sexual exploration" in the orphanage. On online forums parents exchanged stories of children manifesting inappropriate behaviors and their suspicions of lasciviousness in the children's actions. One mother on a listserv claimed that her adopted son had told her, "In Liberia we did sex all the time, how do you expect us to come to America, be around your beautiful children and not try to have sex with them!"

"I think it's important to understand that children are exposed to so much more here [in Africa]," Acres of Hope's Patty Anglin told me. "With many of these kids who grow up in orphanages, they don't learn parameters because they're basically raising themselves. Many times we would see in a twelve- or thirteen-year-old behavior that we would consider normal in a six-year-old."

The parents complained more broadly about behavioral issues. They called Liberian children manipulative and wild, compulsive liars or thieves, and sometimes violent. "When I share that I trust a particular person in Liberia I say 'as much as you can trust a Liberian,'" wrote one adoptive mother. "There are two languages in Liberia," another wrote. "English and lying." Families described the distressing reactions of Liberian children to scolding, as they fell from pouting into an unresponsive state or sometimes began to wail uncontrollably. Some parents regarded it as the manifestations of PTSD, whereas others saw it as defiance. Some claimed they feared for their own or their family's safety.

Tama Covert, a New Mexico mother who adopted two Liberian children and who also learned about adoption through *Above Rubies,* became pen pals with Elizabeth Schatz after she was charged with Lydia's murder. Before the Schatzes entered a plea, Covert wrote to the district attorney prosecuting the case to offer a counter-perspective on how she felt Liberian adoptees could "push parents' buttons" by, for example, willfully refusing to enunciate. Having disrupted one of her own two adoptions, Covert wrote, "It is only by God's Grace and Mercy I am not sitting in a cell next to Elizabeth now."

"Most of us who have adopted these children have come from Christian homes and have a strong faith," Covert told me. "We felt God was telling us, 'This is what I want you to do.' And I know that Elizabeth and

Kevin said 'Yes' to God. They tried to get these children who are so unbelievably damaged to be able to enter into society."

IN ADDITION to the Pearls' prescriptions, some parents in the forums
began trading suggestions for treating Reactive Attachment Disorder
(RAD), a severe and uncommon disorder that traditionally results when
children's early bonds are disrupted. Although attachment problems are a
legitimate issue, and there are legitimate and respected treatments for
RAD, many critics say the disorder is greatly overdiagnosed in adoptive
children; some quoted in the *Los Angeles Times* compared it to "the 'attention deficit hyperactivity disorder of the 1990s.'" "These kiddos are ex-
hausting and you need a break," one adoptive parent wrote. "Make sure
you take him to a therapist who has experience with RAD . . . traditional
therapy does NOT work." Others recommended methods like "holding
therapy," in which children are physically restrained within a caregiver's
or surrogate's embrace for prolonged periods of time while forcing them
to maintain eye contact and sometimes being fed sweets, "power sitting"
sessions of making the child sit in one location for many hours, and a restricted diet—standbys of attachment therapy that seem to resonate with
methods like Pearl's.

Rachael Stryker, an anthropologist of human development and
women's studies at California State University and author of *The Road to
Evergreen: Adoption, Attachment Therapy, and the Promise of Family,* said
there's a common language between one school of RAD therapies that became prominent in the '90s, the "Evergreen model," and methods like
Pearl's. Both present parenting "as a battle." "The synergy comes from a
'spare the rod, spoil the child' perspective," Stryker continued. "The RAD
therapies are really all about taking control of the children, under the aus-
pices of keeping them safe and helping them trust adults." In Stryker's
survey of a number of families seeking RAD treatments for their children
in Evergreen, Colorado, the industry center of the Evergreen model,*
enough parents identified as strongly religious to give these secular RAD
therapies a sense of being imbued with Christian teachings. "Even though
they couldn't articulate it, there was something about the philosophy that

---

*There are other practitioners in Evergreen who follow different models of
RAD treatment.

matched up with their intuition and their folk wisdom about parenting," she said.

Dr. Jean Mercer, a psychology professor emerita at Richard Stockton College and a critic of attachment therapy, said the language of these RAD therapies—like the language that became common around Liberian adoptions—opens the door for more aggressive tactics. Descriptions of RAD carried an extra urgency, with warnings that RAD children will grow into criminals, sociopaths, addicts, or, in an odd equivalence for women, prostitutes, unless they receive extreme intervention. "The phrase, 'these children,' is something said again and again. They're saying, 'we're talking about a special kind of person here, not an everyday child. This is a person who will grow up to be a serial killer.' This is beyond pathologizing—it's demonization."

The demonization could be quite literal. On some attachment disorder websites one indicator listed for RAD is "a darkness behind the eyes when raging." Renee Polreis, a Colorado adoptive mother convicted for the 1997 beating death of her two-year-old son, and sentenced to 22 years in prison, had defended herself by claiming her son had RAD; she'd earlier described her fear of her son's home country, Russia, as a nation filled with atheists. Liberia's Ministry of Health and Social Welfare heard about one case of an adoptee beaten because his adoptive parents believed "he had a devil sitting on him." And Tama Covert told me that she had always wondered whether the daughter whose adoption she had disrupted—and who she said she fears may one day return to harm the family—had refused to submit because her birthmother had used her in a tribal ritual and the girl had thereby been "sold out to the devil."

"The very basic idea of attachment therapy is that you want the child to be obedient, and the child must recognize your authority," Mercer continued. "They equate attachment with obedience. When you have that point of view, you go on to all the nasty kinds of things that human beings do to each other."

Experience from other adoptions gone awry indicates what this could mean. A little-understood corner of the adoption world is the realm of ad hoc respite caregivers who take in adopted children whose parents have declared they can no longer care for them. Although respite care at its best can be a temporary break for both child and parents who have reached their limit, at other times the term can be used to cover "dumping" kids in paid or unpaid group homes. Among these facilities is Montana's the Ranch For Kids Project, a church-owned residential home where international adoptees, mostly Russian, are sent for "horse therapy" and farm work at a cost of approximately $3,500 to $4,000 per month. For some parents sending children to the Ranch is a means to effectively disrupt or end the adoption. For others, like one Christian couple who began fundraising online for Ranch tuition just a few months after adopting a teenage girl from China—whose $30,000 adoption they had also financed almost entirely with donations—it was presented as another step in saving their daughter's soul. "We are battling for our daughter's heart," they wrote in block letters on their website, *Hope. Believe. Obey.* "We will do whatever it takes until she is healed, complete and full of joy!"

In 2012 officials from Russia, angry over a stream of cases in which Russian adoptees were abused, neglected, or killed—to date, US adoptive parents have been accused of having killed nearly twenty children adopted from Russia—staged a photo op outside the Ranch, demanding entry to see whether the children were safe.

Other options for parents seeking a respite from their adopted child or to dissolve the adoption entirely are even less savory, including a series of homes run by private families who function as an underground network for what has come to be known euphemistically as "rehoming" children of failed adoptions.* Operating largely by word of mouth, these families put out a shingle as self-declared experts on attachment therapy and large adoptive families. They take in dozens of children, sometimes in exchange for payment from the disrupting adoptive parents and sometimes as a means of adopting more children if they can't afford adoption fees, if they've failed a home study, or if state foster care or home study agencies have cut them off for having too many children already. "There are homes all across the United States that transfer kids from one place to another. No one's keeping tabs on this," Tennessee Sheriff Joe Shepard told *USA Today* in 2006.

Incredibly, many of these homes have focused particularly on children with intensive medical or emotional needs, to the point at which their homes begin to resemble therapeutic group homes rather than the family life that adoption advocates say they're working to provide each child. While in some cases, that may be a beneficial arrangement, in others, it can shade into abuse. In one case a fundamentalist Christian family in Oregon, Dennis and Diane Nason—Diane is the author of the Christian adoption book *The Celebration Family* and the family was featured on an

---

*"Rehoming" is a euphemism for all disruptions, not just those that go to these sorts of homes.

eponymous ABC made-for-television movie as well as on *60 Minutes*—adopted an astounding seventy-eight children (in addition to their six biological kids). Many of these adopted children had high medical needs and three of them died, allegedly of neglect. When their family inevitably fell apart, more than sixty children were sent to other homes, and the Nasons were charged with the children's deaths. The couple was cleared of manslaughter and child abuse charges in a 1995 trial, but convicted of lesser charges of forgery and racketeering for falsifying records so they could adopt more children, and using their family as a "criminal enterprise" to maintain a flow of donations from supporters. Some children were reportedly left "damaged beyond repair," while the Nasons served 60 days for their sentence.

While Stryker was conducting her research in Evergreen, she encountered some people running private respite homes, taking in dozens of special-needs adoptees or foster kids whose adoptions were disrupted. They had come to Colorado to observe attachment therapists work, learning a modicum of technique to apply at home.

Some homes in this mold were later shut down for severe child abuse, including, in 2006, that of Debra and Tom Schmitz of Tennessee. The Schmitzes had eighteen children, mostly disabled, at the time of their arrest, and they were accused of locking them in caged-in beds, depriving them of physical aids like braces, and bizarre punishments resonant of those allegedly inflicted on other adoptees: holding children's heads under water or forcing them to "dig their own graves." The line between families that are simply large and religious and those that tip into abuse is not always clear, even to those on the inside. Years before the Schmitzes were arrested, Patty Anglin wrote about helping the couple, who then lived in Wisconsin—they reportedly later moved to Tennessee after they were investigated on child abuse allegations—to navigate a tricky interstate adoption in her 1999 book, *Acres of Hope: The Miraculous Story of One Family's Gift of Love to Children Without Hope*. Initial charges against the couple resulted in a mistrial. On the second trial, the Schmitzes pled guilty. Debra received a six-month sentence and her husband, a year of probation.

IT SEEMED EQUALLY difficult for adoption advocates to recognize the potential for abuse inside the comparatively smaller families conducting Liberian adoptions, families that averaged just ten or twelve kids instead of the eighteen or twenty common to the unofficial respite homes. Although Anglin referred to Pearl's book as "a religious cult" she would never recommend to her clients, she had sympathy for other parents, whom she saw as simply in over their heads, unprepared "for the devastation that these children were suffering from." The *Above Rubies* families that adopted from Liberia were "good, good families, but oftentimes they have the heart, but not necessarily the background or education to understand what is involved," Anglin told me. "It's not just about an orphan child. It's an orphan child who has gone through trauma and who may have posttraumatic stress disorder or has obviously seen and experienced things that we can't even imagine."

There was a wide-ranging assignment of blame. Facilitators chided parents for not being patient enough with war-traumatized children. Parents blamed facilitators for abandoning them with problems beyond what was disclosed. Anglin suggested a further failure by home study agencies for not educating families, and she has publicly noted that Acres of Hope did not conduct the home study for the Schatzes, the California family that killed their Liberian daughter. At a 2012 panel on disrupted adoptions Dr. Jon Bergeron of Hope for Orphans excused parents who dissolved their adoptions with a dehumanizing portrait of the children they had taken in. Sharing an anecdote about his family's adopted dog, Bergeron said that a house break-in had traumatized the dog, which then became dangerous as a result of the trauma. "We couldn't just step back and try harder and do more to work with him. We had to make the hard decision," he told the audience, referencing their eventual decision to give up the dog, "and that's where these families are at."

Lydia Sherman, of Liberia's Ministry of Health and Social Welfare, had little patience for arguments like these. "You're adopting a child from a third-world country that went through fourteen years of civil war. What exactly do you think you're adopting? The whole idea of sending them to the United States is because the US is more advanced and has all the different treatments there. *You're* supposed to help them," she told me.

Cheryl Carter-Shotts, whose adoption agency has had no disrupted adoptions from Liberia, said parents need constant support and reminders—that their child was coming from a war zone and would need a full year to recover from every year they were in danger, went hungry, or witnessed violence. But instead of encountering this patience, many, perhaps even most, of the older, traumatized children coming from Liberia went into families in which attachment and love were defined as immediate and unqualified obedience. It was a mismatch of the needs of children and the capabilities of adoptive parents on a nearly epic scale, with many Liberian adoptees going to exactly the wrong sorts of families.

Even Patty Anglin admitted the pairings were sometimes off. "In adoptions, even in America with foster care or anywhere in the world, you are going to have a certain percentage of adoptive families that just probably shouldn't have adopted to begin with," she told me. "And [yet] they make it through the system—they don't have any criminal record, they're well intended. Many of the families were—and I want to be careful in saying this because I myself am a Christian—but those far-right wingers oftentimes, are more narrow in their tolerance level and understanding. And they're probably less prepared, because they live in a more protective environment."

Stories began to pile up of children being returned to Liberia. "You heard about the Tennessee case that returned the child to Russia?" Edward Winant, former vice consul in charge of adoptions at the US Embassy in Monrovia, asked me. He was referencing the adoptive mother in Tennessee who had sent her seven-year-old Russian son back to Moscow in 2010, with a note pinned to his coat charging that he was violent and mentally unstable. "We've had at least three similar cases, where the parents took the child, for some reason they couldn't handle them, and sent them back." In one case, Winant said, a Liberian girl between seven and ten was found wandering the Brussels airport with $200 in her pocket.

The disruption rates were probably similar to those for neighboring Sierra Leone, Winant thought—another country recovering from civil war, where some reports found that overwhelming majorities of children surveyed had witnessed someone being killed or injured or had seen a dead body—but the disruptions were happening at a much higher volume with Liberian kids.

The Department of State announced that in 2008 the Liberian government began to carefully review all Liberian adoptions after the country's government had learned about the growing number of adoptive families who had disrupted or dissolved their adoptions, ending their relationship with the child. Bishop Emmanuel Jones, a Liberian evangelist who runs an orphanage and a home for street children, has taken in at least four children adopted through ACFI who were later returned to Liberia, and he knows of five others who were sent back. Some families sent him children—mostly boys—to "get reorientation" after they displayed sexual behavior; girls were returned because of perceived resistance to authority, said Jones, because "they don't want to submit." Some of the families wanted Jones to counsel the kids and return them to the United States. "But some of [the families] don't even know how to help," said Jones, "so in their frustration, they just say, okay, we'll send you back to Africa."

Among the boys playing in the walled-in compound outside Jones's Monrovia office when we met in 2011 was one who had been sent back nearly two years earlier. Jones still gets requests to help parents repatriate their children. Other children who are "rehomed" simply drop off the map, as little adequate tracking of disrupted adoptions exists. General statistics for the United States hold that between 6 and 11 percent of all adoptions are disrupted, with the rate of failure climbing to nearly 25 percent for children adopted as adolescents. Sometimes it's because of serious issues of family safety—problems with children behaving sexually or violently—and sometimes, several adoption workers told me, it's for much more benign frustrations: grinding teeth, repetitive behaviors, or even irksome medical problems like ringworm. "There's no protocol when a disruption happens," said Maureen Flatley, an adoption oversight expert who has lobbied for adoption reform legislation. "There's almost no knowledge of where these kids go when they leave the families that originally adopted them."

In 2011 I learned the answer for one, an eighteen-year-old young man named Saah Fayiah who had been adopted from Liberia through WACSN in 2007 to a US couple in Pennsylvania. As an infant during the early years of the civil war, Fayiah had been shot in the head while his mother held him. His mother died, but Fayiah lived with the bullet embedded in his skull for years—until his adoptive parents had it removed in the United States. The injury left Fayiah with some atrophied muscles on one side of his body and undetermined cognitive and emotional wounds. Further, at some point during his first year of adoption he was accused of making a violent threat, though the details are unclear and Fayiah denied it. Within a year after his adoption Fayiah was returned to Liberia—though his sense of the timeline is shaky, and his adoptive family, who requested not to be named, said that Fayiah's brain injury and emotional issues had left him with an impaired memory.

Since the quiet disruption of his adoption, Fayiah, now a thin young man easily overwhelmed with grief, has lived with other impoverished young men, former employees cast off from WACSN when the adoption business closed, in an unfinished building miles outside Monrovia. Fayiah receives no financial support from either his adoptive or biological families, is unable to afford school fees, and faces the additional stigma of having returned to Liberia from the United States without any money or advantages to show for it. People who know his story think he squandered his opportunity to prosper in the States and mockingly call him, "American man, American Fayiah."

"I have people who used to tell me I had a green card," Fayiah told me in the back room of a makeshift café off Monrovia's Old Road, a crowded strip of shanties and markets, "but I haven't seen it. I'm a citizen of America, but I have to be back now in Liberia." He eagerly showed me an outdated US passport that he carries around everywhere and asked whether I could help him find a US sponsor. "I don't really understand what I did in America that I had to be sent back," he said.

Although Heather Cannon-Winkelman, a founding WACSN board member who resigned from the agency over disagreements about its adoption practices, has tried many times since 2009 to help Fayiah reestablish his claim to US citizenship, she has been repeatedly told that the adoptive family is still responsible for him—or at least that they had been until he turned eighteen—and that there's little that US or Liberian government bodies can do. In 2012, despairing of ever getting him support from US officials, and suspecting that his adoption had never been finalized in the United States, Cannon-Winkelman personally sponsored him and several other children to go to school full time in Liberia.

The number of Liberian children whose citizenship was in question after their adoptions were disrupted has led some people familiar with the stories to suspect that adoptive parents intentionally failed to complete the adoptions so as to make disruption easier if it became necessary, as parents who disrupt and send their children into foster care can be liable for child support. In 2012 Johanna, the adoptive mother who had watched the Liberian adoption phenomenon grow among *Above Rubies* families, received an e-mail from a fundamentalist homeschooling family that at one time had had twelve children, including three adopted from Liberia. By the time they contacted Johanna, who lives a few hours away in New York, they were down to ten. The family, so conservative that the women wore head coverings, had already "rehomed" their other two Liberian adoptees—one to a family who had previously failed their home study when they had sought to adopt themselves—and they explained on a family blog that they believed God had used them to bring the children to the families He ultimately intended them to have. Now the family was threatening to send the last child, a fifteen-year-old boy diagnosed with PTSD with psychosis whom they had adopted four years earlier from Daniel Hoover Orphanage, back to Liberia. They cited his nonviolent but emotional outbursts, which were almost certainly a result of the trauma he endured during Liberia's civil war, during which he saw people get killed and was enlisted to clean up the bodies when fighting broke out at the orphanage. They were convinced that this behavior—yelling and punching walls, threatening to harm himself—indicated he might become a sexual predator and harm their biological daughters. "Right now our options are your family, trying to turn him over to the foster care system, or returning him to Liberia," the family wrote to Johanna. The boy, like so many other Liberian adoptees, had been punished by having food withheld or being put outside overnight, and the family had additionally tampered with his psychiatric medications in an attempt to control his outbursts.

"They were never prepared to bring these children home. They're not bad people, but what they've done is extremely wrong," said Lisa Bates, another Ohio Christian adoptive mother who had cared for the boy temporarily before he went to Johanna's family. "They did it out of ignorance [and a desire] to be seen doing good." When he came to Bates's house, the teen had only a third-grade education and was so underweight that he gained twenty pounds in two weeks.

The family told Johanna that they had knowingly never gotten around to re-adopting him in the United States, meaning their son wasn't a US citizen. "He said he felt fear every day he was in that home, waiting every day to be thrown out," said Johanna. An attorney they spoke to in New York about handling the custody change as they prepared to adopt him had apparently worked on an almost identical case, for another Liberian child, and believed that a number of families had intentionally failed to complete adoptions to leave themselves a legal loophole.

Bates and Johanna agreed. "If he's not a US citizen and he just disappears, what can [the authorities] do to the family?" Bates asked. "Somebody was thinking about this. Why else would so many of these people not re-adopt?"

It doesn't seem out of the question, given the open conversation around disruption in the *Above Rubies* community. At one point the Liberian adoption discussion forums frequented by families like the one that adopted Johanna's new son were abuzz with adoptive parents seeking to find other homes for their children, and foster care postings featured new Liberian kids every few months. Families called for a suspension of judgment for parents undergoing disruption, which was beginning to seem like just another part of the process. "Let's be a community of support for ALL adoptions," wrote one, "in any aspect of their journey."

WHEN KATE AND ROGER Thompson learned that Isaiah had been sent back to Liberia, they frantically called relatives and government officials. In desperation Roger, a software engineer who created the popular

security program Link Scanner, posted a note on an adoptive parents' forum, and within hours a woman who had adopted Isaiah's cousin got in
touch to say that her mother, a missionary nurse, had sworn she had seen
Isaiah in Monrovia. Her mother knew Isaiah's uncle and put them in
touch. "We didn't really want to be bothered," said Roger, a quiet man in
his sixties with a dry, patient wit. "But when they send a kid back to
Liberia, in my mind that was a death sentence. I didn't want to get involved, but I couldn't stand by."

Through Isaiah's uncle, the Thompsons were able to track him down
in River Cess and bring him back to Monrovia, where he stayed until his
paperwork could be arranged. Sam Allison began calling Isaiah there,
telling him to demand that the Thompsons fly him back to Tennessee. To
the Thompsons he offered to return Isaiah's passport only if Isaiah was
sent back to them. The Thompsons turned to ACFI and later Acres of
Hope to intervene and said that only after the facilitators threatened to report the Allisons did they agree to relinquish custody.

Acres of Hope director Patty Anglin, whom Isaiah visited while waiting to return to the United States, defends the Allisons. "No one was
wrong in that situation. They just felt that for their particular family, it
was not going to work out and was not appropriate," she said, adding that
Engedi's adoption, conducted through Acres of Hope, has been a tremendous success. "I think Sam knew that it was a very dangerous thing he was
doing," said Isaiah. "He said, 'I could get in very big trouble for this. The
Thompsons are going crazy about you and trying to adopt you, and I'm
not going to let that happen.'" When it became clear that Isaiah would go
to the Thompsons, Sam warned him not to answer their questions.

The Thompsons had an escort take him to Brussels, where Kate met
him as he was waiting in a room of other unaccompanied children at the
airport. He had lost twenty pounds since he had left Tennessee and has
since been diagnosed with PTSD. When he started school he tested for
grade 1.8. He's struggled to learn in a few years the foundational lessons
most students learn over a decade.

In July 2009, just before the Thompsons brought Isaiah home, the Allisons e-mailed him care of Anglin. "We had so many dreams and hopes
together," they wrote, "but you must now go on and complete them yourself." They assured Isaiah they had forgiven him as well as the Thompsons
"for this interference," but they said the Thompsons would most likely
want no further contact with them. They warned him against CeCe, whom
they called an angry person and the reason they had to be separated. "We
do not know what you will be told there, but remember the beautiful times

we had together, remember we loved you always," they wrote. "No one can ever take away the truth of what really happened here."

CeCe found the letter in his bag when he returned to Atlanta and was so angered that she tore it up; Kate taped the pieces to save. Isaiah had never read it because he hadn't learned to read at the Allisons'.

IN A MODEST APARTMENT complex behind a hospital in Monroe, North Carolina, a suburb twenty-five miles from Charlotte, CeCe lives with her husband, Samuel, a fellow adoptee she's had her eye on since they lived together at the Daniel Hoover Orphanage. Their twenty-month-old son, Sammy, and Samuel's sister, who was adopted by the same family as her brother, live with them. Samuel, a slim and quiet twenty-one-year-old with a face full of middle-aged worries, was among the Hallelujah Chorus boys adopted to North Carolina. Many of the couple's former fellow orphanage mates live nearby, as did the orphanage director until recently. When CeCe and Samuel married in 2011, all of CeCe's bridesmaids, dressed in alternating red and white strapless gowns, were Daniel Hoover adoptees. Although CeCe's story stands out, they count a number of friends who are estranged from their adoptive families and have limited job or education prospects. "Most of them, when we came to America, there was some part of us that a lot of adoptive parents didn't understand, that we would never be the same like their own kids," said CeCe. "If someone said to me again, do you want to be adopted, I'd say never. . . . I don't feel like we were adopted. We were sold."

Samuel works days at a Tyson chicken processing plant, and in the winter of 2012 CeCe began working nights in the same division to make ends meet and intermittently tried to make extra money through a direct sales jewelry business. She had applied once for cosmetology school but didn't have the adoption papers to demonstrate citizenship nor, at the time, education records to prove she had received at least a seventh-grade education. She's asked the Allisons for them, but for several years they did not return her calls.

On a sunny November morning in 2011 CeCe sat with me in her living room, its sliding door looking out into a field of other apartment developments, while Sammy crawled after the family dog, a black Cocker Spaniel, nervous with love. As CeCe fed Samuel, he began to fuss. She coaxed him with loud air kisses until his chubby face, covered in baby food, erupted into fat-cheeked chuckles. "He's the first baby, he's going to be spoiled," CeCe said. "You want a child to have what you didn't have."

The Allisons, like a number of other adoptive parents of Liberian children, never completed the stateside process of their adoptions, leaving the children's citizenship in jeopardy. Kula found that out when she was re-adopted by Pam Epperly, a longtime foster mother in Oliver Springs, Tennessee, just before she turned eighteen. It was an opportunity no longer open to CeCe and Alfred, who, by the time they left the Allisons' home, were both already too old to be adopted.

Just before Kula's adoption, there was a routine court case to assess her remaining needs. "While in court, Kula made disclosures that disturbed our court staff as well as the judge," a representative from a Tennessee children's service provider, who cannot name herself or her organization, told me. With the judge's backing, she called child protective services to start a new investigation of the Allisons. "I've spoken with both CeCe and Kula as well as Kate," she said, "and all of these stories are more than enough to corroborate themselves and personal enough for me to say they didn't just get together and rehearse." The local Hickman County CPS office opened two cases. The staffer also made a referral to Tennessee's human trafficking authority—the life of labor and abuse at the Allisons' fit the bill, she said—but by the time she had enough information to register the referral, the family had moved.

In 2011, after the investigation had progressed several months—closing one case because the remaining Allison children did not make any disclosures of abuse—the Allisons appeared to leave the state. They told CPS in Tennessee that they were planning to move to Maryland, but one of the Campbells' adoptees told CeCe they had instead gone to Texas, where Sam has family and the "Texas Rubies" are strong. In July 2011 *Above Rubies* announced that Serene was moving "up country" to be with her husband, who had an unspecified military contract. Campbell told me simply that they had left Tennessee. The staffer requested an attachment—a police order to return the children—but the county did not acknowledge it. Unable to find the Allisons, the local CPS office closed the second case.

CeCe worried about her sister Cherish and Engedi, who are still with the Allisons, and feared she had broken her promise to their mother to always keep her siblings safe. At some point after their disappearance the Allisons seemed to quietly return to Tennessee, and in the summer of 2012, CeCe befriended them on Facebook. Her adopted brother Alfred, who lived on his own and worked as a caregiver, had already reached out to them months earlier, explaining to me in early 2012 that he was trying to forgive and move on. CeCe also said she had forgiven them, but more importantly, was trying to keep her promise to her mother to always protect Isaiah and their sister, Cherish. "If I had to see them before I see Cherish, I'll do that," she told me in October. The Thompsons were hurt and so was Isaiah, but a distance had grown between them anyway over what began as minor family disputes: how CeCe had left the Thompsons' house when she became pregnant before marrying her husband as well as a more recent fight about Isaiah when Kate had tried to bring him for a visit. In the wake of that fight, CeCe contacted the Allisons, asking to see Cherish, and heard back for the first time in years. When they spoke by phone, CeCe says, the Allisons asked her if she was "ready to come home and let God take control of things."

The turnaround was unsurprising to the children's social services worker who had requested that CPS investigate the family. "When children are abused in a situation, there is the establishment of control, over time, over the children, which is why they don't want to talk and make any disclosures. It's very similar to battered wives syndrome. If the children at any point established a connection, they're going to want to return. Even though it ended badly, it's still a connection they have."

The Allisons did not return requests for an interview or to answer questions other than several late 2012 e-mails from Sam Allison that denied the allegations the children had made and attested that the family had since reconciled. "Me and my wife have made peace with our children and enjoy a good relationship with them now," he wrote. "By dredging this up you are not letting us put the past behind us and go on [with] life."

In September 2012 CeCe traveled to Tennessee to visit them and see her sister for the first time in years. Cherish was nearly a teenager, and Engedi had begun to talk. The Allisons cried, and Serene apologized, saying she had been young and hadn't understood how to raise CeCe and her siblings. CeCe later posted a picture to Facebook of the thirty-something Serene holding baby Sammy on her lap. "First grandchild!" CeCe wrote. By the next week, CeCe had resumed friendships with the entire Campbell clan. In October, CeCe stopped responding to my phone calls—Alfred later told me that the Allisons had instructed him, CeCe, and Kula to stop discussing their story—and when she returned for Thanksgiving, Alfred and Kula came too. The Campbell family proudly posted photos of the reunion online.

IN 2008 A SMALL Texas-based nonprofit named Addy's Hope got into a tense dispute with Liberia's Ministry of Health and Social Welfare. The unlicensed agency had been accused of child trafficking, and the government insisted its clients did not have permission to take children out of the country—a charge disputed by the organization, which said it had obtained permission before. The organization's co-founder, a devout Christian named HollyAnn Petree, rushed the children onto a plane, just missing some Save the Children staffers who attempted to stop them at the gate.

The next year Liberia imposed an emergency moratorium on international adoptions, citing "gross mismanagement" by both Liberian and US personnel as well as the need for a new adoption law. "We got reports that children were being put in foster homes in America because the adoptive parents in America did not understand the different behaviors of the children," said Lydia Sherman. Green-carded children began arriving in Liberia, stories of abuse began to filter back, and public opinion turned against adoption. Rumors flew that children were being taken to America to have their kidneys harvested or to be trafficked for prostitution. Lydia Schatz's birth parents learned about their daughter's death, and Sherman had to tell them that they had forfeited their legal rights long ago. Other adoptive parents told me that the birth parents of their Liberian children tracked them down, frantic about rumors that their children might be being beaten or could have even been killed. "It just really got out of hand," Sherman said.

Jerolinmek Piah, former Deputy Minister for Public Affairs, had headed the campaign for an adoption moratorium earlier in his career as a children's advocate. "We don't even know how many kids have been adopted or where they are," he told me. "If we are hearing now that someone has been abused, and now instances of death, how sure are we that many kids are not in trouble that we don't even know about?"

In the United States adoptive parents and agency supporters protested the moratorium in apocalyptic terms. Petree blogged about the mounting tensions, including a feverish dream she had about herself and her country director, the former WACSN staffer who had reportedly bragged of relinquishing his own children for adoption. In Petree's dream they rolled in an inflatable tube through a pit in the earth, "from village to village gathering children" and returning them to their headquarters while a hostile army gathered around. Another adoptive parent blogged that she had dreamt about a procession of child-sized wagons carrying unwanted African orphans to hell. Sherman became a target of frustrated adopters. "I've been called the antichrist," she told me. "I've had my life threatened."

Dirk Helmling, the North Carolina pastor who had preached at WACSN's "How Big Is God?" crusade and whose wife took over WACSN's US operations as its adoption coordinator, began e-mailing

Sherman fiery condemnations in 2010, accusing her of deliberately preventing adoptions to qualified US homes. When I contacted him in 2011, within minutes he copied me on a fresh missive to Sherman, accusing her of wanting bribes and comparing her to Satan on the verge of a fall.

Outside her office window at the ministry, Sherman pointed to a four-story concrete skeleton—an unfinished hotel WACSN began building during the adoption boom. The hotel, which was to have been named New Destiny, was now strung with squatters' laundry, flapping gently in the damp air of Liberia's rainy season, smelling of sodden earth and smoke.

Heather Cannon-Winkelman, the founding WACSN board member who resigned after she saw clients returning adopted children like Saah Fayiah and other adoptees being abused, had, together with her ex-husband, lost nearly $500,000 in the hotel venture, which she had been bankrolling to make WACSN's child relief work self-sustaining. When it became clear to her that WACSN's operations weren't working in the best interest of children, she turned information over to the Liberian and US governments about children living in abusive conditions and personally escorted the Forder children—who'd been living at the WACSN compound—to the embassy after Kimberly Forder returned to the United States and was arrested. She tried to fix what she could, supporting children left worse off for WACSN's intervention. "I came here to help kids, and I felt like my money was dirty money," she told me. "What we had invested went into something that was bad."

Liberia is in the process of deinstitutionalizing children in orphanages, most of whom can be returned to families who relinquished the children only because of poverty. Those who can't return home, Sherman said, will be put in foster care or a limited number of orphanages. In 2011 I visited Addy's Hope's old orphanage, located in the dirt side roads between Monrovia and the airport. In a bare but tidy concrete building a pastor and his wife cared for the remaining wards—nineteen children, aged two to fourteen, whose adoptions were halted when the moratorium was established. Like we were playing roles remembered from before, when the heyday of Liberian adoption brought hundreds of US parents on regular visits to homes like this (or at least brought their letters and promises to the orphanage wards), I photographed the children and showed them the images. The little ones peered around taller legs then came to take my hand. There was no surprise at our visit in a country where many Western visitors have come specifically to tour orphanages, and the pastor, Baryee Bonnor, had no request in return besides some confirmation from past US sponsors that the program was over and that they shouldn't wait anymore. "The [US] parents stopped supporting [the children] when adoptions closed," Bonnor told me, and few Liberian parents have yet returned to claim their children. "They should say that they will not adopt them so the children can go home to their parents."

AFTER NANCY CAMPBELL'S early adoption promotion, the cause slowly grew in more mainstream churches, where the story of the failed *Above Rubies* adoptions was long forgotten or never known. In 2010, at Russell Moore's Adopting for Life conference at the Southern Baptist Theological Seminary, the fifteen-child Ahlers family of Kentucky, profiled years earlier in *Above Rubies* for their five Liberian adoptees, performed for a crowd of hundreds and were lauded as "heroes" of adoption. Meanwhile, disrupted adoptions have become such a common occurrence in the Christian adoption community that the panel on disruption at the 2012 Christian Alliance for Orphans Summit drew one of the event's largest crowds to discuss how disruption fits into God's plan for children to find families—sometimes an indirect route, advocates say, that goes through one or more failed adoptions first.

The rate of failure made even dedicated adoptive parents scornful of the movement that was treating adoption as a form of mission work. "Adoption is supposed to be about giving a child a family. When that happens, adoption becomes this amazing thing. But when adoption is not about the child, then it becomes very twisted and disgusting," said Johanna, who had become one of the secondary adoptive parents enlisted to clean up after the wave of disruptions. "Adoption isn't wrong, but adoption done wrong is worse than nothing at all."

LIBERIA IS FINALIZING its Reform Adoption Bill, and when the country reopens, children will be processed under much more stringent requirements. Only three agencies have been approved so far to work in the country, including Cheryl Carter-Shotts's AFAA and Acres of Hope, which now partners with a licensed agency. Anglin anticipates that tight regulation will likely keep the number of adoptions to around one hundred per year, but the agency has since moved on to other opportunities as well: in 2011 Acres of Hope announced that it is beginning adoptions from the Democratic Republic of Congo, where fighting continues in its own fifteen-year civil war.

But even in Liberia the process remains in question. Winant said that when he started at the embassy in 2009, after the moratorium was in place, there were thirty-five "pipeline" adoption cases on the books that would still be allowed to go through. "Since then," he said, "we've processed over eighty," including cases they had never heard of before.

My first full night in Liberia, as I ate at a hotel restaurant popular with ex-pats and development workers, a Lebanese logging executive, several drinks into his evening, came to my table to tell me about famous and accomplished Lebanese Americans. When I told him why I was there, he asked if I wanted to adopt a child, and offered to take me the next day to the interior, where he would help me find a baby to bring home. I declined, but he was excited by the prospect, and already forming a plan. "They all need adoption," he said, his eyes growing misty at the beauty of the idea. "It would be viewed as a miracle."

CHAPTER 6

Pipeline Problems

In 2008 Caleb David and his wife, Becca, young missionaries from Tulsa, Oklahoma, adopted their first Ethiopian child, an infant daughter they named Sakari. Caleb and Becca, who are both biracial—he half-Indian and she half-Mexican—had always intended to build their family through adoption, figuring it would be easy to further "internationalize" their family and believing that having biological children was selfish when there were so many orphans in need. At first they worried that, because they were adopting just one child, they weren't making a real difference. They grew to believe that "changing the destiny" of their daughter was important enough, and it was an example they could share with others: that if everyone helped one child, the orphan crisis would end.

After they brought Sakari home, Caleb, a hip thirty-two-year-old in a checkered keffiyeh scarf, with artfully mussed hair and an open smile, got a tattoo to mark the occasion. In lower-case letters across the back of his neck, it reads "adopted." Not because Caleb was adopted in the way his daughter was but for his adoption by God.

The couple also began a ministry upon their return, the One Child Campaign. They had previously made their living organizing short-term international mission trips for thousands of young Christians through Tulsa's Big World Ventures. In 2010, however, they quit to work full time on their new ministry, offering mission trips of their own. Today, One Child brings groups to Ethiopia to raise awareness about the orphan crisis in the hope that visiting US Christians, who pay roughly $1,500 per trip plus airfare, will return home not just with Facebook photos from a "poverty tour" but also a commitment to stay involved.

Caleb has another tattoo, a lyric inked in cursive on the soft part of his forearm that he took from an Australian Christian rock band and put to further use as a One Child T-shirt slogan: "Break my heart for what breaks Yours." "They're as addictive as adoption," Caleb joked of his tattoos when I met him in Addis Ababa in June 2011.

He was there with Becca, thirty-seven, and Sakari, four, for the family's second adoption, this time of an eleven-month-old infant they had named Huxley. On a warm morning late in the month I met Caleb and his driver at an Addis supermarket, then drove with them to the transition home their agency, America World Adoption, runs. At the home, a cozy, gated compound on a quiet side street, a dozen US adoptive parents in their thirties and forties played soccer with older kids in the driveway or lounged on the front porch, watching children's laundry dry on a clothesline strung over a painted jungle gym. The adults were a casual group. They all knew each other and the children they were each adopting. AWA staff walked through cheerfully, stopping to get signatures on paperwork or confirm appointments families had scheduled with local bureaucrats. Sakari, a bright-faced girl with a toothy, mischievous grin, darted between her parents and the home's "baby room," wearing a T-shirt with an image of Africa and the words, "Go. See. Love." that her parents had bought to support a friend's adoption.

The Davids had conducted a similar fundraiser, appealing to Facebook friends to sponsor a painted wall hanging for Huxley's room, "Hux's Canvas of Love," at $20 per square inch. Through it they had raised more than $11,000 of their adoption fees. But though the process of funding a $30,000 adoption had become somewhat smoother in the United States, as Christian families creatively crowd-source the small fortune each adoption costs, the process of actually completing an adoption was becoming harder in the wake of 2011's adoption slowdown. When I met the Davids they had already been in Ethiopia for nearly six weeks since receiving a rejection letter from Ethiopia's Ministry of Women's, Children's and Youth Affairs (MOWA) over a technicality in their adoption application. Theirs was a negligible problem—an expired notary signature on one page of their home study paperwork—but overriding the objection took weeks in the midst of Ethiopia's adoption processing slowdown. After having changed flight plans for all three once already, the family couldn't afford to reschedule flights for the entire family yet again, so Becca and Sakari were reluctantly preparing to fly home to Oklahoma that week, leaving Caleb to wait on the court.

The Davids had met Huxley's mother—a fiery and empowered woman, Caleb said—and after a frank conversation about expectations, they were confident that she hadn't been coerced into adoption. And although the problems with adoption agencies operating in Ethiopia were certainly widespread, child protection experts privately praised the agency they were using for behaving more ethically than most.

Still, Caleb and Becca recognized the broader problems behind the slowdown and their own delays. They weren't really comfortable with what the adoption movement had become: self-glorifying in the United States and an enabler of corruption abroad. They had seen problems even in the organizations they had ties with: a forty-five-child orphanage One Child supported had been found diverting donations, including a cow Caleb had bought to supply milk for the children, as well as offering to US parents children whose families had never expressed interest in giving their sons or daughters up. "[The orphanage director] was promising kids from his community," Caleb said incredulously. One adoption agency Caleb had spoken to continued to partner with this organization despite knowing these details, because of the agency's conviction that "the kids needed to get out." "If you place a child that's not really an orphan, then you're just making a family's dream come true. And it's not just about that." He sighed. "It used to be so easy, and Ethiopia was the easiest."

ETHIOPIA WASN'T the only place where the adoption process was slowing down; other countries' programs were floundering as well. The growth of the evangelical adoption movement has occurred against the backdrop of a global fall in international adoption rates. From a peak of nearly 23,000 international adoptions to the United States in 2004— America consistently accounts for about half of all intercountry adoptions worldwide—numbers have plummeted to just 9,319 in 2011 and a projected 7,000 in 2012.

As country after country has slowed or shut their programs, adoption advocates have rallied around families "stuck in the pipeline"—those who are waiting in bureaucratic limbo after adoption programs have been suspended. Parents got "stuck" in nations like Guatemala, where abuses ranging from DNA fraud to kidnapping were legendary; Kyrgyzstan, where officials were accused of bribery and observers feared adoptive parents weren't being adequately vetted; and Nepal, previously shut down over child-trafficking charges and then stalled again, just months after reopening, over State Department suspicions that 90 percent of "orphans" offered for adoption had been bought and sold. Many of them appeared frequently in the media, describing how the closure of long-troubled programs had caught them off guard and how they had become stranded in a foreign country, unwilling to leave without their children. Christian adoption advocates dismissed the specifics and lauded these "pipeline families" as martyrs of the movement, referring to them in the same terminology used to describe jailed political dissidents: the Kyrgyz sixty-five, the Guat nine hundred.

Sympathetic politicians pled their cases both to the United States and foreign governments, asking them to make exceptions and speed grandfathered or pipeline cases through. Senator Mary Landrieu, an adoptive mother and co-chair of the Congressional Coalition on Adoption Institute and sponsor of at least seven adoption bills, has been among the most active. She traveled to Guatemala four times after its adoption program closed in 2008 as well as to countries in Asia, Africa, and Eastern Europe where US adoptions have faltered.

The larger context for these individual stories is the overall decline in adoption numbers, which may be the real problem with the Christian adoption movement. Assured by leaders like Southern Baptist author Russell Moore that "there are more children needing homes than loving Christian parents who are willing to take them in," thousands of Christian families have sought to adopt. In fact, however, the international adoption industry is drying up. The drop is often attributed to changes in a few "big" countries: the closure of Guatemala over corruption charges and the concurrent slowdown in China, which is becoming a wealthier country with substantial domestic demand for its own adoptable infants.

Professor and author Kay Johnson, who has written extensively about adoption from China, told me that although Chinese orphanages filled up during the '90s because of the government's One Child Policy, these days there's a dearth of children available for adoption in the nation, and middle-class Chinese are rightfully at the front of the line. International adoption agencies continuing to work in China are now turning to special-needs children, mirroring developments in numerous countries where adoptions have slowed.* "Any healthy child that's adopted internationally is now

---

*As the pool of international children available for adoption has diminished, hopeful adoptive parents in the United States are increasingly adopting a

being taken out of the arms of a waiting Chinese adoptive family—leaving aside how it was separated from its birth family," Johnson said. "It's long past time to stop this international adoption program. And it will happen because the supply of children will vanish."

Similar shifts to limit international adoption programs are taking place in other countries, many not just in response to increased domestic demand but also to problems that have arisen in adoption ethics or the care of adopted children once they arrive in the United States. Russia has voiced increasing anger over numerous reports of adopted Russian children being abused, sent into foster care or ad hoc respite programs, or, in a few cases, repatriated to Russia. After several years of scandals out of

---

category of children who have fewer restrictions when it comes to international adoption: children with special needs. By 2012 the percentage of special needs adoptions—an overly broad category that includes children with extreme medical needs that can't be met in their own countries as well as children who are simply older or who come with siblings—has risen notably. A 2009 survey by the Joint Council on International Children's Services found that 27 percent of all adoptions by its member adoption agencies were for special-needs cases.

However the term is defined, Christian adoption advocates have rightfully pointed to this shift as proof that evangelicals aren't just adopting healthy infants. Indeed, within the Christian adoption movement adoption of children with high medical needs has become a distinguished category of its own. As Rachael Stryker, author of the attachment therapy study *The Road to Evergreen,* observed in her interviews, "People who adopt special needs children, particularly in the evangelical community, are almost given a higher place in the moral order . . . the harder the adoption is, the more they're proving their love for God."

Many prominent families in the adoption movement have adopted multiple special-needs children, including Patty Anglin from Acres of Hope, whose family of eighteen children includes eleven adoptees with special needs, ranging from fetal drug addictions to quad-amputees; and Kiel and Carolyn Twietmeyer, homeschooling Illinois parents to fourteen, who were profiled in *People* magazine for their six adoptees, including two who are HIV-positive and one with Down's syndrome. When their state cut them off as they attempted to adopt a fifteenth child, a Ugandan boy with Down's syndrome, the Twietmeyers claimed religious discrimination. Examples like

Ethiopia, Liberia, and other African countries, the African Child Policy Forum in 2012 called for a halt to adoptions from Africa as well.

"I think the days of a large sending country, like we had in the past with Russia and China and now Ethiopia, are over," said National Council for Adoption (NCFA) President Chuck Johnson. "I don't think we're going to see that anymore." Tom DiFilipo, president of the Joint Council on International Children's Services (JCICS) described a broader collapse, of eight or nine countries either closing or functionally suspending adoption programs in recent years, whether through actual policy or as the result of increasing bureaucratic restrictions.

But adoption advocates don't see the falling numbers as a result of the recurring controversies around intercountry adoption. Instead, they blame familiar scapegoats, like UNICEF or recent reforms, like the Hague Convention, because countries that suspend their programs to implement the Hague standards often will reopen, if at all, to perform far fewer adoptions at much slower rates and prioritize domestic adoptions over international.

In a 2010 paper Harvard law professor Elizabeth Bartholet, perhaps one of the most polemical adoption advocates in the field, charged that "International adoption is under siege" by child protection groups citing ethical abuses as well as by misinformed nations asserting "rights to hold onto the children born within their borders." Bartholet argues that a child's right to a family should trump issues of state sovereignty and that instances of

---

these led Russell Moore to proclaim that one day only Christians would parent children with Down's syndrome or other special needs.

But even in these adoptions—of children with needs or disabilities that make them largely unadoptable in their home countries, to families eager to provide care the children won't receive in institutions—there are signs that special-needs adoptions may constitute the next wave of adoption corruption. In interviews with a number of families who adopted special-needs children from Eastern Europe, I heard multiple testimonials from parents about being shaken down for thousands of dollars by unscrupulous adoption facilitators brokering special-needs adoptions in Ukraine, parents or rival adoption facilitators facing intimidation and threats of violence from brokers who had become territorial over "their" stable of special-needs children, and families who had been openly told they needed to pay thousands of dollars in bribes. The growing number of these stories makes it clear that no category of adoptions, even the most seemingly heroic, is exempt from commercialization.

corruption should be handled individually by punishing perpetrators instead of shutting down a country's entire adoption system. Bartholet expanded her argument in 2012, arguing to the Associated Press that the
implementation of the Hague Convention guidelines was another reason
for falling adoption numbers, that although the Hague "should have been a
real step forward," it had instead become a pretext for the US government
to shut down adoptions from countries that are not compliant.

The idea that adoptions are declining not because of corruption but because of an overzealous response to corruption has become a common refrain. At major evangelical adoption conventions leaders continue to insist
that there are no real problems with international adoption, but that forces
ideologically opposed to adoption are falsifying, fabricating, or exaggerat-
ing stories of corruption. "Despite all the things you read in the media and
the different international claims to the contrary, the process of international adoption is generally working very well," said Chuck Johnson at
Saddleback Church in 2012, arguing that claims of fraud had been blown
out of proportion. "We have no indication of real, true corruption."

What that leaves room for instead is an enemy, and Johnson proceeded to indict one: people who think that children shouldn't be
adopted. Although Johnson is frequently described as a moderating force
at the NCFA, a man who has helped shift the group from its hard-right associations with the Family Research Council to a more even-handed approach, he was all red meat at Saddleback; directly after discussing
adoption critics who don't want some children to be adopted, he added,
"We have to realize as Christians that there is evil in the world and there
are forces that take great delight in the suffering of children."

It was a stunning escalation of rhetoric, from describing adoption critics as misguided to suggesting they might be evil and antichild. But by
2012 adoption had unambiguously become its own culture war issue.
That spring the evangelical *Christian Post* published a series of articles on
the international "adoption crisis," arguing that adoptive parents were
facing hurdles "that could only have been created by either incompetence
or an intentional desire to reduce adoptions." These hurdles were unsurprisingly blamed on the familiar trifecta of UNICEF, the State Department, and Hague. When a family's adoption from Vietnam was halted
after the child's birth family was found, the family complained to the *Dayton Daily News* that "State Department officials believe that all international adoptions are human trafficking." In December 2011 the
Washington Times, which had developed an international adoption
column for its largely conservative Christian readership, called for a

boycott of UNICEF's holiday cards on the grounds of UNICEF's alleged adoption obstructionism.

UNICEF chief of Child Protection Division, Susan Bissell, dropped her head in her hands when I asked her in 2012 about criticism the organization routinely faces over adoption, and in exasperation she protested that UNICEF doesn't control sovereign nations' adoption policies. UNICEF's mandate is to work on overarching child protection systems that impact exponentially more children than the handful who get adopted overseas. But the adoption wars consistently overwhelm that larger conversation. "It's pitched as though it's a battle. It's very sad because it's incredibly time consuming to have to focus on that when we should be focusing on building systems and making sure that those who are available for adoption can access that in a transparent way," Bissel said. "If you really want to help children and you really respect the sovereignty and democracy and good governance and the rule of law that we enjoy in our home countries [in the West], why wouldn't you want the same for other countries?"

But instead of suspending countries' adoption programs so they can implement the Hague and other national reforms, most advocates call to prosecute wrongdoers individually while keeping adoption programs going—to not punish the families, they say, let alone the children, for the mistakes of a few unethical players. As Senator Landrieu quipped to *Newsweek* in 2005, after US missionaries caused an uproar trying to adopt Muslim children following the Southeast Asian tsunami, "When someone robs a bank you don't shut down the entire international banking system." Or as Bartholet echoed to *The Globe and Mail* seven years later: "We don't shut down the stock market because of Bernie Madoff."

But Bernie Madoff's ponzi scheme didn't arise in a vacuum, and neither do the cyclical headline scandals regarding international adoption, as is evident in the very durability of Landrieu's and Bartholet's common defense. As each adoption scandal erupts, painfully similar to those that have occurred before, advocates rush to make the same defense, repeated year after year: that the problem is a few bad apples, not systemic weaknesses in the adoption system.

The analogy is instructive in other ways, though. As Madoff thrived in a culture of deregulation that rewarded risk and turned a blind eye to wrongdoing, so have international adoption agencies benefited from an industry regularly compared to a legal Wild West, where wrongful, corrupt, or failed adoptions have come to be viewed as the human cost of doing business.

PART OF THE REASON ADOPTION is so inadequately regulated is that adoption agencies, through their representative trade groups and advocacy organizations, have had a heavy hand in crafting the laws and institutions that govern their own behavior, amounting to what critics call systematically weak oversight: the fox guarding the henhouse.

For most politicians adoption issues exist primarily as a concern of constituents who have adopted or want to. Eager to please voters with a warm story about helping to bring families together but with little understanding of the complexities of adoption ethics, many legislators sign on to help make adoption easier. The experts who get called in to guide them, quite often, are trade groups representing the adoption industry.

"Whenever you allow an industry to dictate public policy, there's an inherent conflict of interest," said child welfare advocate Maureen Flatley, who has lobbied the government extensively for adoption reform and helped pass "Masha's law" after a Russian adoptee was used extensively in child pornography by her adoptive father, a single man who was allowed to adopt her after specifying the looks he wanted the child to have. "We're not turning to oil companies to draft the safety regulations, but in adoption and child welfare it's always the industry that gets called on. So there's no oversight, no accountability, no real penalties for anything."

Adoption bills have also provided a rare opportunity for bipartisan cooperation. So many Democrats are partnering with right-wing Republicans to support what seems on the surface a benign "profamily" issue that adoption legislation seems to have become a covert conservatizing force. Joint declarations that adoption is a common ground solution to entrenched abortion debates bolster Democrats' credibility with "values voters," who see adoption as a "life" issue. In the process, however, Democrats also implicitly confirm conservative definitions of family. Adoption agencies have hitched a ride on this political calculation, winning featherweight regulations for an industry that purports to work on children's behalf.

As Niels Hoogeveen of Pound Pup Legacy notes, the easy optics of supporting groups that "help orphans" is too appealing for many legislators to turn down, even when the reality is far more complex. "People don't think critically when children are involved," Hoogeveen said. "Everything that is being done for children is good, even when it's actually bad."

In 2000 the US Congress passed the Intercountry Adoption Act, legislation cosponsored by Senator Landrieu with the hard-right North Carolina Senator Jesse Helms that implemented the Hague Convention.

Before its passage, however, adoption agencies and lobbyists, including the JCICS, argued for and won a substantial number of provisions that functioned as loopholes to proper enforcement of Hague principles. The bill as edited by adoption lobbyists held that adoption agencies could not be held responsible for what their foreign partners, contractors, and employees did; that there would be no consistent cap on money associated with international adoptions, making international adoption more lucrative than finding local solutions for children; that it was permissible to make payments for the purpose of locating children for adoption, thereby essentially legalizing the role of child finders; that agencies are not liable for misinformation given to clients; and, most significantly, that Hague rules simply don't apply to adoptions coming out of non-Hague countries, from which adoptions were not only permitted to continue but account for approximately two-thirds of all intercountry adoptions to the United States. Added to the fact that US law does not recognize or track trafficking for adoption as a crime, these loopholes are large enough to accommodate the proverbial truck and make it easy for agency misconduct to go unpunished. As a State Department staffer speaking off the record to an adoption reform group remarked, the government's hands are largely tied when it comes to preventing corrupt adoptions.

In the adoption lobby community that helped craft these exemptions, there's substantial crossover between the Christian adoption movement and supportive politicians. Kerry Marks-Hasenbalg, the co-founder and former executive director of Senator Landrieu's Congressional Coalition on Adoption Institute (CCAI), a nonprofit organization composed of hundreds of members of Congress that bestows annual "Angels in Adoption" awards on adoption industry figures and parents, went on to become an early partner of the Christian Alliance for Orphans. Her husband, Scott Hasenbalg, is executive director of Steven Curtis Chapman's Show Hope and a past Christian Alliance board member. CCAI regularly supplies staff to speak at Christian Alliance for Orphans events, frequently including current CCAI Executive Director Kathleen Strottman, a former Landrieu staffer.

"There are a lot of fingers moving into each others' organizations," JCICS's Tom DiFilipo told me, noting that the Joint Council has significant formal and informal partnerships with the Christian Alliance for Orphans and Hope for Orphans on different advocacy goals. "There's a lot of synergy." In 2010 the Christian Alliance began a campaign called Bloggers for Orphans, asking Christian bloggers to repost their articles, including

policy notices from JCICS that call for action on proposed adoption legislation the Joint Council had helped draft.

ADOPTION ADVOCATES' urgency about falling adoption numbers
isn't due just to the lost opportunities they envision for children finding a
family; they're worried about business losses as well. As the numbers of
adoptions have dropped, the adoption industry has constricted, and 25
percent of US agencies have closed or merged since 2000, according to the
National Council for Adoption. The shuttering of Guatemala in 2008—
what America World Adoption's Brian Luwis called "the gravy train" for
many agencies—was a major factor. "In the last few years a bunch of the
top placing agencies in the US met together kind of clandestinely," Luwis
told me in 2010. "To me it was a 'saving our rear' meeting. For me, it's different: I'm not invested financially. But some of the others, this is their
livelihood: they place thousands of kids. This is the way they've done it,
and they're not going to change. Ninety-some agencies closed [in 2009]. I
think it's squeezing a lot of people out."

In the new, leaner international adoption market adoption lobbyists
have felt the squeeze as well. In internal meeting minutes leaked to the
website Pound Pup Legacy in 2009, Tom DiFilipo's Joint Council described financial shortages that had forced them to halve expenses and reduce staff by 60 percent and that they warned could lead to their closure
altogether if the numbers continued to fall. (The leaked minutes also
pointed to larger problems with JCICS's public image: that they were seen
by policymakers, NGOs, and potential partners as serving adoption agencies' interests only, as a trade organization that harbors unethical agencies; and they suspected these perceptions may have cost them valuable
partnerships with respected nonprofits and philanthropies. The minutes
suggested strategic reconfigurations of the Joint Council's leadership so
they could instead rebrand themselves purely as a child welfare advocacy
organization.) The internal documents laid out a path to survival: highlighting "the collapse of IA" (intercountry adoption) as "a public policy issue requiring significant and effective advocacy"—that is, raising the
alarm about a new crisis: a crisis in adoption itself. "If the Joint Council is
still here," JCICS wrote to their member adoption agencies, "we can help
you be here."

They carried a more alarmist message to their public supporters,
however. "If we don't change the environment in which we're trying to

serve children," DiFilipo told an audience at the Christian Alliance for Orphans Summit in 2010, urging them to activism, "we won't be able to serve children."

A compact, energetic man who sometimes bubbles over into hot-headed passion, at the 2012 summit at Saddleback Church DiFilipo was even more forceful. He appeared at the gathering's annual advocacy panel alongside Chuck Johnson, Brian Luwis, and CCAI's Kathleen Strottman, suggesting to the Saddleback audience that without some form of financial incentive, tying foreign aid to pro-adoption policies, international adoption might sink into obscurity. He appealed to the audience to mobilize behind an initiative that would limit US foreign funding through donors like USAID to groups that had a stated policy that "all children belong in families"—a seemingly innocuous piece of language that could be used to promote international adoption in countries with substantial "orphan" populations.

Without such a policy, he threatened, adoptions numbers are "crashing and burning this year." He warned families adopting from non-Hague countries in Africa that their adoptions would likely fall through and that those countries would "close" within a few years. "Country after country, that's our projection. Within a few years you won't have hardly any adoptions out of Africa anymore."

"[If] you value families, based on the gospel, [then] move it from theory into 'touchable grace,'" he continued. "Use your passion to demand, not ask for or suggest, that the US government establish a policy that children belong in families. I'm talking about international aid money, whatever it is related to. Can't we have as a core principle that money should be used to put children in families?"

It sounded reasonable, but DiFilipo didn't mean just any families. He warned adoption advocates not to be appeased by alternative forms of orphan care that focus more on development and antipoverty work than solutions explicitly about family "permanency"—a word that adoption advocates almost universally interpret to include international adoption. "If you hear that [an aid group is] 'doing family preservation,'" he said, referencing the term for keeping families together to prevent the need for adoption, "by building schools or putting in water wells—which does help keep kids in schools—I get that, but it's not based on policy." Implicitly he was arguing that efforts to serve poor children by serving their families and communities—helping create the conditions that could prevent many children from being placed for adoption in the first place—are not targeted enough to deserve the Christian adoption movement's support.

It wasn't the first time that adoption advocates had proposed that the US government create policies that would effectively promote more international adoptions under the guise of vague language about all children deserving homes. One of the most significant such proposals that gained attention in the wake of the Haitian earthquake was the 2009 Families for Orphans Act (FFOA), drafted by the Families for Orphans Coalition, a startup organization led by several familiar faces: Brian Luwis, Tom DiFilipo, and Chuck Johnson. The bill, which ultimately did not pass, would have created a special office in the State Department, the Office for Orphan Policy, Diplomacy and Development, to oversee adoptions. It would also offer developmental aid to countries that help provide permanent parental care for orphans, including international adoption. In a joint op-ed the bill's Senate cosponsors, Senator Landrieu and right-wing darling James Inhofe, a Republican senator from Oklahoma, argued that such an office could have facilitated tens of thousands of additional adoptive placements from Haiti—and beyond.

One of the key aims of the legislation was enshrining adoption advocacy principles into US foreign aid: in the wording of the bill, to "ensure that all aid efforts receiving funding from the United States recognize and support the need for the preservation and reunification of families and the provision of permanent parental care for orphans." It was the same sort of open-ended language that DiFilipo used in his call to condition foreign aid on countries' policies on orphan permanency, and adoption reform groups worried that it would be interpreted solely to mean inter-country adoption. Words like "permanency," a child-protection term used since the 1980s to indicate getting a child into a permanent family situation, whether by reuniting them with their family or placing them for domestic or intercountry adoption, have been used in the past to emphasize adoption over family reunification. It seemed more than likely that the term would again be interpreted to privilege adoption over broader community aid, like the wells and schools DiFilipo disparaged, that could keep children from being given to orphanages in the first place.

Adoption reform groups, including PEAR and Ethica, worried that the bill would cut financial aid from countries that couldn't meet its requirements, such as conducting a biennial orphan census, and would enshrine an overly broad definition of "orphans" that seemed to make any child living in an orphanage available for adoption, including many children who had parents. "The Families for Orphans Act, if passed, would give the United States unilateral power to develop global child welfare strategies by providing financial incentives for other countries (including through debt and trade relief) to send their children abroad for international adoption," argued a statement from Ethica. "This bill augments existing financial incentives for countries to favor international adoption by offering additional financial incentives, including technical assistance, grants, trade, and debt relief from the United States, which may sacrifice established child welfare principles by favoring international adoption over local solutions." Niels Hoogeveen of Pound Pup Legacy believed that the real impetus for the bill was an effort to stop the decline of international adoption—as well as the collapse of the adoption agencies whose trade groups, like JCICS and NCFA, helped draft the legislation. The makeup of the bill's drafters—adoption industry insiders all—convinced Hoogeveen that the bill was an adoption bill masquerading as broader orphan care. "We give you ten million in foreign aid, and you give us one hundred children for adoption," he said. "That's not aid; that's trade."

"The Families for Orphans Act de facto means the United States is going to pay foreign countries to provide orphans for the American adoption market if these bills are signed into law," he argued on his website.

The Families for Orphans Coalition responded to criticism by pointing out that the bill only mentioned international adoption six times. DiFilipo elaborated to me that the bill did not require countries to actually do intercountry adoption to get aid but rather make more of a symbolic acceptance of adoption, agreeing that it was one of a range of services needed to place children in permanent homes. Likewise, he said, the expanded definition of orphans was never intended to be legally enforceable for immigration purposes but only for broadening the pool of children qualified to receive services. Despite the fact that both aspects of the bill seem more or less a legalistic bait and switch, DiFilipo dismissed critics' concerns as hysterical. "The fact that people are seeing international adoption and therefore assuming the whole bill is about international adoption means they didn't read it."

Indeed, as DiFilipo and Johnson eagerly pointed out, other pro-adoption advocates, who felt the bill didn't sufficiently prioritize international adoption, challenged the legislation as well. The American Academy of Adoption Attorneys, which drafted a letter signed by Bartholet, suggested revisions to the bill that added close to sixty additional references promoting adoption and restricting references to reuniting biological families. If the bill was being criticized on both sides, the adoption lobbyists suggested, that must mean they had gotten it just right.

While the Families for Orphans Act did not pass before the close of the 2010 session and the bill finally died in committee in 2012, the idea behind it seemed destined to live on.

ALTHOUGH THE ADOPTION movement went on the offensive with regard to the "adoption crisis" in 2012, its leaders hadn't always been so unwilling to acknowledge their own role in international adoption's slow death. Just two years before, adoption advocates had expressed concerns that their own movement might be spiraling out of control.

In 2010, when the Christian Alliance for Orphans held its summit in Eden Prairie, Minnesota, at the Grace Church, the recent lessons of Laura Silsby and her fellow missionaries arrested in Haiti seemed to have chastened participants. In an overflowing classroom at the summit's advocacy panel, audience members raised their hands to ask how they could avoid hiring an unethical agency or how they should respond to the growing association of international adoption with child trafficking.

Speaking from the audience, DiFilipo responded that parents' own adoption demand can exacerbate corruption. He gave the example of some adoptive families who recklessly partnered with unethical agencies in Guatemala in the last few months before that adoption program closed, even after most other agencies had ceased operations in the country, the government had issued warnings, and the handwriting was clearly on the wall. "Let's say you've been referred a child from any country, and then you start to suspect that things aren't on the up and up," DiFilipo later said to me. "What do you do? Do you walk away, do you report it, or do you close your eyes and pray that nothing is really going wrong? In some instances we know that families have closed their eyes."

DiFilipo wasn't alone. "We're killing ourselves with these ethical lapses," Johnson told the crowd. Before he worked at the NCFA, Johnson ran an adoption agency in Alabama, where he gained a reputation as a straight player who tried to separate adoption from profit as much as possible, with the intent of transforming it into a pro-bono mission. In conversations with me he had noted that many adoption agencies are marked by an "imperialistic colonialism" that rationalizes improper adoptions with their belief that "to be an American or to be prosperous is better than to be poor and in another country." In the Grace Church classroom, so full that some audience members were sitting on the ground, he offered the audience another hard truth. "I think Christians are the worst at this sometimes," he said, "about the ends justifying the means. 'I will do some-thing to save this one child's life, no matter what it costs everyone else.' We saw this in Haiti, we see it everywhere: 'I will rescue this child.' . . . 'I will falsify a visa application if I have to.'"

Brian Luwis agreed, telling me that ardent adoptive parents can wreak havoc for those coming after them. "I call them 'adoption crazies.' They're such strong advocates, they'll do things in desperation to have a child they think is their child. Some are really unlawful, falsifying an adoption or something like that. Many won't get caught, but once you get caught, what have you done to the system?"

Before the Minnesota summit, in early 2010, the NCFA held an online seminar on adoption ethics for agencies, both religious and secular, that representatives from the State Department also attended. As part of the webinar, NCFA took a blind poll of participants' responses to various eth-ical situations. Through either ignorance of adoption law or a willingness to bend the rules, 20 to 30 percent of the agency representatives partici-pating gave answers that would be tantamount to committing visa fraud or other serious ethical violations. With State Department staff watching, it was embarrassing. "And these are good agencies," Johnson told me sadly. "It's really one of the most hurtful issues we're facing today. You'll hear people saying 'I'm following God's law, not man's law,'" he contin-ued. "In the heat of the moment, people will feel led to break the rules, which is a feeling I encourage them to question, because it really is hurt-ing the process."

Despite this capacity for more measured self-reflection, after Ethiopia began to shut its doors, the Christian movement seemed to shift to more strident activism, highlighting the stories of parents encountering obsta-cles in their adoptions and sinking its teeth into the idea of adoption as culture war.

TO JEDD MEDEFIND of the Christian Alliance for Orphans, the fact that adoption numbers are falling just as the ranks of prospective parents are surging is a "tragic irony." For adoption critics like Hoogeveen, how-ever, the timing is more suspicious. "It begs the question," Hoogeveen wrote, "why the Christian Alliance for Orphans keeps inflating the de-mand for adoptable children, when at the same time there already is a de-clining supply. This doesn't seem fair to all those people being made enthusiastic about adoption, while knowing the increased demand can never be fulfilled."

Part of the rationale can perhaps be found in the strategy of an upstart adoption advocacy group dedicated to the very idea of the "adoption crisis." In late March 2011 Craig Juntunen came to a Chandler, Arizona, home to tell Christian adoption advocates about his plans to increase international adoptions fivefold. In an online video of the meet-up Juntunen, a tall, broad-shouldered man with a darkly tanned face and a neatly trimmed beard, stood in the living room of a Christian adoptive family, between an immense flat-screen TV and a white board covered with a "trinity diagram" depicting the relationship of God to adoption. International adoption is in "a freefall," he told the audience, as though breaking the bad news. But he was on a mission to fix it by embarking "on this crusade . . . to create a culture of adoption." As part of that crusade, his organization, Both Ends Burning, was creating a documentary called *Wrongfully Detained* (later retitled to the pithier *Stuck*) to simplify adoption's labyrinthine ethical complexities to their emotional core: showcasing "the full depth and breadth of the tragic crisis in international adoption" with emotional stories about orphans consigned to teeming institutions after adoption programs shut down. The solution Juntunen proposed was a new "clearinghouse model" for international adoption that would raise the number of children adopted into US families to more than fifty thousand per year.

In Arizona Juntunen was speaking alongside Dan Cruver, editor of *Reclaiming Adoption* and head of the Christian adoption movement group Together for Adoption. The event was the first of Together for Adoption's new "house conferences"—small-scale meet-ups to mobilize adoption advocates at the local level. And the choice of Juntunen to launch the campaign was telling.

Juntunen, a former pro quarterback now in his early fifties and the adoptive father of three Haitian children, is a new and somewhat rogue figure in the adoption world since he founded the Both Ends Burning Campaign in 2010. He tells a folksy story about how he got involved in adoption advocacy after going through the process himself. As Juntunen's story goes, he and his wife, Kathi, had retired early after he had sold a consulting firm serving the tech market at the end of the '90s dotcom boom, and he had retired to a life of golfing and house parties between Arizona and Colorado. Leisure left him feeling "chronically empty" and disillusioned with his lifestyle. When a golfing buddy talked about adopting his own children from Haiti—telling Juntunen, "Think of the worst place you have ever seen. Haiti is much worse than that"—Juntunen was moved to imitation. "Haiti is the antithesis of this," he told his wife, meaning their present life.

He visited a Haitian *crèche,* or orphanage, in the mountains and found one boy he described as "the pick of the litter," who hadn't been chosen for adoption because his photo on the agency website was unattractive, as well as a little girl who did a silly walk that reminded Juntunen of himself. Then, while on a business call to another orphanage with his crèche's director, Juntunen encountered a sickly infant who would become his and Kathi's third child.

Visitors to orphanages in Haiti, which are often considered among the worst children's institutions in the world, frequently describe it as a radicalizing experience, and that seems to have been the case for Juntunen. "Until you see it and smell it, it's hard to describe," he told me. "If we're tolerating this as a society, we should be ashamed of ourselves."

After his adoptions Juntunen self-published a book about the experience, *Both Ends Burning,* which he describes as "the *Marley and Me* of adoptive parenting," tracing the transformation of his kids into "alpha dogs." He and Kathi would go on to start a foundation, Chances for Children, to support an "underperforming" crèche in Haiti—meaning one that was not producing enough adoptions—and to support increased international adoptions generally. Along the way Juntunen realized that what he had initially thought was a "demand problem"—a lack of willing adoptive families to take in these children—turned out to be a "process problem": an inefficient system, marked by unnecessary delays, expenses, and restrictions, such as age limits for adoptive parents that Juntunen finds discriminatory. He also came to learn about what he sees as ideological opposition from international NGOs. "We have families knocking on our door, and we can't put those two things together because of some sort of government rule, some sort of dispassionate policy?" he said to me. "I see that as a tragic social mistake. Really, these governments are the ones that are wrongfully detaining these children." He figured if the US government could move quickly to get kids out of Haiti after the earthquake, there was no reason they couldn't move like that every day.

Both Ends Burning hired strategy consultants from Bain & Company (the same corporation that 2012 Republican presidential candidate Mitt Romney helped found; a Bain management consultant educated at the Mormon Brigham Young University is on Juntunen's board of directors) to help propose a new adoption system that would cut costs and wait times while increasing safeguards. The organization aimed to gather one million signatures on a petition to the UN to demand policies that promote international adoption as well as plan a Summit of Nations meeting to launch the new adoption system Bain helped the group devise.

The launch of *Wrongfully Detained,* or *Stuck,* advertised with a picture of two golden-skinned toddlers peering from behind the barred windows of an orphanage, would be a key selling point for the plan, featuring families in the adoption process in Ethiopia, Vietnam, and other countries with broken adoption systems. In the well-produced film, released in 2012, pipeline families wander at farmers markets and sadly open the doors to rooms they've furnished for children they thought would be here by now. Further in, an adoption attorney from Both Ends Burning's board of directors coaches a family to present the human face of stalled adoptions while on a lobbying trip to DC, and Senator Landrieu bemoans her role in passing the Hague, apologetically saying she had thought it would increase adoptions, not the opposite. In a newsletter update Juntunen described filming on location, in an unnamed country that seemed to be Ethiopia, when an adoptive family was told their paperwork would require additional scrutiny and that the three-year-old boy they wanted to adopt would have to return to the orphanage until the process was complete. On hearing the news, the mother fell to her knees crying in the parking lot of a government office, Juntunen wrote, while he focused in on the little boy, who looked scared and confused.

Another mobilizing moment was meant to be a planned 2011 march on Washington, "The Empty Stroller March," also later rebranded as the "Step Forward for Orphans March." It was to be comprised of prospective adoptive parents pushing empty baby strollers that were wrapped in red tape from the Children's Carousel at the National Mall up to the Capitol. The march was canceled because of bad weather—it fell on the weekend of Hurricane Irene—but Both Ends Burning's influence was growing, however fitfully. Juntunen acknowledged that many adoption experts find his tactics and his proposed solutions naive, particularly at a time when few adoption programs are functioning without scandal, but his common-sense frustration appeals to others.

In March 2011 Juntunen addressed the elite Adoption Policy Conference at New York University Law School, an annual gathering for academics and policy experts hosted by the Center for Adoption Policy and focused on adoption law. It was generally a pro-adoption crowd, charging that "cultural ideologues" are harming adoption, but still a wonky crowd, making its prescriptions in policy terms too arcane for many lay activists to follow. Juntunen, a comparative naïf, spoke alongside a bevy of adoption lawyers, academics, and multiple State Department officials, including Ambassador Susan Jacobs, whom Secretary of State Hillary Clinton had appointed in 2010 to the newly created role of special advisor for children's issues. Jacobs admitted the obvious, "Adoptions have decreased. There's no getting around that fact," before offering the official State Department position on the falling numbers: "We don't believe there's any right number for ethical adoptions."

When Juntunen later addressed the crowd during the lunch session—donning a pair of glasses for the presentation and his hands trembling slightly as if he had found himself in the belly of the beast—he launched in with self-deprecation, acknowledging the awkwardness of "an ex-quarterback speaking to a room full of lawyers." "That said," he continued, "simple ideas do lie within the reach of complex minds."

Delivering what seemed like a corporate motivational speech, Juntunen diagnosed the inability of the conference's attendees to rescue adoption as a problem of battle fatigue, a "can't-do attitude," and a failure of creativity. "International adoption is still in the Dark Ages from a process standpoint," he had explained to me. "That's because we have continued to look at it in bureaucratic terms, and I'm suggesting we begin to look at the process in entrepreneurial terms [instead]."

The entrepreneurial approach he suggested was vague and consumer oriented: streamlining the process of approving adoptive parents and confirming children's orphan status with simple electronic background checks, harmonizing each country's distinct adoption requirements to create uniform standards, trimming redundant safety checks, speeding up results, and eliminating high costs. It was an adoptive parent's wish list—no matter if it disregarded the failure of many adoptions despite the current, more onerous safety checks in place, or the fact that tracing children's family status was so time intensive that, in the first year after the earthquake in Haiti, UNICEF's project to track whether institutionalized children had living relatives had only managed to clear fewer than one thousand kids. Not to mention that Juntunen's plan essentially called for countries around the world to change their individual child protection laws to better accommodate US adoptive parents.

In Juntunen's description of the plan to me, he suggested a goal of adoptions costing just $5,000 and taking only months to complete. When he spoke of this plan at NYU, he preempted any titters in the crowd with a posture of defiance. "As I look out amongst you, I see headshakes. . . . Many of you have already told me that [creating a uniform global system] will never work. Many of you have said that my vision of this central place, where process could be more efficient, is unrealistic. I used to tell employees that no one gets to greatness thinking in realistic terms,"

Juntunen said. "Gandhi said 'First they ignore you, then they ridicule you, then they fight you, then you win.' Since I'm up at this podium, I guess I've passed the 'first they ignore you' phase."

He shifted to an equally bombastic conclusion, describing his adopted daughter's recent book report on Rosa Parks and how he viewed the slow adoption process today as an equally outrageous injustice. He looked in the audience for UNICEF's Susan Bissell, who had spoken earlier that day, once again defending UNICEF from allegations that they were blocking adoptions from Ethiopia. "I say with respect to Dr. Bissell that on January 19, 2010, a UNICEF spokesperson said that the last resort [for Haitian children] is international adoption. Hopefully one day our society will look back at those who held that belief and think they were dead wrong, just as wrong as those who believed that Rosa Parks belonged at the back of the bus." Around the room some members of the audience looked at each other with raised eyebrows and quiet smirks. But when Juntunen finished his speech, others in the audience broke out in enthusiastic applause, and several gave him a standing ovation.

In part the enthusiasm might reflect the other plan Juntunen has in mind: that the bottleneck created as newly mobilized evangelicals enter the constricting adoption market will spark outrage that will transform the system. To hear him tell it, that "chokepoint" is actually a strategic stage in getting laws to change. "So we've created this culture of adoption, and now more and more people want to participate in adoption and are left frustrated because they're denied the opportunity to pursue what they want to pursue," Juntunen told me. "Well, that's where social change happens. I think that . . . this culture of adoption, and this idea that more and more families are going to be raising their hands, that's going to be the catalyst for change."

Since his speech he's won the ear of other adoption proponents: on his board sits Kim Brown, CEO of Holt International Children's Services. (Harvard law professor Elizabeth Bartholet has been on the board since 2010.) The *Washington Times*'s pugilistic adoption columnist championed Both Ends Burning, highlighting Juntunen's thoughts on how adoption will lead to the end of racism through the "cross-pollination of races and cultures." The Congressional Coalition on Adoption Institute (CCAI) joined a planning call for Juntunen's Empty Strollers March in 2011. And in 2012 CCAI Executive Director Kathleen Strottman urged Christian advocates at Saddleback Church to help promote Juntunen's film, *Stuck,* to teach outsiders about the "under-belly" of the adoption world, by which Strottman meant not corruption but rather families caught in the pipeline.*

Stuck was completed with a half-million-dollar donation from Foster Friess, the conservative evangelical multimillionaire who sustained Rick Santorum's 2012 primary campaign and suggested that women keep an aspirin between their legs as a means of contraception. "It's not my money," he benevolently declared at the film's July 2012 premiere, hosted by Senator Landrieu at the US Capitol Visitor's Center Theater. "It's God's money."

ALTHOUGH MUCH of the adoption movement charges ahead with the narrative outlined by Both Ends Burning, some evangelical advocates admit the system needs another kind of overhaul. In 2012 Jedd Medefind told me bluntly that he thought the movement had misstepped in empha-sizing adoption over other forms of orphan care. "One of the mistakes I think the US movement made early on was in terms of it being focused primarily on the beauty of adoption rather than the beauty blended with the difficulty and complexity that comes with adoption," he said. But since then, he said, the movement is increasingly "maturing" to present a more holistic vision of the "continuum of care" needed to address chil-dren's varying needs—international adoption for some, local adoption for others, family preservation for most.

To that end he said the Alliance had hired a new staffer to promote adoption within developing nations rather than international adoption and had supported a conference in Ethiopia in 2011 to encourage local

---

*Earlier in 2012 the Congressional Coalition on Adoption distributed a sur-vey that was at first represented as though it were an official USCIS question-naire, asking prospective adoptive parents to answer questions about their interactions with US officials during the adoption process. JCICS and the Christian Alliance for Orphans promoted the survey online, with the Alliance blog announcing that the results "will be made available to the Senate Foreign Relations Committee for use in an upcoming roundtable on inter-country adoption." To adoption reform advocates like past PEAR board member Pam Veazie, the campaign was really an advocacy tool to collect stories from prospective adoptive parents facing roadblocks in their adoptions, mislead-ingly represented as a neutral government survey.

Ethiopian Christians to adopt. Likewise, in the United States he hoped Christians would shift to adopting or fostering from their own communities as well. "It might not be as 'exotic' as international adoption," Medefind told me, "but the need is every bit as pressing on the other side of the tracks as it is on the other side of the world." In the summer of 2012 Medefind released his white paper, pushing back against the use of the misleading "orphan crisis" numbers like 143 million. He continues to highlight noninternational adoption in his writing and speaking.

In other corners of the orphan-care movement, a smattering of churches were beginning to focus on helping communities care for their own children by addressing the root causes that lead to children being put in orphanages, like The Ethiopia Aid Mission Network (TEAM), a group of Baptist churches in Texas that works on development projects like drilling wells or providing training for local leaders instead of volunteering in orphanages. (These exist in addition to the significant aid work evangelical groups do outside the adoption and orphan care movement.)

Other churches, like the Cooperative Baptist Fellowship, a moderate denomination that split from the Southern Baptist Convention in 1990 over the SBC's increasing conservatism, began working with the Better Care Network, a coalition supported by UNICEF, USAID, and Save the Children that seeks to address orphaned and vulnerable children issues with local solutions. The Better Care Network's faith-based arm seeks to match Western churches and volunteers with local leaders and churches already on the ground, operating from the principle that local leaders know best how to address their own orphan problems.

In late July 2011 Caleb and Becca David finally received word that their adoption from Ethiopia had been approved, and in August they were able to fly home to Oklahoma with their new son, Huxley. With their extended stay and multiple trips, the adoption cost the family a total of more than $42,000. That and the delays they had faced left them conscious of the need for a shift. "Adoption, as incredible as it is, we'd be naive to think that was the only answer. Especially now with it bottlenecking," Caleb had told me while they were still waiting on approval. "As hard as it is for us to be here, we feel like our eyes are being opened about the importance of holistic orphan care. Because ultimately, it's not about us having our child—though obviously that's a huge part of it."

The Davids' observations of the Christian adoption movement in the United States had left Caleb determined that the entire movement had to be transformed from what he described as advocates' eagerness to be recognized as heroes—doing work to gain notice or creating hundreds of redundant orphan-care organizations rather than support the ones already there. "The fastest way for our organization to be shut down would be for me to say what I really think," he told me, with a laugh, in 2012. "You have too many renegade do-gooders with the best intentions who, when push comes to shove, the temptation for glory is just way too much." He eyed the growth of adoption movement conferences skeptically, saying that most of the attendees seemed to be from organizations that had booths set up in the exhibit hall. The trendy issues that were flogged from year to year, like child sex trafficking, didn't seem to reflect sincere engagement so much as marketing. "Are we taking the time to really understand what trafficking is and how that ties into orphan care and adoption?" he asked.

Caleb's hope for the cause is not in the large movement but rather the innovations of a few friends doing different sorts of work in Ethiopia. One organization, Embracing Hope Ethiopia, had begun a day care center for women who needed to work, so they wouldn't have to choose between making an income and keeping their children. Another, Bring Love In, was creating local "families" out of orphanage wards and Ethiopian mothers who had lost their own children. Both of these groups seemed to approach child welfare in Ethiopia with the same sorts of programs that the United States and other developed nations benefit from and, thus, seemed to offer a rare level of respect for Ethiopian families: in need of support, but not the "rescue" of their children. "Those people don't get nearly enough credit, but they are digging deep into the community, dealing with social issues," Caleb said.

But to adoption reform advocate David Smolin, these efforts to shift the discourse remain private discussions that aren't being adequately reflected in the public presentation of the cause, in which adoption leaders still frequently dismiss more holistic development goals as insufficient and in which a foundational problem in the movement's mission continues to corrupt its charity.

Not only has the Christian adoption movement displayed willful ignorance of the long-standing problems in domestic and international adoption, Smolin said, but its ideology—fixated on the symbolism of adopting children into new families and how that mirrors the Christian conversion experience—explicitly exacerbates the problems. "It is not merely a matter of doing the right thing for the wrong reason, but quite often that of doing the wrong thing for the wrong reason," he wrote. Seeing adoption as a divine mission leads people to embrace an industry in which they routinely spend $20,000 to $40,000 to adopt a child without being willing to spend several hundred dollars to preserve the original family. Taking children from the poor becomes normalized standard practice, justified by the sense that adopters are emulating God. A truly just orphan-care movement, he said, would be a poverty alleviation movement.

That's not just a humane principle, Smolin said, but for Christians, a biblical one as well. The Bible's James 1:27 call, Smolin repeats, urges Christians to help widows and orphans together, as a unit. But many people find it both more appealing and easier to assist children alone. Smolin calls that "the biggest mistake that runs through the whole movement: a discarding of the adults and a willingness to sever any connection the child has to adults other than to the adoptive parent." For example, he told me, when one major Christian charity, World Vision, tried to shift its child sponsorship program to a family sponsorship model—largely a change in name alone, as funds for large aid groups' child sponsorship programs routinely benefit the wider community—their donations dropped by half. The complexities of working with the adult poor—the real risks of perpetuating dependency and disempowering aid recipients that are recurrent issues in international development—aren't there in the same way when groups work only with children. Whereas needy adults are often perceived negatively—at best as sacrificial victims, and at worst as welfare queens—orphans are blank slates, uncomplicated objects of charity.

Smolin's initial 2012 law review article critiquing the Christian adoption movement became the focus of a dedicated issue from the *Journal of Christian Legal Thought* in spring 2012, in which Jedd Medefind and Dan Cruver were invited to write responses. Medefind, a thoughtful and diplomatic advocate who frequently invites outside criticism, responded that although Smolin's critiques were valid, he missed the forest for the trees, focusing more on the incidence of individual scandals than the overwhelming problem of parentless children living in orphanages and what happens to children who don't get adopted. "Any movement seeking to reflect God's heart for justice and mercy is highly vulnerable to excess and error," Medefind wrote. "This is as true of today's Christian adoption and orphan care advocates as it was with those championing Abolition and Civil Rights." It echoed what he had told me in the past: that "Christian groups don't have the market cornered on poorly designed efforts to help the needy," and people uncomfortable dealing with ethically complex issues shouldn't try to tackle complicated global problems.

But Smolin said that even as many adoptive parents in the larger adoption community are becoming attuned to the issues of corruption that his family encountered, the root problem remains the same: the unwillingness to recognize that the need is less children requiring adoption than poor families desperate for support. Although movement leaders may acknowledge that reality among themselves, as of late 2012 they've done an inadequate job in getting the message out. "I think behind the scenes these people understand that most orphans aren't adoptable and aren't going to be adopted, but that's not what the majority voice of the movement is saying," Smolin told me. "They're responsible for what people are hearing, and the majority message is really still focused on the theology of adoption, which makes people feel that adoption is at the center."

"It took a long time for adoption to become as prominent as it is now," agrees Caleb David, "and now we're going to have to undo some things."

ON THE LAST DAY of the 2012 Christian Alliance for Orphans Summit at Saddleback Church, Rick Warren came on the stage with a panel of government experts: Minister Inyumba Aloisea, head of Rwanda's Ministry of Gender and Family Promotion, the entity that oversees all adoptions from that country; Dr. Sharen Ford, manager of Permanency Services in the Children's Services Division at the Colorado Department of Human Services, one of the two US accrediting bodies for the Hague Convention on Intercountry Adoption and a foster care system that had worked closely with local churches; and the State Department's Ambassador Susan Jacobs.

Ambassador Jacobs, a diplomat praised by some child welfare organizations for acting almost as a mediator between the different factions of the adoption debates, seemed wary of the fact that many in Saddleback's audience see the State Department as "anti-adoption" for its unique gatekeeping role. She offered the crowd a promise: "The State Department completely supports international adoption, full stop." She followed up with a testimony. "Adoption is as old as time itself," she said. "There are many stories in the Bible about adoption. Moses, of course, is the most famous adoptee, though it might not have worked out as well for his adoptive parents. We might consider that perhaps an abandonment." The crowd rewarded her with a hearty laugh, and so she continued, discussing the "adoption" stories of Esther and Samuel.

Jacobs went on to claim that the United States has never had a problem with fraud or misrepresentation in adoptions from a Hague country, something that advocates like David and Desiree Smolin say is demonstrably untrue, considering the scandals from Hague-compliant countries like India and China. This claim also neglects the reality that most US adoptions come from countries that are not Hague-compliant, such as Ethiopia. But Jacobs's assertion was nonetheless greeted with applause.

Dr. Ford, who is also a board member for the Alliance, amplified the spirit of Jacobs's scripture citing. "I'm trusting there are a lot of people here with hearts of mercy who want to collaborate with the government," she said, continuing in a light-touch evangelicalese, alluding to biblical stories popular among evangelicals, such as the parables of the mustard seed or the sower. "In the long run we know that you are planting seeds that will be harvested, maybe not in front of your eyes, but in the days to come they will be harvested and we will see tulips and daisies and roses, yellow, red, orange, tie-dyed roses. We will see them, shorthaired and longhaired and no-hair, we will see them because you planted seeds and they eventually were harvested. And we love these seeds."

With a belly laugh, Warren whooped at Ford's near-sermon, riffing to wild applause and laughter, "Before Pastor Ford here gives the altar call . . . " And Ford delivered, preaching what indeed amounted to an altar call for Christians to push the government on adoption. "All across this nation our kids want to be connected, and government wants to be connected to you," she called. "All across this nation, we want to be connected through collaboration. We can't do it alone. Will you come and walk alongside?"

The audience swooned and rose for a standing ovation. Standing next to Ford, Jacobs beamed. Warren called on the crowd and those watching online to pray for all three leaders for the next seven days. Nearly all the advocates in Saddleback's worship hall, still on their feet, raised their hands and closed their eyes while Pastor Rick prayed a blessing and the government officials bowed their heads.

CHAPTER 7

A Thousand Ways to Not Help Orphans

In May 2011 Dave and Jana Jenkins, US missionaries living in Kigali, Rwanda, began fostering a two-month-old baby named Gabriel Mugisha. Gabriel had been born ten weeks premature, then abandoned by his mother at the Rwamagana Hospital in the country's rural eastern region. After an eight-week stay in the hospital, where the staff gave the child one of his names—Mugisha, meaning "Blessed Boy"—family friends of the Jenkins asked whether the couple could care for the child.

Dave, an athletic-looking, bespectacled forty-five-year-old, was the senior pastor of Christ's Church in Rwanda, which he had helped establish atop one of the rolling hills that make up Kigali and on behalf of an Oklahoma church-planting group called Rwanda Outreach and Community Partners (ROC). Jana, a forty-four-year-old redhead with a practical, straightforward demeanor, also served with ROC as a missionary in addition to working as an independent facilitator for US parents trying to adopt from Rwanda. Rwanda did not allow adoption agencies to work within its borders, so all prospective adoptive parents applied independently, either handling the paperwork themselves or with the help of an independent facilitator—choosing mostly among a small group of evangelical women, like Jana—who serves as an in-country power of attorney.

In 2011 that was a complicated job. The year before, Rwanda had closed its adoption program amid a flurry of applications, mostly from

US Christians, so it could overhaul its old adoption legislation. In its place Rwanda was drafting a comprehensive family law in line with the Hague Convention that would establish a new adoption authority and oversee a program of deinstitutionalization, emptying Rwanda's orphanages and placing vulnerable children in family settings instead. In part, it was Rwanda's answer to the Way Forward Project, a pilot international development initiative established by the Congressional Coalition on Adoption Institute to promote family-based child care over orphanages, whether at home or abroad. Perhaps more importantly, it was a reflection of Rwanda's deep-seated wariness of international adoption.

While those reforms were being finalized, the only adoptions still being processed in 2011 were the roughly 130 cases still "in the pipeline" from before the 2010 closure, three of which Jana was facilitating. No new applications were accepted, and later in 2011 Rwanda's government announced that it was putting a cap of six months on all pipeline applications, meaning if a family wasn't matched with an adoptable child within that timeframe, the government would send them a "letter of regret" and close the case. Considering that Rwanda only placed adoptions from one orphanage in the country, the Catholic "Home of Hope" in Kigali, and that those adoptions often moved at a glacial pace, a number of prospective parents feared that the adoptions they had been working on for years were about to fall through.

In many other adoption-sending countries a situation like this would have all but ensured that the child who had come into the Jenkins' care would be quickly whisked to an international adoption placement. But Rwanda's government insisted that adoptions undergo individualized, plodding scrutiny instead of permitting the booming free-for-all that characterized the adoption process in nearby Ethiopia. And under Rwanda's influence the Christian adoption advocates at work in the country seemed to behave differently as well.

Unlike many Christians who have begun working on orphan-care issues in Africa in recent years, the Jenkins were longtime missionaries of the old school—immersing themselves in a foreign culture until it became their own. An American woman raised in Kenya as the daughter of missionaries, Jana had lived most of her life in Africa before moving with her family to Texas. She had returned to Africa with Dave in 1993 so the couple could themselves serve as missionaries: first in Uganda for eleven years and later in Rwanda until 2012. In Kigali the couple built Christ's Church around a plan to expand the Rwandan middle class, a small demographic comprising just barely over 10 percent of the largely agricultural country.

Reestablishing a middle class was an integral part of rebuilding Rwanda after the devastation of its 1994 genocide, when nearly one million Tutsi ethnic minorities and moderates among the Hutu majority—two groups composing much of the old middle class—were slaughtered in one hundred days. In a country where it's been said that "if there's a next time," violence will erupt over class divisions rather than ethnic ones, economic mobility was a serious matter for the church to take on.

Pictures taken of the Jenkins in younger years show a slightly fussy, conservative couple, Jana with big hair in a tie-front blouse and Dave looking like a Mormon doorknocker on his first mission. However, their portraits from Africa show a couple who had relaxed into themselves: Jana's hair cut short to flatter her strong jaw and Dave in shorts and a T-shirt, casually wearing Gabriel in a backpack carrier. The Jenkins seemed to have learned other important lessons from their adopted countries as well. Dave blogged with respect about Muslim and atheist friends and wrote bitingly about the sort of "Afro-pessimistic" Western fundraising campaigns that featured images of suffering orphans in donation appeals, "turn[ing] a child's dignity into a marketable commodity." When the "Kony 2012" campaign went viral in early 2012, with US Christians presenting an ahistorical picture of the warlord Joseph Kony's role in Uganda, Dave condemned the video as akin to "violent pornography" that made him want "to crawl outside of my white skin," so exoticizing and bleak that it insulted the reality of the Jenkins' longtime home.

It wasn't surprising that when Rwanda's Ministry of Gender and Family Promotion, known by the acronym MIGEPROF, announced its plan to start moving children out of orphanages, the Jenkins' Christ's Church—which had a long history with the ministry and was invited to its planning meeting in 2010—lined up to help in the way that their host country saw most fit. On Dave's blog, he affirmed that he and his church thought the government's plan to deinstitutionalize Rwanda's orphanages, and find families for the children living in them, "displays the ultimate truths of God."

Orphan-care and adoption issues were something the Jenkins and their church colleagues had already been thinking about. "For the last several years Christ's Church in Rwanda leaders have been praying about how to engage Rwanda's problem with Orphans and Vulnerable Children," Dave wrote. He repeated an estimate that, including victims of genocide, HIV, and poverty, there might be as many as one million "vulnerable children" in Rwanda. Without intervention, he warned, this aging class of children would be a weight that could break the economic gains

made in Rwanda since the genocide, harming the prospects of the stabiliz-
ing middle class the Jenkins hoped to build.

But the adoption rhetoric that had taken off among evangelicals back
in the United States wasn't lost on the Jenkins either. Quoting Calvinist
theologian J. I. Packer's book *Knowing God,* Dave wrote, "'Our understanding of Christianity cannot be better than our grasp of adoption.
Adoption is the highest privilege that the gospel offers.'" Jana told me that
"I think as Christians, God gave us the perfect example of adoption by
adopting us into his family." The couple had themselves adopted two
Ugandan children during their long years of mission work in the country,
and they led their church in observing Orphan Sunday, the annual adoption movement event originally inspired by a church in Zambia but transformed into a widespread multimedia campaign and church highlight in
the United States.

Following the planning session at MIGEPROF, the Jenkins came up
with one idea to complement deinstitutionalization: a pilot program
called "Spoken For," in which children found abandoned would not go
into orphanages but instead directly to a network of foster parents recruited from Christ's Church's congregation, either Rwandans or resident
ex-pats. They would thereby prevent children from being institutionalized in the first place and avoid the harm that orphanages have been
shown to do to children's development. The church would support the
families with a "baby kit" of basic supplies and trainings, and the government would learn that they could turn to the church when they were faced
with a child care emergency. The foster families, envisioned as a temporary solution, would care for the children until a permanent solution
could be found, whether that meant reuniting them with their parents or
extended biological family or placing them for adoption with Rwandan
parents. International adoption would be the last resort. "It's a temporary
system while we find Rwandan families that are ready for adoption," Jana
reiterated to me in June 2011, rocking Gabriel serenely in a paisley-print
recliner in the living room of her Kigali home, surrounded by cardboard
boxes as their oldest daughter prepared to depart Rwanda for her first
year at Wheaton College, a prestigious evangelical school outside
Chicago.

The premise of Spoken For—basically, recruiting and training foster
parents—was an idea foundational to child care systems in the United
States and many other developed nations but one that could be revolutionary in a country like Rwanda, as that nation still struggles to establish
its social and child welfare frameworks. In contrast to orphanage life, Jana

said, the children would be treated as though "you are spoken for, there is a plan for you."

The baby the Jenkins were caring for, Gabriel Mugisha, represented the project's trial run, and the stakes, they seemed to feel, were high. As Rwanda reformed its adoption system, many eyes were watching: from US adoption agencies on the lookout for a new country to work in; to the country's large population of visiting evangelical missionaries, who have invested heavily in postgenocide Rwanda; to international development agencies; to Rwanda's own government officials, wary of following in the footsteps of other adoption boom-bust nations and determined to find a way to care for Rwandan children within their own country. The Jenkins themselves seemed to support this domestic solution, as David sermonized on his blog: "Rwanda's churches and families are the answer for Rwanda's vulnerable children. It is time we say, 'This is our responsibility. These children are ours. You will not take our children away.'"

Given these conflicting interests, where baby Gabe would go next— abroad to an overflowing waitlist of would-be American adoptive parents or to an extended family member or domestic adopter in Rwanda—reflected something larger than his own case. "Since there are fifty-plus [international] families that have been approved by the ministry to adopt and there are no children," Jana told me, "I'm thinking that this time you might end up with an international family. But I'm holding off to see if some Rwandans [come forward] or if he could be integrated back into his family." The Jenkins gave the boy his second name, "Gabriel," meaning a messenger from God, and they looked to his unfolding story for an answer. "In our sprits we sensed Mugisha Gabriel would be a blessed messenger to teach our community what we were to do for [orphans and vulnerable children]," Dave wrote. "But how do we practically proceed? A messenger named Gabriel Mugisha will show us the way."

FOR A TIME, as Ethiopia's adoption boom started to slow down and savvy adoption agencies began suggesting other countries to prospective clients, Rwanda had looked like it would become the next hotspot "source country" in international adoption. The ingredients for a boom seemed to be there. Compared to the flood of children leaving Ethiopia, the adoptions out of Rwanda had been a mere trickle. Between 2000 and 2011 fewer than 150 Rwandan children were adopted by US families, starting from just one adoption in 2000 and rising to a "peak" of 57 in 2011. Further, the country's efforts to expedite clearance of the "pipeline cases" before its new adoption law took effect likely inflated that number. To many adoption agencies searching for the next market supplier, that Rwanda's "export" numbers could be increased likely seemed reasonable, especially given the extensive role US evangelicals had come to play in its public life.

The Jenkins weren't the only American Christians tapped to sit in on MIGEPROF's November 2010 planning meeting about deinstitutional- ization and the new adoption law. National Council for Adoption (NCFA) President Chuck Johnson also traveled to Rwanda for the meet- ing, accompanied by representatives from Rick Warren's Saddleback Church and Bethany Christian Services as well as another large agency with substantial ties to evangelicals and conservative US politicians, the Texas-based Gladney Center for Adoption. All were present to help ad- vise on the creation of what would become the central adoption authority in Rwanda in the coming regime.

This wasn't the first time these groups had spoken to the Rwandan government about adoption. In 2008 representatives from Saddleback and Gladney had also accompanied the Joint Council on International Children's Services (JCICS) delegation to Rwanda on a two-part mission to gauge the country's interest in permitting adoption agencies to work there and also to collaborate with Rwandan church groups in promoting adoption. The evangelical orphan-care ministry Hope for Orphans recog- nized their efforts, writing in 2009, "A few short years ago, virtually no children were being adopted out of Rwanda. Thanks in part to the efforts of our friends at the Gladney Center for Adoption, as well as Saddleback Church, that is now changing, and more children are finding forever fam- ilies as a result."

The reasons for adoption agencies like Gladney or Bethany to court Rwanda's government were obvious, but Saddleback's involvement wasn't random either. In 2005 Rwanda's President Paul Kagame, a con- troversial military leader who helped end the genocide, had invited Sad- dleback Pastor Rick Warren to implement the lessons of his best-selling book, *The Purpose Driven Life*, in Rwanda. Warren's book had been as popular in Rwanda as it was elsewhere in the world, and more than one hundred thousand copies had been distributed in the local language of Kinyarwanda. Creating a program in Rwanda based on the ambitions of Warren's P.E.A.C.E. Plan, a missionary empire that places local churches at the forefront of global development work and that uses trained church volunteers to augment or replace government social services, would mark its first nation-scaled implementation. The plan's programs, such as its "clinic in a box"—giving churches the basic ingredients to provide rudimentary medical care to their community—did triple duty by helping citizens, easing the government's burden, and evangelizing the public by boosting the credibility of the local church providing the care.

"There are more churches than Starbucks or McDonald's combined in the United States," Elizabeth Styffe, founder and director of Saddleback's HIV/AIDS and orphan care initiatives, told me. "And more people went to church last Sunday than will watch every single football, basketball, or other sporting event all year long in America. So there's a labor force in this. All over the world there may not be civic government or school, but there will be a church."

The plan was based on the same premise of a united, global Christian community—ready to be tapped for a joint effort—that informed the Christian adoption movement's formula for solving the orphan crisis: the number of Christians in the world far outweighed the number of orphans, so the solution to the problem was just a matter of mobilization. As Styffe put it, speaking at her home church at the 2012 Christian Alliance for Orphans Summit, "Who's going to end the orphan crisis? The church."

In exchange for giving Saddleback's missionaries unparalleled access to the country, Kagame, who stated publicly that he was not personally devout, hoped that Saddleback's involvement would attract investors to Rwanda. His own goal was to turn Rwanda into what the *Economist* called, "the Singapore of central Africa," and he clearly thought that Warren's influence could help. Warren joined Kagame's presidential advisory council, and Rwanda was hailed as the first "Purpose Driven Nation."

"I've never seen that kind of situation before, where the government has really partnered so closely and so openly with a private organization, whether a religious one or not," the NCFA's Chuck Johnson told me. "You see a lot of public partnerships here in the United States," he continued, noting the "seat at the table" the US State Department has afforded American adoption lobbyists, "but this looks like nation building, where there's a plan to make [Rwanda] an English-speaking, Christian African nation."

Although Kagame was more interested in the business connections Warren could bring to bear than his evangelical message, the proselytizing came along with the thousands of volunteers Saddleback sent from Orange County to Central Africa's Great Lake region. After all, the "P" in Saddleback's P.E.A.C.E. Plan initially stood for "Planting churches," and even though it has since been updated to "Planting churches that promote reconciliation"—a particularly resonant message in Rwanda—Saddleback maintains that all reconciliation begins by reconciling with God.

That was also a message Rwanda was primed to hear. After some Catholic leaders were found complicit in the genocide and Catholic churches became the sites of some of its worst massacres, with many asylum seekers killed inside the churches where they had gone to seek refuge, a massive wave of conversions to US-style born-again Christianity had swept the country. "We had statistics that over 90 percent of our population was Christian, but it didn't stop the genocide from taking place," Eric Munyemana, the executive secretary for Saddleback's P.E.A.C.E. Plan operations in Rwanda, told me. "That's a sign that there [was] something wrong with our Christianity."

Many Rwandans apparently agreed. Today Rwanda is an intensely evangelical country: US missionaries dominate its airport and hotels; the rooftops of Kigali buildings sport massive testimonials to Jesus; and church membership is the focus of any introduction between strangers. The impact was apparent everywhere. In Kigali's sparse but efficient airport a group of postcollege youth missionaries from Oklahoma, training in Rwanda's burgeoning hospitality industry, compared notes with an older Oregon woman who ministers to Rwanda's jailed *genocidaires*. "There's so much *light* here," one of the youth missionaries said. The older missionary nodded. "You can do things here you could never do in America," she said.

It followed that Saddleback's prioritization of orphan and adoption issues became influential in Rwanda. Saddleback staffers, including Styffe, were among the first families to adopt Rwandan children to the United States. And Archbishop Emanuel Kolini, the influential head of the Anglican Church in Rwanda as well as a partner in the P.E.A.C.E. Plan, having visited Saddleback three times, believes that Saddleback's prominence has aided individual adoption applications. "Rick Warren is well known" and the Rwandan government trusts Saddleback, Kolini told me. "Otherwise, [Rwandan government officials] are not sure what [adoptive parents are] going to do with the children."

In 2012 Warren invited the head of MIGEPROF, Minister Inyumba Aloisea, to the Christian Alliance for Orphans Summit in California to participate in a discussion forum with Warren and US government officials on adoption. Minister Aloisea, a woman who had overseen both the burial of the dead and the placement of children for domestic adoption directly after the genocide, explained Rwanda's orphan history to participants. After the genocide, with nearly a million dead in just a few months, family structures had been destroyed and hundreds of thousands of children were orphaned. Some of these children were placed with extended family or other domestic adopters in situations that often resembled indentured servitude. Some families taking orphans were unprepared for the behavior of children who had been traumatized by the violence they had witnessed as well as the loss of their family. Many children were sent to new orphanages built in the wake of the carnage. "We had half a million orphans scattered around the country," Aloisea told Warren. "I have to be honest with you, pastor, we didn't know what to do. We collected all the children in orphanage centers. From 1994 to1996 we had 104 orphanages."

Now Rwanda had cut that number to around thirty-four, and the official number of children housed in those orphanages as of mid-2012 was just over three thousand. "Rwanda intends to be the first country in the world to have no orphans and no orphanages," Warren crowed from the stage, adding that "3,050 orphans are all that's left in Rwanda! From half a million! Teach us how to do that in five minutes. I want to do that in every country!" But there was a disconnect between how that had happened in Rwanda and the support for massive international adoption programs backed by many attending the Saddleback conference. Despite the abundant factors portending yet another "perfect storm" adoption market in Rwanda, no adoption boom came. Instead, Rwanda's government maintained a tight grip on its adoption process, scrutinizing each case extensively and effectively challenging prospective parents to demonstrate why they deserved to adopt one of Rwanda's children.

This level of control, a sharp contrast to the disarray and corruption that took hold in other war-torn and desperately poor countries, is not actually surprising in the context of modern Rwanda, today so well ordered a nation that outsiders hail it as Africa's "biggest success story." While politically the government's control over public life has been condemned as authoritarian, with opposition journalism and dissent stifled under the pretext of postgenocide laws against ethnic divisiveness, and national elections have been dismissed by the *Economist* as "a sham," the positive effects of the new regime's policies are apparent in many other areas. Rwanda is a country where women represent more than half of Parliament, where corruption is rare and a bribe can quickly land both parties in jail, and where once a month all Rwandans, including the president, are expected to pick up litter during a communal cleanup day.

Rwanda is also a place where the rigor of bureaucratic formalities can take on an absurdist air, as was obvious during a 2011 visit to the offices of MIGEPROF. In a hallway of their utilitarian offices in an airy hilltop compound, cranky ministry officials shook their heads at what seemed to them an unmanageable glut of pipeline adoption cases. "We have a huge number of demands, but few children that are adoptable," protested Benilde Uwababyeyi, the child protection officer in charge of MIGEPROF's overseas policy, gesturing at a database for waiting parents—most from the United States and many, Uwababyeyi noted incredulously, asking for more than one child.

In 2011 only one orphanage in the country was allowed to offer children for adoption: the small Home of Hope orphanage run by the Missionaries of Charity, the Catholic order founded by Mother Teresa (its entryway graced with a large poster declaring in English, "We fight abortion by adoption!"). The reason was procedural. It alone, of all Rwanda's orphanages, had implemented a routine process of having the police investigate and declare children legally abandoned so they could be eligible for adoption. Rwanda does not allow children with families to be adopted abroad, and any children sent for adoption must have their family connections traced first to ensure they don't have living relatives. The rules are strictly enforced. When one California couple wanted to adopt an older girl they had met in an orphanage, they were refused because the girl's mother, despite being committed to a mental institution, was still alive, meaning the daughter might have a chance to know her.

Diligently following principles like this can make for a long wait for prospective adoptive parents. Even with a waiting list numbered in the tens, not the hundreds or thousands, parents who are thirtieth in line may stay at the same ranking for many months while officials conduct a full investigation of each child's background before moving on to the next case. It's a task made more complicated and slower by the fact that abandoning a child is illegal in Rwanda, so few parents leave enough identifying details to easily verify the child's status. Compared with this trickle of vetted orphans, the demand from the United States overwhelmed the small MIGEPROF offices.

Not only that, Uwababyeyi said, but by policy, Rwanda wanted intercountry adoption to remain a last resort, coming only after efforts to reunite families or find domestic adopters had been exhausted. "We want children to remain here in Rwanda, because we want them to be Rwandan. To stay in the Rwandan culture and learn Rwandan values," she said, "that's why we are building this campaign." The campaign she meant was the government's nascent effort to encourage domestic adoption, which had entered public awareness via a billboard series sponsored by Rwandan First Lady Jeannette Kagame's Imbuto Foundation, exhorting Rwandans to "treat each child as your own."

International organizations have gotten Rwanda's message. "What we know is that the current minister of MIGEPROF is not supportive of inter-country adoption at all, thinking adoption should be the last resort for a few cases," said Damien Ngabonziza, a UNICEF official assigned to work with MIGEPROF. "They don't want children to be sent out unnecessarily."

In part Rwanda's reticence is a result of recent cautionary experiences. During the chaos of the genocide in 1994 a small number of children were sent abroad to European countries like Italy and France. Some were relin-quished for adoption by desperate parents who saw no other way to save their children, and some were taken out of the country during emergency evacuations by orphanage staff desperate to save their wards. The out-comes were mixed. In the case of a group of children adopted to Italy, the children never came home, and Rwandan families and government repre-sentatives attempting to check on them, including Ngabonziza, were de-nied access. "I visited in Milan in '95 or '96," he recalled. "They would not even allow us to talk to the kids. Later on we tried to get them back, with no results. I understand that after ten years they have probably settled down, but they might like to know who they are and where they come from. Some of their parents survived and may not be aware of where they are."

Some government officials had personal reasons to be suspicious of adoption, such as one ministry official who, one adoptive mother heard, had temporarily lost her own children during the genocide, only to find them later in an orphanage in the neighboring country of Burundi. "I think in her eyes, it was a good thing they didn't have open adoption policies," said the mother. "What if her children had left the country [for good]?"

Alfred Munyentwari, national director of SOS Children's Villages-Rwanda, a nonprofit that works on family preservation and family-based foster care, agreed that the impromptu adoptions that took place during the genocide left their mark in the minds of many Rwandans. In 2006 he was contacted by the guardians of a nineteen-year-old woman who, with a sibling, had been adopted by a German family as a seven-year-old girl af-ter her parents had been separated during the genocide. The father, left alone with the children, had feared they would be killed if he kept them, so he allowed a German couple to take them out of the country. When the adopted daughter felt drawn to rediscover her heritage as an adult and came to Rwanda under Munyentwari's care, she found that her adoption had led to her parents' divorce, as her mother blamed the father for "sell-ing the children" and his community turned against him. "They said, 'You are terrible, you are foolish,'" Munyentwari recalled. "'How can you sell children? We sell cows.'" The father was shunned in his town until his daughter's return cleared his name. "This story is to tell you that sometimes children can go and when they go, they will get homesick," Munyentwari told me. "They will say, 'I am well fed, well clothed,' but no one can feed that need."

"In some countries there is acceptance of adoption, but in Rwanda we think only God can know the future," he concluded, arguing that Rwandans are afraid of not knowing whether their children are okay after they leave the country. "There are some people coming and saying, 'the Rwandese are stupid because they don't want the good life for their children.' But people have to think twice. I may be in a miserable situation today and not able to educate my children, but maybe tomorrow can be better. It's easy to say, okay, you want the child, take the child. But maybe my children will not forgive me. I think it is better to say I'll keep my children."

This cultural skepticism of international adoption has required prospective adoptive parents to learn to accommodate themselves to Rwanda instead of the other way around. In 2008 Jennifer Jukanovich, an adoptive mother of two in Seattle and a six-year board member for the Christian adoption movement group Children's HopeChest, embarked on an adoption from Rwanda. As she was leaving an appointment with MIGEPROF, a young law student standing outside the ministry offices stopped her and asked to see her paperwork, explaining that she wanted to ensure that Rwandan children were going to good homes. Jukanovich didn't share her paperwork, but the demand, hard to imagine taking place in a country like Ethiopia, impressed upon her that things worked differently in Rwanda. Many who have been through Rwanda's adoption system have also encountered the government's determination not to let the country develop a baby business that trades in the offspring of the nation's poor. "When I first moved there, it drove me crazy," said Jukanovich, who has since spent time in Rwanda working on business development. "But now I really do understand that they're trying to protect you and trying to protect their country, making sure there's no corruption. It's a struggle, but Rwandans don't want to become an Ethiopia. They want to do things right."

Many others in the small community involved with Rwandan adoptions agreed. "I know that the previous minister of gender went to Ethiopia and it just turned her against international adoption," Jana Jenkins told me. She noted the existence of bad actors—"a lot of hokey groups"—among the many adoption agencies working in Ethiopia. By comparison she didn't think Rwanda's "proactive government" allowed the same room for bad behavior. "It's easier to do your own thing in a country that's loosey-goosey and doesn't know what they're doing.

There's a vacuum. But there's definitely a direction that Rwanda's going and it's moving pretty fast, and if you come, you just jump on board and see what you can do."

Those who have made it through the process also often admire the country's refusal to conduct easy adoptions. "At times it's hard to explain to waiting families," said adoption facilitator Tina Harriman. "They see the statistics of how many millions of orphans are in the world and they want to help, and then you have to wait for over a year to find a child that's available. But it's because [Rwanda is] very selective and wants to ensure that everything's done very appropriately."

Jaya Holliman is a Vermont mother of two who adopted from Rwanda in 2009. She and her husband decided to adopt after losing their newborn son in 2006 due to a uterine rupture during labor that also left Holliman infertile. After grieving, Holliman approached an agency that was then starting a pilot program in Rwanda. At the time the number of US parents who adopted Rwandan infants each year could be counted on one hand. Holliman induced lactation so she could breastfeed the child she hoped to adopt, and on her agency's recommendation, went to Rwanda to try to shepherd her paperwork through. But the government, suspecting her of lying about her son's death because of the fact that she was lactating and also, she later learned, because they didn't approve of the agency and lawyer she was using, denied her application. "They refused to work with agencies—they flat out refused, which I hadn't been aware of when I signed up," said Holliman.

On a tip from a friend who had successfully adopted from Rwanda previously, Holliman fired the agency, which had misled her about their standing with the government, and applied again on her own, providing documentation about her son's death and her decision to induce lactation. Perhaps more importantly, however, she assured the government that she was now working alone. She was rewarded with a second chance and shortly adopted an infant boy she and her husband named Pacifique. The intensity of the personal scrutiny each case received remained with her. "They were very wary of places like Ethiopia. They were so adamant about the integrity of each case to the point where, when they thought I was lying, they didn't even open my file," she said.

"The impression I got in Rwanda is that they literally take each case on face value," agreed Megan Biehl, a California mother who adopted in 2008 and the friend who advised Holliman on reapplying without an agency. Biehl, who also adopted following the death of one of her biological children, had been advised by contacts in Rwanda that MIGEPROF judged adoption applications on an extremely personal basis—whether the ministry "felt that your story was compelling enough that you deserve to have one of their children"—and that they were fiercely opposed to working with agencies. "The minister told me: do this yourself. We will not work with agencies. You do it yourself and you show me why you want to be a parent for a child from Rwanda, and I will look at your paperwork."

While Biehl and her husband were in the middle of their adoption application, in 2008, they met with then-MIGEPROF head Dr. Jeanne d'Arc Mujawamariya. The minister, Biehl recalled, held up a book about international adoption that an adoption facilitator working for a US agency had given to her, "kind of shook it a bit, and said, 'We do not sell our babies.'"

"I think that [book] infuriated MIGEPROF. It was not a route that she appreciated—this kind of backdoor route of trying to adopt," Biehl said. She asked the couple to be advocates, spreading the word when they got home that Rwanda doesn't "'want any money for our babies.'" "Rwanda should be honored for trying to hold strong to their roots," Biehl reflected, "and not letting the machine get to it."

The difference was so striking that when both Biehl and Holliman traveled through Ethiopia to finish paperwork at Addis Ababa's larger US embassy, the hostility they encountered from Ethiopians who assumed they were adopting Ethiopian children shocked them. Rwanda's smaller system had largely insulated it from that kind of popular backlash.

Rwanda's concerns about allowing agencies access to its process are such that, according to Ngabonziza, MIGEPROF even second-guessed its decision to invite agency representatives to its planning discussions for the country's new adoption law. "One of the mistakes we made as we were preparing the instruments was we invited an adoption agency from the states to help out with the definitions [of best practices in intercountry adoption]," Ngabonziza recalled. "The staff that were sent here did a good job and had good tools that we'll review, but the way they outlined those tools could probably make the United States privileged in adopting from Rwanda above other countries, in terms of what we require from adoptive parents, the criteria they should meet, the support they should have processing the application—things that are not universal." Were they to do it over again, he said, he would have instead requested policy-drafting help from a more neutral body, like the Hague bureau, rather than representatives from any particular country, "especially not the one that has the majority of applications to adopt from Rwanda. It's a conflict of interest."

Harriman, who worked in intercountry adoptions herself, echoed some of Ngabonziza's worries. "What I have loved about Rwandan adoptions from day one is the integrity with which the government works. I don't know of anything that could slide through in terms of unethical practices. I remember when they were talking about moving towards the Hague convention, I kind of chuckled, thinking, they are so there already!"

But, she continued, "When they open up under the Hague, I fear that you're going to get all the Hague-accredited agencies pouring in and inundating the system even more, with even more people seeking adoption, when even now there's a shortage of children able to be referred. I don't know how that's going to look when they really open back up and how they're going to maintain the supply and demand. I'm glad that Rwanda is doing all they can to ensure the protection of their children, but on the other hand, part of me feels like they already were."

CHRISTIANS INVOLVED in adoption and orphan-care work in Rwanda also seem to have taken a different approach from the rest of the movement. And interestingly, that might be thanks in part to Saddleback's evolving pattern of involvement on the world stage.

Ten years into the P.E.A.C.E. Plan, Saddleback leaders say they have come to see their global work differently than they used to. As Warren cheerfully admitted, in offering to help other churches replicate Saddleback's model, "We've learned a thousand ways to *not* do missions, to not help the poor, to not help the sick, to not help orphans." But along the way, he said, they came upon a few dozen things that do work "unbelievably well." In so doing it seems that Saddleback Church, one of the earliest leaders of the adoption movement, has rediscovered some of the "best practices" that traditional development organizations like UNICEF hold to.

This shift is perhaps best exemplified in the advocacy of Saddleback's Orphan Care ministry director, Styffe, an effusively friendly woman who laughs and cries easily and peppers her public speaking with self-deprecating jokes ("I'm more blonde than I pay to be," she riffed at the Christian Alliance Summit). Styffe is a nurse by background who had cared for HIV-positive children in California before Saddleback became involved in global HIV/AIDS work. Also a mother of seven, including three Rwandan children, Styffe arguably planted the seed for Saddleback's development work, showing Kay Warren the article on African HIV/AIDS orphans that famously gave the pastor's wife a newfound sympathy for victims of the disease.

Beneath Styffe's warm demeanor—she invites all new acquaintances to consider her a close, personal friend—the Orange County mother has developed a depth of field experience beyond that of many of her peers in the evangelical adoption community. Too often, she explains, well-intentioned mission groups will launch themselves into a local community in a developing country, determined to complete a simple, concrete plan; instead, they end up dominating the process without taking local opinions, talents, or labor into account. She urged volunteers at the Christian Alliance Summit not to bring money—or at least not at first—and not to perform projects that local people and local churches can do for themselves. Rather, she said, they should tap local human resources and support local goals. Saddleback, for example, had learned to support local churches in Rwanda in completing whatever project was most important for their community—in one instance, building a public soccer field—so that those churches reaped the credit, not the international volunteers.

This strategy certainly reflected the P.E.A.C.E. Plan's principles and evangelizing aims—local citizens happy about the soccer field were more likely to join the churches that built it—but also embodied broader principles from the development community, such as replacing drop-in charity with self-sustaining local leadership. And after the soccer fields are built, Styffe said, churches can begin to tackle other challenges, like encouraging their flocks to see the orphans in their community as a problem that they themselves must address. "The way we measure our success," Styffe said, "is who is the hero [when the NGO leaves], and it's the local church." It was a lesson she meant for the adoption community as well: "If the hope of the world is the American church adopting," she added at Saddleback, "then we will never end the orphan crisis. But if the hope of the world is adoption in the local church, then we'll do everything to mobilize every believer and some will adopt." It's a slower process, she said, but one that will last.

Following this plan, she said, when American Christians go abroad to serve, "they [should not] go play in an orphanage. Or if they go play with kids in an orphanage, they'll take people from the local church, so when they leave, the local church is still there, still engaged."

Styffe's remarks invoked the charges brought against "AIDS orphan tourism" in the 2010 report by the Human Sciences Research Council. This report warned that Westerners mixing exotic vacations with volunteer work in orphanages—an apt description of many short-term mission programs—were doing more harm than good. Not only did "voluntourism" trips chip away at the local economy by preempting possible jobs—volunteers actually paying to do low-skilled work that locals could instead perform for a wage; they also risked hurting children in orphanages whose stability and development were disturbed by a rotating cast of visitors forming intense but short-lived bonds that inevitably were broken at the end of each mission trip. It was a pattern that centered more on the donations volunteers could bring and volunteers' sense of emotional fulfillment, the report found, than on the needs of the children.

Styffe's broader view of the complexities surrounding orphaned and vulnerable children—ultimately, the problem of global poverty—may also have led Styffe to another of her unorthodox views. Unlike most of her colleagues at the Saddleback summit, Styffe had nothing but praise for UNICEF, which she commended for taking more concrete steps to get children out of orphanages than Christian groups have ever done: "It makes me angry that people not in church are doing more to end the orphan crisis than us," she told the crowd. Styffe's surprising message seemed to demonstrate that, whatever failings the Christian adoption movement has had in the past—placing self-serving goals above the best interests of children and lending their power to a frequently corrupt industry—the community is capable of working in ways that lead not back to the familiar cycle of adoption boom and bust but instead toward sustainable development in partnership with local leaders.

But as well respected within the movement as Styffe is, as of late 2012 her perspective is not reflected in the dominant message of the movement. As the adoption reform advocate David Smolin noted about other fledgling efforts to broaden the movement's aims, what matters most is the message that Christians on the ground are hearing from movement leaders. And that message is the one that even Styffe's boss and pastor, Rick Warren, repeated in the promise he made to a cheering audience at the same Christian Alliance Summit: "When I say orphan care, it's adoption first, second, and last."

SOME FACILITATORS in Rwanda believed that MIGEPROF's reluctance to embrace international adoption obscured a larger orphan problem than the country acknowledged. Although MIGEPROF officials told me in 2011 that there were just a paltry thirty-eight hundred orphans in the country—a figure reflecting only the wards of the country's officially recognized orphanages—Jana Jenkins countered with an estimate of one million orphaned children, based on UNICEF's toll of vulnerable kids.

As in other countries, neither the government's likely underestimate nor the misapplied UNICEF number give any indication of how many Rwandan children need to be adopted. But to adoption advocates, the knowledge that there are children in the country's other thirty-three orphanages, which are not authorized to conduct adoptions, can amount to the frustrating conviction that there are many more children just out of reach. "The ironic thing is there are children, they're just not in that one orphanage," Jenkins told me, referring to the Home of Hope. "At the Noel orphanage, there are tons of babies."

She meant the Noel Orphanage at Nyundo Rwanda in Gisenyi, a border town in the far northwest corner of Rwanda, its hazy skyline ringed by a range of jagged volcanoes and its city edge marked by a long fence and two checkpoints, separating it from the shanty-town sprawl of the Congolese city of Goma. A steady trail of vendors walked across the border in both directions, their heads laden with bundles of branches, sacks of onions and cabbages, and eggs nestled in trays, stacked ten rows high. The plastic bags that have been outlawed in Rwanda since 2005 as part of an antilitter campaign flew freely on the Goma side, catching in the fence, and Goma's corrugated metal shacks stood in sharp contrast to the McMansions that the smuggling class *nouveau riche* in Gisenyi had built.

Across town from the border is the Catholic-run Noel Orphanage, the oldest and largest children's home in Rwanda, which housed nearly six hundred children in 2011. The orphans at Noel range from just months old up to twenty-six years, explained assistant administrator Augustine Twagira, a soft, kindly man in high-waisted jeans and a neatly tucked polo shirt. Because children in Rwanda are traditionally considered part of their parents' homes until around the age of thirty, older orphans, including children old enough to have survived the genocide, may live in institutions until their late twenties.

In a series of clean and cheerful rooms babies grouped by age lay in orderly rows of well-cushioned cribs, swaddled in heavy blankets and tended by nurses with infants strapped tightly to their backs. Toddlers pretended to nap, giggling, laying on mattresses that had been taken off their bed frames and arranged on the floor to accommodate more kids. Auxiliary dormitories had been crafted in the medical clinic because there were simply too many children for the space, and in the foyer of each room nurses sat on the floor, quietly feeding children who had just woken up. In the fields outside, older children played soccer or worked in a spacious woodshop set next to the orphanage vegetable garden. Near Noel's library, outside a building designated for residents with developmental disabilities, a young woman reached out to hug Twagira fiercely, and then both my Rwandan guide and me.

It's a massive orphanage, run by a minimum of seventy-one regular staff members and volunteers—sometimes more. The line of well-tended, quiet babies would likely make any prospective adoptive parent sputter at the idea that Rwanda has no children for them to parent. But, as Twagira explained, only a small proportion of the children in Noel could ever be considered for adoption. Of the six hundred, MIGEPROF tallied only eighty as possibilities. Twagira put the number at half that—forty.

When I visited in 2011 nearly 250 children at the orphanage were eighteen or older; only 150 were under five. And of that number some children not only had families but had families who were involved. While I visited, one father from the local community, dressed sharply in a crisp lavender shirt, came to visit his infant daughter. As a young widower, he had followed the local custom to put his baby in the orphanage for care and feeding until she grew to around three years old, because infant formula was prohibitively expensive and, culturally, young children are considered too difficult for single Rwandan men to care for. Beaming and holding his daughter's finger as she sat with a nurse, the father posed for a picture with the child he would one day take home.

"There are about forty children here who have fathers," Twagira told me, noting that high maternal mortality rates made this visiting father's situation relatively normal. "When they are three, he has to come back and pick her up, or we will go to the local authorities," Twagira continued, suggesting that parents who don't return for their children will be reported for abandonment.

It was a scenario—reintegrating children into their families—that Twagira was also preparing to deal with on a larger scale, as Noel, like the rest of the country's orphanages, readied itself for the coming deinstitutionalization project that would largely clear their home of its wards. "It's very nice," Twagira said philosophically, considering the plan. "It's better to be in the family than in an institution. Many children here will go to their families—those that have relatives."

Noel's resident children, like those in the rest of the country, had been assessed by Hope and Homes for Children, a UK-based organization that has consulted on orphanage de-institutionalization programs in countries like Romania and Bosnia and that Rwanda's government commissioned to collect accurate data on all of the country's institutionalized children.

Twagira estimated there were about 250 children at Noel who had lost both parents. Some of those might go to extended family, and for others, a government plan to establish several older children in a joint household might apply.

For the others, said Vianney Rangira, country director of Hope and Homes for Children, the government hoped to foster domestic adoptions by Rwandans. To that end the government had embarked on an educational program to explain the process of domestic adoption to local citizens—a markedly easier process than international applicants face—and was working with churches to replicate more emergency foster care systems like the one the Jenkins' Christ's Church had begun.

In December 2011 Rwandan Prime Minister Pierre Damien Habumuremyi had visited Noel Orphanage and publicly announced that he was adopting a child from the home. "Leaders should serve as examples in giving another chance to less privileged children," he declared. "I will take the lead by adopting a child myself from this orphanage." He proposed that if more Rwandans adopted, within the year there would be no more orphanages. Habumuremyi asked local leaders to help promote adoption by including it as a consideration in their performance contracts.

"Now the problem we have is to set up a campaign to encourage people to adopt," said UNICEF's Ngabonziza. He and other leaders as well as the government had decided the best place to start would be in the churches, "because of their contact with the population and the prestige of their word."

Churches have responded, including Saddleback's Rwanda team. Styffe told me that some of Saddleback's partner churches in Rwanda had been helping to trace children in orphanages to see whether they have families and, if so, what support the families need to bring their children back home. And Munyemana said that Saddleback has established a pilot initiative in the Western city of Kibuye, where an initial group of one hundred families has taken in orphans through informal foster care arrangements, and local churches were trying to help support them with donations to offset the additional financial burden they had assumed. The arrangements weren't full legal adoptions, with families committing to the children as new sons and daughters; that was a step Munyemana thought would have to come down the line. "It's the first major step of willingly going and bringing a needy person into your home," he told me. "It may eventually go to that [next step of legal adoption], but it's a process. It's not just telling people, 'Now adopt.' There is an education process to make them understand all the implications."

When Munyemana traveled to Saddleback Church in April 2012 for the Christian Alliance Summit, he gently told the American crowd to consider Rwandans as capable partners in orphan care and to support their efforts to increase adoption at home rather than just see Rwanda as another source for international adoptees. "Trust that the local church leaders know their context better than you," he said.

By the end of 2011 only a handful of children had been reunited with their families, MIGEPROF's Uwababyeyi told Rwanda's the *New Times*. Some children in orphanages feared that communities they were returned to would reject them, as Rwanda's small size and dense population means that inherited agricultural land comes at a high premium. (Indeed, one aspect of the 1994 genocide was an effective land grab from the dispossessed minority.) The first orphanages began closing in June 2012, shortly after the launch of the new oversight body for Rwandan adoptions, the National Commission for Children (NCC). But the process was extremely slow.

Many in the adoption community were skeptical about how well deinstitutionalization would work. "It sounds great in theory," Jana Jenkins said, "but does Rwanda really have what it takes to follow up on all those cases? A lot of times kids come running back to the orphanage. They haven't been around for years, and they're kind of strangers to their families." Domestic adoptions, she worried, could prove even harder. "Africans are very good at taking care of extended family, but it kind of goes against the grain to take care of a child that's not blood-related."

Jenkins suspected the government had already given up on the prospect of many Rwandans adopting. Further, because few families had initially volunteered to adopt—perhaps due to the legacy of failed adoptions after the genocide—and the Rwandan adoptive families she knew were secretive about their adoptions, the government was shifting their push to long-term foster care instead. A more obvious explanation might simply be Rwanda's widespread poverty and the hardship to poor families of taking on additional costs for food, education, clothing, and health care. Noel Orphanage's Twagira said that, by July 2011, Noel had received only four requests for domestic adoptions. "I think it's the poverty—when you have a daddy who is not able to care [for his child], how will someone else be able to come and take them from the orphanage?" he asked. "The government wants to make more demand, but it's a process to sensitize the population."

Rwanda's situation is not unique. These same sorts of hurdles—or, more optimistically, growing pains—have impacted other countries attempting to increase domestic adoptions over international. Dale Edmonds, a director of the Riverkids Foundation, an NGO dedicated to fighting child trafficking in Cambodia, blogged about the resistance he had encountered in promoting domestic adoption in that country, as international colleagues objected that domestic Cambodian adoptions tended too often to fail. "I think this is a case of theory and practice," Edmonds wrote. "We can say in theory [that] kinship, then local, then international adoptions are best. But if we don't give enough support at each stage, we're going to default to international where the adoptive families in general have way more resources." Considering the financial incentives international adoption already has on its side, bringing thousands of Western dollars into a developing economy every time a child goes overseas, breaking the cycle of adoption boom and bust will require not just support but also patience as well as the understanding that domestic adoption and other local solutions aren't a step too far rather but something that can be learned, slowly by slowly, as Rwandans say.

IN MARCH 2012, after ten months of being fostered by Dave and Jana Jenkins, baby Gabriel Mugisha was adopted to an American couple from Texas, Mark and Chelsea Jacobs, who ran a Christian organization called His Chase Foundation that supported various orphan care projects across Africa. Jana had been representing the Jacobs as power of attorney in another, failed attempt to adopt a child from Noel Orphanage, and the Jacobs referred to the Jenkins as "good friends."

Gabriel became the first child Rwanda's new NCC had matched. The Jenkins had visited the region of Gabriel's birth to assist in a local government investigation of whether he had extended family who could care for him, and when no family was found, they documented his status as abandoned in the same way the Home of Hope adoption orphanage would have done. Because his story had become so central to Christ Church's young orphan program—and such a frequent focus of Dave's writing on his blog and for local Rwandan newspapers—they determined they should have a community send-off for the boy. This was another first: the church's "first ever Adoption Hand Over Ceremony," at which the Jenkins and other church leaders spoke as the boy's "uncles and aunts." In pictures on Dave's blog, the Jacobs, a young, white couple, sat in white plastic chairs inside the church, holding Gabriel, who was dressed in an argyle sweater, as the congregation reached out their arms in blessing and the Jenkins family knelt in front of them, their heads bowed in prayer.

On his blog Dave explained that Gabriel's health issues had convinced them and Rwandan officials that the boy needed to be raised either by a Rwandan family with the financial capacity to take him on regular trips to advanced hospitals in Kenya or South Africa, or by an international adoptive family from North America or Europe. In the fall of 2011 Gabriel had begun having convulsions and seizures multiple times a day, seemingly due to a brain injury from his birth and requiring treatment that couldn't be found in Rwanda.

A brief statement attributed to the Jacobs' Facebook page reaffirmed that special circumstances drove their adoption. "We are amazed by God's story that is unfolding with our adoption . . . with what could only be explained as God's absolute plan for his life and ours, we have been given an official referral for Gabriel Mugisha!" they wrote. They emphasized that their adoption was "completely different than other Rwanda adoptions" but also suggested it could bode well for the future. "We were processed through the new National Commission for Children office, and are hopeful this means great things for the future of adoption." Dave wrote, "My hope is that the Hand Over will begin a new culture among Rwanda's youth of embracing the adoption of orphaned and abandoned children."

But for some the ceremony and the adoption it marked was not a mile marker on the forward path that Rwanda had been looking for nor an inspiration toward domestic adoption. Instead, it seemed like a return to the status quo in other countries—international adoption as the default solution, a surrender to the familiar system of supply and demand.

Among the critics was Nyanja Nzabamwita, a Rwandan who was raised in US foster care after the genocide and today lives in Sweden and has worked frequently in Rwanda as an adoption power of attorney for America World Adoption. In a strongly worded letter to her clients and contacts—a letter immediately forwarded around the small Rwandan adoption community—Nzabamwita compared the Jacobs' adoption of Gabriel to a benevolent form of child trafficking, as the Jacobs hadn't been next in the line of waiting parents, and she argued that the Jenkins' personal connections with the NCC had secured an unfair advantage for Jana's client. She warned that irregularities in the process had the potential to stop other adoptions from being completed, as other pipeline families passed the six-month cutoff without being matched with a child, and that Gabriel's adoption could taint the system going forward. Nzabamwita wrote,

As happy as we may be for Gabe to find a forever family, we as a Rwandan adoption community must be strong enough to question the ethics in this case. . . . The definition of a Black Market adoption is one where prospective parents use influence (like that of Christ's Church Rwanda with the NCC) or payments (to POAs, like Jana Jenkins, and to attorneys, like the one to whom the Jacobs paid money to represent them) to avoid complying with a country's established guidelines.

Although whether the Jacobs' adoption had any bearing on other pipeline cases was unclear, the implication that the Jacobs' adoption was divinely ordained nonetheless bothered Nzabamwita, a consummate adoption movement insider as a Christian who attends the Christian Alliance for Orphans Summit, a former intern at the Congressional Coalition on Adoption Institute who had worked in Republican Senator James Inhofe's office, and an employee of a leading evangelical adoption agency. "It is disturbing that they make this into a Godly story," she wrote. "When God calls you to something, He does not ask you to take matters in your own hands."

"If I had done the same thing when I was in Rwanda, I would have gone to jail," she added to me, arguing that Jana Jenkins' dual role as foster parent to a child and power of attorney for the family that ended up adopting him was highly irregular. "For me this was a reminder that just because Rwanda is trying to do the right thing, it's not exempt from having these things happen."

Jana, who said she had considered Nzabamwita a friend through Rwanda's small adoption community, responded that Nzabamwita refused to understand the complexities of the case. She said they tried for months, without success, to find Gabe's extended family, then waited for a Rwandan family to step up. After the extent of Gabriel's medical needs were known and MIGEPROF helped the Jenkins get the paperwork to take him to Kenya for treatment, domestic adoption options seemed limited. "I think what it boiled down to is that Gabe was placed from a foster family into an international adoptive family, and that was different from what had normally taken place," she said, speculating that those differences had led people to the wrong conclusions, like that she had gone and "found a baby" for the Jacobs. "Normally a child is taken from an orphanage, but that was the whole program that MIGEPROF was trying to go away from. We were trying to start something new."

Speaking from Chicago, where the family moved in 2012, Jana laughed sadly at what she saw as a regrettable misunderstanding of a process that had been above board. The entire adoption, she said, had been overseen by MIGEPROF and then the NCC, which in the end was the body that made the match between Gabriel and the Jacobs family. "You cannot manipulate things in Rwanda," she said. "You can't force things to go your way. It's not like in other African countries."

In the end the NCC's executive secretary, Nyiramatama Zaina, came to Gabriel's Hand Over ceremony at Christ's Church and was "very affirming of what we had done," said Jana. The First Lady's Imbuto Foundation also approved, announcing that it would award both the Jenkins and the Jacobs families its *Malayika Mruzinzi*, or "Guardian Angel" award of one cow each—a traditional ceremonial African gift—in recognition of those who care for orphans.

Since he had come to the United States Gabriel has been diagnosed with cerebral palsy but taken off the strong antiseizure medicines he had been given in Africa; so far he has remained seizure-free. The Jenkins visited him in Texas, as did other families from Christ's Church who had traveled through the United States since his adoption and wanted to check in on a baby they still considered family. "That was the wonderful thing about the whole Gabe story," said Jana. "We did it in the African way, with those who'd been involved in his life. There's a strong connection, and I felt that was a good example—a different way of doing international adoption."

Although the Jenkins have returned to the United States for several years at least, they hoped to interest some Rwandan diaspora families in the US Great Lakes region to consider adopting—internationally, but within their own culture. Back in Kigali families among the Christ's Church congregation were fostering two new infants—at first just the church's new senior pastor, another ex-pat couple from the missionary organization the Jenkins served, ROC, but later a Rwandan family as well.

"I'm not yet ready to give up on Rwandans adopting," said Jenkins, who noted that she had witnessed a rise in local adoptions in Uganda and Kenya in recent years and cited the great changes in US attitudes toward adoption over the last century. In time, she suggested, Rwanda will be a leader among other countries in caring for its own children. But, she added, "It's going to be a slow journey. That's why I think there's still a place for intercountry adoption as a last resort." Gabriel's case, at this early point, might not have leant itself to the ideal solution of finding willing and qualified—and sufficiently wealthy—Rwandan parents, but to Jana it still demonstrated an intermediate way forward: involving the local community in addressing the problem firsthand and in envisioning different solutions. "I wish I could say there are all these Rwandan families lining up left and right that want to do this," she said, "but these are just the first, initial steps."

Saddleback's Munyemana conveyed the same message about Rwanda's slow shift to care for—and keep—their vulnerable children at home. "We are not yet there," he told me, "but we may definitely get there."

CHAPTER 8

Going Home

In August 2005, the day after she gave birth, a South Korean hairdresser in her midthirties named Hyoung-Suk Choi picked up the phone to ask for her baby back. Choi, still a young-looking woman at thirty-nine, with dimpled cheeks and wearing tortoiseshell glasses when I spoke to her online through an interpreter, had found out she was pregnant shortly after she had broken up with her boyfriend of many years. Her brother pressured her intensely to abort the pregnancy, to spare their parents shame. A gynecologist she visited told her that if she gave the child up for adoption, the birth fees would be covered and Choi would receive $500. She kept working until she was in her last trimester, but then, when her pregnancy could no longer be concealed, Choi quit her job at the salon to avoid talk that she, an unmarried woman, was about to have a child.

For single, pregnant women living in South Korea, life is a lot like it was in the United States during the Baby Scoop Era, when millions of women were sent to maternity homes to give birth to their children in secret and relinquish them for adoption. Korean single women who give birth and keep their babies are often disowned by their families and shunned by society. According to a survey conducted in 2009, unwed mothers were the second-most stigmatized group in the entire country, second only to gays and lesbians. Just as in the Baby Scoop Era, the availability of secretive adoptions is seen as a way for women to start anew and leave their mistakes behind. Even the infrastructure is the same, with ubiquitous maternity homes throughout South Korea, maintained by domestic and international adoption agencies and referred to by some mothers as "baby farms."

After Choi quit her job she went to a counseling session offered by an adoption agency in Seoul and was advised to go to a maternity home in the country, Ae Ran Won. She moved there in June 2005 and lived among twenty other women, traveling in groups of five or six to the doctors' office for prenatal checkups. Most, like Choi, were in their late twenties or older—not the teen mothers who had filled the homes in years past and who still represented the public's idea of unwed moms. Twice a month the women fielded visits from representatives from some of the four adoption agencies licensed to work in South Korea. The agency representatives would explain the adoption process, urging the residents to see adoption as a chance for their children to be well educated and emphasizing the grim prospects facing a single-mother family: the mothers would be discriminated against by family, neighbors, customers, and even strangers; their children might be segregated away from the rest of their class at school, with some teachers not giving them snacks and even putting them in a separate room; and other parents likely wouldn't allow their kids to play with "illegitimate" children. Further, when the children reached adulthood, employers would be less likely to hire candidates whose mothers hadn't been married and the parents of anyone the children might seek to marry would likely forbid the match. The sense of public condemnation of anything associated with unwed motherhood is such that, in 2009, a *New York Times* article noted that "Koreans often describe things as outrageous by comparing them to 'an unmarried woman seeking an excuse to give birth.'"

It was a powerful message for women who wanted to parent their children themselves: that to keep their baby would only cause the child real and lasting harm. What that left for many, then, was a secondary decision: between their child being adopted domestically or going overseas. Many women at Ae Ran Won who met with adoption agency representatives came to think of international adoption as the "open adoption" option, through which they might receive updates and keep in contact with their child. Although that sort of contact was far from guaranteed, international adoption at least held out more hope of one day hearing from their children than did domestic placement through so-called "secret adoptions" within South Korea. Given the cultural stigma surrounding children born out of wedlock, adoptive parents in South Korea sometimes go to elaborate lengths to conceal the fact that their child is not biologically their own—faking a pregnancy to coincide with the completion of their adoption or planning a strategic cross-country move to present themselves to new neighbors as an already intact family. What's more, because in South Korea's independent birth registration system children are sometimes not registered until several weeks after a child is born (rather than being automatically registered at the hospital), most adoptive parents will document their adopted children as though they had given birth to them instead.

In addition to the agency visits, groups of adoptees periodically would come to the home as part of an adult adoptee "homeland tour," organized by a US or Western adoption agency, to share their own experience of being adopted. As those visits were translated by agency staff, said Choi, all the adoptees seemed to have been placed with wonderful families, with doctor fathers and teacher mothers, to have grown up happy and have gone to college.

"It was basically a message," said Choi, "that if you send your child for adoption, they're going to be sent to a wealthy family and raised well." The unspoken part of the message was an invitation for the women to compare what they could offer against the resources and advantages of a rich Western family. The messaging paid off. Although Choi said many women enter maternity homes hoping to raise their children, by the time they give birth only a small percentage actually do.

After Choi told her counselor at the home that she was considering adoption, in short order representatives from three adoption agencies visited her. During the half-hour meetings she had with each, all three agencies pressured her to sign a preliminary consent form, authorizing the adoption of her future child. Two of the agency counselors admitted that if she sent her child for international adoption, she would only see him, if at all, after he became an adult, but the third promised to find a family who would keep her involved. She chose that agency, and they gave her the adoption forms, requesting biographical information about her and the father. When she hesitated to sign it and authorize the adoption ahead of time, they urged her to at least fill it out so she wouldn't be bothered with details after birth. Choi completed the form, and the agency representative left. That thirty-minute talk was all the counseling she would ever receive.

TODAY NEARLY 70 PERCENT of unwed mothers who give birth in South Korea—approximately six to ten thousand women per year—relinquish their children for adoption. In 2011, children of unwed mothers accounted for 88 percent of international adoptions from South Korea and

almost 94 percent of official domestic adoptions within the country.*
Only 8 percent of South Korean adopted children did *not* come from single mothers that year.

These statistics don't tell the whole story, though. Of one hundred unplanned pregnancies to single women in South Korea, the Ministry for
Health, Welfare and Family Affairs has estimated that ninety-six will be
aborted. Although abortion is illegal in South Korea, illegal abortions are
widespread and used frequently to conceal unwed pregnancies. Hyoung-
Suk Choi's brother even found a facility that would perform an abortion
when she was eight months pregnant. Of the four in one hundred pregnancies that single women carry to term, roughly three of the mothers will
relinquish the children for adoption and only one will parent—just 1 percent of all unplanned pregnancies to unmarried women.

The primary reason why this is happening in South Korea (when, by
contrast, only about 1 percent of single mothers in the United States relinquish for adoption) is South Korea's intensely conservative sexual culture,
in which women engaging in premarital sex have long been subject to a
strong double standard. Although that prohibition has relaxed in recent
years, as women marry at older ages and many do have sex before then,
social censure for women who "get caught"—by getting pregnant—is severe and even peers roundly consider unmarried pregnant women as irre-
sponsible or stupid. Adoption agencies tell American adopters that so
many South Korean women relinquish children for adoption because of
the country's "Confucianism." By this they mean the country's tradition
of strict family hierarchies and expectations of filial obedience, its way of
defining virtuous womanhood by whether women are submissive to the
men in their lives, and the country's painstaking documentation of family
lineage, historically tracked only on the father's side. In this context "Confucianism" is shorthand for institutionalized patriarchy, a system in
which, until 2008, only fathers could register children. This means that if
a father didn't acknowledge a child born out of wedlock, in order for the
child to legally or socially exist, a grandfather might have to register his
grandchild as his own son or daughter, or a mother might have to take the
dramatic step of starting her own family registry.

The pressures on single women who keep their children aren't just
social. Naming conventions and the open availability of family registries

---

*Informal, undocumented domestic adoptions in South Korea are believed to
occur at as high as three times the rate of those that are documented.

in the country make it easy for employers to tell when a woman has a child out of wedlock. Because Korean women traditionally keep their own names after marriage whereas their children take those of their fathers, in most cases a mother should not have the same name as her child. If she does, a prospective employer can see, as soon as he checks on a job applicant, that she may be an unwed mother. In a country where huge majorities of women who have children out of wedlock either quit or are fired from their jobs, single mothers face extreme difficulty when trying to find work. Child support legislation is often unenforced, and poverty-based welfare assistance is restricted to only the neediest cases— with that need determined by assessing the financial resources of an unwed mother's family, even if that family has cut her off. What little help the government supplies to support children born to unwed mothers tips the scales in favor of adoption: assistance for single parents is between just $50 and $100 per month, depending on a mother's age, whereas foster parents caring for children until their adoption get $250 per month in compensation, and government-run orphanages for abandoned children receive $1,000. "It's not just the social aspect, of people not wanting to be your friend," said Choi. "It's to the point where we can't even make a living for ourselves."

Many turn to maternity homes and adoption instead. Of the thirty-six unwed mothers' facilities in South Korea, seventeen are affiliated with adoption agencies; in some cases agency offices are within maternity home walls. Unsurprisingly, these homes have much higher rates of relinquishment from the women who reside there than do unaffiliated homes. Choi's home, Ae Ran Won, is among those that are not agency affiliated, and today fewer of its resident mothers tend to relinquish for adoption. However, when Choi was there, she estimates that nearly 70 percent of her fellow residents were planning to give their children up. It wasn't much discussed, as the pale of shame about being pregnant out of wedlock lingered even in the home, but the evidence was in the air. Choi would frequently wake up in the morning to find another woman gone; everyone would know she had left to deliver her baby. The women would return by themselves, their faces puffy and drawn. Choi didn't understand why until she returned to the home after her own labor, empty handed and red eyed, after a night of crying alone.

Choi went into labor early, and in August 2005 she gave birth to her son, Junseo, prematurely. The hospital staff wasn't cruel or rude, she said, so much as merely distant. They assumed all the women coming from the home would be leaving their babies behind. "So they didn't do any of the extras," Choi said, like show her how to feed her baby or allow her to hold him after birth.

Ten hours after Choi gave birth the adoption agency came and took the baby. Choi's brother came to the hospital to make sure she gave him up. The agency let her hold Junseo for a minute before they took him, and Choi arrived back at the unwed mothers' facility before lunch. That night, however, she felt that nothing was different in her life except that she no longer had her son; she felt like she had thrown him away.

In the morning she called the agency to say she had made a mistake. They told her it was too late and that changing the paperwork now would be a serious inconvenience. When she pressed them, arguing that nothing could be settled so soon after Junseo's birth, an agency staffer claimed her caseworker had gone on vacation and she would have to wait four more days for his return.

When she called on the fourth day, the agency refused to give her directions to the home and told her to find it herself. When she got there she found Junseo in a crib in a room as bare as a Plexiglas box: white walls, with no pictures or mobiles or toys. The antiseptic surroundings made Choi want to cry. She took her son out of the agency after the staff had her sign a receipt, as though, she said, she was receiving a package in the mail. But as she carried Junseo back to Ae Ran Won, she told him he now had a second birthday: one when he was born, and one five days later, when she got him back. "I said to my child, 'You are born again.'"

CHOI'S EXPERIENCES weren't uncommon, although her victory was. "I know when people hear my story, they realize it's hard," said Choi, "but I want them to know it's two hundred times harder than people are even thinking."

Many South Korean women who have tried to reclaim their children from adoption agencies have faced a variety of roadblocks, such as imposed delays or demands that they pay between $20 and $30 per day for the time their child was in the adoption agency facility. This cost can rise to the thousands in some women's cases but is probably less about the money than an additional way to discourage mothers from changing their minds. Other mothers have faced requirements that they produce letters of consent from their parents or the father of their babies, giving permission to reclaim their children; that they demonstrate that they've found jobs or apartments or reconciled with the baby's father; or, in one case, that a mother write a letter of apology to a US adoptive family that the agency had selected for her child. "A mom shouldn't have to feel sorry about taking her child back," that mother told me, "but at the time, I would have done anything. If the parents were there and I had to bow and say I'm sorry, I would have done it."

IN THE 1950s international adoption came to South Korea—as it would for other countries in the future—during a period of intense social upheaval. Years of civil war and Japanese occupation had shattered much of Korea's traditional lifestyle. Millions of people had died in the fighting—between 10 and 15 percent of the entire Korean population, both North and South. Many others were displaced from their homes. The eight biracial children that Oregon evangelicals and adoption pioneers Harry and Bertha Holt had adopted were among the thousands of "Amerasian," "Eurasian," or "GI" babies who were born of US and UN troops stationed in Korea during the war and unwed Korean mothers. The GI babies had blond or brown hair and light eyes, marking them as different in a homogenous nation that abhorred miscegenation—Koreans called such children "honhyulah" or "mixed blood"—partly as a result of Korea's Confucian culture and partly in response to Japan's long occupation of the country. After WWII ended Japanese rule, Koreans took pride in "pure" bloodlines, coining a new nationalistic slogan, "One family, one blood," that bespoke their independence. Some "Amerasian" children arrived in orphanages with their hair still sticky from dye—evidence of their mothers' failed attempts to pass them off as purely Korean.

Although the Holts' evangelical mission to adopt all "Amerasian" babies out of the country had first popularized the idea of international adoption, leading to approximately six to ten thousand adoptions in the early postwar years, the flow of children out of the country didn't stop after the GI babies had found homes. As the number of biracial children declined, a critical International Social Service report noted in the 1960s, agencies began competing to locate other potential adoptees, seeking out mothers living near military camps, where sex work was prevalent, to relinquish, as too few women were approaching agencies themselves. In 1966 a potential turning point came and was surpassed, as the demographics of the children being sent for international adoption shifted to full Korean children, now drawn from poor or broken families and increasingly from unwed Korean mothers facing discrimination if they kept their children at home. It could have been a moment for South Korea to recognize that its society was changing, as evidenced by the fact of children born outside of marriage. Instead, however, those children were sent overseas. "Pray for these dear mothers who choose to give up their babies," wrote Henry Holt, as he began to process the children of unwed mothers for adoption.

As Korea industrialized with what historian and Korean adoptee Tobias Hübinette calls "astonishing speed and horrifying efficiency" between 1962 and the early 1990s, people moved from traditional life in the countryside to factory work in the city. Inevitably women's roles changed with the economy. But the social mores that governed their behavior did not keep pace with the realities of their modern work lives, and unwed motherhood was still considered a deep stain on a family's honor. Child abandonment began to increase, and the adoption agencies working in South Korea built institutions to house this new class of orphans, as well as homes for disabled children and unwed mothers. Beginning with its origins with the Holts, international adoption began to take on other roles. It became a form of population control in a growing island nation, a way for the government to build alliances with the developed nations adopting its children, and, as Hübinette notes, a way to "regulate, control, and discipline women's reproduction" at a time when women were no longer living the traditional, home-centered lives of their mothers.

By 1967 more than seventy thousand children were listed as living in more than six hundred institutions in South Korea. Although these numbers were padded to increase foreign donations and the true figure was somewhat lower, they still illustrated the reality of a new system in which orphanages had become dependent on foreign aid and institutions needed to maintain high numbers of children in their care in order to justify continuing aid. Sponsors, after all, weren't interested in supporting "orphans" in their families' homes but rather in orphanages or on their way to being adopted.

Eleana Kim, a Korean-American anthropologist and author of *Adopted Territory: Transnational Korean Adoptees and the Politics of Belonging*, explains that agencies were given subsidies from the state to perform some of these social services, but the more important form of compensation they received was the government's permission to conduct overseas adoptions of South Korean children. "Essentially the state would allow them to send children overseas for adoption if [agencies] would also provide certain welfare services [like supporting maternity homes and orphanages]," said Kim. "It put the agencies in this position of having to generate revenue in order to support all these welfare recipients, meaning they had to send more children overseas."

It also allowed the South Korean government to outsource its child welfare problem while ignoring the larger social issues at its root. With the adoption system effectively taking care of the problem of unwed mothers and their children—sending some abroad and financing the institutions that cared for the rest—the government had no need to build a welfare or child protection system of its own, as the adoption program that had originally been created to handle the pariah children of wartime unions had become, ten years later, the most easily accessible means to deal with an unplanned pregnancy. And because adoption provided an easy way to cover up the proof of premarital sex—the "illegitimate" children themselves—Korean society could maintain old ideals of gender roles for women while ignoring the reality that traditional lifestyles had been forever changed. These factors created such a symbiotic relationship between South Korea and international adoption agencies that even as the country broke out of poverty to become a global economic force, international adoption remained embedded in the country's child-care system, and children continued to flow overseas year after year, by the tens of thousands.

Adoptions from South Korea increased through the 1960s and '70s, helped along both by the government's fear of overpopulation as well as growing financial incentives that made profits for agencies and fed revenue to the government through mandatory fees. South Korea would dominate all international adoption programs almost every year through the 1980s and 1990s—peaking in 1985 at nearly nine thousand adoptions in one year—even as the country's economy steadily grew. Today, although South Korea is a G-20 member and among the most technologically advanced nations in the world, it still remains a "top five" sending country as well, fielding the oldest and largest international adoption program in the world. It also maintains a sterling reputation beyond its borders for its uniquely "clean" system: the model adoption country, nearly sixty years on, where the system runs predictably and well, and adoptive families are rarely surprised. Around three babies leave the country each day.

INSIDE A COUNTRY that has become one of the world's strongest economies, however, the persistence of a huge international adoption program has become an embarrassment. In 2011 South Korea's government revised its adoption law, partially in the hopes of promoting more domestic adoptions and decreasing the number of children sent overseas. It wasn't the first time they had tried to do this.

During the 1970s North Korea condemned South Korea for having sold out to capitalism so completely that it was now selling its own children. During the 1988 Olympics in Seoul publicity around the country's continuing adoption trade besmirched South Korea's image with a stark question: why should a country that could afford to host the Olympics have an adoption program that dwarfed that of third world nations?

In response to the first criticism, in 1976 the government imposed quotas on agencies to reduce international adoptions by one thousand per year. Then, in 1989, a rash of fraudulent adoptions of children who had gone missing from their families and who were wrongly adopted out of the country as "abandoned" led to a crackdown on abandonment adoptions. In response, the government restricted international adoptions instead to the children of women who relinquished directly to agencies, and those agencies reacted by quickly setting up maternity homes to make such handovers smoother. In 1994 a quota system was implemented to make the number of international adoptions agencies were allowed to broker dependent on the number of (much less lucrative) domestic adoptions they completed first. The country's adoption agencies also took their adoption pitch to the public, launching ad campaigns featuring South Korean celebrities holding babies, described as "orphan angels." In 2006 the government designated May 11, falling in a month already replete with Korean family holidays, as national Adoption Day.* And in 2007, the government decreed that children relinquished by their mothers should be reserved for domestic adoption for at least the first five months of their lives. But after every effort, domestic adoptions failed to increase enough to take the place of international adoptions. Many Koreans were still resistant to admitting publicly that they had adopted and, more broadly, to acknowledging nontraditional families.

---

*Not only embarrassment over adoption rates but also the emergence of a troublingly low birth rate drove the government in these more recent efforts. After years of fearing overpopulation, today South Korea faces the threat of depopulation and a country imbalanced on both generational and gender lines. In 2007 and 2008 the country had the lowest birthrate in the world—attributable in part to the fact that illegal abortions are so prevalent that they nearly equal the number of Korean births each year and perhaps occur at a much higher rate—and that international adoption remains the standby solution for most remaining unwed pregnancies. (Ironically, as adoption reform activist Jane Jeong Trenka notes, the department in charge of addressing the

After the 2011 law indicated that South Korea's support for international adoption was waning, Christian adoption advocates in the United States mobilized a counter-campaign. In January 2012 Hope for Orphans and a Korean-American pastor called on adoptive parents to make thirty-second videos to lobby the South Korean government, "describing how Korean adoption has blessed your life."

Dawn Davenport, a respected adoption blogger, considered the law's greater significance for all of international adoption: Was South Korea, the program from which all contemporary international adoption had sprung, now signaling the institution's decline, the "canary in the coalmine"? Davenport wrote about her conversations with South Koreans about the remaining challenges to open acceptance of domestic adoption. South Koreans just weren't ready, she was told. In the end she came down where many adoption advocates do: that although there were many justifiable reasons to seek to reduce Korean adoptions, in our nonideal world, where children were still being abandoned, it wasn't yet possible. "Artificially limiting international adoptions before domestic adoptions and acceptance of single motherhood has caught up with the demand is not in the best interest of children," she wrote.

Supportive readers chimed in with a more enthusiastic defense of the program than Davenport had offered. "We could boycott the process and not adopt, we could wait for Koreans to adopt domestically at much higher rates than they currently are, or we can adopt," wrote one. "We chose to adopt." In a way, it was the same argument that had been made for decades. 1988 Molly Holt, who inherited her father's work in South Korea, regretfully told the *Progressive* that, of course, ideally Korean children should stay with their families or at least within their country. However, with so little domestic adoption, she argued, international adoption agencies had to continue their work. Agencies protesting that they would love to "work themselves out of a job" routinely voice similar sentiments. But missing from all these equations was the source of almost 90 percent

---

country's low birthrate also oversees the country's adoption programs.) Although antiabortion advocates have frequently used depopulation threats in other countries as an excuse to crack down on women's reproductive rights, arguing that a dearth of babies justifies a return to patriarchal sexual morality, the experience of South Korea instead starkly illustrates how systemic gender discrimination has left many modern women in the country with no real options besides illegal abortion or secretive adoption.

of the children being adopted and, seemingly, the ready-made solution to caring for many of these so-called orphans: their mothers. That many such mothers would like to parent is evident in the fact that in maternity homes where unwed mothers are given support to raise their children, more than eight out of ten have done so, compared to just three out of ten in maternity homes run by adoption agencies.

To many adoption reformers, the advocates' regretful insistence that international adoption from South Korea must continue obscured the reality that the adoption system has benefited from the stigma against single mothers in South Korea. Agencies that have highlighted South Korea's Confucian heritage as the reason so many mothers must relinquish did nothing to challenge the stigma, critics said, but instead used the stigma to justify continued adoptions. Sometimes, they said, the agencies even helped perpetuate that stigma by reinforcing the status quo. When adoptive parents and agencies defended adoptions that existed because of a coercive system on the grounds that children would suffer in institutions in its absence, to critics, this suggested a circular logic: women relinquished because adoption offered an easy way out of the stigma, shame, and economic peril they faced in Korea's traditionalist society, and agencies seeking to find adoptable children told women they shouldn't keep their babies because of the stigma, shame, and economic peril they and their child would face.

Jennifer Kwon Dobbs, a Korean American adoptee and a creative writing professor at St. Olaf College who studies trends in the Korean adoptee diaspora, wrote in response to Davenport's article that "Adoption agencies are benefiting from the mothers' shame and lack of knowledge, and even encouraging both as a way to ensure a steady supply of children—the very orphan crisis that you're asking us to consider." She criticized some of the adoptive parents commenting on the blog for displaying "a sense of ownership" over Korean children of unwed mothers. "Speaking in the child's 'best interests' has too often become a segue to speaking about the children as if they belong with foreigners."

Kwon Dobbs wasn't alone. A stream of similar critiques from other adult Korean American adoptees who have dedicated themselves to studying international adoption flooded Davenport's comments section, many suggesting that the real challenge isn't increasing domestic adoption but fostering a cultural shift in which South Korean society will increasingly recognize and welcome more diverse forms of family, including single-parent families.

"They say, 'They are so Confucian. They have an ancient culture that can never change; they're kind of backward.' But actually, [culture] changes really rapidly," said Jane Jeong Trenka, president of the adoption reform group Truth and Reconciliation for the Adoption Community of Korea (TRACK). "What it really is is patriarchy, and how the patriarchy was legalized and institutionalized in a certain way on the family registry."

From the perspective of Trenka, Kwon Dobbs, and their colleagues in the adoption reform movement, South Korea's adoption problem is in fact a women's rights problem. Although the economic role of women in South Korea has changed dramatically, social traditions and hierarchies have not yet caught up, leaving unwed mothers to face a massive double standard that punishes them severely while letting their partners off the hook. Although South Korea's economy has rocketed, progress in gender equality has lagged far behind. A 2012 World Economic Forum report on the global gender gap ranked South Korea 108th of 135 countries, between the United Arab Emirates and Kuwait. It's that reality, reformers say, combined with continuing Western demand for adoptees, that undergirds the adoption industry's continued survival.

"The mothers don't want adoption," wrote Kwon Dobbs. "They want their children. Their children are not at home in the US with paying strangers, but rather with their mothers in Korea." Rather than US parents saying how sorry they felt about the circumstances that led unwed mothers to relinquish, she wrote, adoptive parents could instead become their allies, helping change the system that compels them to do so. "Korea is not a canary in a coal mine—as if overseas adoption is a dark tunnel that's about to collapse," she continued. "Let's look at the flickering at the end of the tunnel instead."

THE CHORUS OF ADOPTEES responding to Davenport's article was itself a demonstration of a changing reality with regards to South Korean adoption: adoptees who were once mute recipients of international salvation have become independent adults, and many of them are astute critics of the international adoption system through their activism, scholarship, or writing. To some dismissive adoptive parents and agencies, the children who grew up to criticize the circumstances of their adoption were "angry adoptees," driven by emotion or bitterness toward an irrational backlash. Others treated critical adoptees as perennial children, responding to them with the clucking condescension of parents who know better, even when the adoptees in question were the same age or older than people trying to adopt. Indeed, in one response to Kwon Dobbs's comments, one reader chided her, saying she should express "a little more gratitude" to her American mother and father.

Adoptees were used to hearing this expectation of gratitude. Whether they had grappled with challenges in their childhood—dealing with ambient racism that their usually white parents couldn't or wouldn't understand—or had largely been happy in their adoptive homes, many commonly experienced their adoption as loss. Many felt they had become "church projects" in their undiversified communities. (Of the 150,000 Korean adoptees in the United States, a full 10 percent were sent to Minnesota, which adopts more children internationally per capita than any other state in the United States, thanks in part to the tradition of adoption among the state's heavily Scandinavian population.)

Although JaeRan Kim, former author of the adoptee blog Harlow's Monkey, described her childhood among Minnesota evangelicals as "idyllic in many ways" and maintains a good relationship with her adoptive family, she nonetheless grew up feeling at times that her parents had adopted her to score points for "their heavenly tally." When her family's church talked about mission work in other countries where people were "unsaved," it felt like the comments were directed at her, intentionally or not. "I always felt there was this underlying sense of, 'Aren't you lucky that you were saved, and that you're here, and that you're not one of those heathens in fill-in-the-blank country.'" Kevin Vollmers, a Korean adoptee who began the adoption reform group blog Land of Gazillion Adoptees, agrees, saying, "Once you save somebody or when you are 'saved,' there is always a power dynamic with the people who saved you."*

Driven by this complicated mixture of experiences, starting in the 1990s many Korean adoptees began to visit their ancestral home. Among them was Jane Jeong Trenka, raised in a Minnesota Christian home after her adoptive parents' pastor exhorted them to adopt. In 1995, forty years after Harry Holt's late-night epiphany in the Tokyo hotel room, when he felt God was calling him to rescue South Korea's children, Trenka returned to the country she was born in on a postcollege trip, a "Motherland Tour" organized by a US adoption agency. Among other tourist destinations the trip took adoptees and often their adoptive families to a Korean

---

*Sometimes the tension goes beyond power dynamics. A number of adult adoptee activists I spoke with have received hate mail, including death threats, or personal harassment and worse over their criticism of international adoption.

market, an orphanage, and an unwed mothers' home. Though today Trenka views the preponderance of agency-sponsored homeland tours with a cynical eye—"They'll make money off us until we die," she told me—at the time it was a way for her to meet her birth family, including her mother, who had been writing Trenka and her older biological sister, also adopted to the same family, ever since their relinquishment.

Although Trenka's adoptive parents had been told that the two sisters they adopted from Korea were the children of an unwed mother who had abandoned them, in reality the girls were two of several children born to a married couple; their abusive and alcoholic father had forced their mother to give the girls up. Afterward the mother had wept inside the adoption agency until the staff gave her the address of her children's adopters, to whom she wrote letters to be given her daughters for nearly two decades. She even strapped a dog to her back to replace the feel of her missing youngest child, Trenka. All the while, Trenka said, "my American adoptive parents thought they were getting these completely unwanted children." Trenka returned to Korea several times, including for an extended trip to care for her mother while she was dying. Ten years after her first trip, in 2005, Trenka returned to stay.

Because South Korea is the oldest international adoption program, its alumni constitute the oldest class of international adoptees. And with between 166,000 to 200,000 children adopted overseas from Korea since 1955—nearly 100,000 of them from unwed mothers—there are more adoptees from Korea than any other country. As this massive population of adoptees ages, many, like Trenka, come back to Korea. They started returning in the late 1980s, sometimes on short visits or homeland tours, sometimes to teach for a year, and sometimes as a complete repatriation to learn to live in their mother country for good.

Starting in 1999 a new series of reunions for adoptees began. The Gathering of the First Generation of Adult Korean Adoptees, cosponsored by Holt International, was extensively documented by Korean media, which portrayed adoptees as glamorous and cosmopolitan. Even though individual birthmothers who relinquished for adoption were often invisible in Korean society, adoption was undeniably a part of the cultural landscape in a country that had seen a quarter of a million children adopted away from their families (including an estimated seventy-five thousand domestic adoptions). As shown in the 2009 South Korean documentary film *Resilience,* about an adoptee from South Dakota finding his Korean mother, adoption reunions play an interesting role in Korean pop culture. In the film, directed by Tammy Chu, an adult adopted

man travels to meet his mother with the financial support of a sentimental Korean talk show called *Beautiful Forgiveness* and is finally reunited
with her after a countdown in a booth in front of a studio audience as he
decided whether or not he forgave her for letting him go.

His search was not unique. According to one tally, adoptees submitted
76,000 requests for birth family searches between 1995 and 2005 alone.
And more than thirty-six-thousand adoptees and their adoptive family
members have come on trips like the "homeland tour" Trenka attended.
But when most adoptees managed to reunite with their birthparents or
met pregnant Korean women in unwed maternity homes on agency-
sponsored tours, they were effectively left speechless, staring at their family or their countrywomen across the chasm of a language barrier.

In the late 1990s and 2000s that began to change, as groups of
adoptees began to organize on their own, forming several groups, including Global Oversees Adoptees' Link (G.O.A.'L), which helps adoptees
track down their birth families; and Adoptee Solidarity Korea (ASK),
which advocated against international adoption and for single mothers'
rights. In 2006 some of the birthmothers who had been reunited with
their children through G.O.A.'L's work formed their own organization,
Dandelions: Adoptees' Families of Origin, to advocate against international adoption. In 2004 Reverend Kim Do-Hyun became manager of another organization, KoRoot, which runs a guest house to help adoptees
visit Korea, and politicized its mission, urging adoptees to consider the
plight of single mothers and to cast single mothers' rights as a matter of
social justice and spiritual solidarity. And in 2007 TRACK was founded to
establish a truth and reconciliation commission to look at adoptions and
to highlight the issue of illegal and corrupt adoptions with the government; soon it also joined ASK to work toward unwed mothers' rights.

This network of overlapping groups helped lay the groundwork for
some adoptees to make Korea a more permanent home. By 2012 rough
estimates held that there were several hundred adoptee expatriates living
in Korea again, forming a tight community in which activism blossomed.

As Kim Stoker, the representative of ASK and a professor at Duksung
Women's University in Seoul explains, adoptees who returned began to
connect the dots from their own isolated experiences into a more global
critique of adoption in Korea. They began to see it as something operating
in a system of racial, gender, and class inequalities combined with religious drives. "Nobody comes to get involved in advocacy," said Trenka.
"But they may get involved later after they've spent a lot of time sharing
stories with other adoptees."

To grapple with the stark language barrier that left adoptees as outsiders in Korean culture, some adoptees started teaching English classes, sometimes to birthparents seeking to communicate with their lost children and sometimes to unwed mothers who wanted to know more about adoptees' stories than the sanitized stories they heard at maternity homes. Some less overtly political adoptee groups provided translation services that helped establish a link between adoptees and unwed mothers—single women who, for many adoptees, were coming to symbolize what their own mothers might have endured.

In 2007 members of Dandelions demonstrated during one of The Gathering's meetings: a group of 80 mothers and their supporters held signs in a subway near the conference hotel that read, "Raising our children with our own hands," while adoptees wore bandanas in solidarity. The loose web of adoptee and mothers' groups had become a movement.

ASK then began offering another kind of trip to unwed mothers' homes like Ae Ran Won. Instead of the "zoological" tour that Trenka had gone on years before, ASK brought in groups of adult adoptees for translated discussions about what each groups' experience had been. "Here were all these young women, pregnant, and having to decide if they're going to keep their kids or not," recalled ASK's Stoker. (Stoker was adopted privately, not through an orphanage or agency, and so belongs to the tens of thousands of undocumented adoptions that took place in addition to official government tallies.) "Some have all these fantasies about what would happen to their kid if their kid got adopted to America. We were maybe the same age as they were, and we got to share our stories and say, 'Actually, this is what my life was like, and I'm back here in Korea now. I'm looking for my mom, and I can't find her.'"

The resonances were strong for adoptees, even if their own personal histories didn't exactly resemble the circumstances of unwed mothers today. "Adoptees were being asked to support these women as kind of the generic birth mother who has suffered and might even stand in for their own birth mothers," remembered Eleana Kim, who documented the early history of the coalition in her book *Adopted Territory*.

At one meeting of coalition members, recalls Trenka, an unwed mother who had nearly relinquished her child to adoption went around to every adoptee in the room, apologizing for almost making her child an adoptee like them. "She was crying, and there's this certain hand-rubbing thing that Koreans do when they're really sorry, and she was just apologizing and rocking back and forth," remembers Trenka. "It was terrible.

But there's definitely this feeling among the adoptees, that this could be my mother. And among the unwed mothers, that this could be my child."

What to some seemed an unlikely coalition—of adoptees, birth mothers, and unwed mothers, coming together across generational lines and language barriers—struck the activists as the natural result of the Korean adoption system. Slowly, in time, wrote Trenka, "An environment started to grow where single mothers also were able to become activists."

IN 2009 CHOI and three other mothers, including one she had met at the unwed mothers' home Ae Ran Won, began an online Internet forum for unwed mothers called Miss Mama Mia. The simple message driving their early activism was radical in its way: demanding that Korean society acknowledge its hypocritical approach to sex in a modern society—looking the other way at premarital sex but condemning those whose lives proved its existence, through unmarried pregnancies or childbirths. The fact that there was proof Choi and her colleagues had had sex out of wedlock didn't make them immoral women, they insisted; they were just women who wanted to keep their kids after doing the same thing everyone else had done. On the group's Korean-language website a banner reads, "We have not chosen to be a social minority, but to raise our children."

Choi's group isn't the only single mothers' group in Korea, though it is the only one run by unwed mothers themselves. They were preceded in 2007 by an ally group named Korean Unwed Mothers' Support Network (KUMSN), started by a US adoptive father from Connecticut, Dr. Richard Boas. He was inspired to action after accompanying his Korean daughter on her own "homeland tour" and meeting a group of pregnant women at a maternity home, every one of whom was planning to relinquish her child for adoption. Boas imagined his adopted daughter's mother in their places and realized that the adoption that had completed his family had been a zero-sum game. "Our family's gain was truly this woman's loss—forever," he wrote. "I began to understand why I, like others, had found it difficult to be aware of the reality of unwed mothers. . . . Once you 'get' this, it changes you forever."

KUMSN also reached out to allies from outside the Korean adoption community, including birthmothers organizing in other countries. Among them was Evelyn Robinson, a "first mother" activist in Australia who helped lead the campaign that forced nearly all of Australia's provincial governments to apologize for "forced adoptions" during Australia's own Baby Scoop Era and who has become an ally to South Korea's adoption reform community. In 2011 Robinson came to South Korea to meet with KUMSN, TRACK, and KoRoot as well as to help bolster the call for unwed mothers' movements advocating for themselves. "Adoption has always been largely a women's issue and has been linked to the status of unmarried women in society," Robinson wrote after her South Korea trip. "In countries like Australia we take these freedoms largely for granted nowadays, but they only came about because women were prepared to fight for change."

In 2010, Miss Mama Mia became the Korean Unwed Mothers' Family Association or KUMFA, for which Choi served as planning and publicity manager. Today they work first to try to bring unwed mothers—mostly women in their late twenties and thirties—out of the closet. This is no easy task, considering that when they started their work several years ago even other classes of single mothers, like divorcees, shunned unwed mothers. KUMFA also hosts joint family holidays for unwed mothers and their children, as many of the women have been disowned by their parents and have no place to go for celebrations that most Koreans spend with family. They also provide emergency support to mothers facing pressure to relinquish.

One such mother was Suzie, a thirty-year-old single mother to a three-year-old daughter who requested I not use her real name because she is not yet one of KUMFA's "public moms." After a birth control failure with a boyfriend left Suzie pregnant, she broke up with him out of fear that he would pressure her to abort. When coworkers at her office began to suspect her weight gain was really pregnancy, she went to an agency-run maternity home, where nearly all of her fellow residents relinquished. Although she had first planned to raise her child, after several months of counseling sessions (and mandatory six a.m. daily worship services), she said she would consider adoption. Her file was then transferred to the in-house agency offices.

She hadn't realized how painful relinquishing her child would be until after she had done it. She visited her child in foster care once a month every month for the half a year she stayed at the maternity home, trying to get back on her feet. At each visit she tried to gather her courage to say she had changed her mind, but she always lost her nerve. Instead, she looked online and found KUMFA. She read about other women who had challenged their children's adoptions, and then she asked for advice: "I gave my child for adoption and now I want her back," she wrote. KUMFA members responded with information about her legal rights.

Shortly after she went online the agency called her to say her daughter was being adopted and she could see her one last time. But when Suzie arrived at the agency offices, she instead was greeted by a social worker with a tape recorder, who scolded her for posting questions online and said she would record their conversation in case it was needed for legal proceedings. When Suzie asked to take her daughter back, the social worker said she had to wait a week and ask again. When Suzie returned, a supervisor came instead of her daughter, badgering her with pictures of the adoptive family, emphasizing how much better off her daughter would be. When Suzie didn't back down, they forced her to write a letter of apology to the family as a last means of discouragement. But after she wrote it they allowed her to take her daughter home, for the first time in nearly eight months, to an attic apartment with an understanding land-lady. Although people in the neighborhood sometimes glare and keep their distance, Suzie has found a part-time job and said that one day she will come out publicly as a single mom.

It's a sign that some things have begun to change. A 2009 survey co-conducted by KUMSN on issues facing unwed mothers found that unwed mothers' self-advocacy had increased "tremendously" since 1984 and that more women are trying to keep their children in spite of how hard it can prove merely to support themselves and their child. In 1991, according to Ministry of Health figures, 472 single women officially kept their babies; the number rose to 2,464 in 2007 and likely higher still in the years since 2008, when women were finally allowed to register their children's births themselves.

Other changes are in the air. KUMFA's Choi has begun conducting education exercises for civil servants in public offices that interact with single moms, hoping to change the hostile government attitudes that many unwed mothers have encountered. And two homes for unwed mothers, out of the country's thirty-six, have shifted their focus from adoption to helping support women who want to raise their children. In one of the homes, the percentage of mothers who keep their babies when given some help is 82 percent. (It wasn't all positive though: in late 2012, rumors circulated that the government might cut its already negligible support for single parents.)

The coalition of single mothers, adoptees, and birthmothers has also taken aim at the larger culture of stigma in South Korea. When Trenka became president of TRACK, the group began incorporating some of the political theater and activism traditions she was familiar with from Minnesota. On South Korea's May 11 "Adoption Day" in 2009, TRACK commissioned a Korean artist to create two enormous puppets, one a bride and one an unwed mother who lost her child to an adoption, and the two figures soared overhead as TRACK members held picket signs calling for

"Real choices for Korean women and children." Two years later, on the 2011 Adoption Day, the coalition held a counter-ceremony: South Korea's first Single Mother's Day, marked with an array of donated birthday cakes to celebrate the children of unwed mothers, so long considered shameful. At the end of 2011 KUMSN launched a postcard campaign, with cards featuring cartoon children, in the care of their unwed mothers, declaring, "I am not an orphan!"

The coalition's biggest victory came in 2012 after years of organization and work. Four years earlier, in 2008, TRACK and its coalition partners had filed a complaint about irregular or corrupt adoptions with the government's ombudsman, and succeeded in getting the cases recognized on the official record for the first time. After the complaint was lodged with the ombudsman, the documentation of corruption eventually became part of discussions to review the country's Special Adoption Law, the 1961 legislation that had first set the parameters for the country's international adoption program. Reforming the law became TRACK's most important goal, and it partnered with KUMFA, KoRoot, ASK, and Dandelions as well as a public interest lawyers' association to begin the slow push for reform.

With the support of a sympathetic representative from the national assembly, Choi Young-Hee, and strategic organizing advice from Korean American activists, the coalition called for revisions to the bill and, incredibly, fought to have members of their coalition—including adult adoptees who weren't citizens of South Korea—become part of the group drafting reforms to the law. They succeeded, and with the rare input of the people most affected by adoption, they suggested reforms focused on a number of serious recurring problems in Korean adoptions: unclear relinquishments, adoptions that proceeded from kidnappings by family members or orphanage staff, misrepresentation of children's adoption history, and contradictions in adoptees' records that suggested further fraud. They took their struggle through public hearings at the Ministry of Health and argued for it in the public square. The bill was introduced to the National Assembly on Adoption Day in 2010. It passed in 2011, and was to be implemented in 2012.

A companion bill, passed in 2011, provides further protections for unwed mothers. It stipulates that by 2015 adoption agencies will no longer be allowed to run unwed mothers' facilities, that mothers must have a week after birth before they can relinquish, and that single mothers should receive more support in parenting.

Choi warns that although there have been changes in policy, much of the stigma around single mothers remains. Her son, Junseo, is now a seven-year-old boy, and when I spoke to her via Skype in 2012, he came running into view, chattering happily, from a monthly group dinner for KUMFA and its allies. But it took nearly seven years for Choi's own family to invite her and Junseo to come to a family holiday. Further, although Junseo's father has become an active presence in his son's life, he chastises Choi for taking a political stand—just by being out as an unwed mother—that may harm her son's future prospects. So there's more work to do, she said.

"Korea has to become a society where, even if you don't get married, you can be treated with respect as a mother. That being an unwed mother raising a baby isn't seen as a radical thing to do," said Choi. If Korea could create a culture in which women are actually as free to choose to parent as they are to relinquish, she said she would have no problem with adoption. "But the problem is that we're nowhere near that now. The majority of women who are 'choosing' adoption actually have no choice at all."

Adoption advocates aren't letting go of South Korea's adoption program easily, fearing the broader implications its closure could have. Some have criticized the South Korean coalition of adoptees, birthmothers, and single moms as having latched on to unwed mothers' rights to cover an ideological opposition to adoption, and they suggest that single mothers may not really want to keep their children after all. In September 2012 the US House of Representatives passed a bill allowing for pilot programs to adopt North Korean children living in China or neighboring countries, where some women refugees from North Korea have married local men. To reform advocates like Kwon Dobbs, the bill seems like yet another avenue to simplify more adoptions from more groups of marginalized women under the guise, once again, of giving help to children of war.

But despite these continuing challenges, the successes of the reform movement in South Korea have been revolutionary. Compared to the resistance reformers have encountered in the United States, where Trenka said the only successful adoption legislation is that which protects the interests of adoptive parents, the role that adoptees and mothers were allowed to play in Korean reforms was unprecedented. "The whole time I kept thinking to myself, this could never happen in the United States," said Trenka, "that it's so awesome that we can be here, because we don't have any power in the US."

IN THE UNITED STATES advocates like Trenka are often dismissed as too emotional or embittered to have an accurate perspective on international adoption. When adoption law and policy is developed, the voices of adoptive parents and their lobbyists drown out those of adoptees and certainly birth parents or single mothers. For too many parents seeking to adopt, the stories of coercion or unnecessary or failed adoptions—stories that reflect the unintended harmful consequences of Americans' good intentions—amount to information they don't want to know. For many adoption professionals these stories have simply become the cost of doing business in the child-rescue industry.

The actions and consequences of the Christian adoption movement offer lessons relevant to a community much broader than only US evangelicals. Just as South Korea's adoption program, founded as an explicitly evangelical project, developed to become the longest-standing international adoption program in the world, so has the mission-driven perspective of Christian adoption advocates come to infuse the entire culture of modern adoption. The language of rescue and salvation—language that has its genesis and its most literal interpretation in evangelical adoption efforts—now also colors how adoption is discussed in secular society as well. But when even South Korea's adoption program, hailed as the global "gold standard" for ethical adoptions, actually exists because most adoptees' birthmothers have no real choice but to give them up, this religiously infused cultural understanding of adoption as child rescue is hard to rationalize.

Changing this reality in South Korea as well as the circumstances of coercive or fraudulent adoptions in many other countries will require extensive individual reforms in law and oversight. But perhaps most importantly it requires a shift in understanding from those on the demand side of this industry. Change begins with prospective adoptive parents' willingness to look deeply into any agency they're planning to do business with and to take seriously the experiences of other members of the adoption triad who came before them. Would-be adoptive parents must reassess the conception of adoption that has for decades been informed by the myth of heroic Western parents saving "orphans." For adoption to become a more ethical system, everyone engaged in that system must understand that for most children growing up in poor communities, the answer is not adoption but rather sustainable development, that the best interests of the child don't always mean a family with more money, that Western parents are not so uniquely qualified for parenthood that any untrained couple can take on three or six or ten new adoptees and make the children's lives better than they had been before, and that approaching the difficult task of raising children from another culture who may be traumatized from whatever causes brought them into adoption will require more than food, shelter, and love.

Adoption may be a wonderful outcome for many families and many children, but much more often than we acknowledge, this win-win scenario is not the case. Well-meaning people can enable tragedy with their good intentions or their lack of understanding of what an adopted child needs. For adoptions undertaken without preparation, for serial adopters who may be attending to their own emotional needs rather than those of the children they adopt, or for those driven by a sense that adoption is a good deed—or a biblical calling—for which they will be rewarded, the outcomes are often painful. And as those secondary adoptive parents who have picked up the pieces of failed adoptions can attest, for the child a bad or an unnecessary adoption can be worse than none at all.

IN 2011 Trenka wrote a brief history of how her coalition had begun to win change in South Korea, of how the various groups had come to collaborate to reform the larger adoption system. What began for many of the participants as a story of dislocation, even when adoptive parents had the best of intentions; of pain, even if adoptees were sent to loving homes; and loss, even if there were later happy reunions, became a story of movement building instead. What the coalition had achieved was unique: a voice in the political process for society's fallen women and the eternal children that adoptees are often dismissed as. Trenka wanted to leave a record of how the coalition had formed, how its members learned to overcome the differences that separated them, and how they grew to understand the system that bound them together.

Trenka published the paper with an introductory note, stating that she hoped her movement's history might be useful for the rising generations of adoptees who had come and were still coming from other countries—from China, Ethiopia, Haiti, or Vietnam—and who might try to replicate the South Korean coalition's work in their own homelands. Like older brothers and sisters, one of the first generations of international adoptees offered to the future what they had learned as a roadmap and a guide for their younger siblings, who might also one day seek to get back home.

ACKNOWLEDGMENTS

This book owes itself to the help of many people, first and foremost that of Susan Weinberg, Lisa Kaufman, Rachel King, and many others at PublicAffairs, as well as my agent, Kathy Anderson.

The research and reporting for this book could not have taken place without the support of Esther Kaplan and the Nation Institute Investigative Fund; Diane Winston and the Knight Luce Fellowship for Reporting on Global Religion; and Tom Hundley and the Pulitzer Center on Crisis Reporting. Many thanks are due to the MacDowell Colony and the Rockefeller Foundation Bellagio Center for the gift they provide of time and space to think and write.

Portions of this book first appeared or were conceived in association with several magazines, including the *Nation*, the *Daily Beast*, *Ms.*, and the *Atlantic*. I'm grateful for the direction and help I received along the way from editors and staff there, including Max Fisher, Betsy Reed, Kathy Spillar, and Tom Watson. I'm also grateful to past and present colleagues at Religion Dispatches and the Revenue Watch Institute for their support and flexibility through this long process.

Many friends and colleagues generously gave their time to read and help improve early drafts of these chapters, including Lindsay Beyerstein, Katherine Don, Mark Engler, Robert Eshelman, Adam Federman, Kiera Feldman, Michael Fox, Joseph Huff-Hannon, Chris Kyriakos, Ann Neumann, Erica Pearson, Sarah Posner, Dania Rajendra, Robert Ruby, Beth Schwartzapfel, Jeff Sharlet, Meera Subramanian, and others.

I'm also extremely grateful for help with research assistance or fact checking by Laura Bolt, Katherine Don, Connor Guy, Chris Rodda, Pam Veazie, and Elizabeth Whitman; for help navigating reporting in other countries and translation help to Nat Bayjay, Sam Gasana, Yosef Girmai, and Shannon Heit; for transcribing work by Ashley Baxstrom, EllaRose Chary, Abigail Ohlheiser, Holly Samson, and Katie Toth. A number of other friends and colleagues have provided crucial advice in various aspects of this project, including Ruthie Ackerman, Michelle Aldrege, Eve Burns, Anthea Butler, Elizabeth Castelli, Prue Clarke, Leila Darabi, Evan Derkacz, Emily Douglas, Vyckie Garrison, Michelle Goldberg, E. J. Graff, Mary Ann Jolley, Maggie Keady, Courtney Martin, Andy McKinney, Mac McLelland, Jina Moore, Rebecca Morse, Quince Mountain, Molly Page, Jana Prikryl, Erin Siegal, Anna Sussman, Lisa Webster, Ariel Woods, Josh Zeman, and many others.

I interviewed more than two hundred people in the course of my reporting, and while I can't thank them all here, I owe them an immense debt of gratitude for sharing parts of their lives with me. I give particular thanks to those for whom revisiting painful or complicated memories was difficult and to those who spoke to me although we came from different perspectives. I am particularly grateful for the help of "Johanna," "Samuel," Tom Benz, Heather Cannon-Winkelman, Caleb David, Lisa Veleff Day, Maureen Flatley, Marley Greiner, Jessie Hawkins, Peter Heinlein, Jaya Holliman, Tarikuwa Lemma, Jedd Medefind, Karen Moline, Reanne Mosley, Jessica Pegis, Gina Pollack, Evelyn Robinson, David Smolin, Jo Anne Swanson, Kate Thompson, Jane Jeong Trenka, Pam Veazie, Doug Webb, and others I can't name here.

Lastly, love and thanks to my family and friends and particularly my parents, Mike and Bonnie Joyce, and my partner, Chris Kyriakos, for listening to me throughout the four years I worked on this project, keeping me sane and helping me make sense of what I found.

NOTES

"*" *Indicates sources whose real names were not used.*

Chapter 1: New Life

This chapter drew on news articles, websites, blog posts, or publications from *ABC News, AC360,* Adoptees of Color Roundtable, *AFP, AlterPresse,* the *Albany Times Union,* AlbertMohler.com, Alibi.com, the *Amarillo Globe-News, Americas Quarterly, Aspen Daily News, Associated Baptist Press, Associated Press,* the *Auburn Villager,* AWAAblog.org, Baby Love Child, the *Baptist Press, BBC News,* Bridges of Faith.com, the *Canadian Press, CBS News,* ChattahBox, Christian Alliance for Orphans blog, *Christian Examiner, Christian Science Monitor, Christianity Today, CNN, Congressional Quarterly, Courier-Journal,* the Daily Bastardette, the *Dallas Morning News, Digital Journal,* Eastside Baptist Church website, eloranicole.wordpress.com, *Faith Radio in Alabama,* theglobalorphan project.org, the *Guardian, Haiti Vox,* the *Houston Chronicle, Huffington Post, Idaho Statesman,* KTVB, the *Montgomery Advertiser,* the *Miami Herald, Mission News Network,* NPR, *News Observer,* the *New York Times,* 143million.posterous.com, Opelike-Auburn News, O Solo Mama, *Pittsburgh Magazine, Pittsburgh Post-Gazette, Pittsburgh Tribune-Review, Racialicious,* Randybohlender.wordpress.com, *Reuters, Rightwing News,* the *Root,* the *Salt Lake Tribune, My San Antonio, San Francisco Bay View,* SOS Children's Villages Haiti, the *Telegraph, Time,* the *Times of London,* Vision Forum, *Voice of America,* WALB, WBKO, *WFAA, WSFA,* the *Wall Street Journal,* the *Washington Post,* the *Washington Times, World-Herald Bureau,* and *World Magazine.*

It also benefited from several reports, including "Examining Intercountry Adoption after the Earthquake in Haiti," by National Council for Adoption (October 2010); "Haiti: 'Expediting' Intercountry Adoptions in the Aftermath of a Natural Disaster . . . Preventing Future Harm," by International Social Service (August 2010); "Inside the Thriving Industry of AIDS Orphan Tourism," by the Human Sciences Research Council (2010); "Intercountry Adoptions in Emergencies: The Tsunami Orphans" by the Evan B. Donaldson Adoption Institute; "Protecting the Children of Haiti," by the *New England Journal of Medicine* (March 2010); and "Rescued," by Soledad O'Brien on CNN (2010).

I also relied on information from several books, including *Angels of a Lower Flight: One Woman's Mission to Save a Country . . . One Child at a Time,* by Susie Scott Krabacher (2007); *Both Ends Burning: My Story of Adopting Three Children from Haiti,* by Craig Juntunen (2009); and *Travesty in Haiti: A True Account of Christian Missions, Orphanages, Fraud, Food Aid and Drug Trafficking,* by Timothy T. Schwartz (2009).

This chapter also is based on interviews with Pierre Alexis, Larissa Benz, Tom Benz, Susan Bissell, Eric Carr, Wendy Carr, Katya Chislova, Natasha Chyzch, Tom DiFilipo, Karin Dubinsky, Chuck Greever, Marley Greiner, Shelly Greko, Kim Harmon, Senator Amy Klobuchar, Susie Krabacher, the office of Senator Mary Landrieu, Jedd Medefind, Karen Moline, Russell Moore, Chris Rhatigan, Elizabeth Styffe, Pam Veazie as well as a conference call hosted by US Citizenship and Immigration Services and attendance at the Christian Alliance for Orphans Summit VI (2010), and Adopting for Life (2010).

Chapter 2: The Touchable Gospel

This chapter drew on news articles, websites, blog posts, or publications from ABBA Fund, *AFP,* Afterhisownheart.com, America World Adoption blog, amyadoptee.com, *Associated Baptist Press, Augusta Gazette, Baptist Press, Blade,* Blessings from Ethiopia, chalkinscriptions .wordpress.com, Christian Alliance for Orphans, the *Christian Broadcasting Network, Christian News Today, Christian Post, Christian Post Reporter, Christianity Today, Courier-Gazette, Courier-Journal,* Cry of the Orphan, *CNN, Examiner,* Fleas Biting, Focus on the Family, *Foreign Affairs,* Gifts from Afar, the *Globe and Mail, Huffington Post,* Itsalmostnaptime.blogspot.com, knowingnotignoring.blogspot.com, the *Los Angeles Times,* Lifesong for Orphans, *Merced Sun Star,* the *New York Times, OMG Music,* One Million Arrows, *Orlando Sentinel,* Orphan Care

Alliance, OrphanSunday.org, O Solo Mama, ourlittletongginator .blogspot.com, Mothertheworld.com, *Patheos, Philly Burbs,* Pound Pup Legacy, the *Progressive,* rageagainsttheminivan.com, randybohlender .blogspot.com, Reform Talk, The Southern Baptist Convention Resolution No. 2 (2009), The Schuster Center for Investigative Reporting, Scriptorium Daily, Sudesca.org, Teen Missions International, Together for Adoption, *Touchstone, Towers, Tuscaloosa News,* the *Wall Street Journal, Walton Tribune,* welcomechildorphanministry.blogspot.com, Wearegraftedin.com, *WCTV,* and the White House Office of Faith-Based and Community Initiatives.

It also benefited from several reports, including "Adoption Works Well: A Synthesis of the Literature," by Family Research Council (2010), UNICEF meeting notes from session with US faith-based organizations; "A Few Impressions on Meeting the Harry Holt Plane, the 'Flying Tiger,' Which Arrived in Portland, Oregon, December 27, 1958," International Social Service, American Branch Papers, in the Social Welfare History Archives, University of Minnesota (via the Adoption History Project at the University of Oregon); "The Innocenti Digest 4: Intercountry Adoption," by UNICEF (1998); "Korean Adoption History," by Tobias Hübinette, in *Guide to Korea for Overseas Adopted Koreans,* edited by Eleana Kim (2004); and "Of Orphans and Adoption, Parents and the Poor, Exploitation and Rescue: A Scriptural and Theological Critique of the Evangelical Christian Adoption and Orphan Care Movement," by David Smolin (2012).

I also relied on information from several books, including *Adopted for Life: The Priority of Adoption for Christian Families and Churches,* by Russell Moore (2009); *Adoption as a Ministry, Adoption as a Blessing,* by Michelle Gardner (2003); *Bring My Sons from Afar,* by Bertha Holt (1986); *Created for God's Glory,* by Bertha Holt (1982); *Fields of the Fatherless,* by Tom Davis (2008); *Kisses from Katie: A Story of Relentless Love and Redemption,* by Katie Davis with Beth Clark (2011); *One Million Arrows,* by Julie Ferwerda (2009); *Orphanology: Awakening to Gospel-Centered Adoption and Orphan Care,* by Tony Merida and Rick Morton (2011); *Orphan Trains: The Story of Charles Loring Brace and the Children He Saved and Failed,* by Stephen O'Connor (2001); *Reclaiming Adoption: Missional Living through Rediscovery of Abba Father,* edited by Dan Cruver (2011); *Seed from the East,* by Bertha Holt and David Wisner (1956); *Small Town, Big Miracle: How Love Came to the Least of These,* by Bishop W. C. Martin with John Fornof (2007); *The Spirit of Adoption,* by

Randy Bohlender (2003); *This Means War: Equipping Christian Families for Fostercare or Adoption,* by Cheryl Ellicott (2010); and *Too Small to Ignore: Why the Least of These Matters Most,* by Dr. Wess Stafford with Dean Merrill (2007).

This chapter also is based on interviews with Dan Cruver, Tom DiFilipo, Karin Dubinksy, Maureen Flatley, James Garrow, E. J. Graff, Niels Hoogeveen, Chuck Johnson, Kay Johnson, Gale Bernard Kenny, Eleana Kim, Jason Kovacs, office of Senator Mary Landrieu, Shari Levine, Becca McBride, Jedd Medefind, Karen Moline, Russell Moore, Paul Myhill, Jessica Pegis, Sarah Posner, Lisa Marie Rollins, Kelly Rosati, David Smolin, Kathleen Strottman, Brian Stuy, Elizabeth Styffe, Catherine Wagner as well as attendance at the Christian Alliance for Orphans Summits VI (2010) and VIII (2012) and Adopting for Life conference (2010).

Chapter 3: Suffering Is Part of the Plan

This chapter drew on news articles, websites, blog posts, or publications from *ABC News,* America World Adoption, the *Argus Leader, Atlanta Journal-Constitution, Associated Press, Beliefnet,* the *Boston Globe,* CareNet, *Chicago Sun-Times,* A Christian Perspective on Adoption, *Christian Post, Christianity Today, City Weekly,* Crisis Pregnancy Center Watch, *Daily News,* Decisions, Choices and Options, *Deseret Morning News,* Exiled Mothers, website of Glenn Grothman, Heritage Foundation, *Huffington Post, KOB Eyewitness News, LifeSiteNews, Mail Online, National Post, Orlando Weekly, People, PRWeb, RH Reality Check,* the *Salt Lake Tribune,* Sendevelynhome.com, *Slate, Sunday Times,* the *Village Voice,* the *Wall Street Journal,* the *Washington Post,* the *Washington Times, West Australian, Women's ENews,* Youth with a Mission website, and YWAM Adoption Ministry.

It also benefited from several reports, including "The Adoption Option: Adoption Won't Reduce Abortion but It Will Expand Women's Choices," by the Center for American Progress (2010); "America's Orphan Crisis," by Decisions, Choices and Options; "Research: Adoption Facts," by the Evan B. Donaldson Adoption Institute; Baby Scoop Era Research Initiative selective documents; "Birthmother, Goodmother: Her Story of Heroic Redemption," by the Family Research Council and the National Council for Adoption (2007); "Crisis Pregnancy Centers: An Affront to Choice," by the National Abortion Federation (2006); "Crisis Pregnancy Centers Revealed," by NARAL (2010); "How to Start and Operate your Own ProLife Outreach Crisis Pregnancy Center," by Robert

Pearson (1969); "Missing Pieces: Adoption Counseling in Pregnancy Resource Centers," by the Family Research Council (2000); "Of Orphans and Adoption, Parents and the Poor, Exploitation and Revenue: A Scriptural and Theological Critique of the Evangelical Christian Adoption and Orphan Care Movement," by David Smolin in *Regent International Law Review* (2012); "Positive Adoption Language," by the North American Council on Adoptable Children (2001); and "Post-Adoptive Reactions of the Relinquishing Mother: A Review," in the *Journal of Obstetric, Gynecological and Neonatal Nursing* (1999).

I also relied on information from several books, including *Adoption Healing . . . A Path to Recovery,* by Joe Soll (2000, 2005); *Fallen Women, Problem Girls: Unmarried Mothers and the Professionalization of Social Work, 1980–1945,* by Regina G. Kunzel (1993); *The Girls Who Went Away: The Hidden History of Women Who Surrendered Children for Adoption in the Decades Before* Roe vs. Wade, by Ann Fessler (2006); *The Making of Pro-Life Activists: How Social Movement Mobilization Works,* by Ziad W. Munson (2008); *The 7 Laws of Magical Thinking,* by Matthew Hutson (2012); *Unmarried Mothers,* by Clark E. Vincent (1961); *Shattered Bonds: The Color of Child Welfare,* by Dorothy Roberts (2002); *The Stork Market: America's Multi-Billion Dollar Unregulated Adoption Industry,* by Mirah Riben (2007); *Unlearning Adoption: A Guide to Family Preservation and Protection,* by Jessica DelBalzo (2007); and *Wake up Little Susie: Single Pregnancy and Race before Roe v. Wade,* by Rickie Solinger (1992, 2000).

This chapter also is based on interviews with Joan Aylor, Suz Bednarz, Flip Benham, Jess DelBalzo, Grayson Dempsey, Karen Dubinsky, Carol Evans*, Kris Faasse Ann Fessler, Karen Fetrow, John Fredericks, Mari Gallion, Chamaine Hanson, Carol Jordan*, Shari Levine, Lifetime Foundation hotline staff, Corrinna Lohser, Angela Michael, Robin Marriott, Lauren Guy McAlpin, Anne Moody, Reanne Mosley, Cristina Page, Mirah Riben, Cathi Robinson, Evelyn Robinson, Vicki Saporta, Joe Soll, David Smolin, Jo Anne Swanson, Karen Wilson-Buterbaugh, Jim Wright, Sandy Young, one anonymous birthmother as well as attendance at an Adoption Crossroads meeting, a Birthmothers meeting, and the Christian Alliance for Orphans Summit VI (2010).

Chapter 4: Inside the Boom
This chapter drew on news articles, websites, blog posts, or publications from *ABC News* (Australia), *ABC News Foreign Correspondent* (Australia), *CBC* (Canada), *CBS News,* the *Christian Post, Christianity*

Today, Christian World Adoption blog, Daily Independent (Nigeria), *Econlog, Foreign Policy,* the *Houston Chronicle,* Senator Mary Landrieu's website, the *Los Angeles Times, Mission News Network,* the National Committee for Adoption, the *New York Times,* the *Progressive,* the Schuster Institute for Investigative Journalism, *Sendek,* the *Star-Ledger,* and *Voice of America.*

It also benefited from several reports, including "Africa: The New Frontier for Intercountry Adoption," by the African Child Policy Forum (2012); "The Aftermath of Abusive Adoption Practices in the Lives of Adoption Triad Members: Responding to Adoption Triad Members Victimized by Abusive Adoption Practices," by David and Desiree Smolin (2012); "Briefing on Joint USCIS/State Adoption Site Visit to Ethiopia," by US Citizenship and Immigration Services (2011); "Fly Away Children," by Australian Broadcasting Corporation (2009); "From Guatemala to Ethiopia: Shifts in Intercountry Adoption Leaves Ethiopia Vulnerable for Child Sales and Other Unethical Practices," by Karen Smith Rotabi in *Socmag* (2010); "Fruits of Ethiopia: Intercountry Adoption: The Rights of the Child or the 'Harvesting' of Children," by Against Child Trafficking (2011); and notices from the US State Department.

I also relied on information from several books, including *Adoption as a Ministry, Adoption as a Blessing,* by Michelle Gardner (2003), and *Finding Fernanda: Two Mothers, One Child, And a Cross-Border Search for Truth,* by Erin Siegal (2011).

This chapter also is based on interviews or conversations with Asefa Tesfayem Aregay, Susan Bissell, Katie Bradford, Harry Bowers, Stephne Bowers, Nate Day, Allison Dilsworth, Arun Dohle, Karin Dubinsky, Abiy Ephrem, Maureen Flatley, Temesgen Gebraselassie, Yosef Girmai, Terri Hambruch, Mary Hatlevig, Jessie Hawkins, Peter Heinlein, Niels Hoogeveen, Ambassador Susan Jacobs, Mary Ann Jolley, Kelly*, Fanuel Kinfu, Children's Issues officer Jill Larson, Aynelum Lemma, Tarikuwa Lemma, JoAnna Luks, Brian Luwis, Mehari Maru, Dina McQueen, Jedd Medefind, Barbara McGuire, Paul Myhill, Mary Nelson, Gina Pollock, Samuel*, Semayat*, Leslie Schiller, Erin Siegal, Karen Smith Rotabi, David Smolin, Abebe Tigabu, Lisa Veleff Day, Maxine Walton, Doug Webb, Rachel Wegner, Agitu Wodajo, Anna Wright, four anonymous adoptive mothers in the United States and one anonymous adoptive mother living outside of the United States, one anonymous US official, US Embassy officials in Ethiopia, one anonymous former Ethiopian adoption worker, and two State Department conference call/meetings regarding adoptions from Ethiopia.

Chapter 5: A Little War
This chapter drew on news articles, websites, blog posts, or publications from *Above Rubies*, Acres of Hope, Addy's Hope blog, All Blessings International, the *Analyst*, *BBC*, *CBC Canada*, Childmyths, Christian Alliance for Orphans blog, *Charlotte Observer*, the *Charlotte World*, *Chicago Tribune*, Covenant Life Christian Fellowship, the *Free Lance-Star*, Hopebelieveobey.com, the *Lawrence Journal-World*, the *Liberian Journal*, *Liberian Observer*, the *Los Angeles Times*, the *New York Times*, No Greater Joy Ministries, *Nugget News*, the *Oklahoman*, *O Magazine*, O Solo Mama, Pound Pup Legacy, *Reuters*, *SC Times*, ShowHope.org, Spirit Liberia, the *Star Tribune*, Stepsestablishedbyhim.blogspot.com, *Tribune Business News*, *USA Today*, the *Voice of Russia*, WACSN blog, and the Yahoo Adopting from Liberia group.

It also benefited from several reports, including "Draft White Paper and Emergency Policy Reform Intercountry Adoption: Republic of Liberia," by Emmanuel Dolo (2008); "Fact Sheet: Intercountry Adoption—Liberia, West Africa," by Heather Cannon-Winkelman; and "Human Rights in Liberia's Orphanages," by the United Nations (2007).

I also relied on information from several books, including *Acres of Hope: The Miraculous Story of One Family's Gift of Love to Children without Hope*, by Patty Anglin with Joe Musser (1999); *Child Development: Myths and Misunderstandings*, by Jean Mercer (2009); *Liberian Adoption: Preparing for Your Child's Homecoming*, by Angel Rutledge (2009); *The Road to Evergreen: Adoption, Attachment Therapy, and the Promise of Family*, by Rachael Stryker (2010); and *To Train Up A Child* by Michael and Debi Pearl (1994).

This chapter also is based on interviews or correspondence with Patty Anglin, Alfred (Jaban) Allison, Isaiah Allison, Pastor Baryee Bonnor, Lisa Bates, Carolyn Buford, Nancy Campbell, Heather Cannon-Winkelman, Peter Carter, Tama Covert, Emmanuel Dolo, Kula Cole Epperly, Pam Epperly, Julie Everett, Saah Fayiah, Teresa Fillmon, Maureen Flatley, Emily Garin, Vyckie Garrison, Joseph Geebro, CeCe Godfrey, Sam Godfrey, Carl Graham, Chuck Gremillion, Dirk Helmling, Niels Hoogeveen, Melvin Johnson, Rachel Johnson, Teri Johnson, Bishop Emanuel Jones, Ellen Loftus, Jean Mercer, Johanna*, Geoffrey Oyat, Michael Pearl, Jessica Pegis, HollyAnn Petree, Jerelenmik Piah, Gina

Pollock, Leom Russell, Angel Rutledge, Lydia Sherman, Cheryl Carter Shotts, David Smolin, Jill Spicer, Leah Spring, Rachael Stryker, Kate Thompson, Roger Thompson, Pam Veazie, Pastor Richard Wesley, Aloysnec Wesseh, Pastor Atto Williams, Edward Winant, Robert Zoepuegar, and an anonymous child welfare worker in Tennessee as well as attendance at Christian Alliance for Orphans Summit VIII (2012).

Chapter 6: Pipeline Problems

This chapter drew on news articles, websites, blog posts, or publications from the *Associated Press,* Christian Alliance for Orphans blog, *Christian Post,* the *Christian Science Monitor, Chicago Tribune,* Congressional Coalition on Adoption, *Dayton Daily News, Globe and Mail, Huffington Post,* the Joint Council on International Children's Services, *Journal of Christian Legal Thought, People,* Pound Pup Legacy, *Republica,* the *Washington Examiner,* and the *Washington Times.*

It also benefited from several reports, including "Africa: The New Frontier for Intercountry Adoption," by the African Child Policy Forum (2012); "Global Trends in Intercountry Adoption: 2001–2010," by the National Council for Adoption; and *Stuck,* by Both Ends Burning (2012); as well as statements from American Academy of Adoption Attorneys, Ethica, Center for Adoption Policy, Joint Council on International Children's Services, and PEAR.

I also relied on information from several books, including *Adopted for Life,* by Russell Moore, and *Both Ends Burning,* by Craig Juntunen.

This chapter also is based on interviews with Susan Bissell, Becca David, Caleb David, Tom DiFilipo, Teresa Fillion, Maureen Flatley, Niels Hoogeveen, Ambassador Susan Jacobs, Chuck Johnson, Kay Johnson, Craig Juntunen, Brian Luwis, Jedd Medefind, Kathleen Strottman, Rachael Stryker, and five anonymous adoptive mothers of special-needs children as well as attendance at the Adoption Policy Conference (2011) and the Christian Alliance for Orphans Summits VI (2010) and VIII (2012).

Chapter 7: A Thousand Ways to Not Help Orphans

This chapter drew on news articles, websites, blog posts, or publications from *Christian Post, Christianity Today, Digital Journal,* the *Economist,* Gladney Center for Adoption, Hope for Orphans, JenkinsinRwanda.blogspot.com, the *New Times,* the *New York Times,* the *Orange County Register,* the *Ottawa Citizen,* Purpose Driven.com, Riverkids Foundation, *Rwanda Dispatch,* and *Time.*

It also benefited from a report, "National Commission for Children: Enhancing Child's Protection in Rwanda," by the National Conference on Violence Against Children (2011), and a book, *We Wish to Inform You That Tomorrow We Will Be Killed with Our Families,* by Philip Gourevitch.

This chapter also is based on interviews with Meagan Biehl, Tina Harriman, Jaya Holliman, Jana Jenkins, Chuck Johnson, Jennifer Jukanovich, Kapya Kaoma, Archbishop Emmauel Kolini, Eric Munyemana, Alfred Munyentwari, Damien Ngabonziza, Nyanga Nzabamwita, Vianney Rangira, Sophonie Sebazigo, David Smolin, Elizabeth Styffe, Arlene Tautum, Augustin Twagira, Benilde Uwababyeyi as well as attendance at the Christian Alliance for Orphans Summit VIII (2012).

Chapter 8: Going Home
This chapter drew on news articles, websites, blog posts, or publications from *Conducive,* Creating a Family, the *Korea Herald,* the *Korean Quarterly,* KUMFA, KUMSN, *Joonang Daily, Journal of Christian Legal Thought, NPR,* the *New York Times,* and the *Progressive.*

It also benefited from several reports, including "Adoption Counseling Services Experienced by Unwed Mothers in Korea," by Hyoung-Suk Choi (2010); "Internationally Adopted Koreans and the Movement to Revise the Korean Adoption Law," by Jeane Jeong Trenka for *Ewha Journal of Gender and Law* (2011); "International Adoption: Lessons from Korea," by PRB (2010); "Korean Adoption History," by Tobias Hübinette; "Korean Public Opinion Survey on Unwed Mothers and their Children," by KUMSN (2009); *Resilience,* directed by Tammy Chu (2009); and "Reviewing Issues on Unwed Mothers' Welfare in Korea: Intercountry Adoption, Related Statistics, and Welfare Policies in Developed Countries," by KUMSN (2009).

I also relied on information from several books, including *Adopted Territory: Transnational Korean Adoptees and the Politics of Belonging,* by Eleana J. Kim (2010); *Bring My Sons from Afar,* by Bertha Holt (1986); *Comforting an Orphaned Nation: Representations of International Adoption and Adopted Koreans in Korean Popular Culture,* by Tobias Hübinette; *Created for God's Glory,* by Bertha Holt (1982); *Guide to Korea for Overseas Adopted Koreans,* edited by Eleana Kim (2004); *The Language of Blood,* by Jane Jeong Trenka (2003); *Outsiders Within: Writing on Transracial Adoption,* edited by Jane Jeong Trenka, Julia Chinyere Oparah, and Sun Yung Shin (2006); *Religion and Spirituality in*

Korean America, edited by David K. Yoo and Ruth H. Chung (2008); and *Seed from the East*, by Bertha Holt and David Wisner (1956).

This chapter also is based on interviews with Hyoung-Suk Choi, Shannon Heit, Niels Hoogeveen, Eleana Kim, JaeRan Kim, Hee Jung Kwon, Jennifer Kwon Dobbs, Kevin Vollmers, Evelyn Robinson, Jane Jeong Trenka, Kim Stoker, and Suzie.*

BIBLIOGRAPHY

AcPf. *Africa: The New Frontier for Intercountry Adoption.* Addis Ababa: The African Child Policy Forum, 2012.

"Adoptions Home | Intercountry Adoption." Adoptions Home | Intercountry Adoption. http://adoption.state.gov.

Anglin, Patty, and Joe Messer. *Acres of Hope: The Miraculous Story of One Family's Gift of Love to Children without Hope.* Uhrichsville, OH: Promise Press, 1999.

Arons, Jessica. "The Adoption Option | Center for American Progress." Washington, DC: Center for American Progress, 2010.

Askren, H. A., and K. C. Bloom. "Post-Adoptive Reactions of the Relinquishing Mother: A Review." *Journal of Obstetric, Gynecological and Neonatal Nursing* 28, no. 4 (1999): 395–400.

Balsari, Satchit, Jay Lemery, Timothy P. Williams, and Brett D. Nelson. "Protecting the Children of Haiti." *New England Journal of Medicine* 362:e25 (2010). http://www.nejm.org/doi/full/10.1056/NEJMp1001820.

Bohlender, Randy. *The Spirit of Adoption: Winning the Battle for the Children.* Kansas City, MO: The Zoe Foundation, 2010.

Briefing on Joint USCIS/State Adoption Site Visit to Ethiopia. Washington, DC: US Citizenship and Immigration Services, 2011.

Choi, Hyoung-Suk. "Adoption Counseling Services Experienced by Unwed Mothers in Korea." Keynote speech, 60th Women's Policy Forum from Korea Unwed Mothers Support Network, Seoul, Korea, February 24, 2010.

Connor, Stephen. *Orphan Trains: The Story of Charles Loring Brace and the Children He Saved and Failed.* Boston: Houghton Mifflin, 2001.

Crisis Pregnancy Centers: An Affront to Choice. Washington, DC: National Abortion Federation, 2006.

Crisis Pregnancy Centers Revealed. Alexandria, VA: NARAL Pro-Choice Virginia Foundation, 2010.

Cruver, Dan. *Reclaiming Adoption: Missional Living through the Rediscovery of Abba Father.* Adelphi, MD: Cruciform Press, 2011.

Dambach, Mia, and Christina Baglietto. *Haiti: 'Expediting' Intercountry Adoptions in the Aftermath of a Natural Disaster, Preventing Future Harm.* Geneva: International Social Service, 2010.

Davis, Katie, and Beth Clark. *Kisses from Katie: A Story of Relentless Love and Redemption.* New York: Howard Books, 2011.

Davis, Tom. *Fields of the Fatherless: Discover the Joy of Compassionate Living,* 2nd ed. Colorado Springs, CO: David C. Cook, 2008.

DelBalzo, Jessica. *Unlearning Adoption: A Guide to Family Preservation and Protection.* Charleston, SC: Book Surge, 2007.

Dolo, Emmanuel. *Draft White Paper and Emergency Policy Reform Intercountry Adoption: Republic of Liberia.* Monrovia, Liberia: Emmanuel Dolo, 2008.

Ellicott, Cheryl. *This Means War: Equipping Christian Families for Fostercare or Adoption.* Spokane, WA: Sweetwater Still, 2010.

Examining Intercountry Adoption after the Earthquake in Haiti. Washington, DC: National Council for Adoption, 2010.

Family Research Council. "Adoption Works Well: A Synthesis of the Literature." Washington, DC: Family Research Council, 2010.

Ferwerda, Julie. *One Million Arrows: Raising Your Children to Change the World.* Enumclaw, WA: WinePress, 2009.

Fessler, Ann. *The Girls Who Went Away: The Hidden History of Women Who Surrendered Children for Adoption in the Decades before Roe v. Wade.* New York: Penguin Press, 2006.

Fly Away Children. Film. Directed by Andrew Geoghegan. Sydney: Australian Broadcasting Corporation, 2009.

Fruits of Ethiopia: Intercountry Adoption: The Rights of the Child or the 'Harvesting' of Children. Brussels, Belgium: Against Child Trafficking, 2011.

Gardner, Michelle. *Adoption as a Ministry, Adoption as a Blessing.* Enumclaw, WA: Pleasant Word, 2003.

Global Trends in Intercountry Adoption: 2001–2010. Washington, DC: National Council for Adoption, 2012.

Gourevitch, Philip. *We Wish to Inform You That Tomorrow We Will Be Killed with Our Families: Stories from Rwanda*. New York: Farrar, Straus, and Giroux, 1998.

Graff, E. J. "Anatomy of an Adoption Crisis." *Foreign Policy*, September 12, 2010.

———. "The Baby Business." *Democracy Journal*. http://www.democracy journal.org/17/6757.php?page=all.

———. "The Lie We Love." *Foreign Policy*, November 1, 2008.

Holt, Bertha. *Bring My Sons from Afar: The Unfolding of Harry Holt's Dream*. Eugene, OR: Holt International Children's Services, 1986, 1992.

———. *Created for God's Glory*. Eugene, OR: Holt International Children's Services, 1982.

Holt, Bertha, and David Wisner. *The Seed from the East*. Los Angeles, CA: Oxford University Press, 1956.

Hübinette, Tobias. *Comforting an Orphaned Nation: Representations of International Adoption and Adopted Koreans in Korean Popular Culture*. Seoul: Jimoondang, 2006.

———. "Korean Adoption History." In *Guide to Korea for Overseas Adopted Koreans*. Seoul: Overseas Koreans Foundation, 2004.

Human Rights in Liberia's Orphanages. Monrovia: UN Mission in Liberia (UNMIL), 2007.

The Innocenti Digest 4: Intercountry Adoption. Florence, Italy: UNICEF, 1998.

Intercountry Adoptions in Emergencies: The Tsunami Orphans. New York: Evan B. Donaldson Adoption Institute, 2005.

"International Adoption: Lessons from Korea | In the Matter of Cha Jung Hee | POV | PBS." PBS: Public Broadcasting Service. http://www.pbs.org/pov/chajunghee/international_kim.php.

Juntunen, Craig. *Both Ends Burning: My Story of Adopting Three Children from Haiti*. Denver, CO: Outskirts Press, 2009.

Kenny, Charles T. *Birthmother, Goodmother: Her Story of Heroic Redemption*. Washington, DC: National Council for Adoption, 2007.

Kim, Eleana Jean. *Adopted Territory: Transnational Korean Adoptees and the Politics of Belonging*. Durham, NC: Duke University Press, 2010.

Korean Public Opinion Survey on Unwed Mothers and their Children. Seoul: Korean Unwed Mothers Support Network, 2011.

Krabacher, Susan Scott. *Angels of a Lower Flight: One Woman's Mission to Save a Country—One Child at a Time*. New York: Touchstone Books, 2008.

Kunzel, Regina G. *Fallen Women, Problem Girls: Unmarried Mothers and the Professionalization of Social Work, 1890–1945*. New Haven, CT: Yale University Press, 1993.

Martin, W. C., and John Fornof. *Small Town, Big Miracle*. Carol Stream, IL: Tyndale House, 2007.

Mercer, Jean. *Child Development: Myths and Misunderstandings*. Los Angeles, CA: SAGE, 2010.

Merida, Tony, and Rick Morton. *Orphanology: Awakening to Gospel-Centered Adoption and Orphan care*. Birmingham, AL: New Hope Publishers, 2011.

Moore, Russell. *Adopted for Life: The Priority of Adoption for Christian Families and Churches*. Wheaton, IL: Crossway Books, 2009.

Munson, Ziad W. *The Making of Pro-Life Activists: How Social Movement Mobilization Works*. Chicago: University of Chicago Press, 2008.

National Commission for Children: Enhancing Child's Protection in Rwanda. Kigali, Rwanda: National Conference on Violence Against Children, 2011.

Pearl, Michael, and Debi Pearl. *To Train Up A Child*. Pleasantville, TN: Pearl, 1996, 1994.

Pearson, Robert. *How to Start and Operate your Own ProLife Outreach Crisis Pregnancy Center*. Robert Pearson, 1969.

"Research: Adoption Facts." Evan B. Donaldson Adoption Institute. www.adoptioninstitute.org/research/adoptionfacts.php.

Resilience. DVD. Directed by Tammy Chu. Seoul: KoRoot, 2009.

Reviewing Issues on Unwed Mothers' Welfare in Korea: Intercountry Adoption, Related Statistics, and Welfare Policies in Developed Countries. Seoul: Korean Unwed Mothers Support Network, 2009.

Riben, Mirah. *The Stork Market: America's Multi-Billion Dollar Unregulated Adoption Industry*. Dayton, NJ: Advocate Publications, 2007.

Richter, L., and A. Norman. *Inside the Thriving Industry of AIDS Orphan Tourism*. Pretoria, Gauteng Province: Human Sciences Research Council, 2010.

Roberts, Dorothy E. *Shattered Bonds: The Color of Child Welfare*. New York: Basic Books, 2002.

Rutledge, Angel. *Liberian Adoption: Preparing for Your Child's Homecoming*. Charlotte, NC: CreateSpace Independent Publishing Platform, 2009.

Schwartz, Timothy T. *Travesty in Haiti: A True Account of Christian Missions, Orphanages, Fraud, Food Aid and Drug Trafficking.* Charleston, SC: BookSurge, 2008.

Siegal, Erin. *Finding Fernanda: Two Mothers, One Child, and a Cross-Border Search for Truth.* Oakland, CA: Cathexis Press, 2011.

Smith Rotabi, Karen. "From Guatemala to Ethiopia: Shifts in Intercountry Adoption Leaves Ethiopia Vulnerable for Child Sales and Other Unethical Practices." *SW & S News Magazine* (2010). http://www.socmag.net/?p=615.

Smolin, David M. "Of Orphans and Adoption, Parents and the Poor, Exploitation and Rescue: A Scriptural and Theological Critique of the Evangelical Christian Adoption and Orphan Care Movement." *Regent Journal of International Law* 8, no. 2 (2012).

Smolin, David, and Desiree Smolin. "The Aftermath of Abusive Adoption Practices in the Lives of Adoption Triad Members: Responding to Adoption Triad Members Victimized by Abusive Adoption Practices." Lecture, Annual Symposium of the Joint Council on International Children's Services from JCICS, New York, April 18, 2012.

Solinger, Rickie. *Wake Up Little Susie: Single Pregnancy and Race before Roe v. Wade.* New York: Routledge, 1992.

Soll, Joe. *Adoption Healing: A Path to Recovery.* Baltimore, MD: Gateway Press, 2000.

Stafford, Wess, and Dean Merrill. *Too Small to Ignore: Why the Least of These Matters Most.* Colorado Springs, CO: Waterbrook Press, 2007.

Stryker, Rachael. *The Road to Evergreen: Adoption, Attachment Therapy, and the Promise of Family.* Ithaca, NY: Cornell University Press, 2010.

Stuck. DVD. Directed by Thaddaeus Scheel. Washington, DC: Both Ends Burning, 2012.

Trenka, Jane Jeong. *Internationally Adopted Koreans and the Movement to Revise the Korean Adoption Law.* Seoul: *Ewha Journal of Gender and Law,* 2011.

——. *The Language of Blood: A Memoir.* St. Paul, MN: Borealis Books, 2003.

Trenka, Jane Jeong, Julia Sudbury, and Sun Yung Shin. *Outsiders Within: Writing on Transracial Adoption.* Cambridge, MA: South End Press, 2006.

Vincent, Clark E. *Unmarried Mothers.* New York: Free Press of Glencoe, 1961.

Wilson-Buterbaugh, Karen. "Research | Baby Scoop Era Research
    Initiative." Baby Scoop Era Research Initiative.
    http://babyscoopera.com/adoption-abuse-of-mothers/.
Yoo, David, and Ruth H. Chung. *Religion and Spirituality in Korean
    America*. Urbana: University of Illinois Press, 2008.
Young, Curtis. *Missing Pieces: Adoption Counseling in Pregnancy
    Resource Centers*. Washington, DC: Family Research Council, 2000.

INDEX

Kathryn Joyce is a journalist in New York City whose work has appeared in the *Nation,* the *Atlantic, Mother Jones, Slate, Salon,* the *Harvard Divinity Bulletin, Newsweek,* and many others. She is the author of *Quiverfull: Inside the Christian Patriarchy Movement* and an associate editor at *Religion Dispatches.*